The Road to Jerusalem

MATERIAL TEXTS

Series Editors

Roger Chartier   Anthony Grafton
Joan DeJean   Janice Radway
Joseph Farrell   Peter Stallybrass

A complete list of books in the series
is available from the publisher.

The Road to Jerusalem

Pilgrimage and Travel in the Age of Discovery

F. Thomas Noonan

PENN

UNIVERSITY OF PENNSYLVANIA PRESS

Philadelphia

in Association with the Library of Congress

Publication of this book was made possible by the
Verner W. Clapp Publication Fund in the Publishing
Office of the Library of Congress

10   9   8   7   6   5   4   3   2   1

Published by
University of Pennsylvania Press
Philadelphia, Pennsylvania 19104-4112

Library of Congress Cataloging-in-Publication Data

Noonan, F. Thomas.
    The road to Jerusalem : pilgrimage and travel in the Age of Discovery /
F. Thomas Noonan.
        p.   cm. — (Material texts)
    ISBN-13: 978-0-8122-3994-2 (alk. paper)
    ISBN-10: 0-8122-3994-6 (alk. paper)
    Includes bibliographical references and index.
    1. Travel—History. 2. Travelers' writings. I Title. II. Series.
G156. N66   2007
263'.04109031—dc22   2006051478

*To my Mother
and Father*

Contents

LIST OF ILLUSTRATIONS   ix

INTRODUCTION: PILGRIMAGE AND TRAVEL   I

PART I: MODERNIZATION OF TRAVEL

1. MEDIEVAL PILGRIMAGE INTO PRINT   17

2. CONTEMPORARY PILGRIMAGE INTO PRINT: 1450–1500   29

PART II: TRANSFORMATION OF TRAVEL

3. NEW WORLDS AND A NEW VOICE OF TRAVEL   49

4. REFORMATION AND THE POLEMICS OF TRAVEL   84

5. OTHER HOLY PLACES, OTHER HOLY LANDS   101

6. A SECOND VOICE: TERRA SANCTA INTER ALIA   130

7. A THIRD VOICE: PILGRIMS ON TRAVEL AND PILGRIMAGE   154

CONCLUSION: ALIVE AND WELL AND EARLY MODERN   235

CHRONOLOGICAL BIBLIOGRAPHY OF LIBRARY OF CONGRESS PILGRIMAGES   253

ABBREVIATIONS   269

NOTES   271

INDEX   321

ACKNOWLEDGMENTS   327

Illustrations

All Illustrations are from the Rare Book and Special Collections Division of the Library of Congress. Figures 4, 5, 6, 8, 17, and 34 are from the Lessing J. Rosenwald Collection; Figure 7 is from the John Boyd Thacher Collection.

1. John Mandeville, *The voyages and travailes*, M3r   23
2. Noè Bianchi, *Viaggio da Venezia al S. Sepolcro*, 138–39   27
3. Santo Brasca, *Viagio del Sepulchro*, F3v   33
4. Bernhard Breydenbach, *Die heyligen Reyssen gen Iherusalem*, Jerusalem panorama, detail   38
5. Bernhard Breydenbach, *Die heyligen Reyssen gen Iherusalem*, 35r   39
6. Ludolphus de Saxonia, *Dit es dleven Ons Liefs Heeren Ihesu Cristi*, XLIr   52
7. Christopher Columbus, *De insulis nuper in Mari Indico nuper repertis*, dd5v   57
8. Bernhard Breydenbach, *Die heyligen Reissen gen Iherusalem*, Rhodes pl., detail   58
9. *Nova Typis Transacta Navigatio*, title page   62
10. John Hamilton Moore, *Voyages and Travels*, 1, frontispiece   79
11. Johann Theodor de Bry, *America*, title page   80
12. Romeyn de Hooghe, *Les Indes Orientales et Occidentales*, fig. 12   82
13. François Le Gouz de La Boullaye, *Les voyages et observations*, facing dedication   102
14. Jacques Callot, *Les Gueux*, pl. 687   108
15. Bohuslav Alois Balbin, *Diva Wartensis*, facing 159   110
16. Louis Basile Carré de Montgeron, *La verité des miracles*, after xxviii   111
17. *Mirabilia Romae*, 67v   114
18. René Francois du Breil de Pontbriant, *Pèlerinage du calvaire*, 108 & facing image   124
19. Leonhard Rauwolf, *Aigentliche Beschreibung der Raiss*, title page   137

20. Leonhard Rauwolf, *Aigentliche Beschreibung der Raiss*, 129   138

21. Leonhard Rauwolf, *Aigentliche Beschreibung der Raiss*, 297   139

22. Cornelis de Bruyn, *Voyage au Levant*, 2, between 238, 239, detail   151

23. Heinrich Bünting, *Itinerarium Sacrae Scripturae*, cloverleaf map   159

24. André Thevet, *Cosmographie de Levant*, 176   165

25. Jean Zuallart, *Le tresdevot voyage de Ierusalem*, livre iii, 25   170

26. Jean Zuallart, *Le tresdevot voyage de Ierusalem*, livre iii, 1   171

27. Jean Zuallart, *Le tresdevot voyage de Ierusalem*, livre iii, 10   172

28. Jean Zuallart, *Le tresdevot voyage de Ierusalem*, livre iii,15   173

29. Jean Zuallart, *Le tresdevot voyage de Ierusalem*, livre iii, 142   174

30. Noè Bianchi, *Viaggio da Venezia al S. Sepolcro*, 38   176

31. Jacques Florent Goujon, *Histoire et voyage de la Terre-Sainte*, between 136, 137   177

32. Antoine Gonsales, *Hierusalemsche Reyse*, 1, facing 464.   178

33. Noè Bianchi, *Viaggio da Venezia al S. Sepolcro*, 7   179

34. Bernardino Amico, *Trattato delle piante*, between 8, 9   192

35. Philip Thicknesse, *A Year's journey*, 1, frontispiece   194

36. Peter Paul Rubens, *Vita beati P. Ignatii Loiolae*, pl. 27   195

37. Jean de Thévenot, *Voyages*, 2, facing 574   197

38. George Sandys, *A Relation of a Journey*, title page   215

. . . vicit iter durum pietas?

Has piety conquered the arduous road?
—Aeneid 6.688

Introduction: Pilgrimage and Travel

BY SLEIGHT OF HISTORY, conservative-minded restorations sometimes turn out radical innovations. Pilgrimage to Jerusalem experienced just such a tangle of expectations and results at the hands of that early nineteenth-century pilgrim, François-René Chateaubriand (1768–1848), who, in seeking to revive a devout tradition of going to the Levant, helped to close an era of pilgrimage that had lasted from the later fifteenth century to the end of the eighteenth. That early modern era of pilgrimage is our topic. But because Chateaubriand's shadow hovers and intrudes in much that follows—and because his shadow is also the shadow of a future that has become our own time—it may be best to say something at the outset of his ambitions for pilgrimage.

On 13 July 1806, Chateaubriand departed for the Levant. Back in Paris by 5 June 1807, he retold the adventure in his *Itinéraire de Paris à Jérusalem*, which appeared in print in 1811.[1] In the so-called Era of Restoration that would follow Napoleon's fall, Chateaubriand figured prominently, and not least because he seemed the great reviver of pilgrimage *ad Terram Sanctam*. To his task Chateaubriand brought a combination of clarity and muddle (or at least a tentativeness that turned out to be subversive to his agenda). He was reasonably clear about two things.

Situating himself within a medieval tradition that reached forward into the sixteenth and seventeenth centuries (but, in his view, scarcely much further), he was clear that he was resuscitating a defunct past where pilgrimage was concerned.[2] The eighteenth-century plight of pilgrimage documented his larger historical argument that Enlightenment and Revolution had excavated a deep divide between past and present. By his own later telling of his life, he had for some time (at least since the publication of the *Génie du Christianisme* in 1802) been waging revolution (his word) against the legacy of the eighteenth century and not simply bemoaning upsets after 1789.[3] That pilgrimage *outre mer* had disappeared from the European scene and consciousness was, for Chateaubriand, the handiwork of the Enlightenment. The disappearance of pilgrims had dulled Europe's spiritual sensibility and undermined its spiritual unity. Consider, Chateaubriand urged, the Latin West's response to the fire that had consumed the Church of the Holy Sepulchre ("the Church of the Holy Sepulchre no longer exists") in 1808, two years after his journey. "If a similar misfortune had happened a century ago," he remarked (in the *Martyrs*), "Christendom would have come together to rebuild the church; but today I am afraid that the tomb of Jesus Christ would be left exposed to the elements, were it not for the poor schismatic slaves—the Greeks, the Copts, the Armenians—who, to the shame of Catholic countries, do not spare themselves in repairing such a disaster."[4] Twenty years after his two weeks' visit to Jerusalem, Chateaubriand still recalled that the city had been all but forgotten by Europeans when he sailed across the Mediterranean. A "siècle antireligieux" had lost any memory of the cradle of religion. Chateaubriand associated, as closely as possible without directly merging, this eighteenth-century fate of pilgrimage and the eighteenth-century fate of French society: "As there were in actual fact no longer knights (*chevaliers*), so it seemed that Palestine itself had ceased to exist." Jerusalem, close to Europe in geographical fact, had been made to seem, throughout the century, at the edge of the world. So strewn with imagined obstacles and perils had the route become that to go to Jerusalem became an adventure—one which Chateaubriand attempted and from which he learned the usual but valuable lesson. When the object of one's fears is confronted, he tells the reader, "the ghost vanishes." Between publication of the *Itinéraire* in 1811 and its reissue in the collected works in 1826, Chateaubriand was content to have shown the way (*ouvrir la carrière*) and to see others follow his example. The book became a vade mecum for "a crowd of travelers," a grand publishing success in France and throughout the European world.[5] Chateaubriand did seem to have coaxed pilgrimage from a century-long coma.

Chateaubriand was also clear that what he was reviving was as much a literary as a practical reality. An abundant printed literature of early modern pilgrimage to Jerusalem had flourished across three and a half centuries since Gutenberg. Chateaubriand was steeped in this literature, so much so that his response upon seeing Jerusalem was expressed *in reference to* the responses of others who had preceded him: "I now understood that which historians and travelers reported of the surprise of Crusaders and pilgrims at the first sighting of Jerusalem." Borrowing and inhabiting the emotions of others, he is less bowled over by the moment than fortified and carried along by the tradition. Behind this moment lurked "two hundred modern travel accounts of the Holy Land" which he had read, as well as rabbinical compilations and writings from the ancients which he had also consulted.[6] His act of seeing what was before him was at a contemplative and associative remove, his reaction literary rather than radically existential, his emotions cooled and coddled to a fine erudition, his kind of travel a deployment, rather than a detonation, of sentiment. By prior reading, by recall on the spot of that earlier reading, he positioned himself to see through eyes other than his own. He chose to do so as well when he set the scene down on paper. He was not only aware of his second-hand (even third-hand) optics; to see through borrowed lenses was his primary, or at least preliminary, mode of describing his own arrival on the spot. Pilgrimage for him was overwhelmingly a literary and ruminative experience—an act of recall, commentary, referral, gloss, elaboration.

In Chateaubriand's eyes, the demise of pilgrimage in the crush of Enlightenment and Revolution was not only a matter of so few contemporaries making devout journeys. More disturbing was that writers and readers of pilgrimages had disappeared. "There has perhaps never been a subject less known by modern readers," he noted of Levantine pilgrimage, "nor at the same time a subject ever more completely worked to exhaustion." He himself decided to give a thorough description of the holy places partly because "No one today reads the ancient pilgrimages to Jerusalem; a subject that is altogether threadbare (*très usé*) actually strikes most readers as something entirely fresh (*tout neuf*)." In the process, he served up additional paragraphs devoted to thumbnail dissections of specimens of pilgrimage dating as far back as the early decades of printing. Nineteenth-century readers of the *Itinéraire* were being tutored in the literary history of centuries of pilgrimage.[7]

The pilgrimage that had so seized Chateaubriand's attention was a composite of the devotional act of travel and the literary act of (for the most part) actual pilgrims who put down their experiences on the printed page in order to satisfy the devout curiosity of readers. These elements—the traveler's act of pilgrimage, the literary act of some pilgrims, and the literate or listening act of stay-at-homes—were not, however, equally apportioned even prior to the eighteenth century. Levantine pilgrimage, in the early modern European tradition (in contrast to both medieval and later modern traditions) was overwhelmingly a literary phenomenon, a phenomenon of writing, printing, and reading. Few Europeans in these three and a half centuries had ever actually seen Palestine. Even some of the writers themselves had not made the journey—nor even claimed to have done so.[8] The operative experience of pilgrimage had been a reader's experience.[9] Over the previous century, Chateaubriand estimated, there had been no more than two hundred "voyageurs catholiques" in Jerusalem, and that number included Franciscans resident in Jerusalem and other missionaries stationed in the Levant. His own coming to the Franciscan Church of the Holy Savior in Jerusalem in 1806 had been "a genuine event." Earlier in the same year, at Easter, there had been only one European Catholic visitor in Jerusalem.[10] Early modern travel, then, when understood as pilgrimage, turns out to have been a somewhat gossamer affair.

Much of this a reader of Chateaubriand would have expected, the regnant thesis of the *Itinéraire* being that pilgrimage had waned under duress of eighteenth-century *philosophisme*. But Chateaubriand's interpretation reached beyond the near past: "There had never been very many Latin pilgrims, and this can be proved by a thousand examples." He notes that the celebrated Thévenot's traveling group in 1656 numbered a mere twenty-two; that often there were too few Latins in Jerusalem during Holy Week to take the places of the twelve apostles at the washing of the feet on Holy Thursday; that in all of 1589 ("just when religion was so flourishing") only seven Latin pilgrims visited Palestine. How, Chateaubriand reasonably wonders, is one to judge what would be an appropriate number in 1808? "The throng of pilgrims," he sweepingly concludes, "at least as regards Catholics, must be greatly reduced. We are dealing with something quite small, almost nothing at all. Seven, twelve, twenty, thirty, even a hundred pilgrims are hardly worth the trouble of a tally."[11]

Why, then, such a fuss? Why accuse *les philosophes* of sapping pilgrimage when, in reality, such travel had never—or at least not for centuries—been much in fashion? Because—this seems the slant of Chateaubriand's argument—modern pilgrimage to Jerusalem, even in its heyday, had been a popular and much printed *literature* that had risen out of the thinnest soil of *practice*. Paucity of numbers of pilgrims could hardly be ignored, but evidence of popularity lay elsewhere—in pilgrimage's centuries-long prominence as a printed literature for an audience of readers. Relatively few early modern journeys had in fact produced new elaborations of the ancient, archetypal experience of sacred journey. This literary product of printed texts formed the public, living, and enduring voice and profile of pilgrimage. It made pilgrimage a part of general European discourse. Printed accounts that were to be found in the stalls of sellers and on the shelves of readers of books made pilgrimage a part of the history of European devotion, but also a part of the history of European travel. There had existed—

even flourished—a market for the literature of such devout travel. We can look, as we shall, at the history of pilgrimage in print to be convinced of this—or we can read the *Itinéraire* and find not only Chateaubriand's record of his own actual voyage of pilgrimage in 1806 but also his *hommage* to the full historical reality of this cultural phenomenon that he was seeking to revive.

Clear about the eighteenth-century extinction of pilgrimage and about the deeply literary character of pilgrimage in its early modern heyday, Chateaubriand was altogether less clear when he came to characterize the *revivaliste* tome fashioned from his own Eastern travels. The title of the work, *Itinéraire*, announced a book of travel literature; but, it turns out, the title is suspect, insubstantial—and made so by the author's own second thoughts. Words on the page stand in for words that are absent. Chateaubriand apologizes for the title. He had let it stand, he explains in the preface to the first edition, for lack of something better. "I implore the reader"—the remark is celebrated—"to look upon this travel book less as a *Voyage* than as the *Mémoires* of a year of my life."[12] His *Itinéraire*, then, was not really, or not exactly, an *itinéraire*; not, at any rate, a *voyage*. It should be read as a fragment of *mémoires*. His year of travels was a year in his life. The emphasis has lifted from travel and settled on autobiography.

It would have been odd for any traveler—certainly, any *pilgrim*—before Chateaubriand to have proposed that his narrative be taken as something other than an account of travels. Nor were Chateaubriand's words a throw-away line—idle, elegant, inconsequential—to get his narrative idiosyncratically out of harbor. Otherwise, he would not have troubled to repeat the thought, word for word, almost a hundred pages later in the body of the text in the section on Greece.[13] Chateaubriand was emphatic and consistent, if not precise, in the thought he expressed. His correspondence from the year before publication of the *Itinéraire* had stressed the autobiographical character of the work. The book, he had concluded, both by its language and by the brevity of his time in Palestine, should be seen as expressive of his reactions and personality rather than as expert and informational regarding places he had visited.[14] At this period before publication, to pose as autobiographer rather than travel writer allowed him to parry anticipated criticisms. He need not claim to be an expert on the *Oriens*, but only on himself, the true subject matter of his book. But there was more involved. His insistence, expressed even decades later, that his year in the Orient be understood strictly under the rubric of autobiography was strangely enduring long after the book had caught on with the public.[15] Too little should not be made of Chateaubriand's apology and disclaimer—his theoretical tinkering with the title—for he did take pains to point out how his *Itinéraire* should be read (i.e., *not* as a *voyage*), a point that he underscored more than once over a very long period. Moreover, the literary nature of his book, the autobiographical *form* in which it was cast, is highly important in light of the literary character (of a travel account) that had long characterized (and been recognized to do so by Chateaubriand) the overall early modern enterprise of pilgrimage that he was now seeking to revive.

Chateaubriand's hemming and hawing bear crucially upon our topic. His vantage point stands in our line of historical sight. Like him, and partially due to his writings and their subsequent influence, we tend to think of pilgrimage much as he did—as a devout practice, as an episode in larger lives, rather than as a grand example of travel. Our expectations of pilgrimage have been shaped by him. We look over his shoulder, even through his eyes. Nevertheless, it is important to underscore that such expectations were not those of the pious European Levantiners Chateaubriand had read and admired. Early moderns in the Levant were great travelers because they were pilgrims. Their accounts were part of a literature of travel rather than of autobiography. They themselves shared a grand continuity in travel that reached back at least to late Roman times and forward into the eighteenth century. Chateaubriand's restoration was not, it therefore turns out, equivalent to a replication of a form of pilgrimage that had existed in the past. He had switched genres. He had provided pilgrimage with a new literary vehicle, replacing *voyage* with *mémoire*. His revived pilgrimage was not one with pre-Revolutionary, pre-Enlightenment pilgrimages, even though these literary relics had inspired his own travels and writing.

Chateaubriand was (we shall see) both right and wrong about early modern pilgrimage. While he overstated the decline of pilgrimage in the decades leading up to the Revolution, he was right to stress early modern pilgrimage's literary character. Nevertheless, having grasped the literary core of early modern pilgrimage, he seems—from the kind of book he himself fashioned—not to have seen that this voluminous literature of pilgrimage, however much a literature of devotion and meditation (and of autobiography on the part of self-reporting pilgrims), was also and above all a literature of *travel*. This, in fact, is the great divide between pre-nineteenth-century pilgrimage and a future pilgrimage (as articulated by the *Itinéraire*). Earlier pilgrims had little of Chateaubriand's stepping back from travel and towards autobiography. Chateaubriand's pilgrimage turns out to be innovative rather than restorative. Nor did novelty reside in nuance or details or in the margins. The *Itinéraire* presents a discrete practice of devotion within a new framework of autobiography; gone is the narrative of travels shot through with, and held together by, devotions of pilgrimage such as had been typical—again, we shall see—in the centuries before Chateaubriand.

✳   ✳   ✳

Travel's role in human history across cultures and civilizations has been so immense that one is not surprised to discover travel on the agenda of restoration when Europeans sought to reassemble the ancien régime. Whether constitutive or just contributory,[16] the role of travel in the making of civilizations has been crucial. But what do we mean when we speak of *travel*? The thing itself, as well as its prominence in the scheme of civilizations, is obviously grounded in the errant habits and instincts and strategies of human beings and societies. Man has proved fidgety and mobile from the beginning. Human history is dense with displacements. Our eldest ancestors, in their ability to move and adapt, have been likened to "a superior weed species."[17] Restlessness has always been a reservoir of motivation. That human mobility is one of the substratial givens and *homo errans* among the dramatis personae in the history of civilizations—such had become a congenially asserted insight by the eighteenth century, when Europeans were striving to seize whole a human past that itself clearly had much to do with history's actors not staying put.[18] But motion and mobility, migration and colonization, nomadry and footlooseness of every sort—these are not the same things as travel. *Sheer* motion is too abundant a datum, too lush a given. *Homo errans* is more elusive than, say, *homo politicus*. The human scene—always, everywhere—is choked and cluttered, not structured, nor clarified, by ceaseless motion. Only through the handiwork of cultures themselves, through feats of abstraction and focus, has mobility proved susceptible of interpretation, and thus of becoming something at once more intensely itself and yet quite beyond itself. Out of whirling and massive motion emerges that which transcends the gross and humble state of mere phenomenality and pure errancy.[19] Only when abstraction and focus become feats of a high and general order, when the activity of moving about is made to reflect back upon itself, when society glimpses itself moving this way or that across the mirror it holds up to itself, does *travel* emerge. Polished shards of motion—idealized, observed, remembered, pondered, celebrated episodes of motion—signify the presence of travel. Travel, in other words, as both conduct and noetic elaboration, as both doing and pondering, is mobility refined into genre.

Travel is a composite: on the one hand, a particular and delimited species of mobility; on the other, a literature (or some other ratiocinative amplifier) that notes and annotates this isolated range, this extract, of mobility. By means of travel, mobility calls to itself the attention of society. To take our own age and its congeries of careening and kinetic selves as hypothetical example: with all our going through the air and along interstates, it is possible that the only motion that we will come to reflect upon (the only one to be deemed worthy to float into the television's eye or onto the writer's page or into the newspapers' travel sections or even into the individual's own reminiscences) will be travel in space, the only exemplary traveler the astronaut, the only worthy destination another planet or solar system. So much so might this become the way of our world that all other forms of movement—that is, of potential travel—will cease to exist beyond their status as sheer motion. They will fall beneath our notice, drop below the cultural radar. Astronautica might become in the twenty-first or a later century what aeronautica might have, but did not, become at the end of the eighteenth century.

But this is to speculate on futures. Toward the end of the fifteenth century, there actually occurred a seismic shift in Europeans' habits of travel which offers more substantial food for thought. On the eve of Europe's first uses of printed matter as means of public discourse—an innovation that would lead European culture into fundamental upsets and refashionings—European travel had been, for over a millennium, *peregrinatio causa religionis*.[20] Indeed, the first word sufficed to indicate pilgrimage, and especially long-distance pilgrimage to the Holy Land. To be seriously out and about was to be on a devout errand. To travel was to go on pilgrimage. From the late Empire through the fifteenth century, fluctuating (but often large) numbers of pilgrims made the journey to Jaffa. (By the end of the eleventh century, complex societies within Europe had put themselves on something of a peregrinative footing.) And the fact of such travel was prominently reflected in literature—both in the composition of accounts of such travels and in wider forms of literature that also took notice of pilgrimage.

All of this changed during the sixteenth century. Europeans began to take a new measure of travel, to get a new handle on travel. Travel came to mean something different from what it had for a thousand years. Europeans began to go to new places for new reasons. New destinations and motivations were noted and celebrated and analyzed in a new European printed literature of travel. Over more than a millennium, European travel to the sacred Levant had evolved; but the challenges that had activated change and adaptation had been located primarily in the Levant itself: the late Roman Imperial endowment of sacred sites, the Arab conquest of Palestine, the establishment of Crusader states, the fall of those states.[21] From the end of the fifteenth century, however, challenges to Levantine pilgrimage as the great mode of European travel came from deep within Europe itself. The Levant became demagnetized as Europeans were drawn to new interests, new ambitions, new routes, new destinations. But however great the alterations in European travel and however much these changes were both effected and revealed through print, age-old travel did not evaporate under a sun of general indifference engendered by distractions of Atlantic travel and global circumnavigations. That the defining complexity of modernity would be much reduced, and thus modern civilization itself much impoverished, were such survivals as pilgrimage not taken into account— this much at least is clear from the history of travel among early modern Europeans. *Peregrinatio ad terram sanctam* survived throughout the period from Gutenberg to Napoleon, and its survival was magnified by the fact that pilgrimage, too, like newer forms of travel, was both realized and revealed through print. Print is the tell-tale datum.

*   *   *

Printing was crucial to this reshaping of travel. Printed books helped to fashion the age of discovery, which was an era not only in the history of geography and the history of European *imperium*, but in the history of travel as well. Printed books, however, also undergirded the survival of pilgrimage on the eve, and in the midst, of the great discoveries. (Here, as always, chronology is the strongest color on the historian's palette: it makes every possible difference that Gutenberg labored forty years before Columbus sailed and nearly seventy years before Reformers preached. The order of events gave pilgrimage a chance to hold on, a chance that it otherwise might not have had.) How substantially pilgrimage survived in print is suggested in the following pages by reference to works of early modern pilgrimage that are housed in the Library of Congress. These works provide the bibliographic sample upon which this essay is largely based.[22] From such a sample, it is possible to form an impression of the publishing

phenomenon of pilgrimage as a whole. The contours of pilgrimage as a
printed reality—as a vital *presence* in early modern European culture—
become visible in the bare bones of dates of editions.[23]

The flood of printed pilgrimages from the early modern era has long
been established bibliographic fact. Röhricht's great *Bibliotheca Geographica Palaestinae* first appeared in 1890 and remains the most comprehensive
record of such imprints.[24] Röhricht needed 338 pages to cover 1599 entries,
a large proportion of which describe printed pilgrimages that took place
prior to the nineteenth century. The individual entries, moreover, frequently
describe multiple early modern imprints. Such a bibliographical torrent,
however, has not fed into broad historical interpretations, especially in respect to the history of travel. The volume and spread across three centuries
of such books of pilgrimage have been largely left out of later historians'
syntheses. No matter how much in the early modern air (and bookstalls),
pilgrimage has been most prominent by its absence the farther away discussions concerning travel have carried from a "Middle Ages" that has
been judged the heyday of, and nearly the last word on, pilgrimage as a
mode and manner of travel. Even before Röhricht, Titus Tobler's *Biblio-
graphica Geographica Palaestinae* of 1867 could dismiss Juan Ceverio de Vera's
late sixteenth-century book of pilgrimage as "unimportant"—precisely because Tobler was in search of books of pilgrimage as potential mines of
raw geographical and topographical data rather than as exemplars of travel
literature. The present book will argue that when Ceverio is considered as
a traveler and writer of his travels, his account becomes among the least
unimportant of early modern pilgrimages.[25]

More recent interpretations have similarly failed to see early modern
pilgrimages to the Levant as specimens in the history of travel. It is true that
pilgrimage as a broad phenomenon has come to be appreciated as a prominent feature of the world historical landscape.[26] Expanding the category of
pilgrimage across time and space, however, has stirred anxiety lest particular colors of Christian pilgrimage distort an appreciation of non-Christian
historical phenomena that qualify as pilgrimage. It has been observed that
a new appreciation of pilgrimage in Greek and Roman antiquity—"how
central it was to the fabric of national and international politics at all periods of ancient history"—requires that "we divest it of any association with
Christianity."[27] This is sensible enough, though also suggestive of irony.
While alert to prevent Christian discoloration of new-found varieties of pilgrimage, scholars have allowed a whole era of Christian pilgrimage to the
sacred Levant to languish in the shadows of a neglect from which other

varieties of pilgrimage in other cultures are now escaping. Moreover, this neglected era happens to be the chronologically central era of European pilgrimage, stretching from the end of the "Middle Ages" (the classic epoch of European pilgrimage) to the collapse of the ancien régime. A reason that early modern pilgrims have escaped scrutiny may be that students of world-wide pilgrimage have tended to stress the metaphorical and penitential aspects of Christian pilgrimage. What has been missing is an appreciation that the survival and development of pilgrimage in early modern Europe has much to do with its survival as a form of *travel*—something that Christian pilgrimage shares with all other forms of pilgrimage.

Another reason for scholars' neglect of early modern pilgrimage to the Levant is that few were the actual pilgrims journeying to Jaffa and Jerusalem. Chateaubriand testifies to this decline, but so too do early modern pilgrims themselves, many of whom expressed in their accounts a desire to reverse the trend. The profile of early modern pilgrimage is significantly defined by a shifting ratio between the fact (the actual practice) of pilgrimages to the Levant on the one hand and the literature that celebrated actual pilgrimages, however few, on the other hand. A rough comparison might shed light. Pilgrimage over a long stretch of centuries (medieval, premodern) was marked by a vital literature of pilgrimages but also by a vigorous practice of pilgrimage, so vigorous that at times it merged with the concept of a broader undertaking such as the Crusades. In later modernity (our era), however, more pilgrims visit Jerusalem and its environs in a year than visited these same sites in any of the medieval centuries;[28] and yet one could hardly call this period a great era of pilgrim travel since the literature of pilgrimage has been culturally dormant, even moribund. Today's pilgrimage, it could be argued, survives as a vigorous form of piety, but not as a form of undertaking that contributes powerfully to the larger culture's idea of travel. In the early modern era, however, actual pilgrimage to the Levant was rare, but the literature, the *travel literature* that was produced and published and republished and translated kept pilgrimage very much alive as a form of engaged travel in the minds of its readers. And it is this middle era of pilgrimage—pilgrimage of the early modern period—that has been missed by scholarship, because the literature itself has been overlooked while the relative emptiness of the roads and sea lanes to Palestine has been noted perhaps too much.

Whatever the precise reasons, the strong tendency on the part of modern scholarship, especially when at work on large canvases, to view pilgrimage to Jerusalem as so thoroughly medieval as to be forgotten as a

vital form of travel and as a genre of travel literature in early modern
Europe, has been almost unrelieved.[29] The Turners, who more than thirty
years ago gave academical impetus to the topic of pilgrimage, treated Christian pilgrimage at length and in depth across a wide spectrum; but con-
spicuously outside their sustained notice was pilgrimage to Jerusalem in
precisely these three centuries between the Renaissance and the French
Revolution.[30] Sweeping surveys of Christian pilgrimage also give the subject short shrift.[31] It is sometimes granted to be a bridge between a waning medieval travel and modern modes of getting about, even as a root
and inspiration of that later travel, but at the same time as something that
had seen its day.[32] Especially is pilgrimage hurried to the exit when the
subject is the history of early modern travel in general. Thus, Justin Stagl
speaks of pilgrimage losing its legitimacy in the sixteenth century as *pietas*
gave way to *curiositas*. Frowns and smirks on the part of Erasmus and
Reformers are thought to have been decisive and unanswerable. In such a
view, travel only became newly legitimate when devout travel was replaced
by educative travel.[33] And most strikingly, Antoni Mączak, who takes the
history of early modern travel by Europeans as his subject matter, displays
no hesitancy in excluding pilgrimage to the Levant from his topic:

I decided to omit any discussion of journeys outside Western and Central Europe.
The inclusion of the Levant as well as of the Balkans or Russia, not to mention
countries further afield, would have introduced a completely different set of contemporary problems.[34]

Thus the depth, the completeness, of pilgrimage's fall from historiographical notice! Early moderns' travel to the Levant is equated with travel to
the Balkans or Russia, as though Jerusalem and Bethlehem and Nazareth
and Sinai were nothing more than eccentric and out of the way places very
much off the beaten path.[35] It is as though the significance of the Levant
had nothing to do with the sites of sacred history and with a centuries-
long tradition of travel by Westerners to those sites. It is as though there
did not exist three centuries of a large printed literature that described and
encouraged such travel to the Levant. Little wonder, then, that the absence
of pilgrimage to Jerusalem from an integral place in the early modern history of travel has led to its absence from more general syntheses of early
modern Europe, even those which have focused on the religious dimension of European culture.[36]

*   *   *

The contours as well as the context of early modern pilgrimage's survival as a mode of travel are sketched in the following pages. The first two chapters describe pilgrimage to the Levant in the late fifteenth century, when the great operative novelty was the technology of printing and the great robust form of travel remained pilgrimage. Medieval pilgrimages were translated from manuscript to print (Chapter 1). Contemporary pilgrimages also found their way into print (Chapter 2). The ease with which pilgrimage became a subject matter in print suggested that pilgrimage would remain what it had always been—the great form of long-distance travel for Europeans. Then, however, the history of travel experienced interruption and unraveling and the threat of discontinuity. The context of travel grew more complicated. The predictable future dissolved. An arduous road lay ahead for early modern pilgrimage because the overall shape of European travel altered so abruptly at the turn to the sixteenth century. The dynamic and overarching context of this shift, which involved both the transformation of European travel from pilgrimage into something new and the survival of the old way of travel, was the growth of print as Europe's means of discourse and dissemination of ideas. Print eventually became the practical matrix of nearly everything ideational in early modern Europe. But there is other context that, in league with print, pertains especially to travel. Travel could hardly be left unaltered when Europeans began to move across the globe into regions previously unknown. New routes to new places, new motives and ambitions for undertaking journeys—such helped to generate a new voice, in the form of printed collections of travels, to explain these novelties (Chapter 3). Nor could travel remain unaltered when religious reformers directly assaulted the ancient ways of *peregrinatio* (Chapter 4). Even reinvigorated local and regional pilgrimages—themselves in part a Catholic response to Reformation— had a complicating (though not entirely discouraging) effect on the nature and the prospects of long-distance pilgrimage (Chapter 5). The new technology of print gave impetus and energy to these new developments. The ancient travel of pilgrimage gave way to a new multi-form scheme of travel within which pilgrimage held a reduced and less secure position as one among many modes of early modern travel.

In this new world, long-distance travel *causa religionis* became rarer and more difficult when attempted by individuals and groups; it also became far more difficult to maintain its cultural standing as travel. In both respects, pilgrimage entered upon an *iter durum*. Nevertheless, as the practice of pilgrimage declined, the literature of pilgrimage flourished. Unlike early modern pilgrimage to holy places within Europe or pilgrimage to Palestine in prior centuries, early modern pilgrimage to Jerusalem now became an *almost* purely literary phenomenon. Never, on the other hand, did it quite lose its grounding in actual traveling experience. Printed pilgrimages were, for the most part, descriptions of actual journeys. That this literature was a genuine travel literature is suggested by the inclusion of accounts of such pilgrimage in the printed collections of travels of individual travelers who went to many other places than just the Holy Land (Chapter 6). Collected travels of individual travelers (in contrast to the general gatherings of accounts by collectors of travels) can be thought of as a second, and modifying, voice in the early modern discourse on travel. These traveler-writers were interested in much more than pilgrimage, but were nevertheless much interested in pilgrimage itself. The interest of these travelers helped pilgrimage to survive.

Finally, there existed a third voice in the early modern discourse on travel. Levantine pilgrimage survived above all as a live cultural form of travel by serving as the principal subject matter in books of travelers whose main destination was indeed the Holy Land. In such books, early modern pilgrimage appears vital to early modern culture, both because of its flourishing bibliographical record as printed literature and because the books themselves often wrestled vigorously with the meaning of devout travel in the newly complicated and enlarged context of travel (Chapter 7). The striking fact is that such pilgrimage survived precisely through an awareness, on the part of pilgrims themselves, of the troubles they faced. Pilgrimage survived not as detritus or stored furniture or object of curiosity, but as that which it had always been—a vital form of travel—while at the same time undergoing great evolution and alteration because of a changing historical context which included a changing context of travel itself. Early modern culture is unrecognizable without the literature of discovery; but neither is that culture clearly recognizable without the literature of pilgrimage. Together they document much of the ongoing history of European travel.

MODERNIZATION
OF TRAVEL

I

Medieval Pilgrimage into Print

WITHIN HALF A CENTURY of Byzantine Jerusalem's fall to the Arabs in 638, there came to be written, near the western edge of Christendom off the coast of Scotland, an account of pilgrimage to the Levant. The Frankish bishop Arculf, abroad in the East sometime between 679 and 682, had ended up, on his return passage, perhaps aboard a ship blown off course, at the Irish monastery of Iona, where his conversation provided the substance of Abbot Adamnan's *De locis sanctis*.[1] The book was bursting with topographical data, but also yielded up a narrative of travel that included a nine-month stay in Jerusalem which saw its subject "traversing the holy places in daily visitations."[2] Arculf was "a wanderer (*peragrator*) over several regions"[3] who had journeyed around Palestine, on to Egypt, and then to Constantinople.

Where Arculf lodged, how long he stayed in certain places, what he saw with his own eyes, the measurements he took, his swimming across the Jordan river from one shore to the other at the spot of Jesus's baptism, how his guide hurried him around Nazareth and up and down Mount Tabor, the fact that the guide was a native Burgundian and now a hermit in upper Palestine—such things Adamnan's readers learn.[4] Had Adamnan only marshaled topographical information without conveying details of travel, his book would have been unremarkable. Apart from the text's supplementing and seconding earlier traditions—not much in matters of fact separates Arculf from Jerome—the thread that runs throughout is Arculf's experiences (*experientia, experimentum*) in his own travels, experiences with which Adamnan begins, to which he returns, and with which he concludes his work.[5]

In the post-Roman West, pilgrimage was a great subject matter. By Adamnan's day, Western pilgrimage to the Levant belonged to an ancient but interrupted tradition of travel. Pious journeying to Jerusalem reached back to Origen (c. 180-c.253) and probably much earlier.[6] Between the Constantinian settlement of the Church in the fourth century and the Arab conquest of the eastern Mediterranean in the early seventh, Western Christians not only had gone on pilgrimage to Syria, but had produced a literature of such travel.[7] What would become full-fledged travel writing in Adamnan had existed, if only in skeletal form, from very early days. So rigorously single-minded a work as the *Itinerarium* of the fourth-century Bordeaux Pilgrim—the oldest pilgrimage to find its way into print (but not until 1589, and again, in combination with the *Itinerarium Antonini Augusti*, in 1600)—may have austerely listed towns and stops and distances on the way to and from Palestine, but even this bare-bones production blossomed into pages of remarks when describing the holy sites of Palestine and their Constantinian churches.[8] Nor did the author's pious focus distract him entirely from noticing a larger world that included the burial place of Hannibal in Bithynia, as well as the tomb of Euripides and the birthplace of Alexander in Macedonia.[9]

Adamnan's work resumed this literary genre, as did Arculf's the pious practice, after the early Arab conquests in the Mediterranean.[10] Writing up pilgrimages continued until the twelfth century, when new accounts—part historical narratives, part tales of travels—described European Crusades to the Levant that merged soldiering and pilgrimaging.[11] This synthesis (sometimes, in the sources, confusion)[12] of *peregrinatio* and *expeditio* lasted for over a century, from the late 1090s into the 1220s. After that, Crusading grew increasingly less plausible as a mode of conducting any European business, not just military conquest, in the Levant. Such decline led to a renewed separation of *peregrinus* and *miles* which had been long in the making.[13] By the Fifth Crusade (1217–1221), bonds between pilgrim and soldier had frayed beyond repair. Jacques de Vitry, bishop of Acre (1216–1228), in letters reporting back to Europe from the scene of events, described tension between pilgrims and the Crusader establishment. He sizes up pilgrims as incautious, unreliable, naive, and worse. When the Sultan tries to get the crusaders to lift the siege of Damietta by offering a package that includes the return of Jerusalem and the Church of the Holy Sepulchre, and rent for the retention of some fortresses (Crak, Monreale), most of the pilgrims (*multis ex peregrinis nostris*) thought it a good bargain that ought to be jumped at. But everyone else ("especially the Templars and Hospitalers of Saint John and of Saint Mary of the Germans, as well as the legate of the palace together with the patriarch, the archbishops and bishops and all the clergy") and even a "certain part of the pilgrims" saw wolves' tricks aimed at dividing and conquering the Latins. The immediate effect was indeed "dissension and discord" among the Latins.[14] In the same letter, Jacques speaks of robbers and bandits who are "pilgrims in name only . . . They are hateful to God, disobedient to the lord legate, and, just as Achor, utterly blinded by cupidity."[15] His rage against alleged pilgrims threatens to become almost systematic.[16]

A key subsequent date, suggestive if not causative of what was developing, was 11 February 1229, when Frederick II and the Sultan signed a treaty at Jaffa, the practical effect of which was that Latin Christians won safe access to, but not full possession of, or genuine control over, Jerusalem, Bethlehem, and Nazareth.[17] The treaty was reminiscent of what pilgrims welcomed and Crusaders could not stomach just a few years earlier before the walls of Damietta. The treaty of Jaffa, whatever its geopolitical significance, prepared the ground for a revival of pilgrimage unencumbered by Crusade. Once security of Europeans in the Levant, rather than conquest of the Levant by these same Europeans, came to be the realistic goal, Latin pilgrimages to the Holy Land became once again free to come into their own and to flourish, at least until the time of Columbus.[18] Even after the fall of Acre in 1291, European dreams and strategies of conquest of the Orient persisted; but no longer was the martial vision rampant and determinative. It would henceforth be easier to distinguish between pilgrim and holy warrior.[19]

To travel, especially to set upon a long-distance journey, was once again primarily and unambiguously to go on pilgrimage to Jerusalem. Free of martial associations, pilgrimage to the Orient was the kind of travel that was remembered and celebrated and analyzed *as travel*. Two centuries and more between the waning of Crusades and the coming of great voyages of discovery constituted a resumed era of travel defined as pilgrimage. The great travel narratives written down by Europeans throughout the fourteenth and fifteenth centuries were accounts of pilgrimage to Jerusalem. Clearly the kind of journey that merited recognition—that deserved literary shaping, recollection, and elaboration—was long-distance pilgrimaging.[20] And behind this literary fact stood immense numbers of actual pilgrims. Shiploads of Latin pilgrims, setting out chiefly from Venice, annually made their way to the sacred *Oriens* during much of the fourteenth and fifteenth centuries.[21] And behind the numbers stood an impressive infrastructure that made possible pilgrimage on a grand scale. At one end of the journey was Venice, devoting whole ships and even convoys of ships to the carrying of pilgrims to Jaffa and back. At the other end, Franciscans guided and housed the Latin arrivals.[22]

Pilgrimage did more than generate its own literature of travel. So much a part of the cultural ether, pilgrimage penetrated other genres. Long-distance pilgrims—rather than merchants, soldiers, or diplomatists—were exemplary travelers whom *littérateurs* (hagiographers, encyclopedists, chroniclers) noticed to be out and abroad. Jerusalem was the distant location and great destination on which readers of whatever sort needed, or were curious to have, traveler's information.[23] Nowhere is this intrusive role of pilgrimage as claimant of readers' attention more in evidence than in the medieval literature that offered the widest possible of canvases—the literature of chronicles.[24] This was true even long before Crusades had given pilgrimage a high, if somewhat indistinct, profile in the consciousness of Europeans. Ademar of Chabannes's eleventh-century chronicle of France from its origins to the author's own day is only one striking example of how Jerusalem and Europeans' pilgrimages to Jerusalem could suddenly materialize on a large historical canvas that otherwise had nothing to do with the Levant.[25] This broad and pervasive noetic reality of pilgrimage, as well as its specific presence in a descriptive literature of its own and the numerous pilgrimages undertaken by actual (as opposed to armchair) pilgrims—all three characteristics marked the centuries before and after the Crusades as an age of pilgrimage, much as the succeeding centuries would come to assume the coloration of an age of discovery.

After the early sixteenth century, pilgrims became less likely to occupy space in narratives that otherwise had little to do with pilgrimage. Within Europe, new figures—discoverers, missionaries, tourists—became typical travelers who commanded wide notice.[26] In the Levant itself, the waning of late medieval pilgrimage can be seen in Turkish seizure of key places crucial to pilgrimage travel—Modon and Coron in August 1500, for example, and Rhodes in December 1522, all three of which had been prominently engraved in the great 1486 *Peregrinatio* of Bernhard Breydenbach.[27] Numbers of actual pilgrims declined. The infrastructure of pilgrimage weakened. No longer did pilgrims fill entire ships, much less convoys, departing from Venice and destined solely for the Holy Land. What was happening, however, while a profound shift in the conditions of actual travel and in the sensibilities of many actual travelers, was less than a *complete* cultural tergiversation. Something considerable of the old travel and the old sensibility continued. And this something was that other measure of pilgrimage's cultural status—its role as subject matter of its own distinct genre of travel. Nor did such travel literature merely continue. Levantine pilgrimage's early place in the new technology of print strongly indicated that it was more than a cultural fossil.

*   *   *

When printing became a mode of publication, medieval pilgrimages (i.e., pre-print pilgrimages) were printed almost immediately and continued to be so into the eighteenth century and beyond. Early printers tended to look to the thirteenth and fourteenth centuries for printable manuscripts of pilgrimage and did, in fact, find bestsellers in the relatively remote likes of John Mandeville, Joannes de Hese, Burchardus of Mount Sion, and Jacques de Vitry. They sought pilgrim texts with a proven popularity (to judge by the evidence of surviving manuscripts).[28] Mandeville is particularly illustrative of this popularity and vitality of pre-Gutenberg pilgrimages in print. While "preoccupations purely religious"[29]—the longing to see relics, holy burials in churches, and other religious souvenirs—may have begun to fade from travel writings during the fifteenth century, this is far from saying that pilgrimage itself was on the wane. Rather, pilgrimage's frame of narration was expanding. Pious travel had never been purely religious in its concerns. There had always been much on the way to Palestine, as well as much more beyond Palestine to the east, to catch pilgrims' attention. Certainly, on the eve of printing and during the three centuries following its advent, the world-at-large was coming very much into focus for the pilgrim, without thereby rendering the traveler any less a pilgrim.[30] Mandeville, who had been immensely popular in manuscript and who would continue (from the 1480s) to be so in early modern print, is perhaps the best example of this widened frame of attention.[31]

The 1612 London printing of an English version of Mandeville emphasized pilgrimage as the principal and comprehensive subject matter of a work that nevertheless ranged far beyond Europe and the Holy Land and that noticed much more than churches and shrines and relics. The title makes all of this clear.[32] That forty-three of one hundred and nine chapters treat the routes to Jerusalem, the actual journey to Jerusalem, and the traveling around the holy places of the Holy Land, suggests the primary focus of the work The beginning of the preface[33] demonstrates Mandeville's duality of subject matter (peregrinative and non-peregrinative):

Heere beginneth a short treatise of Sir John Mandevile Knight (who was borne in England, in the Towne of Saint Albone) and speaketh of the wayes to Hierusalem, to Inde, & to the great Caane, and also to Prester Johns land, and to many other countries, and also of many mervailes that are in the holy land.

Its circling back to the matter of the "mervailes in the holy land," however, shows that the enveloping concern of the book was pilgrimage. Pilgrimage, moreover, is the purposeful core of the book. The same preface urges

upon a world riven by discord the usefulness of pilgrimage as a means to
a better world. "But would God," is his prayer, "the worldly Lords were
at a good accord, and with other of their common people, would take this
holy Voyage over the Sea, I trust well that within a little time our right
heritage before said, would be reconciled, and put into the hands of the
right heires of Iesu Christ."[34]

Mandeville's Holy Land is a place whose component sites can be connected to appropriate passages of Scripture. It is also a land of marvels
which form common ground with the marvelous *Oriens* that is also his
subject matter. Mandeville's approach is extravagantly superficial. He seeks
to shake rather than to stir his readers. He covers great spaces, getting
from Europe to the Holy Land and from there to the great exotic regions
beyond. His is a narrative defined by places where he is brought up short
by the purely astounding. The traveler's response to all of this is more wide-
eyed than contemplative or philosophical. There is, for example, the Ile of
Dodyn, which is spoken of as "a great Ile. In the same Ile are many and
divers sorts of men who have evill manners, for the father eateth the son,
and the son the father, the husband his wife, and the wife her husband."
Habits are matched by appearances. An entire population of headless men
walks around with eyes in their shoulders and mouths on their chests.[35] If
the substratum of Mandeville's text as a whole (and of woodcuts that illustrate individual passages in various editions) is the marvelous in a general
fashion—whether the wonders of the Holy Land or the oddities of more
remote lands occupied by the weirdly formed and badly behaved—pilgrimage itself acts as a defining coloration of the traveler, obviously in the earlier stages of the book, but also later in the East when he happens upon
the shrine of St. Thomas. He is careful to describe (and the engraver of
the 1612 edition to depict) the tomb of St. Thomas, its chief attraction being
Thomas's hand, which is on display as a religious relic and as a judicial
touchstone which attracts pilgrims and litigants from far and wide (Figure 1). An idol in the church also draws pilgrims in great processions.[36]
There is a lushness to this Indian pilgrimage that Mandeville alleges to
have beheld and that he cannot resist lingering over and underlining. Mandeville's traveler's eye remains, however much of his material seems to us
non-peregrinative, the eye of the pilgrim.

Pilgrimage sped into early modern print precisely because it was travel,
not because it was a narrow, pre-Chateaubriandian religious practice to be
"performed" in a late modern or post-modern fashion. What had been clear
in Adamnan in the seventh century—that the pilgrim Arculf was a devout

Of the kingdome of Mabaron. Chap. liiij.

Rom this land men goe many dayes iourney to a
countrp called Mabaron, and this is a great king-
dome, therein is many faire Cities and Townes.
In this land lyeth Saint Thomas in a faire tombe
in the Citie of Calamp, and the arme and the hand
that hée put in our Lords side after his Resurrection, when

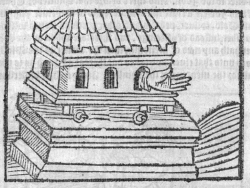

Christ said vnto him, Noli esse incredulus, sed fidelis. That is
to say, Be not of vaine hope but beléeue: that same hand lyeth
yet without the tombe bare, and with this hand they giue their
domes in that country, to wit, who saith right, and who doth
not, for if any strife be betwéene two parties, they wryte their
names, and put them into the hand, and then incontinently
the hand casteth away the bill of him that doth wrong, and
holdeth the other still that doth right, and therefore men come
from farre countries to haue iudgement of causes that are in
doubt.

In this Church of Saint Thomas is a great Image that
is a simulacre, and it is richly beset with precious stones and
M 3   pearles,

Figure 1. John Mandeville, *The voyages and travailes* (London: Thomas Snodham, 1612), M3r.

and experience-enriched *traveler*—remained true of much later medieval pilgrimages that were given new life in print beginning in the fifteenth century. And this was pious travel with a very wide lens. Mandeville's account shows this, but so do other medieval pilgrimages that gained new life as early modern printed books.

Ludolfus of Suchem, for example, was a parish priest of the diocese of Paderborn, who spent five years in the Holy Land in the 1330s and who finally set down his reminiscences years later. While his book provides a dense description of the holy places complete with measurements, depictions of structures (ruinated, surviving, made over to new uses) and their decorations, and the correspondence of particular places to passages in Scripture as well as to traditions that give these places their importance, nevertheless Ludolfus makes emphatically and repeatedly clear in the *Prologue* that he intends not only to write of the state and conditions of the Holy Land, but of the marvels (*mirabilibus*) that are encountered between Europe and the Levant as one sails from port to port across the Mediterranean.[37] Having enjoyed a rich manuscript tradition over more than a century, Ludolfus's book was printed around 1475 and continued to appear in print until about 1485.[38]

Another travel book of the fourteenth century that proved popular in print was the pilgrim Joannes de Hese's *Itinerarium*, the earliest imprint of which appeared in Cologne around 1490. As late as 1565, the same book appeared under the title *Peregrinatio* in Antwerp. Hese himself, a priest from Utrecht, was undoubtedly a pilgrim. In May of 1389, he tells us, he was visiting the holy places in Jerusalem. But was his book an account of pilgrimage? The title, after all, appears an accurate characterization: "A Journey from Jerusalem through various parts of the world." Jerusalem seems nothing but a point of departure for regions far more remote and exotic. A closer reading, however, suggests that the *Itinerarium* continues to offer pilgrimage as the frame, and indeed oxygen, of Hese's further travels. Jerusalem is not so much the jumping-off place, as the initiatory unfolding of all that follows. Hese's Eastern travels flow out of, and are directly consequent upon, his unelaborated pilgrimage to and around Jerusalem. What led him to Jerusalem, and around the Holy Land, led him to continue on. The pertinent passage reads more fully:

> In the year of Our Lord 1389, I Joannes Hese, priest of the diocese of Utrecht, was in Jerusalem in May, visiting there the holy places and making my pilgrimage (beyond the usual) to the Jordan, and across the Jordan to the Red Sea, and on to parts of Egypt and to one city in particular called Hermopolis, which was the

capital city of Egypt where the Blessed Virgin lived seven years with her son Our Lord. And it was in the Red Sea that I saw fishes flying such a distance as one might shoot an arrow.[39]

And then he is off—and yet hardly in flight from being a pilgrim. His journeys taken whole prove more seamless than that. Devout travel is not exhausted by a few syllables explaining the author's being in Jerusalem— "visiting there the holy places." He further says that his pilgrimage extended beyond the norm, leading him to the Jordan and beyond the Jordan, and then much beyond into Egypt, where the first exotic city he mentions fits into a scheme of Marian associations. He remains, in effect, in the land of sacred history. True, he then seizes on odd flora and fauna—at the start, flying fish—which will become a staple of Europeans venturing through the *Oriens*, but the travel log never loses its peregrinative complexion. Within pages, he is telling us about the body of St. Thomas in India: "The apostle's body is whole and intact complete with hair and beard and the very clothes that he wore when alive."[40]

What Mandeville and Ludolfus and Hese all show is that later medieval pilgrimage provided an expansive framework for describing travels, a fact that helps explain the success of their manuscripts in print during the early decades after Gutenberg. The pious adventure—such it was—of Levantine pilgrimage could not but take Europeans (both actual travelers and readers) far out of themselves. It required a long journey to get to the Levant; once there, the terrain of pilgrimage was itself large and complicated, a true field of recordable motion; and beyond the Levant, beyond Jerusalem and Sinai, lay vast Oriental spaces, unknown but imaginable expanses that pilgrims could visit, or claim to have visited, once they had already gotten as far as Jaffa. In the case of Hese, the sense of a change coming in travel is striking. The body of pilgrimage, so to speak, has almost vanished in the breath required for a single mention of Jerusalem; but the soul of pilgrimage remains as the occasion and impetus and atmosphere for further voyaging into the Oriental beyond. *Peregrinatio*—the meaning of the word *almost* alters before the reader's eyes. There is not quite yet a sense of genre bursting at the seams, of new wine spilling from old wineskins, of pilgrimage no longer being identical with travel.

Pilgrimage had for so many centuries been the great form of European travel, the great example of discussable, ponderable mobility, because of its thick religious meaning—ideas of life itself as pilgrimage had deep roots in Latin Christian thought and culture[41]—but also because of this

long-distance character of Westerners' *peregrinatio ad Terram Sanctam* that
made such an undertaking a preeminent occasion for relatable experiences.
Jaffa, Jerusalem, Bethlehem, Nazareth, Sinai—such were sufficiently far
away to stoke travelers' and readers' imaginations, even without tales of
Malabar and Prester John to supplement or overwhelm actual pilgrimage.

The *Itinerarium* of the fourteenth-century Irish Franciscan, Symon
Simeonis, another pilgrimage composed at roughly the same time—but
that found its way into print in the eighteenth century, rather than in the
waning decades of the fifteenth—demonstrates that there was even material rich enough to pass on to the reader just in the getting from Europe
to Palestine. We are given the sights and sounds of London, Paris, and
Venice.[42] Symon tells of seeing the head of John the Baptist in Amiens, of
visiting the city of Nice (which he mistakes for Nicaea in Asia Minor, the
seat of the first oecumenical council), of stopping at the ancient monastery
of Bobbio where he visited the tomb of the sixth-century Irish missionary
Columbanus and saw a stone jar from Cana.[43] Readers learn of the costumes, customs, and relics of Crete.[44] Text is swallowed up, and readers'
attention swept along, by the great topic of Alexandria, details and wonders
and variety of whose history and daily life threaten to swamp the narrative.
Cairo, too, is a magnificent sight for Western eyes (and would continue
to be so throughout early modernity) (Figure 2), the city itself sparking
comparison with Paris.[45] Nevertheless, however great a variety of things
European and Oriental are seen through Symon's eyes, the reader is never
left to forget that Jerusalem is the goal and frame of the long journey.
When his traveling party is insulted by Moslems in Alexandria, Symon
responds: "If Mahomet be the true prophet, then remain in peace with
him and praise him; but to us there is no other lord than Jesus Christ,
whose adopted sons we are and not spies, wishing to visit His glorious
tomb, kneel before it, kiss it with our lips, and moisten it with our tears!"
And upon their arrival at long last at Jerusalem, the holy city is described
as the "port keenly anticipated and long desired."[46]

That Symon's pilgrimage came to printed life only in the eighteenth
century shows that the longing for historical tales of pilgrims' travels, which
we might have supposed to have characterized only the earliest decades of
printing before navigators and Reformers had come upon the scene to
remake travel, did in fact continue well into the eighteenth century. And
what these historical revivals of texts of pilgrimage seem to be about is
in fact devotional travel, and not simply devotions narrowly understood.
A fourteenth-century pilgrimage rescued from the Cambridge University

stacks struck a chord in eighteenth-century travelers and readers of travels. There leaps from a seven-page list of subscribers, for example, the name of Joseph Banks, the great patron and colleague of Captain Cook, as well as the name of Thomas Pennant, the traveler and travel writer.[47]

In the period between the advent of printing in Europe and the upset of eighteenth-century revolution, the printing of pre-Gutenberg pilgrimages represents a foot in the door of early modernity for a mode of travel and a genre of travel literature that had hitherto held sway in Western civilization for a millennium. There was a space of opportunity (of about a half-century) for medieval pilgrimage to become modern. This space existed between the coming of print and the beginning of the great ventures of discovery, which could not but alter Europeans' ideas of travel. And there was additional space (of about two decades) before these discoveries combined with ecclesiastical reformations to place in serious jeopardy the future of pilgrimage both as a practice and as a literary genre within Western civilization.

In the brief meantime—pilgrimage's breathing space—"to become modern" meant minimally to be printed. A crepuscular quality, certainly

Figure 2. Noè Bianchi, *Viaggio da Venezia al S. Sepolcro* (Bassano: G. A. Remondini, 1742), pp. 138–39.

in retrospect, is lent to millennium-old pilgrimages when newly outfitted in print. The best indicator of pre-Gutenberg pilgrimage's presence on the early modern stage is that John Mandeville's book, which had flourished in manuscript before Gutenberg, continued to flourish in print in many languages and often in illustrated editions throughout the early modern period. Medieval pilgrimages printed in early modern times suggest possibilities concerning the survival of pilgrimage on the early modern scene. Printed editions of Ludolfus of Suchem and Joannes de Hese early on, of the Bordeaux Pilgrim in the sixteenth century, of Adamnan in the seventeenth century, of Symon Simeonis in the eighteenth, and of John Mandeville throughout early modernity—all of these reveal the footprint of medieval Europe in early modern Europe. Whether pilgrimage itself had gained a more substantial foothold in early modern culture—more substantial, that is, than as a medieval reminiscence or even as a plausible influence on newer ways of traveling and writing about travel—is a question that requires evidence that is contemporary rather than archaeological.

2

Contemporary Pilgrimage into Print:
1450–1500

AT THE TURN TO THE SIXTEENTH CENTURY, Polydore Vergil lauded Gutenberg and Nicholas Jenson and the city of Mainz for their roles in the invention of printing, but avoided details because he thought the matter common knowledge that would soon be taken quite for granted. The invention had nevertheless been sufficiently marvelous to halt in its tracks Polydore's own dissertation on discoveries in antiquity. The first library, Polydore had observed in his 1499 *On the Discoverers of Things,*

is nothing in comparison with an achievement of our own day, a newly devised way of writing. In one day just one person can print the same number of letters that many people could hardly write in a whole year. Books in all the disciplines have poured out to us so profusely from this invention that no work can possibly remain wanting to anyone, however needy. Note too that this invention has freed most authors, Greek as well as Latin, from any threat of destruction.[1]

Polydore, cheered as he was by a lettered past made permanent and safe by this new invention, would hardly have found inexplicable decisions to print medieval accounts of travel to Jerusalem. Here, as in other areas of intellection and discourse, early printing magnified Europe's cultural inheritances. Even so popular a pilgrim as John Mandeville had never been so widely known as he was about to be. At the same time, and as Polydore also saw, printing was not just a preservative of past intellectual legacies. Books of contemporary pilgrimage were also printed, and perhaps the greatest example—or, at least, the most striking and ambitious—was Bernhard Breydenbach's book of pilgrimage that described his travels to Jerusalem in 1483–1484. Lavish illustrated editions had appeared in print in both Latin and German by 1486. Nor was Breydenbach the first contemporary pilgrim to have had his book printed.

Hans Tucher of Nuremberg (a town councilor who, the year after his

pilgrimage, would become mayor of the city) may be said to have anticipated Breydenbach. The success of his *Reise in das gelobte Land*, a bestseller
of its time, showed the possibilities of contemporary pilgrimage as a subject matter. Tucher's book first appeared in Augsburg in 1479, the same
year as the journey itself. The book reappeared twice in that city in 1482
(once in a corrected edition), and again in Augsburg in 1486 and 1488. It
was available in Nuremberg in 1482, 1483, 1484, and 1486, and in Strassburg in 1483 and 1484. After a pause of nearly two decades, extracts of the
Reise appeared in Nuremberg in 1505 and in Leipzig in 1518. After another
pause, the full text reappeared in print in Frankfurt on Main in 1561. Almost
a quarter century later, Tucher's account was included in Feyerabend's
Reyssbuch of 1584 and in the second edition of 1609.[2]

Much of the content of Tucher's narrative he shared with contemporary travelers and medieval predecessors. Moreover, his "journey and pilgrimage" (*Raise und Wallfart*) do not seem to have caused any rift in his
mind between touristical and devotional components.[3] Similar to the medieval pilgrimages from a century (or many centuries) earlier that were now
coming into print, Tucher's contemporary journey commented on the world
around him. He never lost sight, however, of the journey's spiritual motivation. Touristical distractions scarcely caused him to miss a pilgrim's beat.[4]

That the *Reise in das gelobte Land* was a guide book is clear from passages where Tucher dispenses practical information to the reader, whom
he takes to be a potential traveler. This was, after all, a time when there
still existed the infrastructure for regular travel to Palestine.[5] His detailed
advice on how to travel and what to take (in terms of food and medicine)
suggests how much pilgrimage remained the great option, the great possibility of adventurous travel, for Europeans.[6] Although he himself had
chosen the sea route, Tucher also describes the trek from Nuremberg over-
land to Jerusalem.[7] He is particularly keen to impress upon readers the
rigors of the journey from Gaza to Sinai. Gaza is the last stopping-off
point where provisions can be purchased—a three-day supply of bread,
for example, and two hundred lemons.[8] And at the very end of his text, he
again treats at some length the practical details of travel (expenses, necessi-
ties, distances), and especially impresses upon sea-going pilgrims their
need to develop a good working relationship with their Venetian ship's
agent, upon whom they must rely throughout the journey.[9]

Tucher's book, the first contemporary pilgrimage to the Levant printed
in the fifteenth century, would quickly have become outdated—not because
of its commentary on the holy places (relatively timeless material, to judge

by cited evidence going back to Arculf and Jerome), but because of Tucher's asides on the mundane realities of his day. Age-old features of the traveler's landscape were about to alter so profoundly that there are places in the text where Tucher seems as "medieval" (which of course he was) as pilgrims from a century and more earlier whose texts were also being printed at just this time. With Vasco da Gama's exploits in the near but unforeseeable future, Tucher understandably remains struck by the sight of ships in the Red Sea "coming with all their spices from India." He speaks of Granada as "a heathen kingdom."[10] He celebrates Levantine pilgrimage as an enterprise underwritten by centuries of papal endorsement, reaching back to Pope Sylvester in the fourth century.[11] Such pilgrimage serves as an occasion for celebrating the spiritual unity of Christendom, with its Empire and many Christian kingdoms. For Tucher, one Christian society reaching from England to Italy and from Scandinavia to Iberia manifests itself in the overarching enterprise of devout travel to Jerusalem.[12] Tucher might conceivably have surmised numbered days for Moslem Granada, but was less likely to have imagined great discoverers opening new routes to the East, and unlikely indeed to have contemplated the possibility of a European reformation shivering Christendom and casting a pall of controversy (especially for German travelers) over pious travel to the Levant. Seismic shifts of European culture escaped suspicion in the decades just before cultural ground began to move. A sense of the old order (vigorous because unknowing) on the verge of the new (looming but undescried) defines the winding down of the fifteenth century and makes a printed pilgrimage such as Tucher's a particularly apt reflection of the fog and dynamics of the cultural moment.

Tucher's greatest importance resides in his popularity even in the immediate wake of *conquistadores* and new sorts of preachers in Germany's pulpits. The text's century and more of imprints paved a way into print for other pilgrimages to Jerusalem. Certainly, the astounding lavishness of the production of Bernhard Breydenbach's *Peregrinatio* of 1486 in Mainz is more understandable in light of its coming after Tucher's success in Germany. Tucher's numerous appearances in major centers of German printing before 1486 (the year Breydenbach was first printed in Latin and then in German) would have made Breydenbach's project seem a less risky publishing venture. Tucher, having demonstrated an audience for pilgrimages to Palestine, had set the stage for Breydenbach to produce something more splendid than a simple narrative.

There intervened between Tucher and Breydenbach the *Viaggio* of the

Milanese pilgrim, Santo Brasca, who set out with ninety other pilgrims on ship from Venice.[13] Brasca, too, anticipated Breydenbach, but in a different manner from Tucher. Brasca traveled to the Holy Land in 1480, the year after Tucher had been there, and in 1481 (five years before Breydenbach's book appeared) he published his travels, which much resembled Tucher's, except that Brasca had not ventured south into the deserts and cities of Egypt.[14] The book did not circulate as well as Tucher's, though it did reappear in 1487 (the year following Breydenbach's first Latin and German editions) and 1497 and then one final time in 1519.

Like Tucher at Nuremberg, Brasca at Milan was a member of the urban oligarchy. His Milan publisher addressed him as *ducalis cancellarius*, and he himself dedicated the book to Antonio Landriano, the *ducalis generalis Thesaurarius*. As much interested, if not quite so meticulously, as Tucher in indulgences attached to holy places, Brasca even underscores an indulgence granted by the contemporary pope Sixtus IV (1471–1484).[15] (For him, pilgrimage is clearly a very up-to-date affair.) Much like his German contemporary, he saw his travels as pilgrimage through and through and as an undertaking, moreover, that required of the pilgrim single-minded clarity of purpose;[16] but also like Tucher, he was alive to novelties and exotica that he encountered along his pious way from Milan to Venice, across the Mediterranean, and around Palestine. Residents of Palestine brought him up short. "The customs and costumes of both ladies and gentlemen are much different from ours." And their oddness ran deeper: "They live according to strange laws."[17] And he is censoriously aware of pilgrimage to Mecca by throngs "to visit that disgusting body of Mahomet."[18]

There were differences between the two travelers. For one thing, Brasca's book has about it a liturgical character. He sets down, sometimes at enormous length, hymns, prayers, and antiphons that pilgrims recited at each holy place. Pious travelogue threatens to become prayer book outright, so much so that Latin prayers sometimes quite overwhelm vernacular narrative.[19] For another, Brasca's text offers a first halting step towards the illustrated travel book in the form of a primitive sketch of the Holy Sepulcher (Figure 3). By the 1519 edition, the title page will also be adorned with a rendering of the Pietà at the foot of the Cross and with Jerusalem in the background. The border shows Christ's face on a cloth at the top, and Christ rising from the tomb below. This minimalist visualization of the scene of pilgrimage—realistic and matter-of-fact on the one hand, meditative and imaginative on the other—was soon to come more strikingly to the fore in the literature of pilgrimage.

Queſta ela forma del ſanctiſſimo Sepulchro.El tondo ſi e el mero Sepulchro . quele oue cellete che vedeti vna oenante al tondo. la tra orieto al tondo ſono agionti da la paſſione oel noſtro ſignore in qua.La celleta oenante al ſepulchro fu facta per non laſſare in culto z ſenza reuerentia quel ſaxo quadro che vedeti in mezo ſopra lo quale ſedeua langelo quando introno le Marie oicendo. quis reuoluet nobis lapidem ab hoſtio monumenti.
Laltra celleta oe orieto al ſepulchro e facta oa frati Ethyopi aliter Sabaſini per ſacrificare z oire ſuoi officii z oratione.

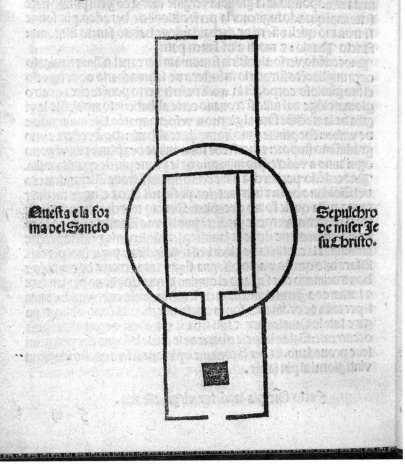

Queſta ela for
ma oel Sancto

Sepulchro
oe miſer Je
ſu Chriſto.

Figure 3. Santo Brasca, *Viagio del Sepulchro* (Mediolani: Nicolai de Gorgonzola, 1519), F3v.

Brasca in print is not quite the same thing as Brasca left to his own textual devices. His Milanese publisher, Ambrogio Archinti, has added a thing or two and thereby altered emphases.[20] While Brasca's text proper (like that of Tucher) is outfitted with advice for the prospective traveler, Archinti's few dedicatory paragraphs to the author stress the immense difficulties and dangers of such journeys. Archinti himself had been greatly worried over Brasca's dangerous plan of action[21] of going to see the Holy Land. The dangers of the sea were uppermost in Archinti's mind ("immense rocks and tossing seas"), and he imagined that "dangers loomed everywhere" once one got beyond the boundaries of the *patria*. The publisher's note indicates the spirit in which the book would be read—not as a guidebook for other prospective Levantiners, but as a great account of adventure for "those of us in our chairs." Archinti's Brasca is offering a traveler's report that puts all in his debt because what he experienced others can now see "in tranquility and safety." And so fine is his account that others, though striving to surpass him, will be frustrated because Brasca has said the persuasively last words on the subject. The unprecedented illustrations may have likewise contributed to the impression that this journey to the Levant was a work of literature that gave spiritual pleasure and aesthetic entertainment (the text itself, Archinti says, allows the reader to see things "just as if they were painted on a canvas"), rather than a practical manual for prospective travelers. Author and publisher had, of course, different immediate goals. Brasca, seized by the quasi-vocation that was Christian pilgrimage, foresaw others in his pious footsteps, while Archinti, at work on producing a book, contemplated readers in the present as well as readers stretching into the future. The slightest difference of coloration (too subtle to be called tension or agitation) between publisher and author does reflect a time when pilgrimage remained popular as the subject matter of travel even as it headed towards a long and gradual decline, not in terms of readership but in terms of popular participation in voyages.

A further difference distinguishes author from printer. Archinti regards Brasca's journey from an explicitly wider angle than does Brasca who, left to his own way of putting things, presented himself as a traveler who theoretically was nothing but a pilgrim (but who in practice, to be sure, showed himself—and not only himself but the genre of pilgrimage itself—to be more broadly and flexibly defined). His publisher, however, while granting that the heart of the matter is pilgrimage, also quickly describes the subject matter of "this holy journey" as "the customs of men and the different regions and whatever are quite remarkable in these regions." All of this is sufficiently vague to be quite inclusive. The *preciosiora* as well as the *exquisitissima quecumque* that are reported back to the sedentary of Milan may be taken to apply to the holy places, but they just as surely refer to other marvelous things observed along the way. Moreover, Archinti is taken with the subject matter of the actual getting to and back from the Levant. A dramatic sense of Brasca bringing forth his account out of the din and dust of travel—this is what Archinti points out as the quality that makes the book deserving of an enthusiastic and careful readership.[22]

Breydenbach's *Peregrinatio*, which overshadows all similar productions of his time, appeared in Latin and German editions in Mainz in 1486, just two years after his return from the Levant. The appearance of these volumes, as well as their subsequent publishing history over the next decade and a half, was a great event that all but established that pilgrimage would have a future in the history of European travels. The journey out from Venice in 1483 has been called the "most famous pilgrimage of the century," and not least because there were among the group at least four writers who wrote up the journey.[23] This was still the era of pilgrimage as *both* a literary and a practical phenomenon. Pilgrims still headed East in crowds, if not in throngs. Breydenbach's shipload of pilgrims, a little over three weeks out of Venice, was overtaken and joined by a second Venetian pilgrim ship at Modon, a coastal town at the southwest corner of Greece and one of the last stops on the mainland of western Christendom.[24] And much later on, while seeing the sites in Egypt before returning to Europe, Breydenbach's party met up with yet another group of pilgrims from Jerusalem who were on their way to Cairo and Mount Sinai.[25]

Breydenbach, recorder of the 1483 pilgrimage who most successfully and rapidly made it into print, was to be read and commented upon throughout early modernity up to Chateaubriand. Even had earlier books such as Tucher's and Brasca's not appeared, Breydenbach's work would have sufficed to show pilgrimage gloriously and robustly surviving into the age of print. His book captured the duality of literature and practice that continued to characterize pilgrimage at this time. Illustrious figure in the Mainz ecclesiastical establishment (long-time canon, and soon to be dean, of the cathedral church when he departed for Palestine in 1483), Breydenbach is described as the book's "principal author."[26] Chief among other contributors to the *Peregrinatio* were Erhard Reuwich, the artist on board whose woodcuts reproduced his eyewitness drawings, and the stay-at-home Martin Roth, the Dominican academic at Heidelberg who learnedly supplemented Breydenbach's diary accounts of his journey. Breydenbach's and

Reuwich's joint eyewitness account could have stood alone, much after the fashion of Tucher's and Brasca's accounts; but in fact, their report served as a jewel at the centre of an intricately and thickly wrought setting. As such, commentary sometimes threatened, by sheer bulk, to overwhelm narrative. In addition to diarist and artist telling us what they saw and experienced at sea, in Palestine, and in Egypt, supporting textual material included, on the one hand, lengthy historical treatments of Palestine and Egypt, the Moslems and their religion, and Oriental Christianity, much of such treatment based heavily on medieval sources; and, on the other hand, the inclusion of reports describing relatively recent events in the Levant. These all but contemporary events—Constantinople's fall in 1453, Negroponte's loss in 1471, the Turks' failed siege of Rhodes in 1480 (just three years before Breydenbach's party passed through), and their attack on Otranto in the same year—had an obvious bearing on, and interest to, Europeans at home who might wish to size up the risks and realities of travel in the eastern Mediterranean.

Breydenbach's book was an intensely traditional work. Much of what he reported on his own voyage through Palestine and Egypt had been told earlier by contemporaries and much earlier by medieval predecessors. From the perspective of the advancing sixteenth century and beyond, the work might come to seem as musty and time-bound as those of Tucher and Brasca. There was the same focus on Eastern wares coming to Europe via ancient routes and beginning their last maritime passage out of Egyptian depots.[27] There was, too, furious and detailed attention devoted to the despicable ways of Moslems and to the doubtful orthodoxies of Eastern Christians—attention on the part of Catholic pilgrims that would have to be recast within a few decades in order to include schismatics and heretics closer to home and thus more to the polemical point.[28] The book's importance was not that it departed from centuries of medieval precedents of pilgrimage, but that it gave ages-old tradition a very modern (and lavish) physical rendering on the printed and illustrated page. While much in the *Peregrinatio*—outside Breydenbach's diaries concerning the Mediterranean, Palestine, and Egypt—had little or nothing to do with Breydenbach's own eyewitnessing, those things that he did see and experience (holy places, flora and fauna, urban scenes and settings, the costumed persons of various ethnic inhabitants of the Middle East) were emphasized to an unprecedented degree. It was not only that the text itself stressed eyewitnessing—"which place [the topography of the Passion] I have seen time and again"[29]—but that a great array of woodcuts illustrated what had been seen and verbally described. The traveler's optical experience was shared twice over with the reader. A whole new (nontextual) lens was turned on, conveying to Europeans what was foreign and exotic about the pilgrim's Levant.[30] Foreign and exotic, but not startling. The aesthetic of Breydenbach's book was reportorial and superficial. The rendering of an object could be meticulous, as in the drawing of Rhodes which included a depiction of damage to the tower of the Church of St. John which had been suffered three years earlier during the Turkish siege of 1480.[31] The images in the book conveyed what was visible and verifiable—panoramas of Venice and Jerusalem, views of Mediterranean cities along the route, costumes and alphabets of peoples dwelling in the Holy Land, structures of holy places, beasts of the region. Images of the latter did contain a depiction of a unicorn, but the *text* made clear that the identification of the animal depended not on pilgrim or artist, but on the insistence of the guide.[32] Breydenbach and Reuwich did, however, take one imaginative step by depicting the pilgrim in the act of pious travel. In the large depiction of Jerusalem and the holy places, the reader can spot pilgrims leaving ship at Jaffa and stepping onto holy ground (Figure 4). And the woodcut of the plaza before the Church of the Holy Sepulchre shows pilgrims devoutly attending to the marked spot where Christ fell carrying his Cross[33] (Figure 5). What the pilgrim primarily saw— the hard data of shrines and edifices and nature before his eyes—retains its importance as major subject matter, especially given the number of woodcuts in the whole production; but these two depictions provide an early, if highly tentative, focus on the pilgrim in the act of his travels, a focus that will grow more prominent in later accounts of early modern pilgrimage. Especially in the seventeenth and eighteenth centuries, the pilgrim will become more and more a character in his travels; and, in the nineteenth century, it will mark the end of an era of pilgrimage when this development loses considerable restraint in Chateaubriand, who will replace genres by housing pilgrimage in autobiography (*mémoires*) rather than in travel (*voyages*).

The visuality of Breydenbach's book, its celebration of the optical, as well as the grand production that results from the combination of illustrations, diaries, and supplemental texts, made the *Peregrinatio* an impressive and unprecedented work in ambition and execution. In the hands of Breydenbach and his collaborators, pilgrimage itself serves as primary subject matter for the book, but also as the highly focused occasion for a wideranging articulation of the historical background to the contemporary scene of much of the Mediterranean. Breydenbach and company had clearly engaged in more than tinkering and titivation of an old genre in a new medium. *Peregrinatio*, without ceasing to be itself, becomes a vehicle of historical and contemporary *interpretatio*—and this as much by its digressions and elaborations, its spotting and filling in blanks of information and meaning, as by keeping to the main spiritual matter at hand. All of this was possible because the work was so focused on pilgrimage. It did not seem incongruous, in a work intent on the personal experience of visiting Jerusalem and Mount Sinai, to treat also of Jacobites and Maronites, of the last days of Byzantine Constantinople thirty years earlier, of Moslems in centuries past and present making their way to Mecca, of the contemporary streets of Cairo and Alexandria, or of the hardships of a town under attack on the heel of Italy.

Even Breydenbach's personal diary account, cut as much of it surely is from available peregrinative cloth, contains a crucial passage that deserves particular notice, because it marks Breydenbach's own contribution to a

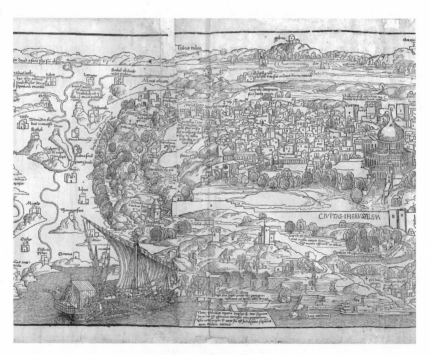

Figure 4. Bernhard Breydenbach, *Die heyligen Reyssen gen Iherusalem* (Mainz: Erhard Reuwich, 1486), Jerusalem panorama, detail.

⟨Hye ist zü mercken das die heylig statt jherusalem an eym höchsten
ende liget· nach der anstossende lantschafft zü rechen· also das man vß
Jherusalem sehet das gantz lant Arabiam·vnd das hoch gebirge Aba=
rym vnd Nebo vnd Phasga· vnd die ebenne deß jordans vnd jericho·
vnd das todt mer byß zü dem velsen der wüsteny eyn statt also genät·
deß halb Jherusalem gar eyn schone vmbsehung hatt· vnd man muß
an allen enden vff stygen dar gegen wan sie höher ligt dan keyn andere
statt yn dem selben lande· vßgenommen Sylo zwo mylen da von li=
gende·
Diß ist die gestalt vnd form deß tempels deß heyligen grabs zü jherusa
lem von vßen·

⟨Vor dem tempel des heyligen grabs lygt der steyn dar vff cristus
viel syn crütz tragen·

Figure 5. Bernhard Breydenbach, *Die heyligen Reyssen gen Iherusalem*, p. 35r.

common narrative and also because it shows with rare emphasis pilgrimage cast as adventurous *travel* rather than an undertaking more narrowly conceived as devotional and liturgical act. On the return voyage from Alexandria to Venice, Breydenbach's ship, along with others, encountered furious weather and contrary winds at sea off the treacherous southern coast of Greece. In the event it took from 22 November to 14 December to manage the passage through rocky, wintry narrows and to end up safely at anchor off Modon. The great fear throughout had been that they would be forced to stay in the Levant far into the next year until season and conditions changed. No other single episode, at sea or in Palestine or in Egypt, consumes comparable length of treatment in Breydenbach's diary (seven double-columned folio pages).[34] Because of the attention and the dramatic rendering employed by Breydenbach, this lengthy passage may be seen as a defining point of the pilgrimage. The great drama of such devout travel to the Orient, it turns out, is the drama of reentry. Moments of elation in such a journey are seeing Jaffa from the sea, arriving at Jerusalem, praying before the Holy Sepulchre, trekking to Bethlehem, climbing Sinai. The crisis in such a journey, however, is just managing to escape the parlous and deeply foreign world of the East and be once again, if not at home, at least within the Christian world. Modon had figured earlier, on the journey out, as the last station where pilgrims joined up for a common voyage. Now, it is similarly depicted as a border town, arrival at which signaled crossing from another world back into one's own world. Here was a convent of Dominicans where one could hear Mass, and a colony of German merchants to offer hospitality. And right on the doorstep were the Turks who came regularly to do robust commercial business with Latins.[35]

Breydenbach graphically (but in words rather than woodcuts) demonstrates, more than any other pilgrim writer, what all of these others also felt—that pilgrimage was a circuit. Its beginning was also its end. However much the goal was to walk in sacred footsteps in the Holy Land, the harrowing return negotiated, in midst of rocks and turbulent waters, through a sea lane with Cerigo on one side and the Morea on the other shows that the guiding intention was to make one's way safely back to Christendom. This drama of reentry defines pilgrimage as above all a travel of return. Pilgrims had crossed a frontier and regained Christendom. This sense of travel—it is one definition of travel—as a circuit that begins at home and reaches home again will remain a shared trait between the old travel of pilgrimage and much of the new travel of discovery throughout early modernity.[36]

The Latin version, which had appeared in Mainz in 1486, reappeared in Speyer in 1490, again in Mainz in 1491, and again in Speyer in 1502. The Latin text also appeared in 1573 and 1577 in Basle (as part of Antoine Geuffroy's *Aulae Turcicae Othomannicique imperii descriptio*). The German version also had a hardy existence after 1486, appearing around 1487 in Strassburg, in 1488 in Augsburg, in Speyer in 1498 and again in 1502. It too, like the text of Tucher, ended up in Feyerabend's *Reyssbuch* of 1584 and in the second edition of 1609. The *Peregrinatio* was also translated—twice!—into French and appeared eight times in one or the other French version in either Paris or Lyon between 1488 and the 1520s. A Dutch translation appeared in Haarlem in 1486, in Mainz in 1488, and in Delft in 1498. A Spanish version was printed in Saragossa in 1498 and a Polish version in Cracow in 1610. The reputation of the work was so great that its appeal, in however enervated (or even eviscerated) a form, managed to reach beyond Catholic Europe once the Reformation got under way. An extract was printed at Wittenberg in 1536. Breydenbach's text, in compressed and mangled form, also appeared in eight pages of the second volume of Purchas's celebrated *Pilgrimes Contayning a History of the World in Sea-Voyages and Land Travels by Englishmen and Others* (London, 1625). This was the only translation of Breydenbach into English.[37]

Tucher and Breydenbach, when we look just to the bibliographical surface of the matter, appear as giants of early printed pilgrimage. Tucher demonstrated that pilgrimage had an audience in the new world of printing, Breydenbach that pilgrimage had not only a place, but a glittering place as a grandly turned out item of illustrated literature. Tucher and Breydenbach together established early on—just prior to the great discoveries and a few decades before the great reformations—that long distance pilgrimage to Palestine was an entirely apt subject matter for printing presses. Without their success in print at this early period—before countercurrents (unanticipated at the time) had developed that might render pilgrimage an unlikely or controversial subject matter for wide dissemination in print—a convincing case for printing accounts of devout journeys to Palestine might never have been made in immediately subsequent times.

Breydenbach's text showed, too, unlike that of Tucher, that an account of pilgrimage was not tied to the author's region or language. The *Peregrinatio* was a great cosmopolitan work that suggested the existence of a cosmopolitan audience. The impact of Breydenbach—the *push* he gave to pilgrimage in print, the case he made for the printability of pilgrimage—was unprecedented and determinative. In the few years from 1486 to 1500 the *Peregrinatio* appeared in six languages and in at least eighteen editions, and by the eve of the French Revolution had gone through fifty-eight printed editions. Chateaubriand was only one of its many later readers.

Translations, perhaps even more than editions and printings, testified to the popularity and vitality of the *Peregrinatio*. Moreoever, in terms of audiences to be reached, translation from Latin into a vernacular was rather like a double translation: a work became accessible not only to readers ignorant of the original language, but as well to a much larger audience of the generally and more profoundly less learned and tutored. Martin Dampies, the translator of Breydenbach into Spanish, had granted that the Latin original was "just the thing for the learned and educated,"[38] but the appeal of pilgrimage, as all translations of Breydenbach show, escaped such confines and thereby explains why Dampies and his colleagues in other tongues had set to work.

Dampies's Saragossa translation of 1498, which was the last of the early translations of Breydenbach, shows how living and supple was the book as a textual artifact. The translation is largely faithful and straightforward,[39] though some passages do compress the Latin text while many others expand the original. Where Dampies more seriously alters Breydenbach's work, however, is by way of major additions. There are three. At the very beginning, he inserts a composition of his own of some seventy pages entitled *Tractado de Roma*, which provides a survey of imperial and papal Rome and, more to the point, a guide to the sacred shrines of Rome[40]. This not only drives home one of Dampies's prefatory arguments, that the way to Jerusalem necessarily led through papal Rome, but also makes pilgrimage to Jerusalem one with all other kinds of Christian pilgrimage, thereby reenforcing the same point implicitly made by earlier pilgrims (and by Breydenbach also, later in the text), when they described their visits to the relic-rich churches and shrines of Venice (not to mention other holy sites on their way to Venice). The second addition is Dampies's own frequent and indicated intrusions in the text by way of commentary. It may be an exaggeration to say that these glosses "form in themselves a new book,"[41] but they do amount to a frequent and ample commentary running through much of the *Viaje*. In general, Dampies is more interested in biblical and classical antiquity (especially in terms of quoting the literature) and less interested in more modern or even contemporary affairs than Breydenbach and company. Dampies, for example, is more keen to discuss the Colossus of Rhodes, and much less so to dwell on the great Turkish siege of Rhodes just a very few years before Breydenbach's journey.[42]

But Dampies's third alteration by way of addition was the greatest and most conspicuous. This was the visual alteration of the original book. Again, Dampies is both faithful and revisionist. On the one hand, all of the original 1486 woodcuts are included. On the other, many new woodcuts are included which tend, by their numbers and purpose, to swamp the original agenda. Even the view of the city of Rome, which most resembles the cityscapes in the original, is quite different from Reuwich's work, in that the Roman view had nothing to do with eyewitnessing, but was simply an adaptation of a woodcut from Schedel's *Liber Chronicarum* (Nuremberg, 1493)[43]—which, in its turn, is the great late medieval (or earliest modern) example of a printed book in which illustrations almost celebrated their utter lack of connection to the object portrayed. Breydenbach's original editions had been relentlessly contemporary books. In addition to showing cities along the route and the wildlife and ethnic life of Palestine, even to the point of showing the alphabets of the languages employed in the Levant, they also depicted specifically religious sites—especially, the grand and labeled panorama of Jerusalem and the surrounding holy places, but also specific holy sites such as the plaza of the Church of the Holy Sepulchre. In all these examples, however, what was depicted was what the actual traveler had seen before his eyes. Reuwich's visual renderings did not utterly lack a devotional aspect—we have noted two portrayals of pilgrims in their devotional acts—but they were products of a recording, rather than a meditative, eye. In the Spanish edition of 1498—just twelve years after the first edition—the outlook has altered. To the original woodcuts have been added woodcuts that depict sacred history. We now find a full-page depiction of the Crucifixion as well as smaller individual portrayals of sacred history that are woven into the text, making a travel book more emphatically than before a prayer book. All of this fits in, moreover, with Dampies's running commentary on the holy places, which stresses more scriptural detail in describing the events of Christ's life that are recalled to mind by sites under foot. It reflects, too, his overall emphasis on the spiritual nature of the journey to the Orient. This is not to say that the Spanish version of Breydenbach was more of a book of pilgrimage than was the original, but only that the two books had different emphases that went beyond mere details in appearance. The notable fact is that the *Peregrinatio* was such a striking innovation in itself—in terms of production values: its sheer exhaustiveness in dealing with the historical and contemporary scene, its manifest sense of display—and then there comes along a translator who does not abandon, or even massively distort, the original, but who nevertheless has his own ideas of how to get this recent work into renewed shape for a new audience. Vitality of a genre is what one recognizes in versions of Breydenbach at the end of the fifteenth century.

*   *   *

The years between Gutenberg and Columbus allowed pilgrimages to find their way into print as the usual travel literature of Latin Christendom. This literature of pilgrimage rested upon the retrieval and dissemination of devout travels that had been undertaken and described centuries earlier, but also on the printings of contemporary voyages to the Holy Land. There was little to distinguish fundamentally the two sets of works. Both were essentially superficial in approach, either relating marvels of the distant *Oriens* or serving as guidebooks to the holy places. Contemporary pilgrimages continued a long tradition set by medieval pilgrimages. Most striking in both cases, however, is the fact that these works were set in print.

Contemporary works in print are more revealing of the fifteenth century by the simple fact of their contemporaneity. Without being utterly transparent, they are far less opaque than works of another time when it comes to revealing the age in which they showed up in print. For example, in the three works cited, it is possible to note the social prominence of the three author/travelers—Tucher and Brasca (and many of Breydenbach's fellow travelers) in society at large, Breydenbach himself in the upper reaches and inner circles of the German church. Pilgrimage was the devotion and diversion of such well-placed figures at the time of printing in the fifteenth century. In addition, publication of such printed pilgrimages followed closely on the heels of the journeys they described. This was true of Tucher, Brasca, and Breydenbach. Such a journey, however well known its general content, was news of the day. The anxiety to get quickly into print is most striking in the case of Breydenbach's book, which required a great amount of labor and coordinated efforts on the part of many workers. This eagerness to get into print may account for some cutting of corners in the end, especially in the matter of illustrations.[44] Moreover, these pilgrimages tended to stay in print over a more or less lengthy span of time. In addition, all these works were guidebooks of a sort. They were tuned to an audience that might actually make the journey. Finally, the lavishness and bibliographical history of Breydenbach as a work of printed literature make it the greatest book of pilgrimage, medieval or contemporary, of the fifteenth century and one of the greatest of the entire early modern period.

Were it the only Levantine travel book to have survived, Breydenbach's *Peregrinatio* would still demonstrate the place of pilgrimage, as does Gutenberg's *Biblia* the place of Sacred Scripture, in Latin Europe on the eve of Columbus and Luther. In demonstrating that place so convincingly, so lavishly, it fortified pilgrimage to Jerusalem against the coming age when such devout travel would cease to be such a newsworthy item and no longer be the only or obvious or most noticed and prestigious way to go far from home.

Pilgrimage as part of the culture (in its traditional role as the preeminent form of European travel) was drifting into a deeply precarious environment. Granted, it says something for its prospects that the elaborate Spanish translation introduced Breydenbach to a wider audience on the Iberian peninsula five years after the publication of Columbus's letter reporting on the 1492 voyage across the Atlantic from that same peninsula. There is also the fact that a copy of Dampies's translation became part of the great sixteenth-century library created by Columbus's son.[45] At the same time, however, there were no further early modern editions of the *Viaje* while, on the other hand, Columbus's *Epistola* inaugurated—it was to turn out—an entirely new era and literature of travel. Already by 1494, four years before the appearance of Dampies's translation, Breydenbach's illustrations had been plundered and put to entirely new uses by the publicists of this new travel.[46]

TRANSFORMATION
OF TRAVEL

3

New Worlds and a New Voice of Travel

DECADES OF LANDFALLS in previously unrecorded places did not mean fifteenth-century Europeans were on the verge of a new age. Just as spectacular voyages into the Indian Ocean by admiral Cheng Ho between 1405 and 1433 had not transformed Ming China into an ocean-going civilization, so at the end of the same century, retrenchment and introversion might easily have been the lot of what in the event turned out to be an expansionist and extroverted Europe.[1] The Portuguese, who arrived at Madeira around 1419, had specialized in explorations and had not been absolutely silent about what they were doing. At least from Diogo Câo's voyage of 1482–84 along the coasts of Gabon, Congo, and Angola, *padrônes* (wooden crosses, stone pillars) had indicated the creeping shadow of Portugese navigators.[2] On the other hand, to announce was not to broadcast. *Padrônes* made a narrow point of precedence-as-possession rather than any broader point of publicity and cultural transformation. Left in the dark, Europe at large remained undisturbed—unpuzzled, unexcited, uninspired—by the deeds of Portuguese navigators. In light of the fact that after mid-century Europeans began to employ printing presses to spread news across Europe, the silence of the Portuguese resembles studied reticence. Without publicity, the pre-Columbian chain of discoveries remained only a chain of events. Had things been left entirely to the Portuguese, and had Europe as a culture not absorbed the significance of its new ventures, Europe's future relationship with the larger world might have come to resemble that of China.

Columbus's voyages and their centuries-long aftermath altered the cultural equation. The preface to the 1493 Latin edition of Columbus's letter describing his first voyage speaks of "Christopher Columbus, to whom our age is deeply indebted."[3] Nevertheless, even accounts of discovery that were printed—some elaborately, like the 1494 illustrated Latin edition of Columbus's letter describing his first voyage, or the 1524 Latin translation of Cortés's Mexican epistles to Charles V—need not have led to a full-dress literature of discovery, much less to an entirely recast European literature of travel, which in turn contributed to a new European civilization. After all, travelers who sound loudly in the modern ear—so loudly in fact that moderns are likely to mistake them for typical examples of "medieval" travelers (the thirteenth-century diplomat and missionary to the Mongols, William of Rubruck; the Castilian diplomat Ruy González de Clavijo, who traveled to the court of Tamerlane in 1403; and Marco Polo above all)— were not typical of their times, nor had they given rise to a new travel literature in the fourteenth century. There were many Europeans abroad in the East in the fourteenth century, but this reality was not reflected in the literature of the time. Reports of a Marco Polo and his like, whether or not harbingers of a future "modernity," were oddities that existed in a sea of pilgrimage notices and narratives. Modern travel literature *in the four-teenth century* remained pilgrimage literature.[4]

A century later, or less than a half-century after the beginnings of European printing, the literature of travel remained pilgrimage. That there was a greater audience for the pilgrim-adventurer Mandeville than for the merchant-adventurer Polo may be partly explained by the wild imaginings of the one being more credible to Europeans than the wild computations of the other,[5] but a more likely explanation is that whereas Mandeville's book was a pilgrimage that included additional wondrous material from the farther East, Polo's was nothing but a book of Oriental wonders that pointedly excluded any serious attention to Jerusalem.[6] Pilgrimage remained the expected subject matter of travel literature, even as Columbus set sail. Well into the Renaissance, travels to the Near East, and especially to Jerusalem, rather than voyages to the New World, remained the popular literature of travel and geography for Europeans.[7] Moreover, Marco Polo had not been able to compete with John Mandeville for an audience before 1500, nor with the pilgrim Villamont after 1500. The latter's thirteen editions swamped the single appearance of Polo in French in the sixteenth century.[8] And if Marco Polo could not compete with Mandeville, the same was true of Clavijo, who had been popular in the pre-print era but who had to wait a very long time from his return to Europe in 1406 from a diplomatic mission to the court of Tamerlane until his first appearance in print in 1582—that is, about a hundred and thirty years after the beginning of Western print.[9] There may have existed an audience-in-waiting for a new kind of travel literature—the manuscript reception of Clavijo and the rapid spread of the Columbian news in print suggest this—but not an audience actively on the spot. It seems, but only in retrospect, that Europe had to have been bowled over by the first discoveries. Even Polydore Vergil, drawn though he was to novelties in antique history and even in his own day (especially in the case of printing), would not give navigators' discoveries the time of day.[10] No wonder, then, that printers were only slowly perceiving a market for travel defined as something other than pilgrimage. The key point is that in a world that, from *our* perspective, was medieval Christendom in the throes of becoming modern Europe, pilgrimage remained the literature of travel.[11] The question is not whether pilgrims were the only ones out and about in the larger world (they clearly were not), but whether pilgrimage was overwhelmingly the kind of movement that was thought of as travel and that therefore deserved notice, a narrative, and a noetic framing. Another way to state the matter is to refer to an early sixteenth-century visualization of the flight into Egypt. In an edition of Ludolf of Saxony's extremely popular biography of Christ, Joseph is presented in the garb of a pilgrim (Figure 6).[12] How else could he be portrayed in a period when to travel was to be a pilgrim?

Columbus himself—for all practical purposes, the first advertised long-distance discoverer—did not see himself as a revolutionary kind of traveler. He placed his voyage into unknown waters within a tradition of pilgrimage (in its Crusading form). In his letter to the Spanish court of 4 March 1493,[13] he spoke of the conquest of Jerusalem as the fundamental purpose of his voyage—"with that as goal, this venture has been undertaken." Columbus, who (like many others) was a reader of Mandeville, was performing a Mandeville-in-reverse. Mandeville told of fantastic journeys, but they began with the journey to Jerusalem and were cast, as a literary whole, in the form of a *peregrinatio*. Columbus simply traveled to the fantastic places first; Jerusalem was the culmination that came at the end—or in the (immediate, anticipated) future. A longing to repossess Jerusalem informed Columbus's expressed thought on his Atlantic undertaking both before and after the first voyage.[14] Indeed, in the very midst of the voyage—on 26 December as he prepared to return to Spain—Columbus thought about the future when he would be returning once again to the New World, but also thought back to the recent past (the eve of his voyage out from Spain), when he, according to Casas's abstract of his *Diario*, had made clear to the court exactly what were to be the fruits of his heroic navigation:

And he says that he hopes in God that on the return that he would undertake from Castile he would find a barrel of gold that those who were left would have acquired by exchange; and that they would have found the gold mine and the spicery, and those things in such quantity that the sovereigns, before three years [are over], will undertake and prepare to go conquer the Holy Sepulchre; for thus

oec haer lede te meerder dz si gae moeste
in vreede lade die si niet en hende en dor=
harde en woeste weghe bossche en wild
nissen daer si sond danc bliue moste wat
si selde huplen vode. Also moste die ioge
sunerlijke maecht en moed maria ende
die oude vad ioseph pelgrimagien gaen
in vreemde lande en niette ioughe rederen
kindeke ihus En si ware arm en nz veel
hebbende. En daer om o mensche alstu
ghetoert wordes soe hebbet lidsaechept
en en meynt niet dat dp va gode die pre=
uilegien gegheue sal worde dpe he selue
noch oec linder moed niet geghenen en
heeft: Ten vierde is te mercke die goed=
nerehept ons here. Diestu wel mensche
hoe gheringe lidten viaecht wou vade
lande sijne ghebooote en hoe goedertie
renlick hp wilet den toert des gheens

die hi in eenen oghenblick mocht doden
Slechts. groot is die lidsaechept des he=
re mer niet nider en is sine oetmoedich
ept: Wat vade aeschijn des vuolghers
vloepdert in die die engele diene. God is
hi meer als een mesche vlieder vade on=
salige herodes hi die een toeiuicht is al=
der mesche Dit is een diepe oetmoedich
hept en woderlike lidsaechept Hi en wou
de sine vuolgher niet verrone: mer vlie=
dede woude hi sin lage seuue: Int welc
hi ons exempel ghegeuen heeft dat wp
ons oeck alsoe punen te doene. te weten
niet wederstane den genen die ons ver=
uolghen of contrarie sin noch van hem
wrake te begheren. mer lijdsaemelijck
verbeiden ende horen toonnen wijcken
Ende dat noch meer is voor hem bidde
also onse here ons leert ute euangely.

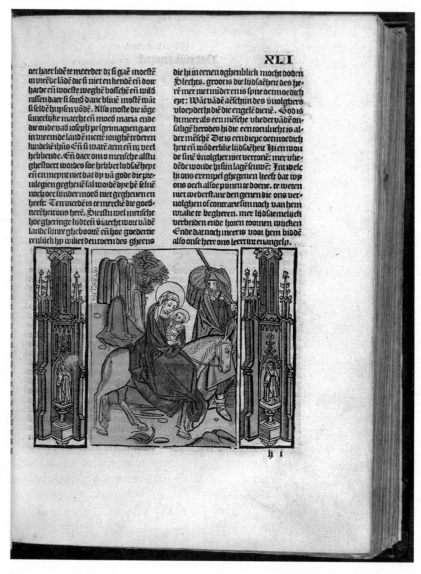

Figure 6. Ludolphus de Saxonia, *Dit es dleven Ons Liefs Heeren Ihesu Cristi* (Antwerp: H. Eckert, 1503), XLIr.

I urged Your Highnesses to spend all the profits of this my enterprise on the conquest of Jerusalem, and Your Highnesses laughed (*se rieron*) and said that it would please them and that even without this profit they had that desire. These are the Admiral's words.[15]

In Columbus's mind, the voyage of 1492, if not itself a pilgrimage, was a prelude and means to a crusading pilgrimage. And what Columbus apparently mused over in December in the New World—the agreed-upon purposes of the undertaking—was what still occupied his thoughts when he wrote to the sovereigns over two months later (4 March 1493) when his feat was accomplished. On that date, he wrote to the court much as he had written in his diary. There is the same context of the sailors he is leaving behind to carry on work that bears on the journey's purpose; and there is expanded emphasis invested in the purpose itself:

> I conclude here: that through the divine grace of Him who is the origin of all good and virtuous things, who favors and gives victory to all those who walk in His path, in seven years from today I will be able to pay Your Highnesses for five thousand cavalry and fifty thousand foot soldiers for the war and conquest of Jerusalem, for which purpose this enterprise was undertaken. And in another five years another five thousand cavalry and fifty thousand foot soldiers, which will total ten thousand cavalry and one hundred thousand foot soldiers; and all of this with very little investment now on Your Highnesses' part in this beginning of the taking of the Indies and all that they contain, as I will tell Your Highnesses in person later. And I have reason for this [claim] and do not speak uncertainly and one should not delay in it, as was the case with the execution of this enterprise, may God forgive whoever has been the cause of it.[16]

One of the defining, if negative, events of European history is that this idea of Jerusalem as the ultimate goal and justification of the entire Atlantic enterprise disappeared from the printed—that is, the public—version of Columbus's communications.

Columbus's focus on Jerusalem meant that his voyage had (in his mind) no autonomous nature of its own;[17] lack of autonomy and novelty, however, was also a potential strength; for an account of a voyage that had retained a Jerusalem-centered focus would have found a ready place in late fifteenth-century travel literature. Such travels of discovery would have made immediate sense. Columbus in manuscript was a figure of transition and continuity in the history of travel rather than of disruption and revolution. Columbus's deeds and thoughts shared a preexistent tradition with Mandeville or with a work such as Pierre Dubois's early fourteenth-century *On the Recovery of the Holy Land* rather than with Marco Polo's *Il Millone*.[18]

The letter that was actually printed for public consumption in 1493, however, and which sped through editions and translations during subsequent years—the tool of "a concerted propaganda campaign"[19]—said nothing about such a Jerusalem-centered motivation. It reflected nothing of Columbus's emphatically restated opinion that the Indies without Jerusalem made little sense. Long-distance travel almost by nature involved travel to Jerusalem. Five years after the letter of 1493, Columbus still clung to his original purpose.[20] And almost five years after that, Columbus wrote to Pope Alexander VI, reiterating yet again the peregrinative essence of his journey across the ocean.[21]

European travel began to be transformed in the aftermath of Columbus. It was not only a practical transformation—a matter of actual voyages to new destinations—but a literary and ideational transformation as well. Peter Martyr Anghiera, who began to write down his commentary-history on the great discoveries in 1494, perfectly reflects the interpretation of the printed *Epistola*. He reports that Columbus's selling points to Isabella and Ferdinand in favor of an Atlantic expedition were the increase of religion and the gaining of wealth. There is not a word on Jerusalem or the Holy Sepulchre.[22] In light of both Anghiera and the printed Columbus, Europe's *explosion planétaire*[23] was accompanied by a literary implosion, the caving in of the idea of European travel as previously understood.

Without the literary and spiritual matrix of pilgrimage, both the voyage of 1492 and the first printing of Columbus's letter in 1493 lacked deep context. Voyage and account of voyage exist on the uncomplicated, undocketed surface of things. If culture is context and pattern, an equilibrium of complexities, a sustainable network of associations, then an *age* of discovery does not plausibly exist on the basis of discrete or random voyages accompanied by a few pages descriptive of such voyages, any more than an age of faith is revealed by a chapel here and a convent there, or an age of industry by a factory or a mill in a landscape otherwise given over to fields and flocks. The preliminaries of Columbus's printed letter may have assumed large proportions for the navigator's deed—casting it as a work of the age, a work that put the age (*aetas nostra*) in his debt—but such words seem vague, grandiose, certainly premature, and more public relations than public reality. Indeed, what was being offered to the public was not mere information—traveler's information—but information that, in passage from script to print, had been deprived of its traditional frame of reference, its traditional matrix of presentation, its motivational pilings.

What such a document portended was less than clear. It belonged to the history of navigation, but not just yet to the history of travel.

All of this is not to deny the reality of an age of discovery in European history (whether hatched in historiographical discourse or produced by self-regarding contemporaries themselves), or even that the age came about in rapid fashion;[24] it is to be careful not to announce its arrival beforehand. And it is to be clear that an "age of discovery" denotes, or requires, not only an increase and rearrangement and deepening of geographical knowledge and perspective, but a transformation of travel itself. That an audience existed that was prepared to attend to such a new travel can be inferred from the reception of Columbus's letter, first printed in Spanish and immediately followed by translations into Latin and the vernaculars and by edition after edition—not to mention editions of the verse adaptation by Giuliano Dati.[25] These printed versions suggest possibilities: that the new discoveries will generate a literature of discovery; that the ethos and ambitions of discoverers will become lodged in Europe's grid of preoccupations. But something more than an echo is required for the advent of a new age, something more than a letter reproduced again and again. Echoes cease to reverberate. They die out.

The age of discovery had not commenced with the navigator's act of 1492 nor with the printer's act of 1493. When, however, the letter came to be reprinted, in Latin in Basel in 1494, that act itself suggested an altered future for European travel. Discovery began to gather definition and find a place within the contemporary world of events and ideas, to become part of the European scheme of things. This edition of 1494, in fact, is among the earliest signs that discovery might be something more than a mere navigational event such as the Portuguese furtively inching and notching their way down the west coast of Africa.[26]

What had changed in 1494 was that the reporting of discovery in the Atlantic began to assume cultural weight. The Basel edition of that year was the product of a convergence of themes, a forging of connections, a complexification of discovery's place in Western culture. Columbus's letter had been previously printed and previously Latinated. It had even been previously illustrated, though the woodcuts are worth pausing over as evidence (along with multiple editions and translations and the Italian versification) of how the interpreted feats of 1492–93 were beginning to take hold within the European consciousness. The Basel edition offers woodcut portrayals of the New World and its inhabitants and of the European discoverers (or at least their ships), somewhat after the fashion of a letter of advertisement, almost a work of public relations, that got out the word to the European world at large. That all of a sudden Castile would allow what Lisbon had not done for decades in the line of publicizing voyages—this is a crucial development. At least part of the reason for advertising the feat of the just-completed voyage—and for filtering out some of Columbus's contribution to that advertisement—may reside in the nature of Columbus's second voyage, which quickly set off from Cadiz (September 1493). Its character was that of a society under sail that was to be transplanted in Hispaniola rather than that of a military and directly exploratory enterprise. This could help to explain suppression of the Jerusalem-as-ultimate-goal concept in the 1493 letter. Colonizers didn't need the distractions of Crusade. Columbus's second voyage imparted a certain gravity to his undertaking and turned it into an enterprise that bore in upon itself rather than flying off, in implication and ideal purpose, towards the Levant.[27]

The 1494 edition brought home to Europeans, not only in word but in picture as well, that which was genuinely new to them, and thus that which was most difficult for the writer to express and for the reader to grasp. There is, to be sure, a difficulty: the pictures are not renderings of the voyage. They represent, but they do not depict, events. Some of the ships, not ocean-going vessels at all, are Mediterranean galleys. The engraver has not even bothered to replace Venetian flags with Spanish (Figure 7). The source of the images is, in fact, the great *Peregrinatio* of Bernhard Breydenbach, which was first printed in Mainz in 1486 and was continuing to be printed, translated, and illustrated at the time of Columbus's exploits (Figure 8).[28]

A twentieth-century historian has interpreted the depiction of Mediterranean merchant galleys in New World waters as a suggestion by the printer of the mercantile possibilities of western seas.[29] The printer may also have been suggesting affiliation between embryonic and traditional forms of travel, between long-distance voyages of discovery and long-distance voyages of pilgrimage. After all, the depicted ship was a pilgrim ship and originally illustrative of a contemporary pilgrimage—and not just any contemporary pilgrimage, but the one most lavishly advertised and celebrated in print and pictures. What these visual borrowings meant is not altogether clear. That Columbus's voyage was a kind of pilgrimage (Columbus's own original view of things) or that it was a replacement of pilgrimage—either interpretation might well have held sway not only in a populace of sixteenth-century readers (some thinking one way on the matter, others

Figure 7. Christopher Columbus, *De insulis nuper in Mari Indico nuper repertis* (Basel: I. Bergmann, 1494), dd5v.

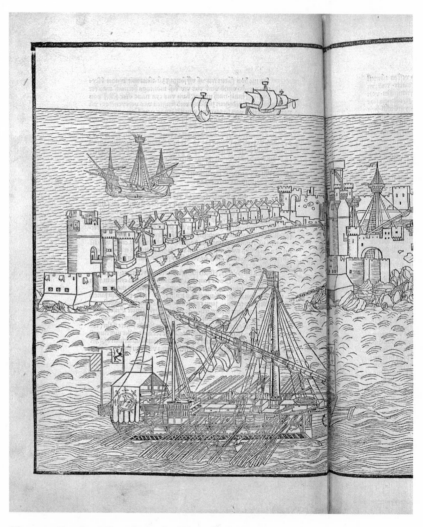

Figure 8. Bernhard Breydenbach, *Die heyligen Reyssen gen Iherusalem*, Rhodes plate, detail.

the other) but even within the minds of individual readers. Equivocation suits an age of transition.

There is a second association being negotiated in the 1494 Basel edition, one that marks off this edition from earlier printings. The book of 1494 does not begin with Columbus's narrative, but with Carlo Verardi's drama on the capture of Granada and the destruction of the last fragment of an Islamic base of power in Iberia. The printer has associated Columbus's voyage with a contemporary (indeed, an all but simultaneous) event of immense resonance. The Basel edition of 1494 interprets the two events of 1492 as being of comparable weight, scale, and dimension on the world historical stage.[30] Columbus's act of discovery, while something grand and exceptional, became, in the printing of 1494, something less out of place; it became part of the *scheme* of things. As a great event, it could be compared to, and associated with, another great event—the expulsion of the Moslems from Iberia. The association, moreover, persisted. Decades later, in 1533 and also in Basel, there was printed a book that again combined Verardi and Columbus, but also included other works bearing on the matter of Europe's conflict with Islam—for example, the Crusader narrative of Robert of Reims, *Warfare of Christian Princes, Especially the French, Against the Saracens.*[31]

Borrowing from pilgrimage to portray the New World as a new Mediterranean, and comparing the internal definition of Europe (Western Christendom rid of Islam) with its external growth, were early steps in normalizing discovery, in Europeanizing (to Europeans) this novel form of travel, and in shaping the times of the discoveries into an age of discovery. Columbus's printed letter had initially been something marginal, exceptional, culturally indigestible—not only because the Atlantic discoveries were novelties in themselves, but because Columbus's own linking of Jerusalem and the Indies had been suppressed before the letter of 1493 had been published. The natural, or culturally predictable, motivations of the account-giving traveler had been erased. Now, however, literature that narrated new sailings into uncharted worlds—shorn of rich (Levantine and devotional) habiliments that Columbus himself would have given to such literature—was to be newly decked out in associations that would give it rank in the European world, a rank and cachet and status that would have utterly nothing to do with the old traditional form of travel. Columbus himself may have seen Hispaniola as a step towards Jerusalem, the printer in Basel may have seen the Mediterranean in the Atlantic; but such were to become almost private insights. Travel itself was being rearticulated, reengineered, reinvented. The *use* of Breydenbach in the Basel edition of Columbus foreshadowed the *replacement* of Breydenbach and his sort of travel by new modes of travel associated with discovery and exploration.

The rapid following up of Columbus's first voyage with subsequent voyages—his own and those of others—shows that there were practical reasons, political, ecclesiastical, economic, that would quickly bring within the general, late fifteenth-century order of things this astounding feat of navigation. News of discoveries, amplified by the new technology of print, became part of the general subject matter of European interests. Over the next three centuries, *les longs voyages* were to be among the greatest undertakings of Europeans and European states. Columbus, Cortes, Magellan, Drake, Tasman, Bougainville, La Pérouse, Cook—these were to be great exemplary figures on the European scene. Nor were their activities and notoriety to be matters exclusive to the world of power and policy—and surely not restricted to the merely technical realm of navigation. There was to be no divorce between the work of the intellect (navigational, geographical, cartographical, astronomical) and wider activity. Such men and feats were to *inspire* an age. Discovery was to be a centerpiece—engine and ornament—of European culture. In 1524, there was offered to the public an elegantly rendered edition of Cortés's epistles to Charles V, translated into Latin and embellished with a large engraving of Mexico City.[32] By the 1660s, the great French collector of travels, Melchisédec Thévenot, commented that for two centuries life had been marked by *les grands revolutions* to which *la Navigation* and *le Trafic* had mightily contributed.[33] Life itself, for centuries a pilgrimage, was now to be an adventure of discovery and exploration. Nor was this new enterprise of sailing into the unknown and undefined to be something restricted to the margins of Europeans' affairs and concerns. The greatest proof of this is that the cultural activity of travel itself, for centuries very largely a matter of pilgrimage, was to be entirely disassembled and reconfigured. The 1494 edition's association of discovery of new worlds with defense and definition of the old world, of Hispaniola with Aragon, of the Carribean with the Mediterranean, opened a door and offered a hint. But it was only a beginning. Much more was in the offing that would demonstrate that discovery was as much a literary (and a spiritual) as a navigational phenomenon.

What the career and (published) thoughts of Columbus had initiated was to be driven deep into the core of consciousness of European culture in subsequent centuries—and this in an increasingly thorough and methodical fashion. Discovery was to become an embedded, integral, and inextricable element in modern Europe, much as pilgrimage had been in medieval Europe. By the first quarter of the seventeenth century, for example, the fact that discoveries had opened up entirely new possibilities for Christian missions offered the opportunity to think—and not in some vague manner—of discovery as a central, indeed as a religious, feature of life. The Benedictines' publication of the *Nova typis transacta navigatio* of 1621, by offering a vividly illustrated account of early discoveries in the New World that emphasized the role of missionaries, could not help but associate one of the oldest institutions of Western Christendom—the Benedictine order of monks, which reached back to the sixth century—with the modern tradition of European overseas exploration that Columbus had initiated barely a century and a quarter earlier. The engraved title page includes two portraits—one of the Catalonian Benedictine, Bernardo Buil, who had accompanied Columbus on his second voyage; the other of St. Brendan of Clonfert, a legendary sixth-century Irish monk and traveler, whose presence also lends an antique religious patina to the enterprises of Columbus and his successors (Figure 9). What the *Nova typis* helps to show is not only that the new enterprise of discovery was able to be knitted deep into the cultural life of Europe but also that the coming of an age of discovery was not a simple victory of contemporary secularity over the piety of an earlier age. Pilgrimage was here replaced by missionary travel, which in turn was more easily connected to new traditions and manners of travel. Pilgrimage was being shunted aside, at least by implication: "Just as Christ our God was greater than Solomon and the Synagogue, he did not build his temple on mount Sion but in his faithful people of every nation and in the hearts of the nations."[34] In this light, it now made more sense—even more religious sense—to travel almost anywhere than to Mount Sion![35] Diversity of souls and nations—that was the pressing *religious* fact of the age conceived of under the rubric of an age of discovery. By the late seventeenth century, this view of the changing of the spiritual guard (from pilgrimage to missions) was all but explicit. Casting back over more than a century of history, the Jesuit biographer and historian Pierre Joseph d'Orléans (1641–1698) could ponder one of the great emblematic figures of Baroque Europe, Francis Xavier (1506–1552), and remark:

Saint Francis Xavier considered China as a promised land (*terre de promission*). All his desires pushed him towards it. Nevertheless, he was only to catch a glimpse of it, dying as another Moses. He saw the promised land but did not enter it. He left his brothers as heirs of his zeal for the salvation of this nation.[36]

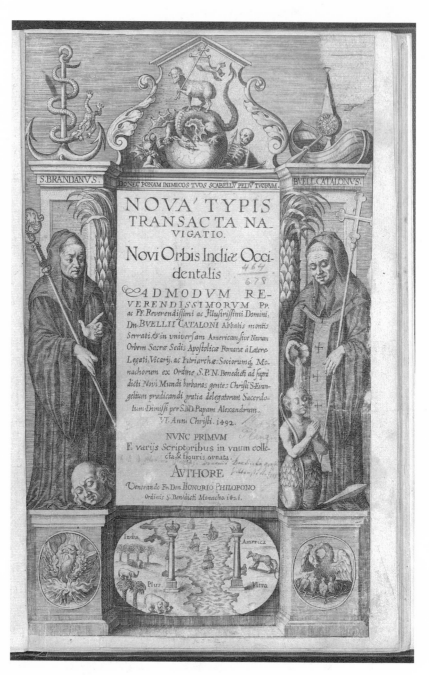

Figure 9. *Nova Typis Transacta Navigatio* (n.p., 1621), engraved title page.

Thus the spiritual weight of pilgrimage was being transferred, at least in some Catholic minds, to the enterprise of missions which had been given great impetus by the new discoveries.

Diversity (of peoples, of data, of possibilities and opportunities) and not mere novelty was what called forth a new age. The work of Columbus (literary as well as navigational) was, in the hands of others, to realize a revolution, a changing of the intellectual guard precisely because there was so much information, and in such great variety, to be digested. We often credit the great discoveries with having an intellectual side. We look to their effects, to the fruits they bore in geography, cartography, natural history, anthropology, astronomy, and to their capacity to produce data sufficient to fill the head of every European reader and the *cabinet* of every European collector. We think of Montaigne—in his ruminations on cannibalism, for example—being fed by the reports of travelers. We think, in other words, of the intellectual effects of travel without always thinking of the intellectual, the literary, nature of travel itself—its intellectual structure and thrust—and of how that too changed when the act and destination of travel changed. Discovery as a cultural phenomenon was far more than an informational upheaval. It was an ideational transformation. Just as different societies have different menus and manners at table, different ways of pitching roofs and planting gardens, so they have different ways of traveling—in terms of where they go, what they look for, what they look out for, what they overlook; in terms, too, of their basic judgments of what shufflings and wanderings transcend the mere animal or diurnal motion of getting from here to there and back again and deserve to become matter subject to intellectual recall and literary shaping and ideational enshrinement.

Columbus's letter is a manifold clue of changes in the offing. First, following so swiftly upon the voyage itself, the letter introduced the factor of publicity. Discovery began to concern, after 1493, not only navigators and courtiers, but a larger public of readers. Second, it is highly significant from the point of view of the history of travel that *printed* versions of Columbus's letter omitted any mention of Columbus's own sense of Jerusalem as inspiration and ultimate goal of such voyaging. Third, as soon as 1494, the 1493 account of the 1492 voyage was beginning to be stitched in multiple ways into the cultural pattern of Europe—having been printed, it was translated; the voyage itself became subject matter for the illustrator; and the whole astounding adventure stood out as a fact that was associated and coordinated with another remarkable fact of the day, namely the expulsion of the last remnants of Moslem power from Iberia (indeed,

Columbus is fully *modern*, in contrast to medieval pilgrims in print, not only in the direction and destinations of his voyage, but in his recording and associating his feat with this other contemporary triumph in Granada). And fourth, the letter of 1494 was (it turns out) an adumbrative snapshot of early modern travel. Not only was discovery replacing, by happenstance of great current events, age-old pilgrimage as the subject matter of travel reportage; the publicists of discovery were making transforming use of the materials of earlier travel. Breydenbach was overshadowed; he was also put to other uses without acknowledgment. Discovery stands to pilgrimage as both heir and scavenger. Discovery shattered and then picked up the pieces of pilgrimage.

The early history of the Columbus letter constitutes the inaugural moment of what came to be Europe's great age of discovery. This early bibliographical history shows discovery beginning to be anchored in and expressive of Europe itself as a non-nomadic civilization of unprecedented mobility. After the reputation of Columbus had taken root and spread, the Chinese option (and Polydore Vergil's as well) of self-restraint grew increasingly less likely or possible. Discovery became a mirror in which Europe glimpsed its heroic self in the foreground of an ever-expanding background.

* * *

Fundamental change in the making was heralded by Columbus's letter— by its omission of Jerusalem from the printed account of his first voyage; by the plundering of woodcuts from pilgrimage to depict events of a voyage that, despite Columbus's own wishes, was being presented as a very different sort of voyage from a *via devotionis*; and by the weaving of the account of Columbus's voyage into a web of associations (linguistic, representational, geopolitical) with the broader culture. Over the longer haul, accounts of other voyages by other navigators, sometimes quite grand productions, deepened and broadened and consolidated this culture of discovery. But the major device for celebrating and popularizing discovery, and for realizing and underscoring a new mode of travel, proved to be the great collections of travels that came to be printed from the early sixteenth century. Early modern Europe, particularly in its later stages, would fashion a range of tools for the intellectual management of new data that rushed in upon it. From around the mid-seventeenth century, lexicons and libraries (that were planned to be "universal") and encyclopedias, as well as learned societies and their periodicals, began to drive general European discourse.[37] But another tool, collections of travels, had gotten an earlier start. They were to prove, almost from the beginning, a great and loud voice proclaiming a new kind and era of travel much different from earlier, pilgrimage-driven travel.

Collectors of travels—literary counterparts to assemblers of *cabinets des curiosités*—set to work almost immediately in the wake of the first discoveries, and by the end of the sixteenth century there existed an impressive roster of printed collections of information and interpretation.[38] The earliest period of this collecting activity culminated in the *Novus Orbis*,[39] which appeared in 1532 in Latin in Basel. Almost four decades earlier in the same city, the humblest first step had been taken towards associating discovery narrative with, if not other works of travel, at least with other works of European literature and with other events of European life. The *Novus Orbis* would go through many editions and translations. Its immediate popularity and dispersion were such that the radiation of the *Novus Orbis* across Europe may be compared to the radiation of Columbus's *epistola* four decades earlier. Though not the very first of such collections, it was the most ambitious and wide-ranging of the early examples, expressing as it did an elegant and reflective sense of the new kind of travel that was uncovering new regions of the world. The *Novus Orbis* was the first to place this new travel in a fully modern context.

The *Novus Orbis* was a work of pragmatic synthesis, a balanced, economical, and comprehensive exercise of account-taking in the aftermath of dumbfounding discoveries. By 1532, sufficient time had elapsed to attempt a calm and expansive view of things. The work's obvious purpose—the title says as much—was to describe the new world uncovered by the earliest discoverers. The first six entries of the *Novus Orbis* are accounts of early Portuguese and Spanish navigations which have been borrowed from an earlier collection—the *Paesi novamente retrovati* of 1507 (translated the following year into Latin with the title of *Itinerarium Portugallensium e Lusitania in Indiam et inde in Occidentem et demum ad Aquilonem*).[40] The purpose of the *Novus Orbis*, however, was also to make sense of this new world created by new discoveries. Unlike the earlier collection, the *Novus Orbis* did not restrict itself to narratives of discovery, but instead fashioned a fuller context of travel, a framework within which these new discoveries were placed. Like the *Paesi*, it included the pre-Columbian navigations of the Portuguese, thereby giving an articulated presence to what had previously, in the pre-Columbian dispensation, gone largely unnoticed (or, at least, unprinted); but the *Novus Orbis* also included a much earlier work, Marco Polo's travels to the Orient, the inclusion of which suggests that it was being seen as a medieval anticipation of what was happening in the fifteenth and sixteenth centuries. The *Novus Orbis* also included the contemporary journey—a touristical kind of travel to the traditional sites of the Orient, an Asia known to two centuries of European travelers—of Ludovicus Varthema, who emphasized the value of the sensible world and the virtues of the traveler as eyewitness of actual places in distant and exotic regions. Varthema preferred to see for himself rather than to read or hear about faraway places. He preferred, too, the practical to the theoretical, the terrestrial to the celestial, the geographical to the astronomical. He was very much in the Renaissance mold of Simon Grynaeus, who had covered much the same ground in the introduction to the *Novus Orbis*.[41]

The *Novus Orbis* even included a work of medieval pilgrimage—Burchardus of Mount Sion's thirteenth-century survey of the geography of the Holy Land. Although only one of seventeen entries—and although the reader was carefully prepared (by the editors) to see in Burchardus a *studiosus explorator* (rather than, say, a *viator pius*)—this inclusion of what might be thought of as the hoariest (and suddenly quite outdated) form of travel is remarkable.[42] How did Burchardus, a European resident of the medieval Levant, provide context for a new world? After all, Grynaeus's introduction, which used the accomplishments of scholars (mathematicians, astronomers, philosophers) and travelers (Odysseus, the Argonauts) in antiquity as background to what was happening in Grynaeus's own time of discoveries, had remained silent on medieval pilgrims and Crusaders who had traversed the Mediterranean in order to make their devout rounds of Palestine. The stretch of centuries (including Burchardus's) that intervened between antiquity and "our century" was absent from Grynaeus's words of introduction. Moreover, the other traveler who forms a part of the *Novus Orbis* and who does not fit the description of a discoverer, the contemporary Ludovicus Varthema, only skirted Palestine on his way to places further to the east. In addition, while it is true that Grynaeus, although he made no mention of pilgrimage, also made no direct attack on devout travel, he may nevertheless have been taking a gloved swipe at the sort of piety of which pilgrimage was a part when he wondered how, in an age (*nostro seculo*) when a part of the world almost the size of Europe has been discovered, those who paid no attention to these startling events could claim to be taking heed of God's other works. In any case, the inclusion of Burchardus in the *Novus Orbis* is doubly remarkable. From the perspective of past centuries when pilgrimage was the very frame and substance of travel, the solitary place of Burchardus within the new scheme suggests a devaluation of pilgrimage (Burchardus, in other words, being given a place in the collection in order to be put in his place); from the perspective of the non-peregrinative travel that was dominating the Renaissance scene, on the other hand, Burchardus's presence showed that pilgrimage was holding on, was still managing, for whatever reasons, to keep a place at the literary table of travel.[43]

Though not the only work of its kind, the *Novus Orbis* was the culmination of the early stage of travel collections, all of which were modest works that were characteristically manageable in their proportions. A page of titles sufficed to advertise the contents of such works. From mid-century, however, things changed. Travel-collecting became a more ambitious undertaking. The classic works of the genre turned into mammoth productions—in many cases, large folios of many volumes. At the very time (1555) that the *Novus Orbis* was undergoing slight enlargement, there began to appear the massive volumes of Ramusio's *Navigationi et Viaggi* which were printed at Venice.[44]

Ramusio was to prove a flagship of the new travel (and also a mine of information for subsequent collectors of travels). From this point onwards, and for at least the following two and a half centuries, collections of travels were marked by nothing so much as a gormandizing spirit in relation to the world beyond Europe. Printed collections sought to take in everything: the Atlantic, the Indian Ocean, the Pacific islands, the interiors of islands and of great landmasses, the realm of the Ottomans, remote Persia, more remote China and Japan, and not even excluding the out-of-the-way fastnesses of Europe itself (the unvisited, or hitherto undescribed, heights and corners of the Pyrenees, the Alps, the strange far north and far west of Europe—Lapland, Ireland). Collectors turned manuscript accounts into print. They translated previously printed sources. They reprinted, excerpted, summarized, or rearranged others already known to the public (either in separately printed books and pamphlets or in the compilations of other collectors). While some collectors concentrated on certain areas or certain periods, the typical works—Ramusio, the Brys, Hakluyt in the sixteenth century, Purchas and Melchisédec Thévenot in the seventeenth century, the immense collections of travels and travel selections that merged into histories of travel in the eighteenth century (when one thinks above all of the shelves of volumes of the abbé Prevost)—were Magellans and Drakes of the study and the print shop. They wished to cover the globe.

Nor did they wish only to devour space. They attended to the history of travel as well as to the news of the most current travelers. They reinterpreted the history of European travel.

Collectors of travels constituted a chain of interpretation across two and a half centuries. There operated, among contemporaries and across generations, a process of continuous borrowing, revision, and updating. Thévenot acknowledged Hakluyt and Purchas in the very first sentence of his "Avis, sur le dessein, et sur l'ordre de ce Recueil."[45] The enterprise of collecting was neither static nor monochromatic. Emphases altered within the tradition.[46] Some collectors, for example, took in the entire sweep of travel throughout history, others the history of voyages since the feats of the Portuguese and Columbus, still others one area of discovery or the exploits of one European nation abroad. Perhaps the greatest difference between earlier and later collectors is that, by the eighteenth century, collections were tending to become histories based on collected extracts or summaries of the data provided by individual travelers rather than collections properly so called of original documents. The hallmark of early travel collections in the sixteenth century was that they broadcast a body of knowledge which travelers had gained through their own eyes and which they had conveyed in their own words. This claim was not given up in the eighteenth century, but it was becoming less plausible. The collective picture of discovery becomes less immediate, less clear and sharp, less unmediated than had previously been the case. This evolution of the genre was itself symptomatic of the defining pressure that typified collections from the very beginning and which only increased with time—namely, the accumulating surge of data that had to be captured, mastered, and conveyed to the reading public.

One glaring constant in this literature of collected travels was the defining position of Columbus as originator of the new travel. Another constant—only less obvious and varying in coloration from work to work—was the diminished place that collectors accorded to pilgrimage. By the time of Jean Baptiste Morvan de Bellegarde (1648–1734), whose *Histoire universelle des voyages* appeared anonymously in 1707 (and reappeared the following year with his name on the title page), pilgrimage was an absence that went unremarked.[47] Indeed, this had been largely so for two centuries during which pilgrimage survived in these rosters of travel as nothing but the smudge that survived erasure. Together these two constants—the preeminence of Columbus, the reduced status of pilgrimage—reveal a new European travel that was the travel of discovery. How powerful was the appeal of this new genre with its new interpretations of travel is shown by the nearly simultaneous appearance of an English translation of Bellegarde's book.

Bellegarde's first volume—which began with Columbus and treated of America (and this, despite his subject being the *entire* history of travel!)—was the only one that actually appeared. The *Histoire* never got close to treating the subject matter of the Near East, much less that of pilgrimages to Jerusalem. We do know, however, the map that Bellegarde had intended to follow. In a lengthy *Discours préliminaire*,[48] his silence on pilgrimage argues that devout travel was neither a feature of the contemporary landscape of travel, nor even an item of its past. Bellegarde's focus is on long-distance travel (*les voyages de long cours, les longs voyages*); but while many shorter journeys catch his attention, the ages-old voyage from Atlantic and western Mediterranean ports to Palestine, not to mention the land routes to the Levant, receives not one word in his comprehensive sweep of human history.

The printer's *avertissement* introduces both the work as a whole and the *Discours préliminaire*, and in doing so grounds Bellegarde's literary effort in its own day and, incidentally, in the grand tradition of collecting.[49] The reader is informed that the work as a whole begins with the New World because the pivotal figure in history is "le celebre Christophle Colomb." Columbus's centrality is just what one would expect in almost any collection of travels. Bellegarde's treatment of Columbus's new world (giving it, as he does, pride of place) is the monumental exception to his planned presentation of *voyages* that promises to be chronological, though the plan itself never gets beyond the stated overall design and this single actual volume. Bellegarde's scope is a universal frame (in time and space), his method the making of *extraits*, his audience the *curieux*, his challenge the sifting of testimony from *une infinité de volumes*. (*Infinité* is a much exercised term in the Bellegardian lexicon. There is mention of an "infinity of known facts" available to the philosopher who travels out into the actual world, an "infinity of voyagers" who have traveled in the name of France, an "infinity of religious" who have worked the mission fields, an "infinity of manuscripts" in the archives of Peru and New Spain which give information on the New World, an "infinity of observations" which travelers to exotic places bring back to those at home.)[50] This overload of experience and data led even collectors themselves—of the eighteenth century (and earlier)—to a dependence on the very collecting tradition that they were continuing and revising. Bellegarde's dependence was profound. According to the *avertissement*, the material of the inaugural volume, first appearing in 1707, had been gathered from the third volume of Ramusio, which had appeared in Venice in 1553. Following volumes were to treat of "all travelers ancient and modern," and Bellegarde himself will tell us that he resorts to the *abregé* and the *relation sommaire* to deal with this tide of information.[51] The *avertissement* explicitly directs readers to the *Discours prélimi- naire* in order that they might get an idea of just how travelers before and after Columbus will be presented.

The subject matter of the great collections was typically dual in nature. There was the massive deluge of new and exotic data that needed to be ordered and presented to the public; but there was, too, the act of travel itself, the very meaning and nature of travel that needed to be addressed. An entire literature of essays (sometimes included in collections of travels, sometimes quite separate) devoted itself to questions of the nature and purposes of travel. This theoretical literature treated questions of how one should travel, where one should go, what one should look for, how one should observe, what benefits should accrue to the traveler and to the trav- eler's own society from such travels. Just like collections themselves, this literature was largely a product of the era of overseas discoveries. It dealt with many varieties of travel, but was largely (though not entirely) unin- terested in mulling over the nature, value, or methods of devout travel.[52]

This desire to work out the meaning and matter of travel had animated the introduction to the *Novus Orbis* early on. It continued to be a live issue at the turn to the eighteenth century in the work of Bellegarde. Bellegarde grounds his presentation in the *naturalness* of travel. The natural desire of man to travel is bound up with his equally natural curiosity and love of nov- elty. A fully natural "inquietude" envelops man and moves him to travel. Bel- legarde opens with such thoughts and then, some thirty-five pages later, returns to the theme. Pliny, who says that "this natural inclination" to travel is due to man's love of novelty, is a theoretical and historical support.[53] Above all, however, Bellegarde has the personal and contemporary example of the great traveler Jean-Baptiste Tavernier (1605–1689), who at the age of eighty—Bellegarde himself would have been thirty-seven—took off for Persia as if he were going to Versailles. After an entire life of traveling, Bel- legarde tells us, Tavernier could not give up the road, could not stay put. It is as if the example of this one man had distilled the natural truth about travel—that men travel because they become bored seeing the same things, that their wonder or curiosity or desire for learning, or even their avarice and cupidity, are aroused, and they themselves are set in motion, by "novelties."[54]

Travel is so inherently a part of the makeup of man in such a view that it helps to provide Bellegarde with a kind of unified theory of man and society. Travel has to do with morality ("Experience shows that youth who lose their way at home through idleness and debauchery become sober, temperate, and virtuous when they travel abroad"), with the nature of man (whose mobility and adaptability mark him off from other animals which are bound to their locales), with commerce (the mechanism by which mobile man insures that the things of the world are spread throughout the world), and with knowledge itself ("a traveler's curiosity" being pretty much the disposition and signature of any true philosopher).[55]

History itself is all but equated with the history of travel. Travel becomes the great common thread that explains nearly everything. Life itself, when elevated to the level of the meaningful, seems travel writ large. The children of Adam, unlike the animals, can live anywhere on earth. They are like the king who moves from villa to villa, or like the city-dweller (the habitable world is "like a great city") who goes down one street and up another.[56] The children of Noe spread across the earth as "these first restorers of the human race."[57] Abraham was one of the first travelers (*voyageurs*) mentioned in history. Socrates was the most splendid example of the cosmopolite. Hercules's journeys were legendary (the Greeks spoke of them "with exaggeration"). Jason and the Argonauts were celebrated for their travels. Strabo based most of his geography on the travels of Ulysses. Virgil made Aeneas a famous traveler. Pythagoras traveled for years on end. Socrates and Plato traveled in search of wisdom.[58] Alexander the Great is a special case: The conquests of Alexander the Great can just as easily be thought of as travels, for he made them with the same rapidity as a traveler (*un voyageur*) who would have been driven solely by curiosity to see, *en passant*, many countries and many different nations.[59] Alexander, Pliny, the Roman Emperors were all travelers, discoverers. The voyages of Christ are something of an embarrassment, but ones quickly gotten over: Christ's voyages may not have been *longs* (a prized attribute in the modern dispensation of travel as represented by collectors), but at least they started almost at birth with the flight into Egypt and were *continuels* during his ministry. The Apostles divided up the world among themselves. Paul, of course, was especially celebrated as a traveler.[60]

After Apollonius of Tyana ("a great traveler"), however, we are rocketed across centuries that do not prompt any comment on Bellegarde's part. We are suddenly "among the moderns," which means face to face with Marco Polo, famous both for his travels and his discoveries (*découvertes*).[61]

It is significant that Bellegarde makes no dark characterization of the inter-
venient centuries. There is no lambasting of whole eras of unenlightened
travel. There is only silence. One more paragraph gets us among the Portuguese. And soon a world prepared by Providence and technology, a
world of hardy discoverers, opens before the reader. Bellegarde lists the
heroes—beginning, of course, with the always hovering Columbus. All of
this—discoveries themselves and the accounts (individual and collected)
of discoveries—has remade the world. "We navigate today more reliably
(*sûrement*) on all the seas going north or south or east or west than they
did in the old days in the Mediterranean or Adriatic."[62] Nothing could seem
more remote to the eighteenth-century collector or historian of travel than
bygone days of voyaging on inland seas that had been left far behind in
the wake of discoverers' marvelous deeds. And most remote of all, it seems,
were voyages from Europe across the Mediterranean to the derelict port
of Jaffa. In Bellegarde's *Discours*, pilgrimage to Jerusalem is the faintest
pulse—in fact, all but undetectable.

It is just detectable. *Terre sainte* bobs to the surface of Bellegarde's
Discours only twice—as a purely historical label for the land from which
the Israelites chased the Canaanites, and as one item in a catalogue of the
"rarities of Asia" that might appeal to a reader's curiosity.[63] Bellegarde
mentions "la Judée, la Palestine," but also "l'Egypte, l'Arabie, l'Armenie"
in the same breath as names of places about which a traveler in the Near
East reports back to stay-at-homes.[64] He mentions that Jerusalem was the
center of Jesus's modest travels, and that the Apostles "marched in the tracks
of their teacher."[65] That is all. The reader is given no hint that this "marching in the tracks" was the beginning of a centuries-long tradition of devout
travelers to the Levant who marched in the tracks of Christ and in the
tracks of other pilgrims. (The same reader would have to resort to a tradition entirely outside travel collecting—the ongoing tradition of early
modern pilgrimage literature—to learn of such an historical context of pilgrimage). Quite apart from pilgrimage specifically to the Levant, even Rome
is presented by Bellegarde as a center of civilization, "this world capital,"
without any reference to its religious weight. It is simply where would-be
architects and painters flock annually to learn their crafts.[66]

Bellegarde might easily have brought pilgrimage into the conversation in his preliminary ruminations on travel. He gave himself openings,
which he then shut down. He announces that commerce and lucre are not
the only lures that persuade a traveler to endure dangers and hardships.
There exist, he assures the reader, higher motives than commerce. The sort

of traveler Bellegarde has in mind, however, is not the *perigrans causa religionis*, but the philosopher who wants to see the wonders of the world for himself, rather than to read about them in books. We hear echoes of Grynaeus and of Renaissance rhetoric in general. Similarly, when Bellegarde mentions journeys of those who "are more like exiles than travelers," he is not preparing to give pilgrims their due, but only to pass on to the reader the bugs (Pythagoras, Empedocles, Democritus, Plato) that Pliny has put in his ear.[67] To appreciate, however, the extent to which pilgrimage had lost its place in a world of travel defined by collectors such as Bellegarde—the extent to which pilgrimage had not merely fallen from its pedestal, but had been swept into the historical dustpan—one need only compare the absence of pilgrimage to the presence of missions in the pages of Bellegarde's *Discours*. Missionaries are a splendid, glittering presence—above all, a fully *modern* presence. The great emblematic figure—comparable in some measure to Columbus himself—is Francis Xavier, who, among the "modern apostles," had made the most voyages:

> Those who have worked things out, and who have reckoned the distance of the places through which he traveled, have concluded, in placing his travels end-to-end, that they covered thirty-three thousand leagues—in other words, more than three circuits of the globe.[68]

Such a *voyageur* partisans of discovery had no trouble embracing. The sheer scale of his activities appealed to them. We are being presented with a revitalization, indeed a revalidation (under the rubric of the modern, no less) of the missionary enterprise—which is also to say the Apostolic enterprise. It need hardly be added that there was nothing comparable under way in the pages of Bellegarde—nor scarcely elsewhere within the collecting tradition that he was continuing—in respect to pilgrimage.[69] Nor was Bellegarde's bow to missions a perfunctory one. He concludes the *Discours* with a nod to the *Collège Louis le Grand*, which was famous for training missionaries who went out from Europe to the remotest corners of the world. Bellegarde has in mind "missionaries to China, Japan, Syria, and a thousand other places." We should not fail to notice that Palestine claims Bellegarde's final attention as an unnamed area of a place (Syria) that is worth mentioning primarily as a field of work for modern missionaries.[70]

The implicit position of the *Discours* on pilgrimage—that pilgrimage scarcely fit into the modern scheme of travel—was entirely within the tradition of early modern travel-collecting. By Bellegarde's day, after centuries in which travel had been collected and characterized (largely in relation to

discovery) with little attention paid to pilgrimage, the once central mode
of travel had ceased to command the attention of collectors of travels. In
such circles (of collectors and readers of collections) pilgrimage had crept
to the margins. To mention at length a pilgrim (even to summarize or
extract, as the *Novus Orbis* had reproduced, the writings of Burchardus, for
example) seems never to have occurred to Bellegarde. It was not only the
obvious realities of the age of discovery—chiefly, the massive quantities of
exotic information (the *infinité* factor) that had poured forth, and continued to do so, from remote corners of the world—that distracted Bellegarde;
there was also a (by now) centuries-old historiographical tradition, a considered and canonical way of looking at travel. Travel collections belonged
to a genre that was governed by certain rules and emphases that depended
on self-conscious traditions reaching back to Ramusio and earlier.

The dismissal of pilgrimage from the *history* of travel—and not merely
from the contemporary scene of travel—is a tell-tale sign of the *mentalité*
of post-Columbian collectors of travels. Bellegarde's vaulting across centuries—from Apollonius of Tyana to Marco Polo—was typical. Marco Polo
and other travelers to the more or less exotic East during the last centuries
of the Middle Ages came to represent an entire millennium of European
travel. The *impression* that modern collectors gave of premodern travel was
that its existence was a shadow of modern travel, but an entirely predictive
or adumbrative shadow. The impression they convey is one of a lean but
just perceptible continuity.

In general outline—emphasis on Columbus, silence on pilgrimage—
Bellegarde belonged to an historiographical tradition that reached back to
the sixteenth century and that would continue throughout the eighteenth.
Almost thirty years after the appearance of his volume, there was printed
in the Netherlands in 1735 a collection of travels, all of which dated from
a period prior to the great discoveries. Nevertheless, and very much in a
Bellegardian key, *Voyages faits principalement en Asie dans les XII, XIII, XIV,
et XV siècles*[71] has its gaze firmly fixed on the present as the highly predictable culmination of those earlier centuries:

Such are the *Voyages* which make up this Collection. They can quite legitimately be
regarded as a necessary introduction to the reading of the prodigious quantity of
writings of this very same sort which the discovery of the two Indies has procured
for us.[72]

That the rigorous intellectual imperium of contemporary discoveries
holds sway in this work of 1735 is clear; that its hold is part of an ongoing
tradition was in evidence from the first of the included works ("a kind of

Introduction to the entire collection"). Its author was Pierre Bergeron, a "writer from the middle of the previous century" (he had died in 1637). His prose was enlisted to provide a capstone to the collected travels. His "Treatise on Navigation and the Modern Voyages of Discovery and Conquest, Chiefly by the French" frames the entire collection.[73] Discovery and modernity are the critical rubrics under which individual works are to be read. Indeed, discovery—or, more exactly and concretely, *les longs voyages*—is part of the repertoire of historical ingredients that make up civilization in the eighteenth (and Bergeron's seventeenth) century. Discovery ranks, for example, with printing and other technological feats, as a constituent of the modern.[74] As we have seen, there was no obvious, certainly no prominent, place for pilgrimage in a scheme that equated travel and discovery. Some historian-collectors of travel simply ignored pilgrimage. Others gave it some slight space. In Bergeron's essay, the nod to pious travel to the Levant is grudging and slight. In a wide-ranging chapter devoted to Catholic missions ("commerce in souls and the propagation of faith") and to their revitalization "in the wake of modern discoveries," he manages to mention a few individual travelers to the Holy Land, as well as a few others who had fitted such a destination into their larger travels. All of this, however, has the odor of an afterthought.[75] And although an *abregé* of Mandeville's travels was included in the volume, the title of Mandeville's work was rendered into an eighteenth-century French that turned it into a discovery-like text and hid any characteristics of pilgrimage.[76]

Bellegarde's volume and Bergeron's essay (and the eighteenth-century collection to which Bergeron's treatise and name were attached), when they are considered specifically as *histories* of travel, or of civilization seen through the medium of travel (the case, especially, of Bellegarde), have enormous cultural significance. Both tomes fabricated an historical continuity to replace that which they themselves (or the tradition of which they were a part) had destroyed. Their silence on twelve centuries of pilgrimage had left a yawning gap in the time-line of history. They filled in that gap with the likes of Marco Polo.

Travel collections helped to shape modern Europe. They served as a loud, if not quite deafening, voice in articulating a new travel. One of the strengths of the genre as a fashioning agent of early modern culture—both mirror and glue for that culture—was that, in place of originality of ideas across three centuries (and beyond), it hammered home many of the same points decade after decade in collection after collection, so much so that it is possible to stumble over an irony—that collections of travels could, after their own fashion, be as repetitive and predictible as were traditional accounts of pilgrimage. In any event, the collections were usually restatements of outlooks on the basis of (sometimes) new travel reports. Individual collections, to be sure, had their individual emphases—especially, nationalist agendas that stressed a kingdom's role in discovery—but there was little disagreement over the historical profile and contemporary nature of travel as a discovery-driven enterprise. The reader is presented over and over with the centrality of Columbus and da Gama, the role of technology in jump-starting modern navigation, the importance of eyewitnessed observations, perhaps above all the role of commerce (commerce in goods, commerce in souls) in leading to the steady and cumulative improvement of mankind. Collections offer variations on an overarching theme of discovery, even though one work emphasizes certain areas of the globe and certain languages and another other areas and languages.

One of the permanent givens in this literature is the sense it conveys of cascading information. By the eighteenth century, the weight of inherited and continuously accumulating data was threatening intellectual chaos—or worse, boredom and vagrant attention on the part of potential audiences. In France, it will take La Harpe a row of volumes just to produce an *abrégé* of the shelves of volumes of Prevost's *Histoire générale des voyages*. In England, at about the same time, tedium reared its fearsome head as a named threat to those who would offer travelers' wares to the reading public. If *infinité* had been Bellegarde's favorite word, tediousness was a key term of choice in John Hamilton Moore's later eighteenth-century collection.[77] And of course the two terms are related. The mass of information, if not carefully handled and predigested, could easily cause readers to nod off in the middle of their overeating. The task, as Moore bluntly put it, was that "much matter ought to be comprised in little space, lest the reader should be compelled to spend a great deal of time in selecting a few pearls from an enormous dunghill." His focus was on acts of *discovery*, which distinguished "the more modern Europeans" from earlier civilizations, including that of the Romans ("Conquest engrossed their ideas"), and from earlier Europeans who were held back by the feudal system at home and by the Crusades abroad. But, again because of the threat of tediousness, Moore chose not to belabor this history.[78]

It takes only a glance at the title page—crowded in eighteenth-century fashion—to see how full Moore's plate was, regardless of how much he sought to rein in his text. What he offered was a combination of history, journalism, anthropology, national celebration, and moral instruction.

Above all, he was defining a world of voyages and travels that extended from the deepest recesses of the past to information on *"newly discovered Isles, and their Inhabitants."* And in the execution of the work, he was— like his predecessors—"assisted by several persons who have made the subjects of voyages and travels their particular study."

It comes as no surprise, despite the sweep of Moore's volumes, that he reserved little place for pilgrimage. The fact that Turkey is part of the world he surveyed means that pilgrimage snuck in after a fashion (thirty pages are devoted to "Travels into Egypt, Arabia, Turkey, Persia, and to many other parts of the East, by Baumgarten, Shaw, Maundrell, Pocoke, etc., etc.").[79] His unfavorable mention of the Crusades as an obstacle to discovery in earlier centuries suggests that Moore was not merely overlooking pilgrimage. He came very close to making an argument for specifically excluding pilgrimages from his collection when, in speaking of the standards for collecting material for the work, he remarked of the collection, that "while it draws the line between the obstinacy of Incredulity, and the folly of Superstition, it omits no species of useful information."[80] We finally get to the nerve ends of the question of pilgrimage's place in the early modern scheme. Superstition, we shall see, was precisely the charge that Reformers for two and a half centuries had been underscoring in their attacks on pilgrimage.[81]

Collections of travels had always articulated a cultural agenda. They had been about heroes (Columbus above all) and about high purposes almost as much as they had been about navigational technology, new-found real estate, and commercial possibilities. Moore brings out particularly strongly the comprehensive cultural claims that could be made on behalf of modern travel. "Having finished this sketch," he observes at the conclusion of the introduction,

we shall now proceed with the work itself, beginning with the voyages of Christopher Columbus and Vasquez de Gama, whose discoveries form an aera the most remarkable in the history of navigation, as they first poured the treasures of the Eastern and Western world into the lap of Europe, and thereby laid the foundation of her present grandeur and refinement.[82]

Moore impressed upon readers that travel, or navigation, had itself constituted an era, which was *almost* identical with, and certainly contributory to, the European era of grandeur and refinement, the very foundations of which were rooted in the triumphs of heroic navigators and discoverers.

The term "age of discovery" probably fits the eighteenth century better than the immediately preceding centuries—not only because great voyages of discovery and exploration continued to be undertaken, but also because in the eighteenth century numerous collectors of travel were able, in a mood of retrospection, to take stock of almost three centuries of navigation and to set it in the grandest possible context. By the eighteenth century, discovery had a lengthy and substantial past. The historical and the contemporaneous were fully connected. One need not rely on the misty travels of Jason and Hercules or on an overly adroit reading of Alexander's wars that interpreted them as curiosity-driven travels. Discovery had an historical record (of three centuries) that was both glorious and workaday. The history of exploratory navigation had become a fully usable past. In some respects, its lessons were intensely practical—how, for example, to get from one place to another.[83] Discovery also taught, however, lessons of bravery and love of liberty, and helped to define national identity in relation both to other European nations and to those outside the European community.[84] Perhaps most indicative of the large role—of edification, of instruction—that travel had come to play is that collections of travel came to be recognized as particularly appropriate reading matter for youth.[85] The splendid frontispiece to Moore's collection of voyages and travels shows the Genius of the work pointing out to schoolboys the meritorious and exemplary conduct of the great navigators (Figure 10). Without this grand illustration, it would not be immediately obvious to us today that Moore's hundreds of pages of text had such an audience even remotely in mind. Nor was this morally instructive note only sounded late in the day of discovery. It had informed Grynaeus's ideas three centuries earlier and had inhered throughout the centuries in which the merits of discovery had been touted. Early in the seventeenth century, an abridgement of Johann Theodor de Bry's collection of voyages to the New World was accompanied by a magnificently engraved title page on which medallions enclosed scenes of the great discoverers, each individual being portrayed in the very act of discovery. The whole is framed by personifications of Prudentia, Fortitudo, Victoria, and Pax[86] (Figure 11).

These collectors of travel had fabricated a new working definition of travel. They had done so by associating one work of travel with another; by including essays, usually by way of preliminaries, on what was the best way to travel, what one should look for, how one should write up one's reports; and by giving to travel of their own day a historical pedigree— especially the pedigree of Columbus, but as well a lineage traceable to a deeper past of travel that also assisted them in reaching such a definition.

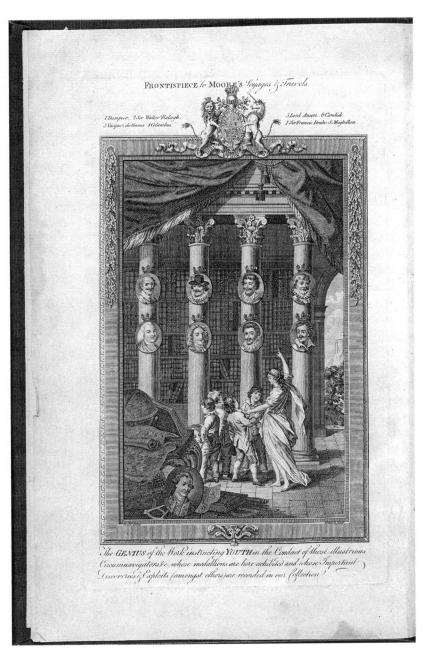

Figure 10. John Hamilton Moore, *A New and Complete Collection of Voyages and Travels*, 2 vols. (London: A. Hogg, 1785?), vol. 1, frontispiece.

Figure 11. Johann Theodor de Bry, *America, das ist Erfindung und Offenbahrung der Newen Welt* (Frankfurt am Mayn: Nicolaus Hoffman, 1617), engraved title page.

If Cook was another Columbus, Columbus himself was another Ulysses. What these collectors were fashioning and refining—those who compiled travels in the wake of Columbus, in the midst of the Thirty Years' War, on the eve of Revolution—was what we today would call a canon of travel literature. Travel literature came to be that which found a niche in a collection of travels.

Other voices of the times also suggest the waning of long-distance pilgrimage. The condescending dismissal by the *Encyclopédie* (as it proclaims the triumph, in matters devotional, of *chez soi* over *outre-mer*) is one such sharp, clear voice.[87] Even more reflective—because less abrasive and tendentious—of an altered world in which pilgrimage to the Levant (and even general awareness of the Levant) began to fade from the minds of Europeans is a work such as Romaine de Hooghe's great book of illustrations, *Les Indes orientales et occidentales, et autres lieux,* which appeared in Leyden around 1700. Its title page is decorated with cameo portraits of Columbus and Vespucci. The book itself begins with detailed and precisely engraved maps that take in the whole world and all its known parts "based on new observations of the Members of the Académie Royale des Sciences." De Hooghe's images are another way, than that of travel collections, to make sense of data and impressions that had flooded Europe's general consciousness in the course of two centuries of wide voyaging and aggressive exploration. (The book's full title shows how ambitious de Hooghe was to gather in and summarize as much as possible).[88] De Hooghe wished to show to Europeans the outer world's customs and habits, its arts and peculiarities as well as its flora and fauna, and also to offer a glimpse of the Westerner himself up and about in exotic worlds (Jesuits being vexed, Spaniards carrying on, through de Hooghe's Dutch eyes, in an uncivilized and brutish manner), worlds of strange religions and variant technologies (Chinese ship-building, for example) (Figure 12), and extravagant costumes. There is nothing exceptional in all of this. The book's tone is largely identical to that of encyclopedists and compilers of *cabinets des rarités* as well as compilers of collections of travels. And like these other cultural sharpshooters and summarizers, de Hooghe gobbled up the world almost whole—but not quite whole, as revealed by the absence of the Levant (except for an interior view of the church-become-mosque Hagia Sophia and a depiction of slavery and imprisonment as practiced among the Turks), that same Levant that had once figured so prominently in the Latin world's gaze upon the outside world.

Nevertheless, it was the great collectors of travels themselves who were the *muralistes*, or the great chorus, that articulated a new world of travel. They explained to the reader the world as it had been made manifest through discovery.[89] Collections of travels offered up a kind of modernity squared: a world of a certain sort and located in a certain present moment, the reader's moment, to which all history—say, from Homer through Apollonius of Tyana to Marco Polo to Cook—was argued to have tended. The immense and elaborate literature of early modern travel collections not only shaped and colored much of the larger context within which writers of Levantine pilgrimage had to operate; it also furnished the background out of which emerged Chateaubriand's novel and ironic (in its effect) surgery upon pilgrimage. It was not the oddest quirk of thought—nor even (or not entirely so) a case of the Romantic finding his proper pose— that led Chateaubriand simultaneously to revive pilgrimage, as pious practice and literary subject matter, and to remove pilgrimage from the universe of travel literature. If we come to Chateaubriand directly from the tradition of pilgrimage literature in which he was steeped, his decision seems eccentric and innovative, even revolutionary to the point of being

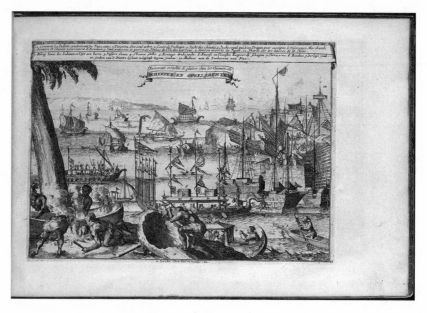

Figure 12. Romeyn de Hooghe, *Les Indes Orientales et Occidentales* (Leide: P. Vander Aa, 1700?), figure 12.

destructive of that very tradition. If, however, we view early modern pilgrims (and Chateaubriand himself) as heirs of a modernity (both Enlightened and pre-Enlightenment) that included much more than matters of pilgrimage, then his maneuver seems less odd and more in the nature of a culmination of three centuries in the development of travel than a departure from that development. It seems a coming to terms on the part of Chateaubriand with certain overwhelming realities. For three centuries, pilgrimage had been under the relentless stress of discovery (not to mention the added and cumulating stresses of Reformation, Enlightenment, and Revolution). The pressures were urging pilgrimage in precisely the direction that Chateaubriand finally, if hesitantly, chose to take—a direction that led pilgrimage away from the literature of travel. Whatever pilgrimage had become by Chateaubriand's day, its role as the main European mode of recollected travel had long passed—at least if one took one's cue only from the great collectors. Were pilgrimage to arise from its pallet, it might best try on new garb. And this was precisely what Chateaubriand undertook to provide for it when he made pilgrimage a moment of autobiography rather than a free-standing experience of travel. He was more cognizant than we might have thought of what were then (or so it could be argued) the prevailing winds.

4

Reformation and the Polemics of Travel

LATE IN THE FIFTEENTH CENTURY there circulated, in both manuscript and print, an account of a pilgrimage to Jerusalem that had taken place around the year 1485. When the book was first printed in 1491 in Venice, pilgrims were the modern travelers (*modernis peregrinis*) spoken of in its title.[1] Pilgrimage was what travelers (whose travels were written down) did. And indulgences attached to sites (also emphasized in the title) were among the preoccupations of such travelers. Columbus had yet to sail. Interpreters of sea-going voyages—historians, collectors of travels—had yet to redefine *peregrinatio* in ways that would usher out pilgrimage as the new travel came into existence. The title of the 1491 imprint stressed both the modernity and the antiquity of pious travel to the Holy Land. Pilgrimage was modern because it was age-old; it deserved to be undertaken today because it had been undertaken in the time of Constantine and Helen and Sylvester.

By the time the same title next appeared in Venice, around the year 1520, the great discoveries were well under way. To a thoroughly contemporary individual, a *modernus*, current events were calling into question the identification of pilgrimage and travel. That pilgrimage had been around for centuries seemed less impressive a claim than it once might have. Nevertheless, however much reasons for travel had begun to alter with the expansion of horizons and introduction of new routes leading to new worlds, the *Peregrinationes* was reissued around 1520 (for the second time; it had also been printed in Angers in 1493, the year of the first appearance of Columbus's *Epistola*). The book was still thought to have appeal and relevance.

The second appearance of the book in Venice did, however, roughly coincide with European developments that would further threaten to displace pilgrimage. Far from Venice, beyond the Alps, 1520 was the year in which Martin Luther burned his bridges, or at least a papal bull. The Pope replied by issuing an excommunication. With Reformation under way, the future constricted for books such as the Venetian imprint. Most who embraced ideas of Luther, Calvin, and other Reformers agreed in their opposition to indulgences and in their challenge to the papal authority that underlay those indulgences, the very things highlighted in the title of the *Peregrinationes*. The title page itself would thus have sufficed, in the decades after 1520, to shrink the audience receptive to reading about a pilgrimage that had been undertaken in 1485.[2]

$*$ $*$ $*$

Reformers in Wittenberg, Geneva, and Zurich, just as surely as navigators from Cadiz and Lisbon and Southampton, undermined pilgrimage as the noetic mold of European travel. And the two forces sometimes acted in unison. Especially in great collections of travels that grew out of a Reformation milieu—the *Novus Orbis* in Basel, for example, or the great tomes of Hakluyt and Purchas in England—there intersected a celebration of new navigational realities and a hostility to old ecclesiastical verities. Purchas's documenting of the great Atlantic discoveries, for example, offered an occasion for confirming history's westward trending away from the geographical locales of sacred events, and thereby made a subtle point of leaving pilgrimage itself in the historical dust:

Jesus Christ, who is the way the truth and the life, has long since given the Bill of Divorce to ingrateful Asia where he was born and of Africa the place of his flight and refuge, and has become almost wholly European.[3]

In Geneva in 1567, for an earlier example of how discovery and reformation were intertwined in the toll that they jointly took on pilgrimage, a ferocious Calvinist satire against the Catholic Church was launched under the title, *Histoire de la mappe-monde papistique*. Indictment of Rome takes the form of a wide-ranging diatribe that pounds away at the entire frame of the Church. The target, moreover, is seen to be as modern as can be, a current creation that has somehow sprung from the new world of European discovery and expansion. Indeed, the pope's world is seen as a malign spiritual universe, a dark and devouring new world, that exists parallel to the new worlds of the discoverers: "It is remarked everywhere how the popes, following the king of Portugal and the Catholic king of Spain, have discovered their papal new world, just as these others have discovered theirs in the East and in Peru." This papal world is, like the other new worlds, made up of parts. The "papistical new world" has twelve subject provinces, seven allied provinces, and six republics (among the latter of which are the Jesuits and the *Sorbonistes*). Pilgrimage figures in this wide-sweeping caricature: among the subject provinces are "devotion to the saints" and "the construction of places of devotion"; and among the allied provinces are "pilgrimages."[4]

When pilgrimage is taken on as a subject in its own right,[5] a point is made of the continuity between ancient pagan temples and the new shrines of the papal world. Loreto and St. James Compostella are cited as specific examples. Jerusalem, moreover, is not apart from, or exceptional to, all of this. It stands at the head of a list of papal shrines as the "the capital city of the province of pilgrimages." Then, at the end of the list, the reader is told that such shrines cover Europe and extend far beyond Europe. Pilgrimage stands forth as a seamless web, a devouring, world-wide menace and conspiracy that fattens the purses of monks, clerics, and the pope himself.

* * *

Pilgrimage remained a fitfully combustible topic through the sixteenth and seventeenth centuries, especially in Germany, where the line was clearly drawn between Catholic advocacy and Protestant condemnation of pilgrimage. On the other hand, the question was not always front-and-center in religious debates;[6] and at least once a serious possibility of positive rapprochement colored the debate. In 1584 in Frankfurt am Main, Sigmund Feyerabend published the *Reyssbuch*, a collection of seventeen pilgrimages written in, or translated into, German and based on materials that reached back as far as the Crusades and forward through the later Middle Ages and into the sixteenth century. The *Reyssbuch* included both pre-Reformation and sixteenth-century pilgrimages, both Catholic and Reformed pilgrimages. (The versatile and entrepreneurial Feyerabend printed during his career both the writings of Innocent IV and the pamphlets of Luther). Feyerabend's tome stands out, because of its serious and exclusive focus on pilgrimages, as the great and towering exception among the great travel collections of early modern Europe.[7]

The *Reyssbuch* is a pivotal contributor, on the German scene, to an earnest discussion of the place of pilgrimage in the modern world, but Feyerabend's unusual collection is more difficult to locate within the broader early modern scene outside Germany. It occupies no obvious niche. The *Reyssbuch* can be interpreted as validating and elevating pilgrimage and solidifying its place within the genre of travel, even in an age of discovery.

It puts pilgrimage on a par with other forms of travel, thus endowing pilgrimage with modern credentials. Feyerabend did make the case for regarding pilgrimages as every bit as *collectible* and publishable as the great voyages of discoverers. Indeed, Feyerabend mentioned his pilgrims in the same preliminary breath with Columbus, Amerigo Vespucci, and Magellan. Discoverers of new lands, he tells the reader, and pilgrims to the Holy Land share a tradition that reaches back to ancient historians and geographers who reported what they had seen.[8] He touted *curiositas* as a motive in its own right for traveling. Feyerabend strove to reconcile the medieval and the modern, Catholic and Protestant, discovery and pilgrimage. He made very large claims for the status, or at least for the uses and the appeal, of pilgrimage in his day.[9] In this light, Feyerabend (who did stand in the grand tradition of European travel collectors) can be seen as offering a serious revision to that tradition, almost a century old by his day, of travel collecting. Pilgrimage, for Feyerabend, was part of modern travel. His unusual take on the world about him was a complicating factor in a time of great change where travel is concerned. While forces of discovery and reformation seemed to push for radical reorganization—even more, radical reconceptualization—of European travel, Feyerabend seemed less sure. He viewed things as going on pretty much as before, with allowances for the feats of the great discoverers, but with pilgrimage holding on to a position of great prominence.

On the other hand, it is every bit as possible to size up Feyerabend's accomplishment in an opposite light. Years earlier, Feyerabend had published Sebastian Franck's *Warhafftige Beschreibunge aller Theil der Welt* (Franckfort, 1567), a more traditional sixteenth-century collection of travels that focused on the great discoveries around the globe.[10] In the light of this earlier collection (which does link Feyerabend to the grand European tradition of travel collecting), the *Reyssbuch* can be seen as not so much Feyerabend's novel enshrinement of pilgrimage in the front ranks of travel in the new post-Columbian world as his sequestration of pilgrimage, his shunting pilgrimage off to the side in a separate volume of its own apart from the great heroic navigational ventures of the age—a feat of abstraction of pilgrimage (vaguely similar, in its way, to that which Chateaubriand would attempt almost two hundred and fifty years later in the *Itinéraire*, when he plucked *peregrinatio* out of a tradition of devout travel and made it over into an interlude or episode in the life of the autobiographer). In any case, Feyerabend gave to pilgrimage an historical legitimacy and visibility and a contemporary life that crossed Reformational boundaries.

Feyerabend introduced nuance and complexity into the heated debate over pilgrimage. From the Catholic perspective, his collection could only strengthen the Catholic evaluation of pilgrimage as a continuing and vital part of life. John Pits (1560–1615), an English Catholic who had studied at Oxford and continued his education in Rome and Ingolstadt (and later taught rhetoric and Greek at Rheims and ended up a canon of the cathedral of Verdun), approached the matter of pilgrimage from a broad and systematic perspective. His *Seven Books on Pilgrimage* (Düsseldorf, 1604), instead of pushing contemporary pilgrimage to the margins or condemning pilgrimage to a purely historical existence that had been discredited and superseded, argued for the close association of *Bildungsreise* and pilgrimage. *Peregrinatio moralis* and *peregrinatio religiosa*, far from being opposites on the spectrum of travel, harmoniously overlapped in Pits's interpretation.[11] Pits's valuation of pilgrimage as a fully modern and engaged mode of travel was at implicit odds with the great travel collections of the day—Feyerabend excepted.

In 1606, two years after Pits's work, Jacobus Gretser brought out his own vast historical treatment of pilgrimage.[12] Among its many other tasks, Gretser's tome answered the Reformed critique that saw pilgrimage as vestigial and shameful. Gretser described a detailed centuries-long history of pilgrimage and documented its continuing life in the early seventeenth century.[13] In both respects, he resembled the outlook of Feyerabend.

Pilgrimage was only one item on Gretser's large plate. Gretser knew many things in a way that most men know only one thing. He was a Counter-Reformation fox, but one not totally lacking the habits of a hedgehog. His range of intellectual curiosity was immense, but so too his powers of application and concentration. Jesuit biographers captured his essential qualities: "we are dumbfounded—as we should be—at the variety, the multitude, and the erudition of his works."[14] He leapt across the surface of things from subject to subject, and then penetrated deep below the surface—historically, theologically, philologically—whatever seemed required—of a given subject. He was something of a stalking tiger. Intellectually tireless, he was always on the move; but he lingered as patiently as need be over a task.

He was unremitting. A colleague, who knew his work well, remarked that Gretser "drained dry all the libraries by his reading, and almost filled them back up again with his writing."[15] He worked deep into the nights. He produced 234 printed books; an additional forty-six works survive in manuscript. He was a playwright (23 dramas), a Greek grammarian, a theologian, a philosopher, an historian. His originality has been questioned, never his energy. His reputation (to judge by a portrait executed a century after his death) suggests the intensity and studiousness of the man—a kind but perhaps remote night owl on a very high limb. We imagine an antiquarian, isolated from his times and fellows.

But not so. For one thing, antiquarians were not then—nor for long after (consider Le Nain de Tillemont, or, from an earlier time, Ambrose de Morales[16])—isolated figures. Gretser held chairs at the university at Ingolstadt, where Pits had studied, throughout most of his productive literary years. His correspondence linked him to people in high places, to people across Europe, to people around the world ("as far afield as the Indies"). He most clearly fits into his time and place, however, as one of the great Catholic polemicists as the Reformation wore on, as the century turned, and as long and bitter war in Germany approached. The titles he collected—*fortissimus* Athlete and *vigilantissimus* Defender of truth, Vanquisher (*domitor*) of Lutherans, Hammer (*malleus*) of heretics, Terror of those who falsely attacked Jesuits—suggest a combative career that began center stage with the Regensburg colloquium of 1601. His Jesuit biographers took more than five closely printed folio columns to list "the various works against the Heretics that he labored over (*elaboravit*)."[17]

The *De Peregrinationibus*, on its own a classic excavation and exposition of the history of Christian pilgrimage, also serves as a perfect example of that intersection of the antiquarian-historical and the contemporary-polemical which characterized much of the erudite battler's writings. Gretser's concerns in this book, in both sweep and detail, went far beyond contemporary upsets; but he was well aware that his subject matter was topical and controversial. He devotes an entire chapter to the question "Whether contemporary heretics even travel to Jerusalem, and in how devout a manner"[18]—a question that Feyerabend's *Reyssbuch*, by its very content (both Catholic and Protestant), would have prompted any reader to raise over the previous two decades. The *Reyssbuch* had implied continuity between travel to Jerusalem before and after the Reformation by both Catholics and Reformed. That Feyerabend found pilgrimage a *collectible* form of travel, as well as that he saw devout travel to Jerusalem spanning the Catholic/Reformed divide—both facts argue for the modernity of pilgrimage and against the general view of Reformers that pilgrimage was at most a fossil, historically interesting (and treacherous) but inapplicable to the moment and the future. Indeed, the vital currency of pilgrimage in Feyerabend's volume is reenforced by two of the collection's most striking features. First, the majority of the eighteen works collected by Feyerabend had, in some form or other, already found their way into print before Feyerabend brought them together. And second, while five works reach back to the fourteenth century or earlier, four pilgrimages were from the second half of the fifteenth century, and eight were from the second half of the sixteenth century (that is, between 1550 and 1584).[19]

Gretser's entire tome, like Feyerabend's, argued that pilgrimage's long historical tradition fed its contemporary vitality. For Gretser, however, pilgrimage past and present was a *Catholic* phenomenon. He could not accept Feyerabend's assumption of pilgrimage as an oecumenical activity. How, Gretser wonders, are the Reformed—Calvinists and Lutherans who abhor (*detestentur*) pilgrimage, who see pilgrimages as "superstitious and contrary to the word of God"—to escape the very same charge of superstition that they hurl at Catholics if they themselves travel (*peregrinari*) to Jerusalem? Nevertheless, the unthinkable has happened. Gretser has read his Feyerabend: "For there exist in that great volume of pilgrimages some travel diaries (*Hodoeporica*) of men who have strayed from the ancient faith and Catholic religion." He lists them: Jacob Wormsber in 1561, Melchior Seidlitz in 1556, Joannis Helffrich of Leipzig in 1565, the Swiss Daniel Ecklin in 1552, and "one whom it is necessary to name above all the rest, the physician of Augsburg, Leonard Rauwolf, in 1573."[20] Why Rauwolf above all? We shall see.

Gretser leads the reader along a path complicated by the equivocal (and perhaps fast-changing) meaning of *peregrinatio*, which can denote either a journey of any sort or a pilgrimage. He recognizes the fact of Reformed journeys to Jerusalem, but not their status as genuine pilgrimages. The second part of his question at the head of the chapter is *quam devote* the Reformed undertook their travels. Gretser contends that Protestants did not travel in the devout manner of pilgrims, but went east with another purpose (*alio fine*) which was twofold. First, the *Sectarii* were merely antiquarians who traveled in order to see antiquities. They entirely lacked the spiritual motivation of a pilgrim ("without any hint of piety or religion"). They only wished to boast that they had seen Jerusalem, Mount Sinai, and other foreign (*peregrina*) places. Second, the Reformed traveler in the Levant seemed keen to make for Jerusalem in order to make sport of (*irrideant*) the piety of Catholics who prayerfully visited the holy places.[21]

The distinction between Reformed travelers (antiquarians, tourists, cut-ups) and Catholic travelers (pilgrims) is critical to Gretser, who is writing in a world in which Feyerabend had clouded the question. Leonard

Rauwolf is singled out ("From this one learn about all the others").[22] He is the Reformed traveler who most arouses Gretser's ire, probably because he acted so thoroughly the part of the genuinely devout traveler:

> How did the physician occupy himself while the pilgrims devoted themselves to their pious practices? "While the pilgrims were occupied in their activities, I stood back"—*not*, to be sure, as the publican in the Temple—"and I recalled to mind what our Savior Christ Jesus endured and performed in these places." Soon he began a new sermon (*concionem*) and declaimed, in a word, "as if preaching a sermon (*praedicantice*)." He forgot, I think, that he was writing a travel diary and not a "commentary (*postillam*)."[23]

Rauwolf's own description of his spiritual demeanor in the Holy Land,[24] not simply the fact of his journey to Palestine, raises the evident possibility that Reformers could perform pilgrimage. It is this possibility that the Hammer of Heretics attacks with vim:

> He [Rauwolf] concludes his sermon with this most fervent prayer (*precatione*): "Bestow on us Lord Jesus Christ your Holy Spirit, that He may maintain us in the knowledge of your Word. May He confirm and habituate us in your Word so that without fear we might freely proclaim it in company with you in the face of our enemies. And if they bring against us vexations, may we bear all calamities, afflictions, and crosses patiently and gently in order that your honor might be completely guaranteed and our constancy be fully in evidence."

This is altogether too much for Gretser. He will not abide it. The hammer lifts and falls:

> How pious is our physician? How ardent are the prayers (*vota*) he solemnly proclaims (*concipit*)? How great a fire does it ignite, this desire of his to defend and propagandize the Lutheran word? I maintain the suppliant was heard. For now he has gone away to a place where there will no longer be an occasion of falling away from the Saxon word. He is confirmed in his very own word, without any danger of losing that confirmation.[25]

Gretser's vehemence suggests many things (apart from the spiked temperature of religious exchange in the later stages of the Reformation just prior to the Thirty Years' War).[26] Certainly, he does his part to quench any Feyerabendian premise that pilgrimage constituted common Christian ground for both Catholic and Reformed. (Nor, we will soon see, was it only Catholics such as Gretser who resisted a Feyerabendian center).

Gretser's dismissal of Rauwolf is worth noting for other reasons as well. He expresses, in his critique of Rauwolf, his view of what is, and what is not, appropriate to a travel account. Gretser's objection to Rauwolf's sermonizing or commentary in a travel diary almost amounts to a literary or aesthetic disapprobation. Such behavior does not, he argues, fit the genre. Gretser, in other words, sees pilgrimage as a species of *travel*, and not solely a more narrow matter of theology. When he speaks of pilgrimage, he has in mind a mode (and literature) of travel—although, to be sure, the fish Gretser was frying in the *De Peregrinationibus* were not primarily literary. Finally, however much time had elapsed for Reformational dust to settle, the gusts of diatribe in Gretser's prose (and in that of the opponents to whom he was responding) over this issue of long-distance pilgrimage to Terra Sancta helped to stir everything up all over again. Peace was not about to settle over Germany, if intellectual skirmishing over the meaning of travel to the eastern Mediterranean was any indication. A work such as the *De Peregrinationibus* seems to foreshadow the long devastation that was about to be visited upon Germany. In 1632, little more than a quarter century after the publication of Gretser's tome, Gustavus Adolphus's armies would march to the very gates of Gretser's academical city of Ingolstadt.[27]

Six years after Gretser's masterwork on pilgrimage, there appeared in Wittenberg in 1612 the *Itinera sex* (*Six Journeys*), composed by the Lutheran scholar Balthasar Menz (1537–1617). Had Menz's book appeared before Gretser's, the latter would very probably have responded to it. An earlier work printed in Leipzig in 1586, the *Grundliche und warhafftige Beschreibung der löbliche und ritterlichen Reise und Meerfarth in das Heilige Land nach Hierusalem des durchlauctigen . . . Fürsten . . . Albrechten, hertzogen zu Sachsen*, written by Hans von Mergenthal (d. 1488) and edited, but very unsympathetically, by the Lutheran devotional writer Hieronymus Weller (1499–1572), had inspired some fine pages of reasoned and wrathful taking-to-task of Weller on the part of Gretser.[28] *Six Journeys* was a similar kind of work. Menz recounted six excursions over the Alps taken by five Saxon rulers during the previous century and a half.[29] Casting back over this period, which included the half-century before the coming of the Reformation, Menz focused on travel and its historical roots in pilgrimage, but was studiously uninterested in the historic role of the great discoveries in reshaping the contours of travel. Menz's collection of travels had scarcely anything in common with the tradition of travel-collecting that we examined in Chapter 3. He seems unaware of Ramusio and the other great collectors of travel of the preceding century. His interests in travel were other and narrower than theirs.

Menz sought to defend the ideals of the Reformation, especially the

Reformation as realized at Wittenberg. By 1612, the past in Germany that seemed (to a German curious about the traditions of national travel) to call for interpretation was not so much pre-Columbian as pre-Lutheran. Menz's *Itinera sex* harvests a patch of such history, a century and a half of Saxon travel. He celebrates, but also performs corrective surgery upon, the historical record of German travel. He labors to isolate, to extract, and to discard the devotional impulses that had informed, defined, and motivated such travel in an earlier, Catholic Saxony. The *Itinera sex* strives to disinfect of any devotional contagions the journeys over the Alps of dukes and electors, Menz's revered ancestral leaders—not an easy task, considering how deeply European travel before Columbus and Luther had been permeated with the religious ideals and practices of pilgrimage.[30]

The very contents of the *Itinera sex* testify to this historical preeminence of pilgrimage. In order to substantiate the history of Saxon travel, Menz turns to pilgrimages—five of the six journeys had been actual pilgrimages, the sixth was a contemporary form of tour that had evolved from pilgrimage. There is no better witness (because an unfriendly witness) than Menz to the devout character of European travel prior to the sixteenth century. If he could plausibly have portrayed Frederick the Wise taking to the road for a far destination in other than the manner of a pilgrim, presumably he would have done so. An absolutely key point about Menz is that he does not disguise or deny the fact that the *frame* of pre-Reformation travel was pilgrimage. Other kinds of travel—such as Henry the Pious's military excursions—come into the picture, but are insufficient or too episodic to stand alone, much less to give overall shape or structure to the narrative of travel. Such are no more than addenda to accounts of pilgrimage. And surviving evidence confirms that a student of travel (such as Menz) could scarcely have looked at things differently. German travels from the mid-thirteenth through the mid-sixteenth centuries were essentially and overwhelmingly pilgrimages, and especially pilgrimages to the Holy Land.[31] Nor is this all. What better shows the (enduring) strength of peregrinative impulses than the fact that Menz himself caught the peregrinative bug? At least after a fashion. He is the celebrator of the great city of the Reformation. Saxony had been the first center of the Reformation, and Wittenberg the center of Reformation Saxony. A century later, Wittenberg remained a university city suffused with reminders of Luther and Melanchthon. Menz may not have been ready to offer indulgences to lure the faithful to Wittenberg, but he did want—the very title of his book says as much—to turn Wittenberg into what Rome and Jerusalem had been for centuries—a center of pilgrimage, of devout tour, a place (comparable to Jerusalem, to Rome) where there were, for the true believer, things worth seeing.[32]

To cast doubt, much less aspersions, on pilgrimage to the Holy Land was to raise questions that went beyond what we today would characterize as a narrowly religious debate. For centuries, the traveler had been a pilgrim (*peregrinus, viator*), his literature of travel a literature of pilgrimage. Travels, voyages, journeys—such counted as notable acts of men long before men took to the Atlantic to redraw Ptolemy's maps; travels were part of a bundle of *res gestae* that made men legendary, heroic, admirable, exemplary, civilized. How, in the polemical wake of Reformation, was an opponent of pilgrimage to salvage, or to put a more respectable face on, this history and these traditions of travel that had always been part of the makeup of the European identity? What constituted memorable travel in an age when old ways of traveling had been discarded in parts of Europe (in reformational Saxony, for example)? As late as the early seventeenth century, this remained an open question. It was the very question that Balthasar Menz entertained, and answered, with his Latin collection of travels.

Menz's first step was to retool these *itinera* from the past—these journeys *causa religionis*—by placing them in a context both antique and literary. Homer, he reminds us, had written of the travels of Ulysses. Julius Caesar's poem (mentioned by Suetonius) described his journey to Nearer Spain. Roman emperors recounted, or had recounted for them, their imperial journeys. Horace wrote up his journey to Brindisium, Ovid his sailing to Miletus. By such precedents Menz had been inspired (*incitatus*) to undertake his own composition (*scriptio*), which was a review (*recensuimus*) of six journeys by dukes and electors of Saxony. Menz's hope was that both his own courageous act of following such a literary path and the example of his subjects' travels would inspire readers. He wrote to celebrate the memory of great Saxon rulers, but also to encourage his readers "to a similar zeal for prudence and humanity and for leading one's life well and happily." Good rulers, he reminded them—and all his travelers were rulers—were gifts of God who insured, among other things, "true religion."[33] Nevertheless, the intended reader for this work—its message combining the moral, political, and literary under a classicizing canopy—was not the usual *lector pius* who pored over accounts of pilgrims, but a *lector eruditus* who would, it was hoped, gain intellectual pleasure from reading this medley of travels, some of its ingredients plucked from the German but all of them recast in the Latin language and in the classical mode.[34]

After reframing the Saxon journeys with the help of classical analogies and references, Menz moves on to a second step by confronting the historical reality of pilgrimage in order to thwart its contemporary impact. His approach to his subject matter is alchemical. By literary manipulation, the Saxon pilgrimages will survive as journeys, but with their peregrinative sting removed. He does not deny that the travels he has collected were pilgrimages. The very title states that three of the six journeys were to the Holy Land; and at least five of the six journeys, including the one that got no further than Italy, were clearly undertaken for traditionally religious motivations. Having granted the central impulses of his travelers, however, Menz then dismisses their pious motives from serious consideration. He changes the very character of the works that their devout motives had wrought. Pious practices of his ducal travelers, he tells the reader, merely reflect erroneous usages of an earlier time. They were inessential to appreciating the travels. His first traveler, Albert, son of Elector Frederic II, set off on pilgrimage in 1476. Piety, to be sure, had led him to the holy places—piety, however, as then understood (*ut credebatur*).[35] On his way eastward through Europe, he is received by cities and given gifts, including at one stop relics of saints—again, "because of the devotion of that age."[36] Menz's third traveler, Duke Frederick III, set out in 1493 for Palestine for the same pious reason—"from the habit of those times." Frederick's motivation, however, is portrayed as somewhat diluted. To religious impulse are added inclinations of the self-improving tourist ("judging that men became polished [*erudiri*] through traveling").[37] Menz's description of Frederick's baggage gives scarce hint of the fact that Frederick was one of the most perfervid of European collectors of sacred relics—by the coming of the Reformation, the possessor of over 19,000 items[38]—or that this 1493 journey was probably the source of a good part of his sacred treasury. In Menz's account, the purely devotional character of Frederick's journey is overshadowed by other considerations, particularly that of Frederick's life "after his return from Palestine": the wars he fought, the architecture and learning he fostered at Wittenberg, and the infant Reformation he protected.[39] Menz singles out two great events of Frederick's rule—the election of the Emperor (Charles V, whose choice Frederick facilitated) and "the reform of the churches." Menz specifically underscores Frederick's relationship to Luther and Melancthon:

He protected by his renowned authority Martin Luther who renovated the celestial doctrine concerning the salvation of souls against the madness of the papists

(*furores Pontificiorum*) and he summoned Philip Melanchthon from Tübingen and
established him as a professor in Wittenberg.

Henry the Pious was a similar case. He set out on his first pilgrimage
to Jerusalem in 1499, "because it was the custom of that time." The very
next year he repeated the journey. He then went to Compostella.[40] But later
still, the Catholic pilgrim became Lutheran and sedentary, setting up a
household relatively late in life in Freiburg in 1518. This traditionally devout
man had been always on the move, whether on pilgrimage in the Levant
and Spain or on imperial business in Germany (following the imperial
court, engaging in its battles). His sudden change—Menz permits no doubt
on this—was not a mere alteration in Henry's circumstances, but a conscious reversal of Henry's habits and thought. Papal ideas had been actively
rejected ("papal absurdities having been put aside"), their underpinnings
seen for what they were ("their superstitions having been discredited"). In
their place Henry took up a "more sincere teaching of celestial truth." And
he did more than take it up; he defended and propagated it, fighting off
the fierce objections of his brother Duke George, who died Catholic and
without heirs. The Reformation in Saxony triumphed under the startlingly
newly evangelized Henry and his sons Moritz and Augustus. In the retelling of Henry's pilgrimages, pilgrimage itself becomes both an image of the
whole superstitious world of papal Europe that has been overthrown—
such it appeared to Lutherans in Wittenberg—and also the pivot on which
the turn from old world to new is executed: Henry the pilgrim becomes
a new man whose decisions and actions cancel the old world that had celebrated pilgrimage, the very world of which he himself had been such a
strikingly visible ornament and exemplar.

Menz had reworked the ducal travels. First, he had placed his book
and subject matter in a classical tradition of travel and travel literature. He
intended contemporary readers to enjoy these accounts as an antique reader
would have appreciated travel accounts of his own time. Second, Menz
celebrated the Saxons' journeys while dismissing their central motivation,
which, for Menz, was simply their following the misguided and wrong-
headed sentiments of earlier times. Such an attitude on Menz's part would
have gained plausibility in light of the fact that two of the most avid and
devoted pilgrims—Frederick III and Henry II—had in fact subsequently
converted to the Lutheran outlook. Finally, Menz's anthology of Saxon
travels offers a third means of updating such travel in the wake of Lutheran
reformation. This third means appeared in the sixth and concluding journey.

Whereas Frederick and Henry had been celebrated pilgrims who had, we may suppose, given up pilgrimage as a decision incidental to their new religious affiliations, the sixth journey shows travel itself remade along lines that Menz could only approve, lines that made it unnecessary for him to tamper with the traveler's intentions and outlook. This final account of travel retells a contemporary journey of the elector John George, who traveled to Rome in 1601.[41] Menz had devoted a hundred pages to the historical journeys; he now gives almost two hundred and fifty pages to John George alone. The earlier accounts, it turns out, are background to John George who "was following the ancient examples which we have reviewed above."[42]

He was, and he wasn't. This last journey is an interpretation of, or evolution away from, those *exempla avita,* which may have been mixed in their motivations but which had been primarily, formally, and unmistakably devotional undertakings. The journey (*peregrinatio*) of 1601 is quite different. John George travels out of touristical passion pure and simple: "Having attained his maturity, he burned with the desire to see foreign nations." This newly minted *peregrinatio* is scrubbed quite clean of pious impulses for setting out on a long journey. Travel has become a rite of passage, not of devotion. We see at its end just how exceptional Menz's collection of Saxon travels had been. Coming nearly a century after the rise of travel collections, it did what travel collectors had rarely done before, and hardly ever would do afterwards: Menz mounted a frontal attack on pilgrimage. After a fashion, he turned pilgrimage against itself—or at least turned it upon its head. While praising his ducal heroes for their travels, he argued that the travels took the devotional form they did because of the dark times in which the dukes lived—the poor ninnies didn't know any better—and that, had they had it to do over again, and had they lived in the wake and light, rather than on the eve, of Luther and Melanchthon and the days of glory of Wittenberg, they would have traveled differently. Menz's thesis found suggestive evidence in the transitional figures of Frederick and Henry and full manifestation in the journey (in 1601) of John George.

John George arrives in Rome and views a ruinated city—"now scarcely inhabited and full of ruins." He is undaunted. The eternality of Rome springs from "the splendor of its glory and the clarity of its name. With the learned (*docti*) fighting on its behalf, it can never be extinguished or abolished."[43] The *eruditus lector* now has been ushered to his place front and center in the writer's audience. If *peregrinatio* still means "pilgrimage," it does so in an entirely metaphorical sense. Menz's volume has turned the stone of ancient pilgrimage into the gold of up-to-date (but also Homeric and Ovidian) tour.

*   *   *

In the Reformation struggles, pilgrimage to Jerusalem was one more or less important item of contention. Its niche in a larger structure of religious contest is highlighted in the *Histoire de la mappe-monde papistique* printed in Geneva. There were those, however, who bore in upon the matter of pilgrimage with greater focus and concentration. Especially in central Europe, where pilgrimage over the Alps and across the Mediterranean to the Holy Land had long been the great recorded way of going on a journey and where the Reformation had originated and been debated with great intensity, both Catholics and Protestants saw the fate of pilgrimage as crucially involved in the religious questions of the day. They also realized, however, that they were talking not only about theology, but also about travel, when they spoke about pilgrimage. To go on pilgrimage was a mode of prayer, but also a mode of travel. When one accepted or rejected pilgrimage, one was pondering the purposes and motivations of the traveler. Where one went and why were under scrutiny—as well as the manner in which the traveler recollected his travels. Feyerabend saw devout travel to Jerusalem as a great tradition and continuity that deserved to be maintained and underscored even in the age of Columbus and Magellan. More surprising was that it made no great difference to Feyerabend that he was also dealing with the era of Luther and Zwingli. Gretser, mindful of the great tradition of pilgrimage and of the bumps and buffets it had endured in the Reformation, was sure of its survival in Catholic Europe and was aware that when he was talking about the literature of pilgrimage he was talking about a literature of travel. The literature of travel was also, and even more clearly, the concern of Weller and Menz. While they disagreed absolutely with Feyerabend and Gretser about the viability and desirability of pilgrimage, they also saw that the debate was about the future of travel. Menz, in particular, wanted to save the Saxon tradition of travel, but could only do so by confronting the historical reality that such travel had been pilgrimage. The great Saxon journeys had been long-distance journeys abroad *causa religionis*. However much these journeys represented a rejected tradition of travel, that very tradition—in the shape of actual journeys in the past—was the only seedbed from which could grow the thoroughly modern journey over the Alps of John George. The logic and presentation of Menz's own anthology makes this point.

The battle over pilgrimage to the Holy Land understood as a battle over travel had greater clarity as an issue, if not greater resolution as a contested issue, in central Europe than elsewhere. Across Europe as a whole, great voyages of discovery were astounding facts of a new life that eventually showed up in a new literature of collections of travels. These collections, without making much of the omission, invested few if any pages in pilgrimage. In the heartland of the Reformation and Counter-Reformation, on the other hand, where *peregrinatio ad Terram Sanctam* had long loomed large, opposition to pilgrimage was not a dumb (though dramatic) fact of life that then happened to find literary expression, but an articulated critique of travel as it had been known up until the sixteenth century. Here, travel was a drawn battle line separating traditional travel from new travel, separating pilgrimage from whatever might be replacing pilgrimage. Hence, it is in this region that we find Feyerabend's collection of pilgrimages, the oddest of literary concoctions in the larger world of Ramusio and Hakluyt and M. Thévenot, but a quite sensible focus of debate within Germany itself—sufficiently so that Weller and Menz would come closely on its heels with their own collections of pilgrimages which, however, served an argument quite contrary to that of Feyerabend. Indeed, from the dates of publication—Feyerabend's *Reyssbuch* in 1584, Weller's book in 1586, a second edition of the *Reyssbuch* in 1609, a versification of Weller in 1611, and Menz's anthology in 1612—it is difficult not to conclude that Feyerabend's method, though not his conclusions, was contagious in the immediate neighborhood. Menz may have even rushed his Latin text into print out of fear that the debate was getting away from him. After all, two of the three new entrants in the second edition of the *Reyssbuch* were Catholic pilgrimages. If the first edition could be read as affirming the ecumenical nature of pilgrimage, or even as asserting the growing role of the Reformed as writers of pilgrimage, the second edition could just as plausibly be read as indicating that pilgrimage remained a predominantly Catholic form of religious travel, and a self-renewing form at that.

Debate over pilgrimage was not simply debate over points of devotional theology, or even over matters that were broadly and deeply ramifying throughout the entire domain of theology. It was also a debate about man-at-large-in-the-world. It was about destinations and about reasons for going far away from home. It was about what one hoped to encounter on the road. It was about travel, and thus about the contours of the cultural landscape. Just as the literature of great discoveries was not only about the expansion of geography and the compiling of new-found data, so the critiques of, and apologies for, pilgrimage were not just about devotions before holy sites. Cortés and Francis Xavier, whatever else they were, were modern types of travelers, but so too were Breydenbach and Santo Brasca and (we shall observe) their successors into the eighteenth century. That the great changes in travel that were under way in early modern Europe were indeed *about travel* is less clear in the context of the great discoveries, where pilgrimage is not being taken on directly, and even in the context of the Reformation, when Catholic defenders of pilgrimage such as Gretser are speaking on behalf of a religious practice as well as a mode of travel taken for granted for centuries. But a Protestant critique of pilgrimage, such as that of Menz, makes the dimension of travel very clear indeed. Menz wanted to preserve the valuable historical tradition of Saxon ducal journeys to Rome and to Palestine. He simply didn't want similar journeys in the present to be pilgrimages, nor did he want those in the past to be taken seriously any longer as pilgrimages. He was reshaping travel, regardless of the theology that drove him to do so, just as were the Ramusios and Thévenots reshaping travel for whatever larger historical reasons of their own.

5

Other Holy Places, Other Holy Lands

EARLY MODERN CURRENTS of immense cultural force—discoveries of new
worlds, reformations of the ancient Church—altered the scheme of travel
among Europeans and especially the place of Levantine pilgrimage within
that scheme. Another, much older but newly energized current—devotions to shrines of pilgrimage within Europe itself—also impinged on the
early modern fortunes of traditional pilgrimage to the Holy Land.[1] Long
before the sixteenth century, holy places closer to home had attracted devout travelers who might otherwise have journeyed to Jaffa.[2] In a time of
Baroque fervor, the prominence of shrines within Europe could only inten-
sify. In any event, the coincidence of the two—novel forces let loose on
seas and in pulpits, familiar presences along pilgrim roads within Europe—
altered the contextual scene in which Levantine pilgrimage assumed its
early modern shape and survival.

*　*　*

More than its remoteness kept pilgrims from the Holy Land. François Le
Gouz de La Boullaye, prominent among a line of seventeenth-century
French travelers to the Orient, happened to find himself at mid-century in
the Syrian city of Sidon, which was only days from Jerusalem. Nazareth's
proximity turned his thoughts to distant Loreto in Italy. And such pondering caught him in an underbrush of rumination (concerning theologians' dispute with philosophers over the matter of Loreto) that abstracted
him all the more from his immediate surroundings of Palestine and its
sacred places.[3] But *Jerusalem*! What other city—and especially since it was
so nearby—would have been more likely to have beckoned a Western traveler who sported a European reputation as *le Voyageur catholique* (Figure
13)? The answer to the question was *Rome*. Le Gouz took a pass on Jerusalem. Several reasons figured in his decision, but one counted decisively.
For Le Gouz to have waited for the most advantageous time (Holy Week,

Portraict du Sieur de la Boullaye-le Gouz en habit Leuantin, connu en Asie, & Affrique sous le nom d'Ibrahim-Beg, & en Europe sous celuy de Voyageur Catholique.

Figure 13. François Le Gouz de La Boullaye, *Les voyages et observations* (Troyes: Nicolas Oudot, 1657), portrait facing dedication to Cardinal Capponi.

when a visitor was allowed to see more things and places of interest than at other times) would have meant his missing the opportunity to be in Rome for the celebration of Easter in the Jubilee year. Le Gouz moved on, returning to Europe by way of Egypt.[4]

Few Europeans, of course, were likely to be weighing travel possibilities in the neighborhood of Sidon and Jaffa. It was churches and shrines closer to home that engaged them in many and deep-seated and often quite complicated ways. Indeed, one of the great distinctions between Levantine pilgrimage and pilgrimage within Europe was that, while travel to Jerusalem meant adventure and escape from the workaday rhythms of life, pilgrimages closer to home were caught in more immediate and surrounding realities. Ambrosio Morales (1513–1591), for example, the great Spanish historian, could not go on pilgrimage to Compostella without Philip II interfering in order to instruct him to make a survey of books, royal burials, and relics on his route to the great shrine.[5] Morales had been prepared "to go on pilgrimage to visit the glorious body of the Apostle James, patron and defense of our entire nation" by the end of May, 1572.[6] However, Philip's other (or additional) ideas arrived on May 8. Almost two pages of instructions outlined what was expected in terms of industry from Morales and cooperation from churchmen and nobles of Leon, Galicia, and the Asturias. The king was not after impressions. He expected the journey to produce a "very specific account," the very sort of thing Philip was fond of poring over.[7]

Morales's journey and account of journey necessarily became less single-minded than he had intended. And when his manuscript came to be printed two centuries later, it was further encumbered with motives and an audience other than, or additional to, those he had originally contemplated. Just as Philip had his own ideas about docketing possessions of his kingdom when Morales traveled and wrote, so Enrique Flórez (1702–1773), the great Iberian historian of his own day and belated editor of Morales's travel report, saw the latter more as a source of archaeological material than as a specimen of devout travel.[8]

Morales's *Viage* shows the close connection between non-Levantine pilgrimage (and its literature) and the rest of life. Composed in the sixteenth century, it remained alive as a document that was read and consulted, copied and circulated, without ever having made its way into print. Then, deep into the eighteenth century, it gained a whole new lease on life by being printed at last. It survived, too, in another sense. Pilgrimage was the motive and substance of a work that, looked at from other angles, had motives and substance of a different order. The *Viage*, whatever else it might be interpreted to be, retained the capability—so its author thought and its editor allowed—of being read as a *santo viage*, a *romeria*. In the end, pilgrimage was multivalent because so organically and inextricably sewn into the social and cultural fabric.

*   *   *

So intimate was the connection between shrines and their societies that even the great discoveries of early modern Europe were sometimes, even if not often, reflected in this literature of non-Levantine pilgrimages. Even the publication of such a traveler as Morales, who evinced no interest in discoveries and New World horizons, prompted his editor to forge a link, however vague, labored, and belatedly noted, between Morales's pilgrimage and the global responsibilities of Philip II, who, weighed down though he was with New World dominions among his myriad concerns, found time to tinker with Morales's pious designs.[9]

The connection between Catholic pilgrimage and European discoveries is closer in a traveler such as Pedro Cubero Sebastián (1645–1696).[10] After a stint as confessor to the imperial army in Hungary, Cubero became one of the notable travelers of the seventeenth century. What set him apart was the variety of his traveler's hats. Most obviously a missionary who had received, in Rome in 1671 under the pontificate of Clement X, the office of Apostolic Preacher with licence to preach throughout much of the Orient,[11] he also became, in executing his missionary task, a representative figure of the whole exploratory enterprise. By circumnavigating the globe in his travels, he was recognized in his own time to be another Magellan, Drake, or Cavendish.[12] In addition, however, Cubero's thoroughly modern traveler was a pilgrim of a very traditional sort, a fact that becomes clear in his *Breve relación, de la peregrinación que ha hecho de la mayor parte del mundo* (Madrid, 1680), which describes nine years (1670–1679) of journeying across Europe and Asia and into America and back to Spain.

What does occasionally cause him to linger over a spot or settle into a digression is not some facet of missionary endeavor or some gem of ethnographical *exoticisme*. Cubero sees things as a pilgrim. He pauses over churches, shrines, and relics and the devotions that attend them. Siena, for example, merits special notice because of its historical layers of local sanctity.[13] "Peregrinación" has for Cubero, however much he himself acts the world traveler and missionary, more than a little of the medieval sense

of *peregrinatio*: to be on the road is to be on pilgrimage. True of his journey from Spain to Rome, it remains true once he has pressed on to the
interiors of Asia and the coasts of New Spain. At the same time that he is
on the lookout for Christian communities scattered across Asia and the
New World and for souls to be converted—expected behavior for a missionary—Cubero is also on the lookout for holy places (Goa, which holds
the remains of Francis Xavier; Ceylon, where Adam may, or may not, have
lived after his expulsion from Paradise; Madras, where the Apostle Thomas
was said to have been buried; the Arroyo de la Himagen, in New Spain,
where nature appeared to have carved a likeness of Our Lady of the Immac-
ulate Conception in the rocks).[14]

Cubero shows that the European pilgrim (and not only the explorer,
missionary, conquistador, and tourist) was part of the European extrover-
sion that was the essence of what we mean by the Age of Discovery. Pilgrims both participated in *and* interpreted the expansion of the European
world. Cuberian pilgrimage—every bit as much as the collections of, say,
the Brys or Melchisédec Thévenot—helped to keep alienation and overload
at bay. Cubero's variety of pilgrimage was yoked to an exploratory task—
not the task of rendering exotic populations submissive to Europe, but that
of making Europeans themselves (Europeans in Europe) receptive to these
strange new lands which turned out to be, like Europe itself, surfaces that
were reassuringly dotted with holy places.

Cubero's outward-bound (and world-encircling) travel represented one
variety of association between pilgrimage and discovery. Another variety of
such association was the voyaging of the European (or Europeanized) pilgrim from the periphery to the center in an act of cultural introversion or
retroversion. An example is Joseph de Castro's account of his 1687 pilgrimage to Rome in one hundred and fifty-six pages of verse narration.[15] This
book by a Franciscan missionary in the Spanish New World was printed in
Europe shortly after his return to Mexico and at a later date went through
a second edition and, in 1745, a third (the latter two printed in Mexico).[16]
Castro made his long journey by sea and land—all the way from San Luis
Potosì to Rome via Havana, Cadiz, Madrid, Alcalá, Saragossa, Lerida,
Barcelona, Narbonne, Avignon, the Alps, Turin, Milan, Loreto, Assisi—in
order to fulfill a pilgrim's vow and in so doing to be part of a hallowed tra-
dition (". . . going to Rome because of a vow / Is a custom most ancient").[17]

There is a third variety of pilgrimage literature that sheds light on
the expansion of Europe, but without involving travel in either direction
between Europe and the New World. Churches in the Indies became

themselves translations, or stand-ins, of shrines of pilgrimage in the old world; and a literature came into existence that had as its role the proclamation of this translation. Indulgences brought the benefits of holy Europe, of Rome or Loreto or of other shrines of the Old World, or even of the Holy Land itself, to the shores and sites of the New World. The very centers of devout European civilization had, for all practical spiritual purposes, and through the agency of indulgences, migrated to the farthest corners of the world penetrated by Catholic Europeans. By the eighteenth century, the tendency was well-worn and came to be crystallized and perpetuated in works such as the Jesuit Antonio Natale's *Tesoro*[18] and the Franciscan Joseph de Avila's *Colección*.[19] Pilgrimage became indigenous to the churches of the New World, not only through the rise of holy places peculiar to the New World (places made holy by apparitions or by native or missionary heroics), but also by these translations of European holy places across the sea, as it were, by means of certificates of indulgence.

From the point of view of the history of travel and travel-writing, pilgrimage had always been—for those who sent others on pilgrimage on their behalf, for those who read pilgrimage narratives in lieu of going themselves—a vicarious experience. It now became a virtual experience. If pilgrims went to a Jesuit church in New Spain on the proper feast day—that is, on the day "when there are Indulgences in other holy places (*lugares pios*)"—and if they prayed accordingly, they would gain indulgences "as if we ourselves (*personalmente*) were visiting those holy places."[20] True, indulgences had been in use for centuries and had long been associated with pilgrims' travels. What was now happening in the New World had for centuries been happening in the old world. Nevertheless, it *was* now happening in the New World. Indulgences became instruments for the widest possible radiation of pilgrimage outward from its ancient centers. The uses to which indulgences were put to save and retrieve sacred locales within Europe for the benefit of those outside Europe now experienced a new wave of application. Indulgences proved more than medieval detritus that had somehow not been entirely swept away by Reformers' brooms. Indulgences, far from being anachronisms, proved the most modern of spiritual instruments for coping with the modern problem of distance.

* * *

Early modern pilgrimage was so involved in its surroundings that anything, even the milieu of conquistadors and navigators, might swim into its literature's range of notice. On the other hand, a writer such as Cubero, who manifested pilgrimage and discovery as two sides of a coin, is not broadly typical of non-Levantine pilgrimage literature. Printed descriptions of shrines and local devotions rarely mentioned the Indies or voyages of discovery—but not because these devotional works were abstracted from the world about them, but because they were so deeply immersed in other, more immediate aspects of that world.

Pilgrimage held up a mirror to Catholic European societies. Jacobus Gualla's *Papie sanctuarium* of 1505 offered Pavia's wealth of holy relics as proof of the greatness of the city itself; and his descriptive catalogue turns out to be a kind of history of the city.[21] A 1513 description of devotions practiced by the fraternity of St. Ursula in Nuremberg provided engravings that depicted great crowds that included every rank of society and seemed barely able to contain themselves within the frame of the picture.[22] In the next century, engravings by Jacques Callot (1592–1635), executed sometime in the early 1620s after he had departed Rome where he had been studying, depicted a parade of down-and-out Europeans who are usually characterized as a gallery of beggars, at least some of whom were pilgrims (Figure 14).[23]

The literature of religious shrines all across Catholic Europe expressed historical profiles and destinies of regions and nations. The capacity of pilgrimage to symbolize the unity of a society, especially one under siege from heathen or heretic, is clearly manifested in the work of the Bohemian Jesuit historian, Bohuslav Balbin (1621–1688).[24] His book on the history, indulgences, and miracles of the pilgrim church of Wartha (or Bardo) in Silesia—one of three works that he devoted to Czech Marian shrines—was printed in Latin in Prague in 1655 and translated into German two years later.[25] The *Diva Wartensis* is grandly illustrated. Title page portrays Virgin and Child watching over the village of Wartha. Angels bear heavenward pilgrims' petitions as well as the church's titles of honor for the Virgin, and they return to the pilgrims with benefits—among which is prominently displayed *Libertas* (represented by an angel with unlocked shackles in both hands). Wartha itself is depicted as a fortress ringed by shields. The words "Mary's benevolence is Wartha's stoutest protection" serve as a protective wall encircling church and village. Throngs of pilgrims flock in ordered legions from all directions with Marian banners at their heads. Later in the text a second rendering of the same scene is more close-up and matter-of-fact.[26] The peregrinative reality is still paramount—the village is described as "visited since the year 1200 because of its miraculous

Figure 14. Jacques Callot, *Les Gueux* (Nancy: s.n., 1622 or 1623), plate 687.

statue of the Blessed Virgin Mary"—but the portrayal is straightforward and topographical. Things are situated in relationship to one another— village to river, both to holy mountain. Places are labeled and dated. Later still, a third illustration reinterprets the locale yet again.[27] Flocks of pilgrims are replaced by savage cohorts of Tatars and Hussites, the former burning and pillaging in 1241, the latter putting Wartha to flames and slaughtering Catholics in 1477. The enthroned Virgin of Wartha who in good times awaits and watches over pilgrims has now become the *Deipara flens et vaticans* who both foretells and witnesses the nightmarish times of troubles of her people. Pilgrims have not disappeared from one portrait to the other, but they have changed from massed and ordered devotees to desperate individuals scaling the mountain on which they learn, upon reaching the heights, the horrible truth of their history ("Catholics come upon [Mary] weeping") (Figure 15). Balbin's interpretation, knitted out of Old Testament references, sees the goal of pilgrimage as a collective goal, and the fate over which Mary presides, whether intercessor or lamenter, as a collective fate.

Balbin's Wartha displays the Marian shrine at the heart of Silesian life— center of popular pilgrimage, center and focus of violent events of history that plagued the region, and center of the day-to-day life of the pastoral landscape in which the church was set.

While shrines and literature of pilgrimage were able, after the manner of Balbin, to serve as a force of cohesion, a theater uniting heaven and earth, high and low, historical past and workaday present, they could nevertheless also serve to dramatize fissures in early modern society. The Jansenist Louis Carré de Montgeron's *La verité des miracles operés par l'intercession de M. de Pâris* (Utrecht, 1737) unambiguously demonstrates how politically detonative and ecclesiastically volcanic could be the expression of pilgrim devotions. His book celebrated and closely described miracles worked at the tomb of the Jansenist abbé de Pâris after his death in May 1727 (Figure 16). The vividly illustrated book gives permanence and resonance to the late and startlingly populist manifestations of Jansenism. Licking its theological wounds, the movement had turned to celebrating the memory and relics of its founders, and particularly miracles associated with defeated heroes. All of this came most dramatically to the fore at the tomb of the abbé de Pâris in the cemetery of St. Médard in Paris. What Port Royal had not been allowed to be—a shrine in the countryside for Jansenist *dévots*—the cemetery of St. Médard was to be, though not in the countryside but in the city of Paris itself. Louis XIV had demolished Port Royal

Figure 15. Bohuslav Alois Balbin, *Diva Wartensis* (Prague: Typis Universitatis Carolo-Ferdinandeae in Colleg. Soc. Iesu ad S. Clementem, 1657), facing p. 159.

in 1711. St. Médard might be said to have been the revenge of Port Royal.[28] With the *convulsionnaires'* seeking after cures and enlightenment through devotional acrobatics at the urban tomb of the abbé, Jansenism's survival into the 1730s and beyond involved a profound evolution that both shook the royal and episcopal order of France and took Jansenism itself far from its early days of rural retreat and elite intellectualism and undisplayed interiority. It was as if the ethos of Champaigne's portrait of Mother Agnès de Saint-Paul and Sister Catherine of St. Susan had been cashed in for that of Bernini's Ecstasy of St. Teresa![29]

Society did show through in its shrines. The vast literature that describes non-Levantine holy sites—their miracles, relics, histories, and ceremonies—documents a variety of connections between the life of a shrine and the life of larger society, whether regional, national, or trans-European, that came within its magnetic orbit of influence. Among vital roles played

Figure 16. Louis Basile Carré de Montgeron, *La verité des miracles operés par l'intercession de M. de Paris* (Utrecht: chez les Libraires de la Compagnie, 1737), after p. xxviii.

by such sites, one deserves emphasis because it figured so importantly in so many shrines. European holy places stood in the stead of the far-off Holy Land. Unlike the world of discovery and exploration, which only occasionally figured in pilgrimage accounts, and then largely because of the coincidence of missionary and pilgrim in the person of the travel writer (Cubero, Castro), the world of the Holy Land—its relics, its replication, the localized indulgences referring back to it—was a central subject matter and constant theme of numerous accounts of European shrines. One can see this even in Morales's poking about the northwestern corner of Iberia. After all, Compostella was an Apostolic shrine and therefore a kind of extension of the Holy Land; and, too, the cathedral treasury of Oviedo, which Morales also visited, contained a wealth of Holy Land relics, among them part of Christ's sudarium, soil from Palestine ("from that holy land which he at one time trod with his pious feet"), and a fragment of the rod of Moses.[30] Nor was it only in the old world that spiritual associations were drawn between local sites and the sacred Levant. When in 1709 a new shrine of Our Lady of Guadalupe was erected at the foot of Tepeyac Hill, Juan de Goicoechea, a Jesuit who preached on the occasion, spoke of the Virgin taking up residence in "new Jerusalem, New Spain."[31]

In an age of radically reduced numbers of actual pilgrims to Palestine, travel narratives of pilgrims who did go to the Levant were more likely to be read than were their calls for imitators to be obeyed.[32] Symptomatic of a basic early modern shift in religious travel were such eminent travelers as Morales, Le Gouz, Cubero, and Castro, who traveled widely and strenuously and out of religious motivations and yet expressed no hankering after Jerusalem. Although there were obvious impediments to such travel—the attraction of new routes and places, the insecurity of the eastern Mediterranean, the decay of the European infrastructure for such Oriental travel—if we focus just on the religious side of the new world that was taking shape both on the globe's surface and in the minds of men during these centuries, the role of missionary travel looms large. Jean Baptiste Gaby, a missionary and contemporary of Cubero, speaks of being on board a ship that had been blown within four miles of the African coast. All on board were afraid of being captured by the inhabitants of what is called "this deadly country." But Gaby adds: "we believe that we ought to ponder and venerate a land which so many illustrious martyrs of our order have soaked with their blood as well as so many others who have made the land illustrious through their sufferings."[33] Similarly, we have heard the sixteenth-century Jesuit Francis Xavier spoken of, by his fellow Jesuits at just about this same time, as a new Moses gazing at the new promised land of China. Missions thus created new holy lands—lands, not just shrines—that themselves became quite new objects of reverence and devotion.[34]

Whatever the reasons, actual pilgrimages through much of this period seem to have flourished as a local rather than as a long-distance phenomenon.[35] This localization of pilgrimage within Europe itself and even within the wider and expanding European world meant that the Holy Land would survive as a place to go, in large part either in the mind (as in the *Spiritual Exercises*) or on actual travels to places that claimed to possess mementoes and fragments of relics from sacred Palestine. The bringing back of pieces of Palestine, the endowing of a European shrine with Levantine relics, and the underscoring of such an endowment in literature associated with the shrine—all of this had a pedigree reaching back to the earliest days of Western pilgrimage. At least since the empress Helena had been said to have brought relics from Palestine in the fourth century and to have scattered soil of Calvary on the ground of Nero's circus, fabricating stand-ins of the Holy Land had been under way.[36] Rome's position as the preeminent destination of pilgrimage for Europeans[37] depended in part on this close association with the memory and artifacts of Jerusalem. Relics were not simply procured. Their presence was indicated, observed, and elaborated across centuries. The popular Roman guidebook, *Mirabilia Romae*, prominently displayed a woodcut of pilgrims venerating the cloth of Veronica[38] (Figure 17). A late seventeenth-century traveler, in describing the Church of S. Croce in Gierusalemme, notes both the ceiling painting of St. Helena's discovery of the Cross and a cache of relics, "amongst the rest one of the pieces of silver for which Judas sold his Master; a large piece of the title which Pontius Pilate caus'd to be fasten'd to our Saviour's cross in three languages, which is so ill written, that I am apt to think they were very bad scriveners in those days, or this was done by one of the worst."[39] Nor was Rome the only recipient of such evocative relics in earlier centuries. Guibert of Nogent (1053–1124) had claimed that Nogent was itself a product of pilgrimage, its very identity as a civilized spot bound up with the relics brought back by a pilgrim from the imposingly distant Jerusalem in the time of Mary and the Apostles.[40] With the advent of printing and the growing remoteness of the Levant from Western life, the replacement of the Holy Land by its substitutes became ever more prominent. With the thinning out of actual pilgrimage to Palestine, all that dramatically remained of the Holy Land was revered bits and pieces displayed in Western shrines and the descriptions of them in the printed literature.

Figure 17. *Mirabilia Romae* (Rome, 151–?), p. 67v.

Loreto is crucial to all of this. It accelerated and emblazoned Europe's cooptation of the sacred Orient. Sometime in the decades immediately after the advent of print, Europeans became widely aware of the story of the miraculous angelic lifting up of the holy house (*santa casa*) of Nazareth and its eventual relocation in Italy, which was thought to have happened a century or two before the news became current in print throughout Europe.[41] Over the next three centuries, the story of Loreto made a huge literary impact—especially in Jesuit historiography, first with Orazio Torsellino's *Historiae libri quinque*, which appeared at the end of the sixteenth century and went through editions and translations until, a century after its first appearance, it was substantially reworked by another Jesuit, Iuan de Burgos Angelopolitano, who, among other roles, served as the Jesuit rector of the College of Saint Ann in Mexico. There had also been the massive *Pèlerin de Lorette* (1604) by another Jesuit, Louis Richeôme, which had helped to launch Loreto's world-wide reputation.[42] The enthusiasm of Loreto's reception in Renaissance and Baroque Europe—quite apart from literature specifically devoted to celebrating the site and broadcasting and defending its cause—was immense and enduring. For one thing, Loreto helped literally (and in two senses) to domesticate pilgrimage. A great shrine of Christendom had been extracted from a remote Palestinian backwater (in Muslim domains) and relocated within Europe; moreover, Loreto highlighted a Christianity of the hearth and home that was reflected in this house which was the home of the Holy Family. The impact on Europe was profound. Erasmus, of all people, wrote late in life the *Virgo lauretana*, in honor of our Lady of Loreto.[43] Artists depicted and decorated the shrine. Caravaggio's Madonna dei Pellegrini, though placed in the church of S. Agostino in Rome, was a portrait of pilgrims in Loreto. Lorenzo Lotto spent the last years of his peripatetic life as a brother of the Santa Casa.[44] The shrine seized the imaginations of Europeans and showed up in unexpected places. An anecdote in Castiglione's *Book of the Courtier* tells of two travelers who trick a third into making vows to go to Loreto.[45] When Pedro Fernando de Queirós set out from Peru in 1605 on his Pacific voyage of discovery which took him almost as far as the Solomon Islands, he dedicated his fleet to Our Lady of Loreto.[46] Similarly, the great Jesuit missionary in the Far East, Alexandre de Rhodes, making his way across Europe to Portugal to commence his missionary travels, made a stop at Loreto in 1618: I went to Loreto to fortify myself in this holy chapel where the Savior began all his voyages."[47]

Rhodes's Loreto was not thought of as a relic or memento of a Holy

Land site—it was that site. It was the place to go to receive inspiration that one would earlier have received by going to Jerusalem or to Nazareth itself. And thirty-one years later, in 1649, upon his return from the Orient, Rhodes traveled again to Loreto, "and there I gave thanks to God, and to the holy Virgin my glorious Mother, who preserved me in such great dangers of body and soul."[48] Loreto, enclosing decades of his missionary travels, impressed the stamp of pilgrimage on the entire enterprise of missions. Indeed, in the book that Rhodes wrote describing his missionary exploits, he casts himself in the dedicatory epistle as "a poor pilgrim."[49] Towards the end of the century, Cubero—even more thoroughly than Rhodes a missionary gotten up in pilgrim's garb—sheds his usual digressive brevity when he comes to Loreto. He tells of pilgrims coming there "from the four corners of the world" and of the "prodigious miracles" that the faithful witnessed there. But above all he tarries in order to describe, for those unable to travel there themselves, the house in which Mary lived and matured, the very house of the Annunciation and the Incarnation. He drives home the reality: the Queen of Angels lived here "in Nazareth, province of Galilee, in Syria."[50] Perhaps one reason Cubero saw no need to go to Palestine on his world travels was that he had already done so by making this stop in Italy. This pious regard for Loreto, at all events, put it at the very center of the major happenings and dramas of the seventeenth century. When the Turks were defeated at the siege of Vienna in 1683, of the two captured Turkish standards, one was sent to the Pope in Rome, the other dispatched to Loreto to be displayed at the *santa casa*.[51]

The reputation and magnetic power of Loreto were long-lasting. It drew crowds throughout the eighteenth century. The great pilgrim, Benedict Joseph Labre, who traveled from shrine to shrine throughout Europe, visited Loreto eleven times before dying in Rome in 1783.[52] A French cleric, on his way to Palestine in the later 1770s and ready to find at Loreto "nothing more than a sequestered place of devotion," was overwhelmed by "a pretty town" of Renaissance architecture, statuary, fountains, and lavish decoration bestowed by princes civil and ecclesiastical. The visitor was exposed to the handiwork of Bramante, Raphael, and countless other artists. The point of all this precious lavishness, of course, was the *santa casa*, "this holy place" which was itself the most precious object. The pious tourist from France tells the reader that he has seen nothing like it anywhere else.[53]

Loreto, of course, did not spell the end of Nazareth, which continued to be visited by the few devout Western travelers who actually reached Palestine. In 1669, Michel Nau, a Jesuit missionary stationed in the Levant, made a pilgrimage to the Galilee in the company of the French consul at Sidon. In this particular visit—unusual among published pilgrimages because restricted to the northern regions of the Holy Land—Nazareth in the absence of Jerusalem became the central spiritual attraction of the journey.[54] As much as Nau was taken with the sites of Nazareth, however, his mind was also occupied with the shrine in the Italian town even as he stood in this sacred town of the Levant. One could not think of the relics of the one (the house) without thinking of those of the other (the foundations of the house). Indeed, this new symbiotic relationship between the two has introduced a whole new slate of doubts and queries—on the part of the *incredules*, on the part of the *Scavants de mauvaise humeur*—with which the conscientious pilgrim must contend.[55] Even for one whose feet were planted on the holy ground of the Galilee, to be in Nazareth was to have one's attention and calculations necessarily focused on the European holy site as well. We have already noted the *voyageur catholique* François Le Gouz (1623–1668) skirting the Holy Land when he was in Levantine waters and thinking of Nazareth not so much in terms of itself as in terms of Loreto back in Europe.

Loreto is the most dramatically thorough example of a holy place within Europe serving in the stead of that Holy Land in the Levant, relics from which did much to constitute the holiness of many a European shrine. Gualla's 1505 itemization of Pavian relics that had been transferred to Milan in 1499 (a meticulous accounting of seven pages) includes at the head of the list numerous fragmentary pieces connected with the life of Christ— the Nativity, and especially the Passion, but also with other moments (a piece of "the rock where Christ stood for forty days without food or drink," or of "the stone upon which Christ was baptized")—so many that one has the sense that the viewer of these *archaeologia sancta* must have felt transported to the eastern Mediterranean.[56] Palestine had become less physically remote for the pilgrim who found himself surrounded by such mementos, whether in Pavia or in Granada (where half of the cloth used by Mary to wipe away her tears at the Passion was discovered along with bones of St. Stephen, part of a horde of sacred riches buried during the Moorish domination)[57] or in some other church of some other shrine in some other part of Europe. Indulgences, too, when attached to a particular church or feast, had the same effect of standing in for the actual Holy Land site.[58] Just like relics, indulgences served as *aides de contemplation*.

In this re-presenting of the Holy Land in the European here-and-now, the *idea* of Loreto was contagious. Not only did the fame of the *casa santa* spread; not only did churches, altars, and devotions in other places become replicas of the actual Loreto in Italy; Loreto itself became a certain *kind* of shrine. When Pedro Gonzalez de Mendoza (1577–1659),[59] the archbishop of Granada, described the shrine of Nuestra Señora de la Salçeda in Spain in the early seventeenth century, he speaks of the Toledan region of Alcarria, over which the shrine on Monte Celia watched, as similar to the Holy Land itself—a humble and compressed region that by all natural rights would be impoverished but that by divine favor flourished. Indeed, the overall force of Gonzalez's argument persuades the reader that the Toledan region with its holy shrines is a *terra sancta* come to current (and sensorially accessible) life. The region, he writes, was famous for its holy mountains just as was the Holy Land; and Mount Celia was the "competidor del Carmelo" and, more, was the analogue of Mount Sion. As the latter was superior to all the other ancient holy mountains, so Mount Celia was superior to the rest of the holy hills of Alcaria.[60] But what clinches this association of holy Spain with the holy Levant is that the Shrine of Nuestra Señora de la Salçeda can rightly be saluted as "Loreto de España la Salzeda."[61]

Example upon example could be cited from the early modern centuries of devotional writers who saw their local holy site as a reflection of the Holy Land. Nor did the claim always rest on the possession of relics from the Levant. One figure of the time, the Spanish Capuchin historian and biographer Matheo de Anguiano, went so far as to style Madrid as the New Jerusalem, and this because there had been found within the city, on the Calle de las Infantas, the Crucifix of the Long-Suffering (Imagen del Crucifixo de la Paciencia) in the royal convent of La Paciencia de Christo. Anguiano's *La Nueva Jerusalèn*, which appeared in Madrid in 1709, was among the most ambitious celebrations of a European shrine as stand-in for the Holy Land.[62]

At the time of Anguiano's writing, the shrine was only seventy-five years old and had arisen from an alleged episode that came to light in Madrid in 1632. Jews who lived in Madrid on the Calle de las Infantas had, according to Anguiano's account, brought from Portugal an image of the crucified Christ which they then abused in an effort to reenact the historical sufferings of Christ. After the outrage was discovered and the culprits punished, services of reparation by the Catholic community were immediately instituted (*annuales, y perennes cultos*) and the house of the Jews was converted, by act of Philip IV, into the Convento de la Paciencia de Christo. The new royal foundation was entrusted to the Capuchins. Thanks, it was said, to the "rage and cruelty of the notorious Hebrews," there was scarcely anything left of the abused crucifix; so another was imported from the Capuchin Monastery of St. Anthony. It was this crucifix that became the object of popular veneration beginning in 1639.[63]

Such was the story attached to the relatively recent origins of the shrine in Madrid. Anguiano may have simply been repeating current anti-Jewish lore that could, in turn, have already been enlisted by the shrine's founders to fit the general and vague motif of a local shrine becoming heir and replacement of the Holy Land. On the other hand, the story may be more specifically rooted. At the same general period of the shrine's foundation, there had been appearing in printed editions the book of pilgrimage of Henri de Beauvau, who had been on his way to Jerusalem in 1605 and had mentioned a similar episode that was said to have occurred in Beirut and that had been memorialized by a chapel in that city.[64] And the same story could be read in earlier accounts of pilgrimage—that of the fifteenth century traveler, Hans Tucher, and that of his contemporary Santo Brasca, who mentions the same anecdote in his account of 1480.[65] A version of the story also appeared in the extremely popular illustrated pilgrimage of Noè Bianchi, which had first been printed in 1566, but continued to be reissued throughout the seventeenth and eighteenth centuries.[66] There were, to be sure, other possible sources for Anguiano's story, the most likely being the frequently printed and immensely popular medieval work, Jacobus de Voragine's *Legenda Aurea*.[67] However, Jacobus's entry, under "De exaltatione sanctae crucis," tells a more nuanced story as well as one less harsh toward the Jews than are most of the pilgrims' versions.[68] It is possible, therefore, that the shrine in Madrid may have arisen out of an active reading, or acquaintance with, the literature of early modern pilgrimage to Jerusalem. There may, in other words, have been the closest connection between the literature of pilgrimage to Jerusalem and the founding of a shrine intended to replace Jerusalem in the city of Madrid, a connection undetectable except for the clue given by the story of Beirut.

Around this notorious tale, whatever its precise source, Anguiano raised a scaffolding of interpretation. Madrid comes to reflect Jerusalem because the historical episode of alleged Jewish perfidy towards the crucifix recalls the actual Passion in the original Jerusalem. It is recent history rather than possession of ancient relics that gives Madrid its new name and rank and right to be thought of and reverently visited as "Jerusalem." Not that Jerusalem itself in the contemporary Levant is out of mind. But as a destination of pilgrims, it is remote and unfrequented by Europeans. It is the distance of Jerusalem itself from Anguiano's Spain that makes the popular naming of the site *Nueva Ierusalèn* so entirely apt (*que tan adequadamente le toca*):

The first [Jerusalem] is very far away from Spain, and there are immense obstacles in the way of Spaniards' being able personally to visit it. This is not to deny that our Catholic kings as well as others have striven to maintain with proper decency, aside from the many years of almsgiving, those holy places where our redemption was worked out. But so that we might not lack completely this spiritual comfort, the Lord in his supreme providence has arranged that there might be another *New Jerusalem* in Madrid (*en esta Catholica Corte*), and a living likeness of the first, in order to stir up devotion and remembrance of his Holy Passion and Death and so that no one should be excused from visiting and frequenting this holy site, where for such a long time the iniquitous wrought such horrendous injury to his sacred image and where he has worked such miracles and wonders.[69]

Contemporary Levantine Jerusalem gets the quickest of reverent nods as the site of sacred history—and is then dismissed as being, for practical purposes, entirely too far away to be a reasonable goal of pilgrimage and spiritual comfort.

Three decades after Anguiano, this bathing of shrines on European soil in the noetical essences of the Holy Land can be seen in Portugal in the work of the ecclesiastical antiquarian of Porto, Antonio Cerqueira Pinto (1679–1744). His *Historia da prodigiosa imagem de Christo Crucificado* (Lisbon, 1737) describes the ancient shrine of Bom Jesus de Bouças in the city of Matozinhos in northern Portugal. Pilgrimages were continuing to be made to the shrine by throngs of the devout in Pinto's own time.[70] Here, the great attraction was an image of the crucified Christ that was said to have come, unlike the crucifix in Madrid, from Jerusalem. Indeed, it was said to have been carved in wood by Nicodemus and to have been done by him after the likeness of Christ that was impressed on Christ's linen burial shroud.[71] Like Anguiano (and like the historians of Loreto), however, Pinto, too, describes and advances a basic thesis of the times: the shifting of the European spiritual consciousness from east to west, from historic Asia to contemporary (and Atlantic) Europe—a trend that includes a shifting of pilgrims' own focus of attention from the Levant to the soil of Europe itself. Pinto explicitly makes the point that this shrine is a holy place not only because of the presence of the image but also because of the *meaning* of its being here rather than elsewhere. If Palestine had been the place of origin of Christian belief, Pinto argues, then the miraculous ending up of this image in Portugal, at the very westernmost edge of Europe, demonstrated how the Christ of the universe was to be praised and known everywhere.[72] The image of the crucifix not only calls to the mind of the pilgrim the holy land of the Passion; the image is also, in its own right, aptly placed (at the edge of the Atlantic) in the modern, hugely expanded world. Pinto's work is recognition that it makes a peregrinative difference that Jerusalem is no longer at the center of the world. Nor, it implies, are other places (Rome, for example) in Europe at the center of this new world. Hence this shrine placed at the *termo Occidental da Europa*. The *exact* center of Pinto's world is not Jerusalem nor even Europe as a whole, but the western edge of Europe. The exactitude suggests a connection between the expansion of the European world and the transference of the attention of pilgrims from the Levant to Europe.

The ground of sacred Palestine—*terra sancta*, *vestigia sacra*—grew remote and its outlines vague even as versions of it within Europe multiplied and clarified. But the Holy Land was not forgotten, becoming in this very period a powerful literary reality, a highly topical subject matter, regardless of how few pilgrims actually visited it. In sixteenth-century France, there were almost as many printed voyages to Jerusalem as voyages to the New World, which certainly indicated a deep interest in the Holy Land if not a readiness actually to go there.[73] But the literary question to one side, Jerusalem was in fact being replaced as a destination of travelers by shrines that themselves seemed, for various reasons, very much like the sites of sacred Palestine. And this phenomenon, while very strongly in evidence in Iberia—consider that Philip II's Escorial was an architectural attempt to recreate the holy city of Jerusalem[74]—was by no means restricted or peculiar to Spain and Portugal. Loreto is striking evidence of that. Moreover, north of the Pyrenees and far beyond the Mediterranean rim, the Baroque culture of Catholic Europe continued and intensified movements of pilgrimage that not only celebrated local saints but also recalled the great events and dramas of sacred history itself. There were above all the Marian shrines throughout Europe. Counter-Reformational Poland became famous throughout the seventeenth century for its crowds of pilgrims visiting Marian shrines but also shrines that called to mind Calvary.[75] But one also thinks of a city such as Cologne that was identified *illo tempore* with devotion to the Magi. There was, too, the devotion of the Stations of the Cross as an alternative to pilgrimage to the Holy Land and as a reenactment of Christ's route to Calvary. Connections were made between such devotional dramas and specific sites on the actual terrain within Europe where the Stations were prayed. Southern Germany, and in particular Bavaria, especially as seen through the interpretive lenses

of Jesuits—the volumes of the *Bavaria Sancta* (Munich, 1615–1627) of Matthaeus Rader, the 1678 *Miraculous Mirror of Divine Miracles from the Old
and New Testament* of Benigno Kyhler—became a holy land of holy places
where the great events of sacred history were enacted. In a work such as
that of Khyler, the very definition of Bavaria was keyed to shrines rather
than to geographical, topographical, military, or other conventional markers. How powerfully these devotional analogies or comparisons between
Palestine and Europe worked can be seen in the very practice of the Stations
of the Cross; for it seems that the Franciscan practice of the fourteen stations was not something that derived from Palestine—that is, from devotional practices of pilgrims marching from site to site in the Levant—but
was a practice indigenous to Europe that was then, during the seventeenth and eighteenth centuries, applied to pilgrimage in the Holy Land
itself. We seem in the throes of disorientation. What was going on, one
might well ask, which was east and which west, which referent and which
antecedent?[76] The very intensity of Baroque pilgrimage on the domestic
scene—and especially when the attention of pilgrims was directed to shrines,
processions, and devotions that impinged upon the conception of the
Holy Land—was a distraction from, and then an alternative to, Levantine
pilgrimage, however much it also served as a reminder of the archaeological and devotional reality of the Holy Land itself.

Shrines that had their focus on a piece of the True Cross or other relics
of the Passion were concentrated on a line extending from the north of
Germany through central Italy, with the heaviest concentration in Bavaria.[77]
But throughout the Catholic West, the reality of the Holy Land was approx-
imated in churches and shrines. France of the fifteenth and sixteenth centuries had been blanketed with monumental sculptures of the entombment
of Christ. Bordeaux, Troyes, and Trier each had three such works; Limoges
had four.[78] A bestseller of the late seventeenth century was a devotional book
by the Jesuit Adrien Parvilliers on the Stations of the Cross "which are
performed in Jerusalem."[79] (Parveilliers was not simply using the Stations
as a means of recalling to the prayerful minds of Frenchmen the historical
Passion, but also as an act specifically in imitation of how that recollection
was made in the contemporary but distant Holy Land itself.) The claims
of shrines to a special relationship to the Holy Land, usually through their
possession of a relic (which need not be a fragment of the True Cross),
were matters of great moment. For decades—from the late seventeenth
century to the middle of the eighteenth—the Vendôme could be thrown
into high controversy by the widespread belief that the Monastère de la

Trinité had in its possession one of the tears that Christ had shed on hearing of the death of Lazarus. The combination of popular belief and intellectualist demurring, as well as the quantities of printer's ink spilled over the entire matter, shows what a live and protracted issue relics and pilgrimage were at this date.[80]

In Paris itself—the hub of eighteenth-century Europe, the filament of *la Lumière*—processions of devout pilgrims who made the Stations of the Cross were a great public phenomenon even in the final decade before the coming of the Revolution. We have evidence of this in René François du Breil de Pontbriant's *Pélerinage du Calvire sur le Mont Valérien, et les fruits qu'on doit retirer de cette dévotion* (Paris, 1779). The shrine had come into existence well over a century earlier. Court figures (including Richelieu) supported the idea of the shrine, and *lettres patentes* were obtained from Louis XIII in 1640. The Confraternity of the Cross was established in 1644, and its statutes confirmed in 1707.[81] What makes Mont Valérien a holy place, a *saint lieu*, is a relic—"a precious receptacle of a fragment of the true Cross."[82]

Pontbriant places the Parisian devotions on Mont Valérien firmly within the context of the history of pilgrimages, which, he says, have always been pious practices engaged in by the faithful. What is different for eighteenth-century Frenchmen, however, is that they are unable to actually visit the Holy Land ("Unlike the earliest Christians, we are unable to make our way into these blessed countries").[83] Pontbriant's book, through highly charged language and through engravings of Christ's Passion, is intent on more than giving the history of the site. He strives to recreate the spiritual and emotional experience of the pilgrim who has never left Paris but who walks in the footsteps of the suffering Christ (Figure 18). We are very far from the antinomian world of the Parisian *convulsionnaires*—Pontbriant emphasizes that this is a shrine of the Diocese of Paris and celebrates its royal pedigree—but Pontbriant does strive, in describing a shrine, after comparable intensity of spiritual feeling. Pontbriant considers Mont Valérien "a plot of land uniquely consecrated to this devotion" and nothing less than "a Calvary that ceaselessly calls to mind that of Jerusalem where Jesus Christ was sacrificed and died for our salvation." One is led by the experience on the mountain to be "inflamed" with love and touched by the edifying sites. One sheds tears. One enters into "transports" of sympathy in imagining the sufferings and triumphs of the Saviour. Pontbriant, in imagining Jerusalem in Paris, turns the pilgrim book into something much more than a description of relics and miracles. It becomes fully a part of devotional literature—

and even something more: "It is perhaps a surprise to the reader to find in a book dealing with the Cross the treatment of ethical questions, which at first glance might seem quite out of place."[84]

Devotional rites performed in Paris and that recalled Jerusalem could be performed, or could be read about and interiorized, anywhere in the world. A copy of Pontbriant's book, an octavo volume of almost three hundred and fifty pages, sat at one time (and still does) on the shelves of the library of the third president of the American republic and notable of the frontier Enlightenment, Thomas Jefferson of Virginia.[85] In the last decades of the eighteenth century, Monticello stood at the outermost edge of what might be called European civilization understood as a community possessed of an organized and institutionalized manner of looking upon the world. Monticello was an elegant outpost before the continent opened out into a vastness of wilderness. That Jefferson was part of the audience for a work of European pilgrimage is a fact both striking and opaque. It shows us that "audience" is an ambiguous category in historical investigation—

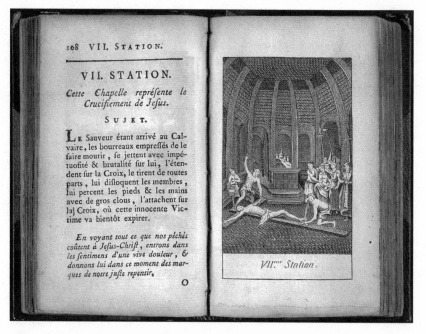

Figure 18. René François du Breil de Pontbriant, *Pèlerinage du calvaire sur le Mont Valérien* (Paris, 1779), 108 and facing image.

a powerful concept, but not one that should be confounded with categories of actual popularity or acceptance or even influence. What did Jefferson think of Pontbriant's guide? We cannot say. Whether he opened the book or made any use of it—for instruction, bemused diversion, edification?— are unanswerable questions. But the fact remains—and it is an acoustical fact of immense if indefinite importance—that report of the devout doings on Mont Valérien in Paris, which were themselves attempts by Europeans to imagine themselves on the Mount of Calvary in Jerusalem, was there to be heard, or read (and pondered and internalized or combated and dismissed), on the Monticello of Mr. Jefferson in the New World.[86]

*   *   *

Beyond Europeans who actually got themselves to the Holy Land—Tucher, Brasca, Breydenbach, their relatively few successors across three centuries— early modern pilgrims to Palestine were either vicarious travelers, who stayed at home and read others' accounts, or virtual travelers who visited Nazareth by visiting Loreto (or, at even a greater remove of virtuality, visited a church in the New World in order to obtain the indulgences of a visit to Loreto) or visited Jerusalem by visiting a shrine such as La Nueva Jerusalèn. These two groups were not necessarily, or even probably, mutually exclusive one to the other. There was likely much overlap between them. To have read accounts of actual travels to the Holy Land might well have led the reader to visit shrines nearer by that recalled the Holy Land. So also, pilgrims to Jerusalem-like sites within Europe may have been inspired by these sites to read about travels to the actual Jerusalem, even if only a few would have entertained a realistic thought of actually going to the Levant. The Calle de las Infantas recalls, even as it replaces as a visitable site, the Via Dolorosa just as does Mont Valérièn (even Mont Valérien on the shelf at Monticello) the Mount of Calvary.

The relationship between pilgrimage to the Holy Land (whether as a practice of travelers or as a specimen of travel literature) and this other universe of pilgrimages that flourished within the European world was marked, above all, by ambiguity. It is tempting to see the advertisers of non-Levantine pilgrimage as simply one more element in a negative context within which Levantine pilgrimage had to exist—in other words, as early modern agents (much like discoverers, reformers, and collectors) who pushed Levantine pilgrimage to the margins of European travel. In truth, there may have been over the centuries some competition for actual

pilgrims. Le Gouz de La Boullaye's experience is anecdotal evidence for see-
ing the asserted claims of shrines as a zero-sum competition. Roman
Jubilees may well have siphoned travelers from Venetian boats booked for
Jaffa. But touristical competition seems an unlikely theme in the face of
evidence, both medieval (e.g., Symon Simeonis) and early modern (e.g.,
Breydenbach, Ignatius Loyola) that travelers perceived a continuum between holy places *en route* to the Holy Land and the holy places of the Holy
Land itself. The seventeenth-century pilgrim to Palestine, Louis Deshayes
de Courmenin, was only typical of many of his early modern colleagues in
his remarking, for example, on the international repute of Bari as a center
of pilgrimage.[87]

In any event, what exactly was going on when a European holy site
was cultivated as a setting evocative of the Holy Land was a live issue, to
judge by remarks of Jacob Gretser, whose great historical summing up of
Christian pilgrimage appeared in 1606 in the very midst of the early modern age of pilgrimage. Ancient exiles, Gretser observed, came into new lands
and erected cities and named places in a manner that recalled their home-
lands. They were thus able to contemplate a kind of likeness (*simulacro*) of
their homeland. This phenomenon of history is all that is going on, Gretser
argues, when Christians create replicas of the Holy Land in Europe:

> Who is going to blame Christians if they substitute, for the eyes of the pious, a
> likeness (*imagine*) of those places which Christ dedicated and consecrated by his
> blood, passion, death, and burial and which not every person can visit for himself?
> In this or that place they devise and erect a kind of model (*ectypon quoddam*) of
> places which actually exist (*vere sunt*) in Jerusalem or Bethlehem or in some other
> place. Such is done to encourage and increase the devotion of the lovers of Christ
> and their pious affection towards our Redeemer.

This act of pious substitution is done in many places, Gretser continued,
including in "our Germany." And it still happens daily where the original
fervor (*priscus fidei ardor*) gathers strength and gains new life.[88] For Gretser,
controversy or scandal did not figure in the matter. To replicate holy places
was a species of universal piety. One found it in the *Aeneid* as well as in
shrines all across Catholic Europe. And yet, there may have been some
element of upset. Gretser did make the effort to drive home his point. His
question—*Quis vitio vertat Christianis*—who would blame Christians who
replicate the holy places?—had perhaps been raised by others and needed
an answer. The question would likely have been hurled across the Reformational chasm. It might also have circulated within Catholic circles.

The connection between the two varieties of pilgrimage, European and

Levantine, was more subtle than one of overt competitiveness. Although it is certainly true that as the early modern era advanced, a pilgrim landing in Jaffa was increasingly becoming a *rara avis*, it would be to put things in the wrong light to say that the more typical pilgrim of the age chose to go to the church on the Calle de las Infantas in Madrid *instead of* to the Via Dolorosa in Jerusalem. Similarly, Loreto was not so much a chosen alternative to Nazareth for such a pilgrim as the only practical possibility of connecting at all with Nazareth. What is of historical interest by this time is the connection between the *literature* of Levantine pilgrimage on the one hand and the evocations of the Holy Land on the other, evocations that were concretized in the European shrines that drew throngs of pilgrims. Since actual travel to the Levant was no longer anything but exceptional, that relationship can hardly have been agonistic. It was more likely to have been symbiotic. Unlike discoverers and reformers, in spite of whom Levantine pilgrimage survived as a travel literature, devotees of European holy sites help to explain the survival of Levantine pilgrimage—again, as a printed literature of travel. They positively (if not quantifiably) contributed to that survival. Europeans who were devoted to domestic shrines (that recalled, directly or indirectly, the land and shrines of Palestine) were likely to be attentive to accounts by the few piously intrepid travelers who actually did make the increasingly unrealistic journey to the eastern Mediterranean. Such devotion to non-Levantine shrines reminiscent of the Holy Land helps to account for the fact that pious travel to Palestine remained topical in an age when travel itself seemed so thoroughly pointed in quite other directions—sufficiently topical that it remained subject matter for a literature of travel that flourished in print. And (we shall see) this topicality endured well beyond the pre-discovery and pre-Reformation era of Breydenbach. Relics housed in European shrines and indulgences attached to them represent an institutionalized cultural longing for the Holy Land and thus an occasion for sustaining its topicality in the minds of readers of travels. Such a widespread longing was the protoplasm of a potential audience of readers who might not have been prepared to go see the Holy Land but might well have been desirous of hearing tell all about it.

Among printed pilgrimages, moreover, those that recorded long-distance travel to the Palestinian Holy Land had a recognizably literary shape. Such works existed within a millennium-long tradition not only of actual travel to the Holy Land but of self-conscious reporting on such travel. That tradition entered the modern stream of civilization through printed editions of medieval pilgrimages (the Bordeaux Pilgrim, Adamnan,

Burchardus, Mandeville) as well as through contemporary pilgrimages (Breydenbach above all) that antedated the great discoveries and the Reformation, and we will see that literary tradition continue to thrive in the midst of discoveries and reformations and well into the eighteenth century.[89] Devout travel within Europe, on the other hand, had less sharply etched literary features. First of all, there was not the same tradition of extensive literary description of pilgrimage as there had always been for journeys to Palestine. To travel within Europe—even all the way from, say, Galway or Vézelay to Compostella[90]—was not the same order of feat as the journey from anywhere in Europe through the Turkish Levant to Palestine. Second, on the modern scene written accounts of domestic pilgrimages were less likely to be finished literary artifacts. Domestic sites left a rich deposit of things—posters, engravings, statues, medals, maps, broadsides, certificates of indulgences, etc.—but were less productive of the strictly literary artifact that focused on the individual's pious journey.[91] Third, literature that did come into existence (and survive) was usually descriptive more of sites and shrines, of miracles and donations, than of events and arduosities of the actual getting to, and back from, shrines. The more local or regional (rather than long-distance) a pilgrimage, the easier the journey and fewer the exotica encountered along the way—and therefore the less likely the pilgrimage was to assume literary shape and find a literary audience. What was often produced, in place of a full-fledged travel narrative, was a vaguer noetic animal that was merely associated—often by way of advertisement or of historical description—with the goal of the pilgrim. Literature of pilgrimage to European shrines was often a literature of some other variety than travel. Even after great exceptions are noted—such as Morales, Castro, Cubero—it remains true that, in an age of long-distance travel (and in an age attuned to long-distance travel narratives), if one were in the mood for reading about *devout* long-distance travel, pilgrimage to the Levant remained the ticket. And that mood was sustained and nurtured by Europeans who went to Loreto or Rome or Madrid, which cities would, among other things, have whetted their interest in the Holy Land. Two things readers back in Europe shared with Levantine pilgrims: they, too, were pilgrims; their pilgrimages often took them to places that were Jerusalems—but only of a tantalizing sort.

In terms of the background and overall history of travel, then, it would scarcely be possible to form any idea at all of pilgrimage to Terra Sancta after the fifteenth century without paying attention to pressures exerted on pilgrimage by the great discoveries, by the Reformation, and by Catholic pilgrimages and processions within Baroque Europe. The third pressure, however, provides the richest context. While it is largely true that early modern pilgrimage to the Levant evolved and endured for three centuries *in spite of* discoverers and reformers, and true as well that early modern pilgrims continued to trickle towards Jaffa *in spite of* the Jerusalem-like shrines of Rome and Madrid and Paris, it is also true that a remarkable printed literature of pilgrimage to Palestine flourished at least in part *because of* the pilgrim spirituality fostered by such shrines within Europe— and by the further fact, negative but not unimportant, that by and large the literature of pilgrimage to shrines within Europe did not satisfy the desires of an audience looking for a literature of *travel*.

6

A Second Voice: Terra Sancta Inter Alia

THE HAKLUYTS, THÉVENOTS, AND BELLEGARDES hammered together a new construct of travel that shared little with the centuries-old scheme of European travel which had been largely constituted by pilgrimage. The major collectors of printed travels may be said, by their choices of inclusion and exclusion, to have acted as great theoreticians and emphatic voices of the new travel that helped define early modern culture. Nevertheless, long-distance pilgrimage to the Holy Land remained a stubborn if beset reality. Contemporary pilgrimages printed prior to Columbus and Luther (and prior to the collectors themselves) had renewed pilgrimage's lease on life. Breydenbach's monumental *Peregrinatio* suggested a future for pilgrimage. Even after the inventions of America and of pristine Christianity, pilgrimages to Terra Sancta flourished as a literary phenomenon. Medieval pilgrimages, for example, which had first appeared in print in the first half-century after Gutenberg, continued to be uncovered and printed well into the following centuries.

A weightier indication of pilgrimage's staying power in the wake of Columbus and Luther is that some contemporary pilgrimages to Terra Sancta throughout the early modern era found their way into print as episodes of travel in larger itineraries of individual travelers. Although the emphasis and design of such books dealt with matters and locales entirely distinct from pilgrimage, the evidence of such works is nevertheless crucial to understanding pilgrimage's place in early modern travel. First, these volumes do confirm and reflect a profound historical shift. Pilgrimages to the Holy Land were no longer the overarching and defining form of travel, but only one among many varieties of travel. At the same time, these accounts of individual travelers' various journeys also show that *peregrinatio ad Terram Sanctam*, however emphatic its exclusion from the great early modern collections of travels, did in fact survive in the broader itineraries and collected travels of prominent individual travelers. By thus setting the record straight on the vital presence of pilgrimage, these works—

a second voice, as it were, in the early modern discourse on travel—render the scheme of early modern travel more complex and various. They also render the early modern discourse on travel less theoretical, inasmuch as these were books of actual travelers rather than books of compilers of travels who were not in most cases travelers themselves. And finally, by including accounts of pilgrimage in accounts of their other travels, these writers show that pilgrimage continued to be thought of as part of a genre of *travel*. This last point is vital. Without these works, it would be much less evident, given the interpretive shadow cast by great travel collections, that separately printed early modern pilgrimages were in fact to be taken as travels rather than just as books of piety in a narrow (and narrowing) sense.

In truth, the distinction between a book of pilgrimage that placed major stress on the journey to Palestine and used pilgrimage as the *frame* of narrative, and a book of travels that merely included pilgrimage *inter alia*, is porous and fluctuating.[1] This is because of the very nature of Levantine pilgrimage, which was a long-distance adventure that took Europeans across, and then far out of, Europe proper. Much of the way, and all the time that they moved about the Holy Land, they traveled *in partibus infidelium*. For pilgrims making their way to Jaffa from Antwerp or Livorno or Venice (not to mention their getting to such ports in the first place prior to setting out on the Mediterranean),[2] there was much more to see and describe than Palestine and its holy sites. Moreover, the fact that Christians considered pilgrimage in terms of a journey—not only the visiting of a holy site, but also the getting there and back, were all part of a spiritual and experiential continuum (a penitential, but not exclusively penitential, *ascesis*)—meant that observations of pilgrims on, say, the landscape of France or the arsenal or glassware factories in Venice or the ancient ruins of Crete or the pyramids of Egypt could well be integral to the pilgrim's actual reportage. How distinguish between a pilgrimage with touristical asides and a tour with a pious detour?

Henri de Beauvau's *Relation iournalière du voyage du Levant* exemplifies the cloudiness of the distinction between a book of pilgrimage and a book of travels that merely accommodated pilgrimage within a broader itinerary. Beauvau was a muscularly learned tourist of the Adriatic and eastern Mediterranean (who appears to have packed his Pliny and Strabo), and it is certainly possible to read him in just that light. His observations and engravings display interest in fortifications and the political situation in the Levant (matters of who held what port or island and how recently they had acquired same), and also in the colors that antique myth and history as well as sacred and Christian history imparted to the places he visited along his route. Were we to judge simply by his general reasons for traveling—ones typical of a highly placed European traveler of the time: "The reason for my plan was curiosity; the goal to make myself more able to serve my Prince"[3]—or by the proportion of his time spent in the Holy Land—departing Venice 1 November 1604, he was in Constantinople from 10 January to 17 May 1605, in Jerusalem from 2–26 August 1605, and back in Naples on 27 November 1605—or by the fifty-five pages out of a total of a hundred and eighty-one that he devoted to the holy sites of Palestine, we would be inclined to conclude that much more than pilgrimage was going on in this book and that consequently this was something less, for our purposes, than a pilgrimage pure and simple.

For all that, Beauvau's *Relation* was a book of pilgrimage. The author's emotional investment in the Holy Land is simply too intense to be ignored. His reaction to Jerusalem is of a completely different order from his responses to any other places along the way—to, say, Constantinople or Cairo, both of which cities impressed him immensely. Moreover, Beauvau may have been in Jerusalem only four out of fifty-six weeks, but it took almost a third of the text to describe that brief time. In addition, when later editions were illustrated (under Beauvau's supervision), his usual method was to allot major places along the way a single bird's-eye view and then to move on. (For Egypt, to be sure, both Cairo and Alexandria were illustrated, but not, significantly, the pyramids, despite their being "so renowned in all books of history.")[4] To the Holy Land, however, Beauvau devoted numerous visual delineations of cities and sites, as well as renderings of interiors and of architectural plans. The sheer concentration, both textual and visual, that Beauveau gives to Terra Sancta is the most prominent feature of the book. The engravings show the Holy Land as the only area on his itinerary that is treated, so to speak, from within—from the perspective of the traveler's visual experience and not as simply shots snapped on the fly. Jaffa becomes a doorway into a fully depicted world. Finally, it is clear that the book's very first readers, the Franciscan censors at Toul, knew what kind of book they were reading—a pilgrimage, the work of a "pious traveler."[5]

At the end of the spectrum opposite to Beauveau's *Relation* (and similar books of thorough-going pilgrimage treated in the next chapter) stand books that present pilgrimage as a subject matter, but in as slight a fashion as possible. Perhaps the most celebrated example is the worldwide travels of the often printed and much translated *Giro del Mondo* of Giovanni

Francesco Gemelli Careri (1651–1725). The holy places of the Levant are
indeed present, but not to very great effect (the French edition of 1727
spared sixty-five out of almost three thousand pages for the Holy Land).[6]
Careri had claimed, but only to quiet his brother's worries, that the goal of
his venture was the Levantine holy places, but in fact his great destination
was China, which had much the effect on him that Jerusalem had on confirmed pilgrims.[7] Such books—there were others before and after Careri's[8]—
show that pilgrimage remained at least a flickering subject matter for travelers in early modern Europe. In taking up these books, readers would have
become aware of pilgrimage, though the same readers would not likely
have taken up these books in the first place had their major interest been
in pilgrimage.

A great middle ground, however, existed between books that offered
only glimpses of pilgrimage and other books, such as Breydenbach's or
Beauvau's, that profoundly occupied themselves with pilgrimage. By the
middle of the sixteenth century—a century after the coming of print and
more than a half-century after the origins of the great discoveries—travelers
whose primary destination was not the Holy Land nevertheless published
travels in which pilgrimage to the holy places was a substantial subject
matter.

The importance of sacred Palestine to French travelers (as well as
French compilers and readers of guidebooks to Europe and the Levant) is
clearly documented by Charles Estienne's wide-ranging 1552 guide for travelers.[9] Estienne's original intention had been to limit his remarks to places
and pilgrimage routes within France "dealing with the pilgrimages (*les
saincts voyages*) and rivers of this country" but in the actual composition,
the work expanded to include "the principal and most popular journeys
through Italy, Spain, and the Holy Land."[10] The entries are brief. They
touch on conditions of roads and bridges, possibilities of brigands in a
region, mileage between stops, places of interest (the chateau de Cham-
bourg, built by the late king Francis; the ancient town of Plaisance, "famous
for the victory of Hannibal over the consul L. Sempronius"; Romont, where
German begins to be spoken), and especially places of pilgrimage (Poitou,
where pilgrims suffering from epilepsy come to the church of S. Jean
d'Orbestier; Baulme, where Mary Magdalene did penance in a cave; Tara-
çon, where one can see the head of St. Martha in the church dedicated to
her and which was a "very popular trip."[11]

Outside France, Estienne lays out the route to Montserrat ("a place
not less visited in Spain than is Loreto in Italy").[12] Rome receives an entry

that economically sums up all its aspects: "Rome—holy city, seat of the Pope, chief city of all Italy. Note Veronica's Cloth, numbers upon numbers of beautiful shrines, not to mention the antiquities of the ancient Romans. Note, too, that the city was in ancient times confined to seven hills."[13] Rome is a place of relics in abundance, an irresistible lure to the sixteenth-century pious Catholic traveler, but also to many Protestants as well.[14] Similarly, the northern Spanish city of Oviedo (where Morales in this same century was surveying relics) is worthy of note: "In this city is the Church of the Holy Savior, which contains [relics] from the crown of thorns, the milk of Our Lady, the skin of St. Barthlemy, as well as many other holy shrines." Estienne reports that some rank pilgrimage to the Church of the Holy Savior ahead of that to St. James Compostella.[15]

Jerusalem holds place of honor in Estienne's continuum of travel that extends from sites of local shrines and local interest through regional and trans-European sites to the Holy Land itself. Jerusalem is the only locale that Estienne treats concretely as the destination of an actual *journey*. He speaks of the journey to Jerusalem "which the ancients emphasized by calling *Voyage d'outremer*." He notes that pilgrims take ship for Palestine at Venice on the feast of the Ascension. He cannot predict expenses of the trip because of fluctuating winds and seas. Such variables, he adds, make it impossible to compute exact distances. He further gives a sense of the route by pausing over Zara, the principal city of Dalmatia and controlled by the Venetians, which pilgrims passed on their way down the Adriatic. Although Estienne has less to say about Jerusalem itself—"see the Holy Sepulchre and other places of singular devotion"—than he has about Rome, Oviedo, or even Zara (which, he noted, possessed antiquities connected with Julius Caesar),[16] on the evidence of Estienne's guide book, Europeans continued to view travel in general as very much bound up with pilgrimage. The major reason that people traveled, to judge by his *Voyages* and other similar works of the time, was still grounded in religious devotion.[17]

Estienne's appreciation of long-distance pilgrimage to Jerusalem—allotting the Holy Land, as he did, an honorable but not central place in his consideration of travel (indeed, Jerusalem in the text and title is something of a glorious afterthought)—stands in fundamental contrast to the evaluation (often left unspoken) given to such pilgrimage by the great collectors of travel who paid scant attention to pilgrimage. Nevertheless, the attitude of Estienne was not a private one.[18] It is reflected in the works of many actual travelers of the time, including those who ranged far beyond the traditional European and Mediterranean destinations with which Estienne was concerned. These travelers were not pilgrims through and through, but they were pilgrims when they were not being (most of the time, it is true) other kinds of travelers.

An example is the French diplomat and naturalist, Pierre Belon, whose *Observations de plusieurs singularitez et choses memorables, trouvés en Grèce, Asie, Iudée, Egypte, Arabie, et autres pays étranges, redigées en trois livres* was first printed in 1553, the year after the appearance of Estienne's guide.[19] His three-year journey (1546–1549), "which has been difficult and laborious, but also useful and enjoyable,"[20] had many destinations and many things on its plate—natural history, observations of foreign peoples, their traits, their customs—but also made time for devout visitation of the holy places. In the same tradition—but in a Protestant tributary of that tradition— stood Leonhard Rauwolf, whose *Aigentliche Beschreibung der Raiss*, first published in Augsburg in 1581, described his lengthy stay in the Levant. Rauwolf was the conscious heir of Belon. He followed in his tracks, not- ing plants in the Levant that Belon had seen before him. More generally, it is worth noting that writers such as Rauwolf, who were not on the face of things pilgrims, were one means by which pilgrimage did secure a niche in the great collections of travels. Rauwolf himself proved a highly popu- lar subject for collectors—not only for Feyerabend's *Reyssbuch*, but for late seventeenth- and eighteenth-century collectors. He exists, for example in full English translation (by Nicholas Staphorst) under the title *Travels into Eastern Countries*, which forms part of John Ray's *A Collection of Curious Travels and Voyages* (London, 1693).[21]

A physician of Augsburg and a naturalist whose original interests in the Levant were not those of a pilgrim, Rauwolf nevertheless hardly turned out to be immune (as Jacob Gretser was sourly to perceive) to the spiritual experience of being in the Holy Land. He had struck out for the Levant in 1573, driven by a natural inclination to travel (especially to Eastern parts) but also by a quite specific plan to see for himself plants that had been described by ancient authors and to collect botanical specimens that might prove medicinally useful to Europeans back home. Pilgrimage had not originally figured in his calculations. Only far along in the journey—at the end of the second part of the text when Rauwolf tells of sitting in Tripoli, musing on the nearness of the sites of sacred history—is he struck deeply and devoutly by the idea of going on pilgrimage, so much so that pilgrim- age turns out to take up the largest section of the work. Pilgrimage indeed *becomes* a sufficiently large theme in Rauwolf's account that his book sheds light—much as had Beauvau's, but from the opposite end of the spectrum—

on the distinction between books of pilgrimage and books that included pilgrimage among other concerns. Just as Beauvau was an example of the former that could easily be taken for one of the latter, so Rauwolf was an example of the latter (a book of tour and scientific enquiry) that could be taken for the former (a book primarily devoted to pilgrimage).[22]

The shift in emphasis can be detected not only in the text, but in illustrations that introduced the three parts of the book. The first illustration, on the title page, shows Rauwolf landing, almost conquistador-like, in the Levant, sword on his hip and ship behind him in the harbor (Figure 19). The Turk, with whom he shakes hands, could be a New World native, were he not so elegantly and heavily clad from turbaned head to shod toe (and except for that handshake). The second part of the book, which tells of Rauwolf's journeys inland, is introduced by an image of a Turkish caravan (Figure 20). The final illustration, introducing the part of the text dealing with Terra Sancta, depicts the Epiphany (Figure 21). These images form a summary triptych for the attentive reader. All three depict travel. The first two document the traveler in his travels. The third is a scene of travel drawn from sacred history, a scene from which contemporary experience has been excluded. It is possible that the Lutheran Rauwolf, though not uncomfortable with the idea of the Holy Land, was hesitant to show what numerous Catholic books of pilgrimage (beginning haltingly with Breydenbach) made a point of showing—namely, the contemporary peregrinative act of visitation and prayer. The images seem to suggest a certain Protestant diffidence on Rauwolf's part. He has allowed himself to be caught in the pious (and questionable) act of pilgrimage. He (or the printer) seems to want to clarify (somewhat), in picture as well as in word, the limits of what he was doing (in contrast to what he thought the Catholics thought they were doing?). He wants to see the holy places, but he adds: "Not that I thought still to find there Christ our Lord, as the two young men Peter and John and the three Maries did."[23] Or, we might add—having gazed upon the third illustration—as the Magi did.

The illustrations are but one hint of the difference between Rauwolf and Catholic pilgrims of his party. The difference did not, of course, depend on hints. Rauwolf was firmly in the Protestant camp. He got in the general and required licks against "Latinists or Papists," (but granted good marks to the hospitable Franciscans in Terra Sancta).[24] He commented tartly upon the doings of Catholic pilgrims. He was pretty much fed up with devotions and indulgences and absolutions and remissions of sin and told his Catholic companions that

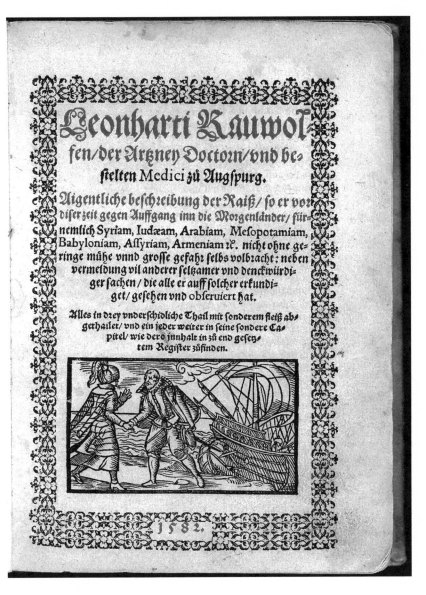

Figure 19. Leonhard Rauwolf, *Aigentliche Beschreibung der Raiss* (Lauingen: Leonhart Reinmichel, 1582), title page.

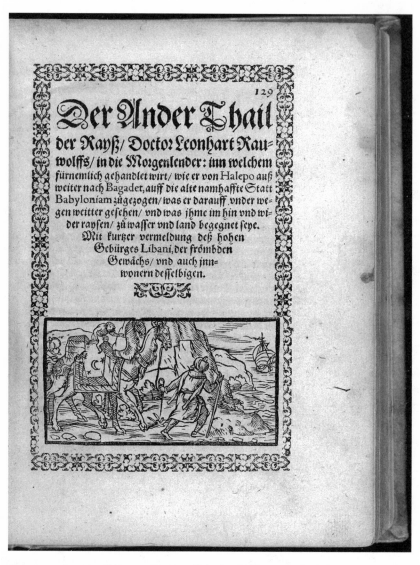

Der Ander Thail

der Rayß/ Doctor Leonhart Rau=
wolffs/ in die Morgenlender: inn welchem
fürnemlich gehandlet wirt/ wie er von Halepo auß
weiter nach Bagadet, auff die alte namhaffte Statt
Babyloniam zügezogen/ was er darauff .vnder we=
gen weitter gesehen/ vnd was jhme im hin vnd wi=
der raysen/ zü wasser vnd land begegnet seye.
Mit kurtzer vermeldung deß hohen
Gebürges Libani, der frömbden
Gewächs/ vnd auch jnn=
wonern desselbigen.

Figure 20. Leonhard Rauwolf, *Aigentliche Beschreibung der Raiss*, p. 129.

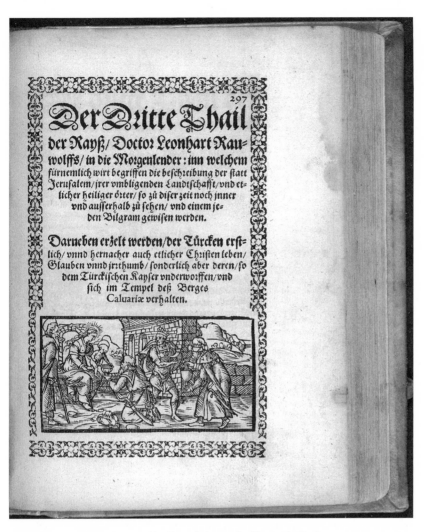

Der Dritte Thail

der Rayß/ Doctor Leonhart Rau=
wolffs/ in die Morgenlender: inn welchem
fürnemlich wirt begriffen die beschreibung der statt
Jerusalem/ jrer vmbligenden Landtschafft/vnd et=
licher heiliger örter/ so zů diser zeit noch jnner
vnd ausserhalb zů sehen/ vnd einem je=
den Bilgram gewisen werden.

Darneben erzelt werden/der Türcken erst=
lich/ vnnd hernacher auch etlicher Christen leben/
Glauben vnnd jrrthumb/ sonderlich aber deren/so
dem Türckischen Kayser vnderworffen/vnd
sich im Tempel deß Berges
Caluariæ verhalten.

Figure 21. Leonhard Rauwolf, *Aigentliche Beschreibung der Raiss*, p. 297.

I expected remission of sin no other ways but only in the name and for the merits, of our Lord Jesus Christ; and that I had not undertaken this pilgrimage as they did, to get any thing by it as by a good work; nor to visit stone and wood to obtain indulgence; or with opinion to come here nearer to Christ; because all these things are directly contrary to Scripture.[25]

Rauwolf had, however, undertaken a pilgrimage of sorts. It is hard to read any other way the traveler's deeds of one who wrote that he visited the holy places in order

to exercise my outward sense in the contemplation thereof, that I might the more fervently consider with my inward ones his bitter passion, death, resurrection and ascension, and to appropriate to myself, and to apprehend the better, and to make my own, by faith and firm confidence, Christ our Lord himself together with his heavenly gifts and treasures, as he has manifested himself in the holy scriptures.[26]

Hostile as he was to the additional—richer, more complicated—meaning that the holy sites had for Catholic pilgrims and unsympathetic as he was towards Catholic devotions, Rauwolf had little or no argument with traditional identifications of holy sites. He shared a sensible spiritual topography with other pilgrims. Nor, even when we read him as primarily a botanical traveler, is it always easy to separate that role from his role as pilgrim. At Rama, he speaks of spices available to Nicodemus for preparing the body of Christ for burial (and still available to be seen by pilgrims). Here a traveler's professional interest—that of doctor and natural scientist—need not be abstracted from, but rather could be intimately combined with, the pilgrim impulse. A bit of natural observation is tied into Scripture in a way pertinent to the scene—a not insignificant sign of pilgrimage's vitality in the modern age.[27]

Rauwolf was a pilgrim, however, chiefly because of what happened to his heart and mind when he found himself "in those places where our dear Lord Christ did walk about."[28] And however sharp the quarrel between Catholics and Protestants over what exactly the truly devout were doing when they traveled about the Holy Land, a sense of much common ground filters through Rauwolf's rendition of his time in Palestine. Through Rauwolf's eyes, much frankness, but also much amity, existed between devout disputants. Each side appears to have had a tolerant and patient disapproval of the other's views: "The next morning my comrades, after they had been at confession, and received the Sacrament upon mount Calvaria, came to me into the church again, with an intention to go round once more. So we saw the holy places once more."[29] His mood seems less exasperation,

or even resignation, than irenic collegiality. There was about his departing figure an almost companionable shrug as he joined his Catholic fellow
travelers within the church.

Somewhat in the fashion of Rauwolf himself, it frequently occurred
to other travelers to the Levant who were already in the neighborhood to
include on their itinerary a pilgrim's stopover at Jaffa. Merchants and tourists could arrange for excursions from Cairo or Tripoli or Sidon. Others,
however, who cut a larger figure on the early modern scene—world-wide
travelers who probed the corners of newly discovered lands and of the far
Orient—also traveled to the holy places and recorded the episode as a devout experience. One such extravagant traveler, the famous Pedro Ordóñez
de Ceballos,[30] devoted three chapters and part of a fourth of his *Historia,
y viage del mundo* (Madrid, 1691; first ed., 1614) to his own pilgrimage to
Jerusalem and Bethlehem. He vowed to go to the Holy Land in thanksgiving for having survived dangers and mishaps in earlier voyages (he claimed
to have begun to travel when he was nine years old). He included in his
roster of travels through Europe, Africa, Asia, America, and "Magellanica,"
his journey to the Holy Land with "all its holy places, the instruments
upon which our Redemption was realized."[31] Ordóñez, in fact, acts the
devout pilgrim wherever opportunity arises. In Rome ("the Holy City,
head and mistress of the world") he kisses the feet of Gregory XIII, from
whom he receives a medal that immediately rids him of a stomach ailment
that had plagued him for four years, and he visits all the churches inside
and outside Rome, churches which have "relics without number."[32] Outside of Europe, he continues to act the pilgrim—for example, in India
"where I visited the Holy Sepulchre of the Apostle St. Thomas."[33]

Ordóñez's contemporary and a similar sort of voyager, Jean Mocquet
(b.1575), traveled wherever and whenever he had the chance. Mocquet was
a restless wanderer—and this despite his comfortable position in the world.
He was ensconced near the very center of European power and influence,
first as royal apothecary to Henry IV and subsequently under Louis XIII
as curator of the royal collections in the Tuilleries (Garde du Cabinet des
Singularitez du Roy). He nevertheless was seized with a perpetual longing to be abroad. On intimate terms with the royal family, he would bring
home specimens of plants and other exotica for the royal collections as
well as stories to entertain the king.[34] And yet, scarcely back in France and
settled in at court, he would start dreaming up yet another foray into the
outer reaches that would remove him from court for months or years.[35]

Mocquet made six journeys, which he described in his *Voyages en*

Afrique, Asie, Indes Orientales, and Occidentales (Paris, 1617). The book appeared just three years after the first printing of Ordóñez's similarly wide-ranging book of travels. After more than a decade of coming and going (1601–1614) between Europe and Africa, the New World, and the Indian Ocean, Mocquet had planned a sixth journey, a *tour de monde* which in the event floundered and ended up as merely a down-at-the-heels stay in Spain. When he had returned from his most recent (fifth) voyage—to the Levant, from which he had brought back a "quantity of rare plants and other remarkable specimens"—Louis XIII and the Queen Regent were charmed by his finds and specifically commissioned him to establish a *cabinet* of exotica in the palace of the Tuilleries. He threw himself into the task but soon—and hardly surprisingly—discovered that he needed to add to the collections by undertaking further journeys and especially to make a "circuit of the entire earth."[36] He went to Seville to try and arrange "the most excellent *voyage du monde*, and after the example of the famous heroes Magellan, Drake, Cavendish, and Olivier van Noort, to make a complete *tour de l'Univers*." It all came to embarrassingly little, and when Mocquet got back to Paris, his traveling days were over, his mood of isolation and unfulfillment all but complete.[37] This was in August 1615. His book came out two years later, by which time his traveler's resilience had kicked in and he was looking forward to future publishing projects (also stillborn) based on his travels, if not to any future travels.[38]

Mocquet reflected the age of discovery under full sail. His own curiosity, wanderlust, and love of novelty—his most striking traits—he himself thought of not as eccentricities but as signs of humanity.[39] They were part of the civilizational ambience of a seventeenth-century Europe that was itself bathed in the achievements and aura of discovery. And discovery was more than something others had initiated decades or a century ago. Mocquet and his contemporaries lived on the edge of continuing exploration. What was called the third continent—"la terre Australe, non encores descouverte"—was a work in progress. Not so many years ago, he tells the reader, the Portuguese navigator, Fernandes de Queiros, had described some of the coasts of the Solomons, "but it remains to wait for a more certain and complete discovery."[40] The early seventeenth century was not merely an age of discoveries, but an age of travels into the wide world that discoverers had opened up, and continued to open up, to travelers of all sorts—travelers such as Mocquet, who were not, nor did they claim to be, discoverers, but who traveled in the discoverers' wake as tourists, examiners of "the universe," and conveyers of data (stocking walls and shelves of *cabinets*) to Europeans from these far-flung places. Travel itself is what had changed in the wake of Columbus (and Queirós), the altered scene demonstrated by the fact that five of Mocquet's six voyages began from Atlantic ports. The lone exception was the fifth voyage when he departed from Marseilles for Syria and the Holy Land.

Mocquet was, as it were, philosophically and spiritually attuned to pilgrimage. True, his "natural curiosity" drove him to travel; but more was at work. Mocquet ponders God's uprooting of Abraham and would have his readers conclude with him, in an ages-old European cultural tradition still lingering in his Europe, that we are all "pilgrims and travelers (*pèlerins et voyageurs*)" on the earth. We are not meant for the pleasures and comforts of home and native land, decides this *voyageur* who time and again gave them up, who all but threw away the cushions and slippers of an anchored and cosseted existence in the corridors and apartments of royal residences. We are meant for the toils and troubles of journeys, adds this highly connected (but strangely solitary) man, this French Spartan who experienced woes aplenty on his wanderings.[41] It seems so much pious boilerplate, except that there is more in the recipe that made Mocquet a pilgrim. Mocquet was existentially attuned to pilgrimage. Pilgrimage, much as it had with Ordóñez, grows out of his other journeys—especially the arduous journey into the Indian Ocean which had begun at the end of November 1607 and only ended with his return to Paris in September 1610—and also out of the shocking news of the assassination of his beloved Henry IV that had greeted him in the waters off Lisbon. He no longer had that royal ear to fill with his traveler's tales. He was suddenly seized with the desire to make "a journey of devotion" to the Holy Land. Within the year (8 September 1611) he was sailing from Marseilles.[42]

An entire book, rather than Ordóñez's few chapters, retells Mocquet's experiences in the Levant. Yet there is both more and less than meets the eye.

To take the less first, Mocquet devotes relatively few pages to the heart of the Palestine venture. *Livre V* accounts for only forty-eight pages out of a total of four hundred and forty-two pages of text.[43] Moreover, many of those few pages are devoted to the winter he spent in Tripoli and the land journey that took him south to Jerusalem by way of Damascus.[44] Having left Tripoli on 9 April 1612, Mocquet reached Jerusalem (without any show of emotion) on 27 April. The time in between was taken up more with describing (and complaining about) the difficulties of travel than with attending to the few holy spots that were passed along the way. In the few days between 27 April and 1 May, when he and his party left Jaffa, Mocquet was shown the holy sites (which meant principally Jerusalem, Bethlehem, and their neighborhoods). All of this takes up only eleven pages. By 6 May, he is back in Tripoli where he remains until 18 May, arranging for the packing of scented flowering plants that he has gathered mainly from Mount Lebanon and the neighborhood of Tripoli. These shrubs are destined for the garden of the Louvre, where the king will be able to see them from his chambers.[45]

Pilgrimage seems to have utterly lost the spotlight, even in the fifth book that specifically takes pilgrimage as principal subject matter. In such cramped textual space, Mocquet's rendition of his pious rounds is rapid-fire and seems more than a bit pro forma. He excuses himself from describing all the sites of Bethlehem out of the usual seventeenth-century reluctance to tread ground already tamped down by observant predecessors.[46] He takes care of the holy places within the Church of the Holy Sepulchre in summary fashion. He travels the Via Dolorosa at breakneck speed ("le lieu ou . . . ou . . . ou.."). The reader reads a hurried catalogue. Mocquet himself may have been winded. He concludes: "Thus in brief are the other holy places in the city of Jerusalem and its environs according to what was shown and explained to us by the religious who conducted our tour."[47] In such a rendition, pilgrimage itself seems worn out, washed out, bleached away. Indulgences are not mentioned. Franciscans, a lively presence (of hospitality and instruction) in other pilgrimages, are barely so in this rendition. Jerusalem itself in its physical look and extent (present-day Jerusalem, to be sure, as opposed to the ancient city that is recalled by the holy sites) calls to Mocquet's mind, of all places, present-day Blois.[48]

Mocquet's time in Terra Sancta was brief, perhaps necessarily so. He may not have controlled his schedule. Such retrospective covering of everything in a few pages, however, was his own doing. The few pages do not explain the rapid-fire treatment, but are themselves explained by such treatment. Mocquet didn't have much to say.

If there is less, however, there is also more than meets the casual reader's eye in all of this. Mocquet, it turns out, is a thorough-going pilgrim, not simply a tourist pushing himself to see things for himself out of natural curiosity, or to see and note, if only at a glance, famous sites that others have seen before him. When he and other pilgrims enter the Church of the Holy Sepulchre it is with devout purpose—"to make our prayers and visitation."[49] And Mocquet suddenly, if only briefly, lets the reader in on the impact that sacred space has had upon him:

And then I heard Mass at break of day at the place of the Holy Sepulchre, making confession and taking Communion the most devoutly as is possible at a place so holy and venerable. And I did this with such contentment and satisfaction that I think nothing comparable has happened to me in life. I offer infinite thanks to my God for having preserved me from so many accidents and dangers and for having brought me to this holy place to perform here the duties of a good Christian and Catholic.[50]

He even suddenly turned moralist. We contemporary Christians who neglect the sacred law, he warned, should be instructed by the sorry state of the Holy Land, a desiccated region that had once been "the most pleasant and plentiful in the world." This ardor and spirituality derive from "ma curieuse devotion"[51]—that is, curiosity about pious matters—which, once satisfied, leaves him prepared to depart. His is a spirituality, however, that (except for rare lapses) is kept under wraps, a veiled spirituality that takes place off stage, off the reader's page, in the heart of the pilgrim who does not divulge many of the secrets of the heart. The essence of Mocquet's pilgrimage remains largely untranslated into print. Mocquet may have been a bridge figure (associated as he and his family had been with the convert-king, Henry IV). Is there a lingering Protestant sensibility at work in the Catholic Mocquet, a sensibility that restrained him from publicly delving into, and dwelling upon, the spiritual experience of pilgrimage, and a sensibility, moreover, that was detached from Catholic emotions (expressed at first sight of Jerusalem), Catholic practices (indulgences especially), and the entire structure of Catholic pilgrimage that was represented and implemented by the Franciscan Custody in Terra Sancta? Such matters occupied so much of the surface of Catholic renditions and so little of the expressed attention of Mocquet. In any case and for whatever reasons, Mocquet suggests the limitations of the pilgrimage genre—the limitations, that is, on what we should expect to find in a pilgrimage. In his hands, pilgrimage serves as a literature of travel—devout travel, to be sure, but not what one would think of as a book of devotional literature. The fact that he has told us just enough for us to suspect that he himself was a devout pilgrim makes those boundaries of the genre all the more striking. So much of his description of his pious journey avoided a public display of the pious experience itself at the very same time, however, as he acknowledged the reality of the experience. Against all odds, the interlinear regions of the text are made over into zones of flagrant possibility (for the reader).

For a century and three quarters after his first appearance in print—from the eve of the Thirty Years' War to the coming of the French Revolution—numerous travelers like Mocquet traveled elsewhere (the rest of the Levant, the rest of the world) but also traveled in more or less devout fashion to Jerusalem. These same travelers reserved at least some space for the retelling of their pilgrimages.[52] The literary reality of early modern pilgrimage—and therefore, in large part, the fundamental historical reality of pilgrimage at that time—was embodied almost as much in works such as these as it was in works of travel whose primary focus was on the pilgrimage to the Holy Land.

Pilgrimage could get lost in such larger works. But not always. At mid-century, Pietro della Valle published an account of his wide-ranging voyages in two volumes. He goes on and on[53] about how he is driven to travel by curiosity, how he fits into the tradition of ancient heroic travelers as well as into that of Columbus, Gama, Magellan, and Vespucci, how the strange things he sees will be "a spiritual treasure," of how he was seized by "an impatient desire to travel widely." In addition to this heated-up rhetoric of curiosity and of the ways to satisfy it through travel, however, Valle suddenly introduces the idea of pilgrimage, but with a twist. Pilgrimage is not seen—as it often is in such travelers—as a journey that flowed out of other journeys, usually as an act of thanksgiving for coming safely through other travels, but as the Christian traveler's payment of a debt of honor, the payment of a kind of traveler's tithe (*un espèce de dixme*). Pilgrimage thus is not simply a devotional act in some general and indeterminate manner, but one that is essentially a traveler's act. It is found to be both peculiar and appropriate to even the widest-ranging *voyageur*. Valle's own overall intention had been to concentrate on the Levant because of his desire to see the greatest parts of Europe, Asia, and Africa, but also because it is the holy places of the Levant that allow the traveler to execute his religious responsibilities.[54]

Some years later, in 1655, Jean Thévenot set out for the Levant, having already been traveling the roads of Europe for three years. Within a decade, his much-reprinted *Relation d'un Voyage fait au Levant* (Paris, 1664) appeared for the first time.[55] Thévenot was a traveler's traveler (an engraved portrait shows him dressed in the Oriental fashion and celebrated as the ideal voyager). Wise in the ways of travelers (his uncle was the famed seventeenth-century collector of travels, Melchisédec Thévenot), he knew a trope when he used it. It was *comme les autres* that he attributed the printing of his book of travels to the pressure of friends who had read the manuscript. And he was well aware of the defining worry of seventeenth-century travelers to the Levant. He is at pains to justify why he is offering yet one more account of travels to the region. He himself, after all, was traveling under the inspiration of earlier travelers who had written of their adventures. What is left to say after the learned and observant have had their say? He picks at the question and settles on some answers. It is worthwhile, he convinces himself, to tell of one's travels. Things don't stay the same. Superficial appearances (*la face des choses*) alter. Habits and practices of today differ from those of earlier travelers' times. One traveler cannot observe everything, cannot remark upon everything. In any case, there has never been a travel book that did not instruct in some way. His own notes contain nuggets ("much that is specific and curious") worth passing on. He can offer many things that have never been written about—"or at least very slightly written about."[56] Interestingly enough, however, when Thévenot takes up pilgrimage in the Holy Land, he reaches a somewhat different conclusion.

He had decided to go on pilgrimage to the Holy Land upon returning to Cairo from a visit to Mount Sinai, his reasons being the usual ones of Christian piety.[57] In the event, the pilgrimages to Sinai and Terra Sancta turn out to comprise nearly a quarter of the entire text. Like Rauwolf's book, Thévenot's sizable pilgrimage-within-a-larger-text serves as a conduit through which pilgrimage does make its way into the great collections.[58]

Like Mocquet, Thévenot is respectful and rapid-fire, but more meticulous and substantial, in his description of the holy places. He gives us somewhat more than Mocquet's schedule of stops. And as regards modern Jerusalem, where Mocquet had vaguely seen Blois in modern Jerusalem, Thévenot sees the walls of Avignon in the new Turkish walls of Jerusalem.[59] Thévenot is a detached and ironic observer. (He undergoes investiture as a Knight of the Holy Sepulchre, but largely as a protective cover for his return voyage to Europe, since he has learned that the Spanish will not arrest such a knight, "even if he is a Frenchman.")[60] Although he is in the Holy Land as a pilgrim, the reality of *his* pilgrimage tends to evaporate as an actual presence in the finished text. This is for the usual reason that everything has been said—and even quite recently—by others who have visited the holy sites. "It is for this reason," he tells the reader, "that I will speak only as a traveler (*voyageur*), only indicating (*marquant*) them [*tous les lieux saints*] in the order in which I have seen them."[61] Thévenot appears to abdicate the role of pilgrim (at least in a formal or literary sense) *in his text* at the same time that he is actually performing the activities of a pilgrim. Nor were pilgrimage and its problems and nuances at the center of his attention as a traveler. What he had earlier argued himself around— this same problem of too many predecessors in the Levant as a whole—

now appears an immovable obstacle in the specific Levantine region of sacred Palestine.

Thévenot has brought us to an important pass. There is no hostility to pilgrimage in his attitude. It is just that, for him, being as he is a writer of travels, the sites of Palestine have been done so often and sufficiently well that nothing seems unsaid. Pious travel to Palestine, in as much as it produced a literary *something* beyond the experience itself—inasmuch as experience fabricated a text that reflected back upon the experience (as gloss, as commentary, as reminiscent celebration)—was now reduced, for Thévenot, to a simple marking of the traditional spots of sacred ground. Thévenot exposed the reader to even less of the peregrinative experience than had Mocquet. We are let in even less on the secret of the author's pious disposition. It is as if the reader were being shown a telling of beads without any suspicion that thoughts and prayers were moving the fingers along the string of decades. Thévenot seems to contribute to a process of impoverishment where pilgrimage is concerned. Fear of being repetitive and redundant, has lead the pilgrim, not to say goodbye to all that, but to say very little at all. Pilgrimage threatens to disappear not only in the pages of some philosophic Levantiner (Volney, for instance), but even in the pages of those very travelers who were, more or less, attuned to pilgrimage.

Is there no way out of these straits of growing, self-imposed silence? Is there no life left in pilgrimage as a form of travel reportage? Is the reader back in Europe—who, not incidentally, has for almost two centuries gotten used to travel tales featuring novelties and exotica—to be treated to nothing more than a succession of printed books that drily itemize traditional sites under the roof of the Holy Sepulchre and along the Via Dolorosa and on either side of the roads between Jaffa and Jerusalem and between Jerusalem and Bethlehem? This might have sufficed in the age of manuscripts when, getting the word out about anything was a much less efficient proposition; but in the age of print it would hardly do at all. And yet, it is asking too much to expect fresh possibilities, new light on visitor-worn holy sites, from the writings of travelers for whom pilgrimage to Palestine was merely an episode of wider travels. Thévenot is an excellent example of a traveler who had his hands full on this very question of what the traveler was to say when so many others had already said so much. The problem met him at every turn throughout the Levant. Perhaps he was exhausted by the need to say something new by the time he had reached Terra Sancta which, after all, was the most visited and most fully described, and thus most problematical, area of the entire Mediterranean.

Yet it is just such a traveler—not Thévenot himself, but his contemporary, the Dutch artist, Cornelis de Bruyn, who traveled throughout the Levant and beyond—who reopens the entire question. He discovers new possibilities by means of the simplest of maneuvers. He points to a way out, and he does so not incidentally nor by chance, but in language that makes clear that he recognizes the existence of a problem.

Bruyn's *Voyage au Levant* appeared in French in Delft in 1700, two years after its original publication in Dutch in the same city. Bruyn had started out from Holland for Italy at the end of 1674, lingered there for several years, and then toured the Levant from 1678 to 1685.[62] There is much to ponder in his book, both text and engravings; but I shall fix on three points.

First, Bruyn was not an artist who happened to be a traveler. He was an artist in order that he might be a traveler. He had, from his youth, wanted to travel, and developed his drawing and painterly skills precisely in order to be a better traveler. Bruyn is absolutely clear about this. Indeed, he brings a gust of new life into the tired prefatory thought of most travelers—the thought, that is, that they had always and passionately longed to travel. What for most was a throwaway line at the starting gate was, for Bruyn, a statement of how he had lived his life and honed his perceptions. Bruyn was one of the great travelers of the European tradition, not only because of the travels themselves and his verbal and visual depictions of his far-flung experiences, but also because of his extreme consciousness of himself as a *traveler*. Travel was his art, vocation, and life. The act of travel informed everything.[63] There was no confusion in his mind (unlike, for example, that which later reigned in Chateaubriand's) in regard to what he was doing when he described his travels. He was a traveler who composed a book of words and drawings that documented his travels. There was no doubt about his writing a *voyage*. That he put his entire self into it did not turn the work into autobiography.

Second, Bruyn did not flinch from the reality, daunting as it was to others, that many travelers had preceded him and had written about their travels. He gloried in their company. He saw immense diversity in the personal inclinations of travelers as well as in their comments and in the style in which they expressed themselves. This *diversité d'inclinations, et de ce différent tour d'esprit* has produced travels to one place that seem to be travels to quite different places. Only the nontraveler would be surprised at this. It is all a question, for Bruyn, of concentration, of focus, of perspective. The traveler who applies himself to this or that facet of a place misses other matters that may be of primary interest to another traveler. The same holds true, Bruyn continues, for the Levant where, "as everyone knows," many skilled travelers have gone and have written up their *relations*. In fact, this diversity is a boon to the contemporary traveler, who thereby has guides to assist him in his own travels. Bruyn boasts that he carries along on his travels copies of Valle and Thévenot and that he consults the illustrations in Olfert Dapper's compilation of engraved Palestinian scenes whenever he can get hold of the volume. And these are not only aids when he is actually on foreign terrain; they are useful, too, when he comes to arrange his own text. What he reads helps to determine what he writes. He is not afraid to abbreviate his own remarks or to borrow from those of others.[64]

Third, how these remarks—on travel in general and on travel in the Levant—pertain specifically to pilgrimage in the Holy Land can be seen in one example of Bruyn's sketch-work in Jerusalem. Bruyn wished to make a panoramic drawing of the city. Others had often done the same; but his was to be a sketch with a difference. He tells the reader that

I went to the Mount of Olives in order to draw the city. The spot that I chose was not the one where Jesus Christ wept over the city. My reason was that others, who had gone there before me, had always represented the city from that vantage point. I went to locate myself a little farther towards the south side of the hill, in order to make my sketch of the city, as much as this was possible, from the south-east side.

Such sketch-making was fraught with peril. Turkish authorities did not want Europeans getting the city down on paper. Bruyn was accompanied by two Franciscans and an interpreter who stood around to hide the fact of what he was doing. They brought with them a picnic hamper so that a show of lolling and feasting might distract any onlooker from Le Bruin's real work with the *crayon*. Because of the danger, his task had to be interrupted from time to time and took three days to complete.[65]

This shift of scene exemplifies Bruyn's theory of travel as an experience and a literature (including an illustrated literature) of diverse insights and inclinations and changing perspectives on the part of travelers themselves. This particular maneuver by Bruyn is all the more striking because it is executed on the terrain of pilgrimage, and is included in precisely the form of travel that seemed most resistant to innovation. What makes pilgrimage a difficult literature for moderns (*us* moderns, not just early moderns) to digest is that it covers the same ground over and over again. So much of discovery-induced modernity is defined by the novel and the exotic—exactly the qualities that are not to be found on the surface of pilgrimage as a literary genre. Not only do all pilgrims haunt the same places (at the very time that other travelers are exploring whole new oceans and continents). They go in the tracks of, and in the spirit of, not only Christ and figures of sacred history, but also earlier pilgrims. It is not only *pietas* in the abstract that rankles the modern sensibility; it is this very particular form of piety that seems grounded in repetition and redundancy. If one longs for diversity in the pages of pilgrimage, one must be prepared to look for it—that is, to squint and peer, not just to glance. Pilgrimage is a literature of nuanced elaborations rather than of startling discoveries. Consider, for example, pilgrim writers' visual renderings of the plaza of the Church of the Holy Sepulchre, which seem so much alike—which seem *essentially* alike—but which are, in fact, far from identical.[66] Or consider Bruyn's startling decision to move over a bit, to locate himself paces away from the usual spot in order to get a new angle of vision on the city of Jerusalem (Figure 22). Pilgrimage may have been resistant to diversity, but it was not immune to it. How could it be? It was a form of pious *travel*.

Bruyn's volumes would be reproduced well into the eighteenth century, and throughout the century there were published accounts of other travelers, especially travelers in the Levant, which also included chapters, or whole sections, on devout visitation of the Holy Land. Laurent d'Arvieux, for example, who derived from a Provençal mercantile world that looked upon the Mediterranean as its Atlantic Ocean and Indian Ocean,[67] began his life as a merchant and diplomat in the Mediterranean in 1653 at the age of eighteen. His *Mémoires* (Paris, 1735), published in six volumes long after his death, gave considerable attention to his time spent as a pilgrim in the

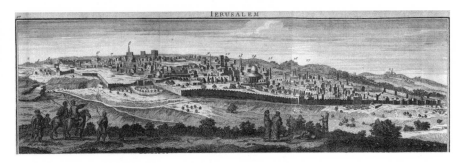

Figure 22. Cornelis de Bruyn, *Voyage au Levant*, 5 vols. (Paris: J. B. C. Bauche, le fils, 1725), vol. 2, between pp. 238 and 239, detail.

Holy Land and was among the most massive testimonies to an early modern life spent traveling in the Levant.[68] Another example of an eighteenth-century traveler whose perspective was broadly Levantine but who gave considerable attention to the Holy Land was Jean Baptiste Tollot, who set out for the East in 1731 and whose account of his travels was published in 1742.[69] And there were other such travel writers who left their mark as the eighteenth century progressed. It was Bruyn, however, who had most definitely saved, so to speak, such travel as a worthy subject matter for the printers to consider. He recognized that the traveler (and the pilgrim) depended not only on data distributed by others—Franciscans, earlier travelers—which one simply repeated. Foreign or exotic scenes were not simply bundles of sensible material external to the observing traveler. One also had to figure into the equation the traveler's disposition, his inclinations, the impressions he formed, the particular angle of vision (literally) from which he took in the scene. The personal factor mattered—the *diversité d'inclinations*, the *tour d'esprit*. Where one decided to set up one's easel on the Mount of Olives made all the difference.

It should be added, however—and the addition is crucial—that Bruyn made the case less for pilgrimage itself than for Levantine travel in general. After all, when he had given his new view of Jerusalem, what struck him most was the mosque on the Temple Mount shining in the sunlight. Moreover, the whole point of previous travelers' sketching the city from the traditional spot was that they were attempting to see Jerusalem through the eyes of Christ bemoaning the fate of the city. To do so had always been a specific act of the pilgrim retracing the life of Christ. One might argue that Bruyn's maneuver was an advance for the aesthetics of the tour, but a loss (or highly dubious gain) for the spirituality of the pilgrimage.

The force of Bruyn's accomplishment as an observant and expressive traveler does, in fact, reenforce two general points. First, his inclusion of the Holy Land on his itinerary and on his agenda of things to be sketched and written about underscores the early modern survival of Levantine pilgrimage *as travel*. At the same time, however, Bruyn's (or any traveler's) inclusion of pilgrimage as only one episode of much wider travels means that the vital and reflective manifestation of pilgrimage as a genre and the answers to early modern problems (aesthetic, intellectual) confronted by pilgrims *as travelers* were not likely to be found in such travelers whose perspectives included much more than pilgrimage. Theirs were the general solutions of general travelers.

There did exist in early modernity, however, other travelers who, unlike a Mocquet or Bruyn, did travel primarily in order to get to and around and back from the holy places, and who did, once back in Europe, write down and publish accounts of their travels. These travelers, even more than those we have been examining, kept alive a tradition of travel that reached back to the likes of Tucher and Breydenbach, and beyond them to medieval pilgrims, some of whom had first come into print in the later fifteenth century. They might be called the third voice in the early modern context, weighing in on the question of where and whether pilgrimage belonged in the scheme of early modern travel. Their single-minded attentiveness to pilgrimage itself established an important line of continuity between Europeans traveling before and after Gutenberg as well as before and after Columbus and Luther. In this line of travelers there stands a contemporary of Bruyn, the Frenchman Antoine Morison, who was not a traveler who merely made room for pilgrimage within a larger agenda. He was a pilgrim through and through. Nevertheless, he did share Bruyn's insight—or at least exemplified the truth of the insight—that the individuality of the traveler was all-important. We might say that he viewed things in much the same light as did Bruyn, but that he shone his lamp more strongly and specifically on pilgrimage itself and on the holy terrain through which the pilgrim traveled. He manifested his own inclinations, his own *tour d'esprit*, as a pilgrim. He saw things very much through his own eyes. His great subject matter was his own *experience* of being in Terra Sancta. But in speaking of Morison, we have gotten ahead of our story.

A Third Voice:
Pilgrims on Travel and Pilgrimage

IN 1595, A LITTLE OVER A CENTURY after Columbus returned from his first voyage, Juan Ceverio de Vera traveled on pilgrimage to the Levant. His *Viaje de la Tierra Sancta* came out the next year in Rome. Editions followed in Madrid (1597) and in Pamplona (1598 and 1613). Ceverio came from a distinguished conquistadorial family in the Canaries, his great-grandfather (Cabeza de Vaca's grandfather) having been the conqueror of Gran Canaria and one of the original Spanish settlers of the islands. From his youth, he was in royal service in New Spain, where he was eventually ordained a priest. After eight further years spent in Spain, he traveled to the Rome of Clement VIII (1592–1605), where he was enrolled as an acolyte of the papal curia.[1] Clement's pontificate was a period of great projects (intellectual, political, spiritual) at Rome that would culminate in the Holy Year of 1600. The intensity and glitter of the times were marked by great Roman personalities—among them, Filippo Neri, Cesare Baronius, Roberto Bellarmino. But despite the excitement and splendor and high ambitions of the curia, the Roman scene turned out not to Ceverio's liking. "I was unhappy over the state of affairs at that great court," he vaguely says of his discomfiture, which may have reflected intense chagrin felt by Spain's partisans in Rome at the approaching reconciliation between Rome and Henry IV in the wake of the attempted assassination of the French king, news of which had just arrived (January 1595) in Rome. Whatever had rendered him out of sorts ("I was weary and desired peace and quiet"), Ceverio looked to return to Spain and in the meantime sought consolation in spiritual reading. Thus did he happen "to spend several hours on an Italian book of pilgrimage to Jerusalem." The effect was electric, freeing him from stupor and insulating him from second thoughts ("idle advice and misgivings") of those around him. He vowed to go on pilgrimage, sought and obtained the pope's licence to do so, and immediately set off on 27 February 1595.[2]

Even after an entire century of grandly reported discoveries of new worlds, Ceverio's *Viaje* showed the vital survival of pilgrimage to the Levant as a focus, and not just an episode, of actual travel. A single book of pilgrimage had inspired him to make the long voyage eastward, and his traveler's experiences led him to leave (as we shall see) his own highly distinctive stamp on the literature of pilgrimage. While the pilgrimage tradition in which he stood was part of a remarkable continuity that reached back over a millennium, by Ceverio's time pilgrimage to the Levant was also a fully modern phenomenon. That the literature of pilgrimage, both before and after Ceverio, was printed is an overarching fact. Pilgrimage's impact would have been marginal, had pilgrims' tales remained, as many did, in manuscript.[3] Print, to be sure, did not suddenly become the sole carrier of ideas in the modern period. Even the distinction between printed books and manuscript books was slow in becoming clear.[4] Long after the 1450s, European public discourse continued to depend on the circulated written word.[5] This also held true in the specific case of pilgrimages. (We do not know whether Ceverio had read a manuscript or printed book of pilgrimage.) A striking instance of fifteenth-century manuscript publication was Jean Adorno's account of a 1470 pilgrimage that was dedicated to James III (1460–1488) of Scotland, for whom a lavish copy was prepared.[6] Even for pilgrimages that were printed, there survives a hint of an afterlife, or parallel life, in manuscript. Deshayes de Courmenin's seventeenth-century pilgrimage exists in an eighteenth-century manuscript, although his travel account had last been printed in 1645.[7] At the end of the seventeenth century, copies of the manuscript account of the 1697 journey to Jerusalem of Henry Maundrell, an English resident of Aleppo, were not only sent back to friends in England prior to the account's first printing, but actually used as a guide book by other members of the Levant Company factory in Aleppo when they made their journeys to Jerusalem.[8] Distribution of the text (i.e., publication) preceded the work of printers.

To have survived only in manuscript, however, would have relegated pilgrimage *as a genre* to the archival lumber room. Pilgrims' accounts would have gone unnoticed as time passed, especially since such devout travels scarcely surfaced in the printed travel collections that were the loud voice of the new travel. The future of pilgrimage, if it was to have a future, lay elsewhere than in manuscripts. It is not surprising that when Chateaubriand went on pilgrimage in the early 1800s the tradition to which he appealed, and out of which he fashioned much of his revivalist *Itinéraire*, had been preserved in printed books of pilgrimage, not in manuscript codices. Pilgrims had long before chosen, however much choice was wrapped in a veneer of formulaic reluctance, to have their texts printed.[9] That pilgrimages were in fact printed—that the legacy of Tucher and Breydenbach carried on and expanded—is the very first clue of pilgrimage's modernity.

Subject matter, moreover, proved inexhaustible, and this despite nearly every pilgrim writer across three centuries claiming to sense exhaustion around the corner. No single work—even the *Viaggio da Venetia*, which first appeared in print in 1500 and continued to be regularly reprinted well into the eighteenth century[10]—served up the last word for Europeans curious about devout travel to the holy places of Palestine. Even ages-old availability of basic data and story-line for such travel did not quiet the presses.[11] From the early decades of printing to the end of the ancien régime, hundreds of printed works retold devout travels to the Levant and described in detail sites that pilgrims found there. Nor was this a literature of single appearances. Editions and translations of the constituents of this body of work multiplied the impact of the genre many times over, even after Europe and its ideas of travel had so altered and enlarged.[12]

In addition to being printed, the literature of early modern pilgrimage operated on a different timetable. Unlike the travel literature of discovery, there existed no urgent connection between date of travel and date of imprint. Decades might intervene between the two. For example, almost sixty years separated journey and publication in the case of the Spanish Francisan, Antonio de Medina, who had arrived in the Holy Land in 1513. He was back in Spain on the feast of the Ascension, 1514; he had finished writing his travel account in 1526; the book itself, *Estaciones y misterios de la Tierra Santa*, appeared in print in Salamanca in 1573 and again in 1575; a richly illustrated Italian translation, *Viaggio di Terra Santa*, was printed in Florence in 1590 and reissued (perhaps) in 1594. Both Spanish text and Italian translation reflect a world of deep and intense Catholic piety that spanned the century—manifested at one end by the actual journey and writing of the *Estaciones*, and at the other by the printing and translation and elaborate illustration of the long-finished work.[13]

Another example comes from farther east. The Bohemian noble Krystof Harant set out for Terra Sancta in April, 1598. At Venice, he joined a small group going to the Levant. He was back in Venice on 26 December. An illustrated edition of his travels was printed in Czech in Prague in 1608. A second edition appeared in Prague in 1668. In the meantime, Harant himself had been executed in 1621 for Utraquist sympathies. Years later, in 1638, his book was translated into German, which text nevertheless was only printed, under the title *Der Christliche Ulysses oder Weit-Versuchter Cavallier*, in Nuremberg in 1678.[14] Ten years from journey to publication, fifty years from first edition to second, thirty years from first edition to translation, and forty more years from translation to publication of translation—all of this suggests a leisurely pace of publication that often characterized pilgrimage, especially in contrast to narratives of discovery. One could not predict the literary birth (or demise) of a work of pilgrimage.

Contrast in timetables between literatures of pilgrimage and of discovery suggests fundamentally different sets of expectations on the part of the respective audiences of each form of travel reporting. Pilgrimage had once been the latest (and almost the sole) word in travel reporting, and thus pilgrims' accounts had been items of news that appeared quickly (Tucher, Brasca, Breydenbach). One of the signals that something had changed in travel was that something had changed in the literature of travel. Ever since Columbus, accounts of discoverers broke news or stirred up controversy or documented rival claims or created a general sensation of adventure, while pilgrimages, even if advertised in their titles as modern and up-to-date (*neu, nouvelle*), were less tied to the moment and the scoop. They might appear quickly; or they might not.

Travel-like books of nontravelers illustrate another general characteristic of early modern pilgrimage—the shifting of the cultural balance, in the case of pilgrimage itself, away from the phenomenal to the noumenal. Long-distance pilgrimage came to involve much less actual travel (no Crusades, increasingly smaller parties, fewer ships) and much more reading and writing about travel. It is a vexed question—of how many early modern Europeans actually took themselves in pious fashion to Jerusalem. That the knowledgeable Gretser, who mulled over the matter in the early 1600s, estimated actual pilgrims by means of speculation vis-à-vis published accounts of pilgrimages shows just how vexed. The flaw in such figuring was that even Gretser lacked a perfect bibliographical handle on printed pilgrimages, much less on those remaining in manuscript. He knew, moreover, that some pilgrims returned to write up their travels, but more after the fashion of a tourist than of a pilgrim. In any event, Gretser knew enough to conclude that pious travel to Jerusalem was not quite a thing of the past and that "not a few" still undertook the journey. He ends up figuring that there were a hundred pilgrims for every published pilgrimage.[15] The number seems optimistic for 1609 (when Gretser's book appeared) and will seem much more so as the years advance during the following two centuries that end with Chateaubriand finding himself pretty much alone as a devout European in Jerusalem. Pilgrimage to the Levant survived into early modernity as an intellectual and literary and contemplative experience of readers rather than as an actual experience of throngs of travelers. The cultural reality of pilgrimage as a form of travel was based on the thinnest layer of actual travelers who then recorded their travels. How thin that layer was can be appreciated by considering works that had the look and feel of books of travel—they were cast in the *form* of travel books and could be read as such—although their authors had not themselves visited Palestine. Indeed, an eighteenth-century traveler to the Holy Land could justify yet one more account of Levantine travels, not only on the usual grounds that travel writers to the same places differ in their impressions and information, but also for the additional reason that some authors of travel accounts had never actually set out upon their travels, much less put foot in the Holy Land.[16]

Fiction is not unusual in the early modern literature of pilgrimage to Palestine.[17] In *all* travel literature of the time, the fit was snug between literatures of imagined and actual travel. After all, Thomas More took pains to portray his imaginary source on Utopia, Raphael Hythlodaeus, as Amerigo Vespucci's "constant companion in the last three of those four voyages which are now universally read of, but on the final voyage he did not return with him."[18] Even in the person of the great Columbus, there had been at work several sorts of traveler—not only the discoverer nor even the calculating pilgrim who saw Jerusalem as the ultimate goal, but as well a kind of utopianist who felt (and feared) himself on the verge, on his third voyage, of reaching terrestrial Paradise.[19] Just as early modern travel literature that had sprung from and documented the events and atmosphere of great discoveries had also produced works of stay-at-home travelers and dreamers, all expressive of "another manner of traveling,"[20] so other works of travel that took form and atmosphere from early modern pilgrimage produced accounts of devout travel that utterly lacked grounding in actual experience of the road by their authors. Both branches of early modern travel, that of pilgrims and that of discoverers, show that travel itself was a genre vague in outline but also bursting at the seams. Utopianists produced a kind of travel literature, just as did desk-bound describers of sacred terrain. Both thought as travelers. The line between imaginative and actual was not absolute in the travel literatures of either discovery or pilgrimage.

A work treating of Palestine in just this fashion was published in Helmstadt in 1581. It enjoyed an immense popularity over two centuries. This was the *Itinerarium sacrae scripturae. Das ist: ein Reisebuch über die gantze heilige Schrift* of Heinrich Bünting, a Lutheran theologian of Hannover.

However much a work of the study, this book could be easily taken and read as a travel book.[21] Bünting, although he had never actually visited Palestine, produced an original work by recasting Sacred Scripture into a *Reissbuch*. Bünting's *Itinerarium* immediately became one of the great permanent texts of Europe, a modern classic that went through at least sixty editions in the years between 1581 and 1757. Moreover, it was printed in a roll call of languages: German, Swedish, Czech, Dutch, Latin, Danish, English.[22] Among the maps that Bünting included, the most famous was the cloverleaf configuration of the world which pictures Europe, Asia, and Africa as three petals joined at the center by Jerusalem which serves as hinge, clasp, and focus of the world. America (*Die Newe Welt*) just barely figures in all of this as a fragment in the ocean that is stuck within the lower left margins of the map (Figure 23). Indeed, this famous rendering of the world presents by visual means an argument that exactly counters the assumptions of the great European travel collections. In the cloverleaf, margin and center (as conceived by the likes of a Hakluyt or M. Thévenot)

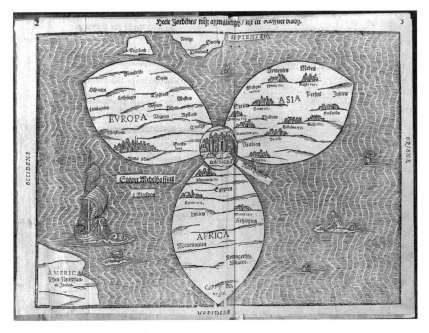

Figure 23. Heinrich Bünting, *Itinerarium Sacrae Scripturae* (Stockholm: Andrea Gutterwiss, 1595), cloverleaf map.

may be said to have exchanged places and the New World to have become small and out-of-the-way.

This travel literature of sorts (lacking only an author-as-actual-traveler) would continue throughout early modernity to hover about pilgrimage as much as it did other varieties of European travel writing. Olfert Dapper, a physician much interested in historico-geographical matters who published a series of lavishly illustrated books on the Near East, Far East, and Africa, never set foot in Palestine. Nevertheless, his *Naukeurige Beschryving van gansch Palestyn, of Heilige Lant* (Amsterdam, 1677) drew so deeply on writers of pilgrimages for information, and so vividly did his many engravings call to mind the historical and actual scene of Palestine, that it would be difficult for the reader not to take his presentation as that of a traveler.[23]

Writers such as Dapper in the 1670s back through Bünting in the previous century—or even back to John Mandeville and Petrarch[24] in the fourteenth century—constitute more than an intrusive aside to our story. Precisely because early modern pilgrimage as a form of travel had become overwhelmingly a *literary* phenomenon that flourished in a world furnished, unlike the world of its medieval roots, with very few actual pilgrimages, pilgrimage itself *as travel* is largely a matter of travel *literature*. These "fictional" pilgrimages are simply at yet one further remove from the (in the case of pilgrimage) constantly thinning actuality of the traveler on the road to and from the Levant. The scenes in Palestine as presented by a Dapper cannot be minimized as part of the literary experience of travel to the Levant as it existed in the minds of early modern stay-at-home Europeans. Long-distance devout travel to the Levant was, after all, largely experienced by early moderns as an experience of readers—a literary experience.

One of the practitioners of this imaginative travel, the Lutheran Bünting, points to another aspect of Levantine pilgrimage in its early modern manifestation, namely the place of Protestants. Indeed, their role as devout travelers to Jerusalem is nearly as important a story as the role of Catholics persisting in pilgrimage in the face of Protestant critiques. Both demonstrate adaptability, and thus vitality, in early modern pilgrimage. In any event, just as the *itineraria* of writers who themselves concocted travels from their armchairs are part of the larger literature of pilgrimage throughout the period, so also the *itineraria* of actual Protestant travelers to the Levant are part of a larger literature of pilgrimage that was predominantly Catholic in inspiration, tradition, and performance.

Mention of a Protestant component of early modern pilgrimage leads into interpretive thickets. We have witnessed Rauwolf acting very much the

devout traveler in Jerusalem, but also the Ingolstadt Jesuit Gretser deny-
ing Rauwolf any place in the grand tradition of Christian pilgrimage. It
is not simply a lengthened historical perspective allowing us to employ a
broader definition of pilgrimage that gets Rauwolf and other Protestant
travelers under the tent. There was, after all, the *contemporary* example of
Feyerabend, who included both Catholics and Protestants in his collection
of pilgrimages. Also, distinctions must be made between various sorts of
Protestants and various sorts of pilgrimage in early modernity. Edward
Gibbon, for example, offers one version in his reminiscences of a journey
in 1755 through Switzerland. Going from Zurich "on a pilgrimage not of
devotion but of curiosity," he arrived at the great Marian shrine of Einsiedeln, the very memory of which still kindled his ire years later. He even
went so far as to say that its devotions offered to him—and to Zwingli
two centuries earlier—"the most pressing argument for the reformation
of the Church."[25] Gibbon's antipathy towards Marian shrines was widely
shared among Protestants.[26] On the other hand, pilgrimage on the European continent was directed toward more than shrines devoted to Mary
and the saints. We have already seen that housing relics associated with
the life and passion of Christ was a principal aspect of many of the great
and small shrines of Europe. Calvin dismissed such piety—"it is an error
of the first order and by all accounts a root of evil that the world, instead
of seeking Jesus Christ in his word, in his sacraments, in his spiritual graces,
is accustomed to amusing itself with his robes, his shirts and his linen"—
but great numbers of Protestants as well as Catholics sought these shrines
out of devotion and in search of spiritual consolation.[27] In July 1640, more
than a century before Gibbon's fit of indignant reminiscence in Switzerland, holy relics that had long been preserved in Germany were brought
from Nuremberg and put on display prior to the sitting of the Imperial
assembly in Ratisbon the following month. A Catholic observer of the scene
singled out eight items for mention: the lance that pierced Christ's side, a
nail that had fastened Christ to the cross, a scrap of the table cloth from
the Last Supper, a fragment of Christ's swaddling clothes, a piece of the
true cross, three links from the chains that had bound Sts. Peter and Paul,
a piece of the tunic of John the Evangelist, and a fragment of the arm of
St. Anne. Thomas O'Corrain of Tipperary, who traveled widely in Europe
during the Thirty Years' War and who served as a chaplain in the Catholic
armies, witnessed this display of relics and was amazed that Luther's followers had preserved such relics from harm for such a long time, especially
since their "pseudo-propheta" had taught his followers utterly to hate "holy

bones of saints etc."[28] The *etcetera* is what pertains here. Lutherans are expected to be opposed in blanket fashion to relics—and yet "holy bones of
saints" are not, with the exception of the relic of St. Anne, what are involved
on this occasion. Instead, the focus is on relics that recall sacred history in
the Levant—precisely the items over which Protestants and Catholics often
shared rapt devotions.

The circle of pilgrims to Palestine (pilgrimage being understood, unlike
its reminted meaning in the Gibbonian lexicon, as *devout travel*) radiated
well beyond the Catholic milieu as the sixteenth century progressed. Joannes
Helffrich of Leipzig, whom Gretser will disapprovingly cite as one of the
Protestant travelers to the Holy Land, traveled to Jerusalem and throughout the Levant in 1565. First printed in Leipzig in 1578, Helffrich's *Kurtzer
und warhafftiger Bericht, von der Reis aus Venedig nach Hierusalem* went
through many printings between 1578 and 1584, all at Leipzig except for a
1580 Nuremberg edition. In 1584, the book was included in Feyerabend's
Reyssbuch. In 1589, there was one last separate edition of Helffrich's book in
Leipzig; and in 1609 it was included in the second edition of the *Reyssbuch*.[29]

Helffrich traveled towards the end of an era when actual pilgrimage
to Jerusalem could still be experienced as a somewhat popular undertaking. Departing Venice on 1 July 1565, his party was an international body
that amounted to the fairly robust number of fifty-two pilgrims of various
nationalities. If not the golden age of pilgrimage from Venice, neither was
Helffrich's sailing the dismal showing of numbers that would be reported
by pilgrims in the seventeenth and eighteenth centuries.[30] In terms of a
wider audience for his account of pilgrimage, Helffrich felt the same unease
that was also being expressed by Catholic pilgrims of the time. His preface makes the point that although there have been many accounts of travel
to the Holy Land, they do not agree on every point. In particular, he emphasizes that difference in the era of one's travels means differences of things
to be seen and reported upon. The Ottomans' seizure of Syria in 1516 is a
case in point. Local customs change; the composition of the inhabitant
population alters; monuments themselves, depending on the vicissitudes
of current history, become more or less visible, undergoing both destruction and restoration. It is such issues—that center more around possibilities of entertainment and readability and less around matters of theology or
spirituality or sacred archaeology—rather than any Catholic-Lutheran conflict over the meaning of pilgrimage, that occupy the Protestant Helffrich
at the very beginning of his work.[31] It seems that any pilgrim (Catholic or
Protestant) is aware, a century after Columbus, that this issue of novelty

is important (perhaps even more so to the Protestant who, unlike the Catholic, is not caught up with pilgrimage as a tradition energized by liturgy and ceremony and public devotions which, by their nature, are unashamedly repetitive).

In a general way, therefore, it makes sense to speak of the tradition in which Ceverio de Vera traveled and wrote in the 1590s, and which would continue for two centuries after Ceverio, as a fully modern (or early modern) tradition, however deep its roots in centuries past. That Protestants recognizably shared in important aspects of the experience of pilgrimage, that an imaginary component of travel writing attached itself to the pilgrimage tradition much as similarly concocted works attached themselves to the new travel literature of discovery, that pilgrims now wrote up their journeys to a relatively and generally unhurried schedule, and above all that the flourishing literature of pilgrimage was based on fewer and fewer actual journeys and that the literature was *printed*—such traits show that while there existed a fundamental continuity in the history of pilgrimage to the Holy Land stretching back at least to the likes of Adamnan's Arculf and the Bordeaux Pilgrim, there also existed clear evidence of pilgrimage to the Levant as specifically anchored and at home in the early modern scene.

*   *   *

Brighter light falls on Ceverio's 1596 book when it is read in the context of the sixteenth-century writing of pilgrimage which he immediately followed. Momentum, fueled by late fifteenth-century printers' resurrection of medieval pilgrimages and even more by their publication of contemporary pilgrimages, was sustained in the following century by further books of contemporary pilgrimage, many of which proved long-lived in print. There is the success, for example, of the French lawyer and Roman curial official, Barthélemy de Salignac, who seems to have been in Palestine around 1518 and who wrote an illustrated *Itinerarium terrae sanctae* that appeared in seven editions in various cities—Venice, Paris, Lyon (twice), Magdeburg (twice, in combination with Burchardus of Mount Sion's text), and Altenberg in Meissen (in a German translation)—across almost an entire century (1519–1612).[32]

The record of Salignac suggests that pilgrimage (and its audience) had survived the immediate turbulence of great discoveries and ecclesiastical reformations. Some thirty years after his journey, André Thevet made an extensive tour of the Levant during the years 1549–1552. After his return he served as Royal Cosmographer to Henry II (1547–1559) and later still (1575) wrote, in addition to other works, the celebrated *Cosmographie Universelle*. He described his journey to Palestine in an earlier book, *Cosmographie de Levant* (Lyon, 1554), which also appeared in 1556 in Antwerp as well as in Lyon, in 1575 in Paris, and in 1617 in Giessen (in a German translation).[33]

Thevet allots only a handful of pages to the Holy Land itself,[34] but makes clear from the start that pilgrimage, far from being just an episode, was the motive and frame of the entire journey, that "my chief purpose was to see the places where the news of our redemption had been preached for the first time by the Savior."[35] Thevet is devout and attentive and firmly within the Catholic tradition of pilgrimage.[36] He is, moreover, in the Holy Land as elsewhere in the Levant, alive to colorful contemporary detail. He not only tells the reader that "Turks, Moors, and Arabs" throw stones at the tomb of Absalom, but actually includes a visual illustration of the rock-throwing (Figure 24).[37] Thevet, nevertheless, devout observer as he is, does not make of his circuit of the holy places a deeply spiritual or interior experience that is rendered accessible to the reader.

What sets Thevet apart is his keen sense of what he was about as a traveler. His preliminaries define issues and problems.[38] Very much a professional writer of travels—a *cosmographe*—who had chosen the Levant and the Holy Land as subject matter, he was anxious to explain how his undertaking fit into a larger scheme of things. He was aware that he operated within a context, a tradition. For one thing, he knew that he traveled and wrote in the wake of the Reformation: "What is more, I heard many condemn pilgrimage as something invented by the devil and extremely harmful." He flicks this aside by answering that "the voyage to Jerusalem is a praiseworthy and honorable thing for Christians."[39]

It is not so much the act of pilgrimage, however, as the writing about pilgrimage, and about travel in the Levant generally, that occupies (and troubles) Thevet. The problem that he perceives here is a matter less easily dismissed than the polemical critique of Protestants. Thevet, in fact, is an early voice within the tradition of printed pilgrimage to express the travel writer's chagrin over the suffocating weight of a long tradition of travel to the Levant and to the Holy Land in particular. It is now almost eighty years after Tucher and others had begun to be printed. Was there anything left to be said by Thevet, anything new to discover, after so many ancients and moderns have gone before him to the same places? Thevet's answer—his justification of what he is doing—is that the world, that nature itself, is able to mix things up, to offer novelties and variations of things

destruit.Là fut menee l'anesse à notre Signeur pour faire son
entree en Ierusalem. Emaüs estoit vne ville loing de Ierusalem quatre lieues, laquelle les Rommains en signe de victoi-
re ont depuis appellee Nicopole, ou fut connu le Signeur
par deux de ses disciples, en la fraction du pain, apres sa re-
surreccion. Bethanie estoit vn lieu loing de Ierusalem deux
mille, prochain du mont Oliuet, fameux tant du recueil de
Simon le Lepreux, que de la sainte famille Marie Marthe,
Magdaleine, & le Lazare: lesquelz furent exposez en la Mer,
sans timons, ne voiles, & diuinement conduis en la Gaule,
pour y fonder la vraye Bethanie, c'estadire, la maison de po-
ureté, douleur, & mespris: ce qui est en ce Monde proposé,
aux vrais Fideles, & Chrestiés. Bethanie est pour le iourdhui

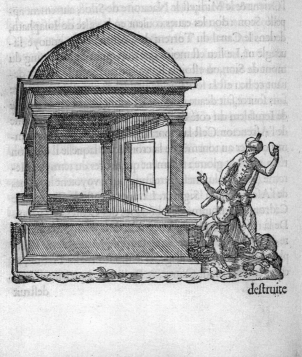

destruite

Figure 24. André Thevet, *Cosmographie de Levant* (Lyon: Ian de Tournes, et Guil.
Gazeau, 1554), p. 176.

described in the classic writings. Otherwise, what would Pliny, not to mention Ptolemy and all the others, have had to say in the wake of Strabo, who had "dealt so completely with geography"? Had men followed those who think everything described has been described once and for all, we would have deprived ourselves of a vast and instructive literature.[40]

Such was Thevet's general answer; but he seemed to recognize in pilgrimage an extreme and particular case of travel writers' woes. He allowed that many men, and especially the learned, described and had printed their journeys to Jerusalem. Still, he insisted, they were only human, they didn't remember to describe all that they had seen, they left *something* for others to write ("to collect the seeds after the harvesters"). Thevet, however, seemed less than happy with this formulation, and he added the observation that readers would find in his book not only pilgrimage in the Holy Land ("something which is common enough among Christians"), but visits to other regions of the Levant and treatments of a variety of subject matter (natural history, different customs, cities, landscapes, and so forth). Finally, he wrapped up the entire matter (travel to the Levant *and* to the Holy Land) by circling back: "After all, Socrates was improved by Plato, Plato by Aristotle, and Origen by St. Jerome."[41]

The expert and renowned traveler thus attempted to counter two threats to modern pilgrimage this early in its printed career—the obvious one of the Reformation's critique of pilgrimage itself, and also the fact that printing ("[they] have described and had printed") had rendered descriptions of pilgrimage all too usual literary fare. Something else, too, was at work. The issue was whether one was able "to discover (*inventer*) new things." Thevet, after all, lived in times of discovery, and his *Preface* opened by addressing the matter in terms that the age would have understood. We could be reading Grynaeus's introduction to the *Novus Orbis* of a quarter century earlier when Thevet described the optics of travel. Vision, he wrote, is the greatest of our senses. We establish and control and develop knowledge by actually confronting the sensible world, by traveling through the world. Books and theories are not enough. We must see for ourselves. We must compare "the almost living image" with "the half-dead letter." And we do this, we rub up against Creation, through travel. "How much God the Creator loves travelers (*Viateurs*)."[42]

Thevet's importance in the history of travel, apart from the travels themselves and his careful reports on what he had seen, is that he was among the early worriers over the role of repetitious devout travels in an age of unprecedented discoveries and widespread printing. He demonstrates that pilgrims were quite aware that they lived in a larger world that prized novelty (new worlds, new routes, exotica of every imagined description), and aware, too, that seeming repetition grew all the more obvious in a world of *printed* literature. (It had taken hardly three-quarters of a century for print to have this effect, to have in some sense glutted the market.) And on top of all this—but a less serious problem, to judge by the amount of attention Thevet paid to it—was the Protestant critique. Pilgrimage, more or less from Thevet to the eve of Chateaubriand, was to live under the shadow—or under the goad—of second thoughts that occupied the minds of pilgrim-writers simply because of the larger and profoundly altered world which they inhabited. Urgency attached itself to the question of why a devout traveler would bother to publish a narrative of his journey.

There is no reason to think that this fundamental worry dissipated. In 1584, thirty years after the first edition of Thevet's account, Sigismund Feyerabend's massive collection of pilgrimages in German was published in Frankfurt. However much this great work may have celebrated and shored up early modern pilgrimage, it may also have exacerbated the problem of *repetitio* which had already thirty years earlier troubled a thoughtful pilgrim such as Thevet (as well as the Protestant pilgrim Helffrich a few years after Thevet). Putting numerous pilgrimages side by side within the covers of a single volume would have made glaring the common ingredients in all of the texts—one reason that may have worked against collections of pilgrimages becoming a popular genre in the first place. That Feyerabend's example of collecting pilgrimages was not widely followed in subsequent centuries may be in part due to this nature of pilgrimage as a form of travel that crossed and recrossed the same lands for the same broad purposes.

Two years after Feyerabend's tour de force in Frankfurt, the Belgian Jean Zuallart traveled to and around Palestine. The following year (1587), his *Il devotissimo Viaggio di Gierusalemme* was printed in Rome. Three additional Roman editions over the next ten years were followed by a silence of ninety years that was suddenly broken by a new printing in Rome in 1687. In the meantime, a French translation was printed at Antwerp in 1604, 1608, and 1626. German and Latin translations were printed in Cologne in 1606. The Catholic Zuallart (like the Protestant Solomon Schweigger) was a new entry in the 1609 edition of Feyerabend's *Reyssbuch*.[43]

Zuallart considerably heightens the tone of Thevet (and other pilgrims in print) when he similarly looks over his shoulder at the work of previous pilgrims and at the critiques of contemporaries. He is acutely, indeed ferociously, aware of those who would discourage the printing and read-ing of pilgrimages. He draws a bead on the "insolent, wrong-headed, and ignorant opinions and objections" of those who hate pilgrimage to Jeru-salem and pilgrimages in general. Such people claim that pilgrimages are "superfluous," that there is no longer anything to see in Jerusalem, even that the city's location has changed since the time of sacred history. All of this is false, Zuallart counters, the work of the devil who strives to abol-ish virtue and true religion and our own salvation. And the devil accom-plishes this by "obscuring and making men forget the holy places where they have been redeemed and where he has been conquered." Zuallart is convinced that there is much more of great interest to be written about the Holy Land.[44] Nor does he answer hostility to pilgrimage in a merely vague and general manner. The devil is not the only one under indictment. Early on, he does something quite unusual by offering an entire chapter entitled "Against those who Hate this Holy Journey."[45] Although the act of pilgrimage spurs pilgrims to depths of devotion and virtue, Zuallart insists that there have always been enemies of pilgrimage in general and of pilgrimage to the Holy Land in particular. Such enemies are "heretics given over to the world and the flesh, men who condemn the ancient cus-toms and holy institutions of the Catholic Church" and who discourage devotion and contemplation ("pious thoughts") by discouraging pilgrim-age. Zuallart dusts off names—"the ancient Arians, Pelagians, Manicheans, and other heretics from the past"—and then turns to his own day, citing "the modern socalled Reformed," but also the *politiques libertins*. The latter have added their two cents: "namely, that such long pilgrimages only serve to squander the time and money of those who make them, and that this is particularly true of pilgrimage to Jerusalem." Zuallart, at the very time that actual pilgrimage to the Levant was waning, argued not only for the reading of pilgrimage literature, but for taking ship to the Holy Land, regardless of the Reformational and political arguments raised by others. His is a combative and comprehensive sizing up of the problematical, when not actively hostile, setting in which the pilgrim traveled.

Zuallart made pilgrimage a live issue of the day. While his rhetoric in defense of pilgrimage had edge and fire and targets, he had at hand, too, a less polemical method of advocating and reenergizing pilgrimage. Here, in Zuallart's use of engravings, which he claims to have been executed after his own original drawings on the spot, the echo is not of Thevet but of Breydenbach. Indeed, Thevet had included only one minor illustration of the Holy Land among his Levantine images, whereas Zuallart's text is filled with the visual. Even the comparison to Breydenbach is limited. With two exceptions—the pilgrim in the plaza of the Church of the Holy Sepulchre and pilgrims as a party disembarking at Jaffa—Breydenbach's subject matter is things, above all surfaces of things, as they were found in the Levant. Things that catch his eye (or Reuwich's under his supervison) are the unpopulated sacred sites, the various groups of residents dressed in costume, their alphabets, the region's fauna, and above all the look of cities along Breydenbach's route. Zuallart's images, on the other hand, are striking because so many of them portray (and identify) pilgrims in the act of their devout traveling about Palestine. Pilgrims become noticeable actors within scenes of the holy places. Pilgrimage itself becomes the subject matter of the book. Emphasis has shifted from the informational to the dramaturgical. Most striking is the image of pilgrims dropping to their knees and then prostrating themselves on the ground at first sight of the walls of Jerusalem (Figure 25).[46] But there are others—pilgrims heading inland from Jaffa; pilgrims traveling through the centre of Rama; pilgrims warily making their way past the House of the Good Thief while Arabs up to no good are visibly lurking about (Figures 26–28).[47]

Among numerous illustrated books of early modern pilgrimage, there were three general categories of material portrayed: (1) objects seen, the surface of things; (2) devotional scenes drawn from sacred history, church history, and liturgy; (3) the pilgrim in his pilgrimage. Breydenbach is probably the greatest of pilgrimage books—at least in the matter of the illustrated book—because he came to include all three categories of illustrated subject matter. The first category was his specialty; the second category came to the fore in other editions, especially the Spanish of 1498; and the third category crept in from the beginning in the two images mentioned above. The category of the devotional shows up early, not only in the Spanish Breydenbach, but on the title page of the 1519 edition of Brasca and throughout the 1525 edition of Salignac. In the case of Zuallart, the emphasis was clearly on the third category—itself the rarest of the three categories—but even with him it doesn't do to overstate the case. Consider that while Breydenbach, who usually did not show pilgrims in his woodcuts, did in fact place them in the plaza outside the Church of the Holy Sepulchre (Figure 5); Zuallart, on the other hand, despite his usual inclusion of pilgrims in his scenes, chose to leave quite devoid of pilgrims his own drawing of the plaza of the Church of the Holy Sepulchre (Figure 29).[48] (It is worth noting that variations in other depictions of this scene of the plaza help a modern reader to appreciate, by analogy, the variation

gnes: l'vn ayant, comme il semble de loing, la forme d'vn cocq, qui furent par nous laissez à main gauche proche du chemin qui vient de Silo, Ramatha, Sophin, autrement dit S. Samuel & autres lieux qui se voyent estant sur le hault de ladite montaigne : mais pource que ce lieu est proche de la Saincte Cité de Ierusalem, nous parlerons au chapitre suyuant de nostre arriuee en icelle.

Silo:
Ramatha
Sophin.

De nostre arriuee en Ierusalem.

CHAPITRE V.

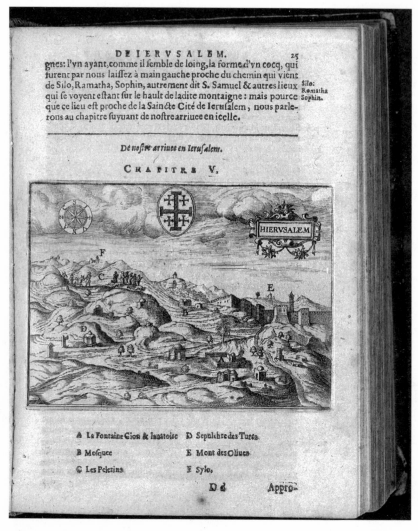

A La Fontaine Gion & lauatoise   D Sepulchre des Turcs.

B Mosquee   E Mont des Oliues.

C Les Pelerins   F Sylo.

D ô   Appro-

Figure 25. Jean Zuallart, *Le tresdevot voyage de Ierusalem* (En Anvers: Arnould s'Conincx, 1608), livre iii, p. 25.

LE TROISIESME LIVRE,

Contenant la defcription & narration de tous les lieux Sainéts
& remarquables, qui fe voyent & vifitent par les Pelerins,
tant en Ierufalem, Bethanie, Montana Iudee, qu'autres lieux
de la terre fainéte, commenceant à la Cité de Iaffa.

De Iaffa, CHAPITRE I.

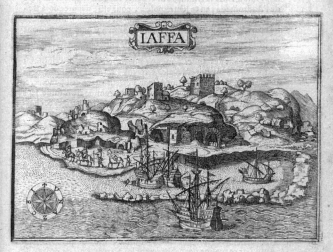

IAFFA

L A tref-antique & defolée Cité de Iaffa, ou Zaffa (felon la pro-
nonciation Venitienne) en la fainéte Efcriture appellée Ioppe, qui fignifie beauté, eft affife à foixante cinq degrez quarante
minutes de longitude, & trente deux degrez cinq minutes de lati-
tude, fur vne coline affez haulte, le long des riues de la mer medi-
terranee, furnommee de Phœnice, ou d'Egypte. Quant à fa fonda-

Iofué. 19.

Plin. lib. 5
c. 13. li. 9.
ca. 13.

A a   tion

Figure 26. Jean Zuallart, *Le tresdevot voyage de Ierusalem*, livre iii, p. 1.

homme seul dudit Soubassa pour nous seruir d'Escorte & Sauf-
conduit, par la grace de Dieu, nous arriuasmes sur l'apres-disner
en la ville de Ramma.

De la ville de Ramma, & ce que y fut veu & fait par nous.

CHAPITRE III.

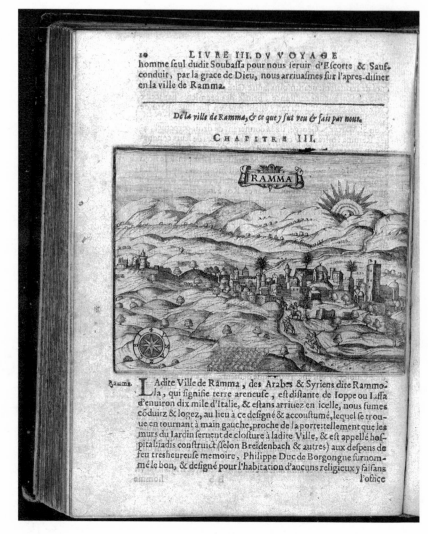

Ramma. L'Adite Ville de Ramma, des Arabes & Syriens dite Rammo-
la, qui signifie terre areneuse, est distante de Ioppe ou Iaffa
d'enuiron dix mile d'Italie, & estans arriuez en icelle, nous fumes
coduirz & logez, au lieu à ce designé & accoustumé, lequel se trou-
ue en tournant à main gauche, proche de la porte: tellement que les
murs du Iardin seruent de closture à ladite Ville, & est appellé hos-
pital: iadis construict (selon Breidenbach & autres) aux despens de
feu tresheureuse memoire, Philippe Duc de Borgongne surnom-
mé le bon, & designé pour l'habitation d'aucuns religieux y faisans
l'office

Figure 27. Jean Zuallart, _Le tresdevot voyage de Ierusalem_, livre iii, p. 10.

Des lieux que l'on voit entre Ramina & Ierusalem.

CHAPITRE IIII.

DOMVS BONI LATRONIS.

A Le Chasteau du bon larron. D Casal.

B Arabes de Cheual courans. E Les Pelerins cheminans

C Le puis S. Iob. F L'eglise de 7. freres Macha-
bees.

Estans ainsi accommodez, & montez sur noz asnes, nous par-
tasmes dudit Ráma le samedy penultiesme dudit mois d'Aoust
audit an 1586, deux ou trois heures deuant le iour, & apres auoir
cheminé vne bonne heure, nous trouuasmes (a l'endroit ou trauer-
se le grand chemin venant de Damas, & conduisant vers Gaza, &
de la

Figure 28. Jean Zuallart, *Le tresdevot voyage de Ierusalem*, livre iii, p. 15.

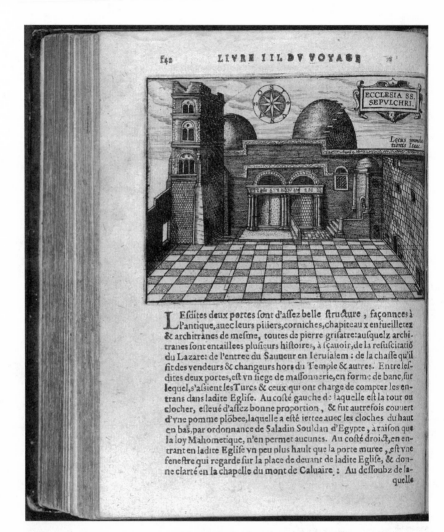

LEsdites deux portes sont d'assez belle structure, façonnées à l'antique, auec leurs piliers, corniches, chapiteaux enfueilletez & architranes de mesme, toutes de pierre grisatre: ausquelz architranes sont entaillees plusieurs histoires, à sçauoir, de la resuscitatiõ du Lazare: de l'entree du Sauueur en Ierusalem : de la chasse qu'il fit des vendeurs & changeurs hors du Temple & autres. Entre lesdites deux portes, est vn siege de massonnerie, en forme de banc, sur lequel, s'assient les Turcs & ceux qui ont charge de compter les entrans dans ladite Eglise. Au costé gauche de laquelle est la tour ou clocher, esleué d'assez bonne proportion, & fut autrefois couuert d'vne pomme plõbee, laquelle a esté iettee auec les cloches du haut en bas, par ordonnance de Saladin Souldan d'Egypte, à raison que la loy Mahometique, n'en permet aucunes. Au costé droict, en entrant en ladite Eglise vn peu plus haut que la porte muree, est vne fenestre qui regarde sur la place de deuant de ladite Eglise, & donne clarté en la chapelle du mont de Caluaire : Au dessoubz de laquelle

Figure 29. Jean Zuallart, *Le tresdevot voyage de Ierusalem*, livre iii, p. 142.

within sameness that exists in the literature of pilgrimage itself—that is, in the text as well as the illustrations.) (Figures 30–32)

Part of Zuallart's importance to the history of early modern pilgrimage is this visual interpretation that he gave to the act of pilgrimage itself. His images had immense influence. They showed up prominently in later works (seventeenth-century travels of Cotovicus and Castillo) and even where one would less expect them (the English Protestant Sandys's travel book).[49] The only other images that might have had comparable impact were those of Noè Bianchi, the influence being due to the remarkable run of editions in print, between 1566 and 1742, that marked his *Viaggio da Venezia al S. Sepolcro ed al Monte Sinai*. Bianchi's book was a kind of everyman's Breydenbach in much smaller format, and thus far more useful as a guidebook than Breydenbach's folio for the actual pilgrim in transit in the Levant. And to the stay-at-home, it would have conveyed more thoroughly and densely the experience of moving about the Holy Land, especially since the volume was as much picture book as text. Many of Bianchi's illustrations seem to have derived from Breydenbach (cityscapes, the plaza of the Church of the Holy Sepulchre, images of animals of the Levant), but there were many more of them (over a hundred and fifty) and their visual treatment was more telescopic (or microscopic) than Breydenbach's. Bianchi offers not only a view of the city of Venice, for example, but also a depiction of the feast of Corpus Christi when Venetian Senators processed with pilgrims about to embark for the Holy Land (Figure 33).[50] Bianchi's woodcuts—almost snapshots of things seen—give a largely contemporary feel to the scenes depicted.

In 1588, the year following Zuallart's appearance in print, Francisco Guerrero set out on pilgrimage to the Holy Land. He was seventy years of age. Behind him was a celebrated career as a composer of sacred music. Indeed, his musical renown had spread throughout Europe and the New World. This world-wide reputation of the choir master of the Cathedral of Seville helps to explain the extraordinary publishing history of his *El Viage de Hierusalem* (Valencia, 1590). The book of travel was published in principal cities of Iberia—Valencia, Seville, Alcalá de Henares, Granada, Valladolid, Madrid, and Lisbon—and across a span of over two hundred years. For a century, from 1590 to 1694, eleven printings are fairly regularly spaced. There then intervenes a ninety-year hiatus (1694–1785), interrupted only by the 1734 publication of a Portuguese translation in Lisbon. The Spanish text then suddenly revives, appearing (under a new title) in Valladolid (1785), Madrid (1790), and Madrid again in 1801.[51]

LA CHIESA DEL SANTO SEPOLCRO.

SEPVLCRO DE CHRISTO.

SOPRA QVESTA PIETRA CASCO' CHRISTO

Ome ſi entra per la porta della Chieſa per lo dritto circa
ſei paſſi in piana terra v'è una pietra di Porfido, di color
verde, laqual pietra, e longa otto paſſi, e più di tre dita, ed è larga
una ſpanna, e più. Sopra queſta pietra fu drizzato il Noſtro Si-
gnor con la S. Croce, e quivi fu unto con l'unguento, che ſi chia-
                                                                    ma

Figure 30. Noè Bianchi, *Viaggio da Venezia al S. Sepolcro*, p. 38.

In Guerrero, there is little entertaining of doubts whether a published pilgrimage could be of any value to readers. Guerrero's desire to go to Jerusalem was too long-standing and his actual experience of the Holy Land too intense for such worries. To be on Calvary, he writes, was so beneficial to body and soul "that we seemed to be in Paradise."[52] Guerrero strives to describe not so much the holy places as what it meant to be in the holy places. He expresses what he can and then retreats into inexpressibility.[53] What escapes words is not the site—not the foreignness, the *exoticisme* of things seen—but what happens at the site, at the *place*, in the interior reaches of the individual traveler. It is the spiritual intimacy and emotional experience of the devout traveler, not the newness or the strangeness of the place to which he has traveled, that poses the specifically writerly challenge to a pilgrim-rememberer such as Guerrero. Guerrero has leapt far ahead of the traveler's ambitions of a Thevet or Breydenbach, and certainly of a Mocquet. (On the other hand, his text has something in common with the pilgrim-centered illustrations of Zuallart).

The immense figure of the day, in terms of the impact of his 1588 pilgrimage in print, was Jacques de Villamont. *Les Voyages du Seigneur de*

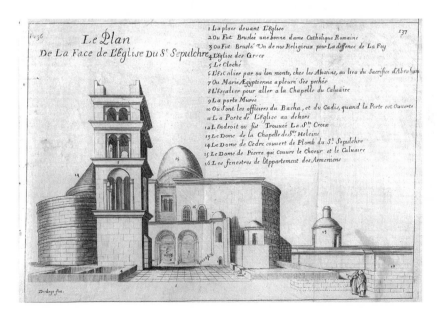

Figure 31. Jacques Florent Goujon, *Histoire et voyage de la Terre-Sainte* (Lyon: Pierre Compagnon et Roberrt Taillandier, 1671), between pp. 136 and 137.

Figure 32. Antoine Gonsales, *Hierusalemsche Reyse* (Antwerp: M. Cnobbaert, 1673), vol. 1, facing p. 464.

Questi sono li principali Senatori di Venezia, quali il giorno del Corpus Domini processionalmente accompagnano li Pellegrini, che vanno al Santissimo Sepolcro.

VENEZIA Nobile, e Ricca Città, della quale non ha un' altra seconda al Mondo, posta come dovete sapere nell' acqua,

A 4

Figure 33. Noè Bianchi, *Viaggio da Venezia al S. Sepolcro*, p. 7.

Villamont appeared at Paris in 1595 and was in continuous print for decades. When the book appeared for the sixth time in Lyon in 1667, it had undergone at least twenty-four editions in seventy-two years in five cities (Paris, Arras, Lyon, Rouen, Liège).[54] Villamont dominated, or at least overshadowed, the pilgrimage scene in France, although his book was never translated into another language or published outside France.

Villamont's volume of almost six hundred pages, closely printed and without illustrations, describes his journeys through Europe, voyage from Venice to the Holy Land (in a party of five laymen and two clerics), visits to the sites of the Holy Land, excursion to Egypt, and return to France. However touristical much of this may have seemed to the casual reader, pilgrimage was at the center of the account and permeated the entire text, even before Villamont's arrival at Jaffa. In Siena, he lovingly described "The superb church dedicated to the Queen of Heaven," and he paid much attention to the shrine at Loreto. He was attuned to relics that anticipated the Holy Land—a thorn from the Crown of Thorns preserved at Bologna, columns before the grand altar of St. John Lateran which had been brought from Jerusalem. A striking indication of how closely a pilgrim such as Villamont associated devout travels in Europe and in the Levant is reflected in his having the Pope bless sixty rosaries which he then took with him ("out of devotion") in order to touch them to the holy places in Jerusalem.[55]

Travel through Europe (all of the first book) was by way of preliminaries to his "main plan," which was to find a ship at Venice that would take him on his long-anticipated voyage to Jerusalem.[56] Villamont's foray into the Levant did, however, trouble him when he came to putting the experience down on printed paper. He was uneasy for vaguely the same reason that other pilgrims worried: there always lurked, just beyond publication, the hounds of criticism. Villamont does not precisely speak of fear on his part that everything he writes will be seen by the public to have been written to exhaustion by others before him; but he does express anxiety that his book will be disdained by "grand and rare minds and wise cosmographers and chorographers who are so prominent in today's France," the very ones who might well have been expected to raise the question of whether yet another travel account to the Middle East was called for. Villamont, however, sidesteps the issue by claiming to have another audience in mind and to "have written this book solely for those who are curious to know that which is beautiful and remarkable in the Holy Land, where the feet of Our Lord have stood, and where his Holy Sepulchre is adored by all, following the words of the Prophet Isaiah.[57] In describing his departure from Venice, he adds something more to the definition of his venture. He traveled across the Mediterranean, he tells the reader, because he had long desired to go on pilgrimage. He is *not* going, however, "because of the obligation of a vow or out of a desire for empty glory, but only because of the singular desire and affection that I had to visit the holy place where the Savior of our souls shed his precious blood to ransom all humanity."[58] Villamont makes the case for pilgrimage as a deeply personal act (and therefore one susceptible to a personal rendering of the experience that would not simply be the same old story told one more time) and, what is more, for pilgrimage as a peculiarly *modern* variety of travel that has jettisoned medievality (pilgrimage as Crusade, pilgrimage as winning of indulgences and fulfillment of pledges) in favor of pilgrimage animated by pure devotion. Guerrero's influence—even Zuallart's—can be spied in Villamont.

*   *   *

In the light of such immediate predecessors, Juan Ceverio de Vera's account appears all the more striking. The same year that Villamont's book first appeared in print (1595), Ceverio was on pilgrimage in the Levant. The publication the next year of his own book suggested a shifting of gears within the genre. Pilgrimage, to be sure, had not been just one thing up to this point. Guerrero was unusual in his depth of response to the holy places. Zuallart's pictures, if not his rhetoric, were all but unprecedented. But there was, and would continue to be, a cloud of defensiveness and second thoughts about written pilgrimage on the part of early modern pilgrims themselves, and it was this diffidence that was gloriously absent in Ceverio. His book's swiftness of publication, while not absolutely unprecedented at this period, recalls printed pilgrimages from an earlier time, before accounts of discoverers and explorers had replaced them as the sort of travelers' news that couldn't wait. One reason for Ceverio's account reaching the public so quickly may have been its show-stopping Columbian coloration—something surprising in itself since the din of discovery is utterly absent from most other pilgrimages (except as an implied threat to what the writer of pilgrimages was about and except for the eccentric precedent of Feyerabend).[59] Ceverio, however, connects the two forms of travel from the very beginning. This is his book's greatest achievement. "That most courageous Columbus" appears in the *Prologo del Autor al Lector*,[60] where Ceverio sets before the reader "discovery of the New World" and "travel to the Holy Land" as comparable examples of long-distance and adventurous travel. One is driven by "the greed for visible gold," the other by the desire "to enrich one's soul with the wonderfully rich minerals of the holy places." The two forms of travel shared, too, the fear that each inspired in the minds of those contemplating either adventure. In the early days of the great discoveries, Ceverio observes, getting across, and particularly *returning* across, "the wide and unknown Ocean sea" cooled the ardor of potential sailors. But fear abated as the sea-lanes became well-known. In Spain, Ceverio argues, pilgrimage remains in the same condition as discovery had been in the wake of Columbus. Although he claims that two hundred pilgrims go to Jerusalem every year along a reliable route ("much traveled and safe"), he also asserts that to treat of Jerusalem among Spaniards is to speak "of another world". If someone actually returns to Spain from the Levant, "it is thought of as a miracle." Ceverio's great hope is that his "copious journey" will show that the journey is safe and will cause "many Spanish to go and give thanks in the name of their provinces to the Majesty of God at the Holy Sepulchre of his Son." In a scarcely opaque reference to the Reformation, this getting to Jerusalem on the part of Spaniards is crucially tied up, in Ceverio's mind, with their ability to "defend Catholic Spain from the contagious infirmities of the soul which besiege it."

But it was Columbus rather than Calvin who occupied Ceverio's thoughts in the *Prologo*. The connection that Ceverio drew between discoverers on the high seas and pilgrims crossing the Mediterranean arose not only from the fact that each kind of travel was in pursuit of a contrasting variety of wealth or even the fact that both journeys were heroic adventures that could not but inspire trepidation at first reckoning. Something more positive was at work. Ceverio concluded his preliminaries by pointing out that both the Indies and the Levant are seats of marvels and wonders: "Moreover, I wished, at the request of friends, to write down some of the wonders (*maravillas*) both of the provinces of the Levant as well as of the West Indies, because by coming to the notice of men they give glory to the Lord." What held all this together was that when Ceverio was pondering one kind of voyage, he was also pondering the other. The two together constituted the complete reality of the European heroically abroad. We are in the presence of a notable synthesis.

That all of this was laid out in the *Prologo* is remarkable enough, and even more so that comments on the New World were carefully woven into the book proper, the primary subject matter of which was the sacred Levant. The *Viage de la Tierra Santa*, to be sure, in both structure and content remains a book of pilgrimage; but to its essential narrative has been added

a significant alloy of what one might call complementary or mutually en-
lightening *maravillas*. Things underfoot in the Levant spark memories of
other things encountered on the far side of the world. For example, when
Ceverio is describing the road from Jerusalem to Bethlehem, he sketches
the habits and character of "Moorish Arabs" whom he characterizes as
"gallant" and "courageous." Coming out of hills and deserts, these nomads
trouble the local population and are the Turk's "principal enemy." Ceverio
devotes about half a page to the Arabs and then resorts to a comparison
in hopes of clarifying his portrait of these odd folks: "Similar to these
predatory Arabs are those daring Indians (called Putimaes), since they also
support themselves by robbery and have destroyed many provinces of the
Indies and even some cities of the Spanish."[61] Almost three full pages then
follow which deal entirely with these "powerful Indians," these "inhuman
Indians" whose most telling cultural features are their general habits of
ferocity and their specific trait of cannibalism.[62] The dropped thread of the
Arabs turns out never to be picked up again by Ceverio. Elsewhere, too,
in the text, the Levant leads to the Indies. Conversation with a Greek bishop
concerning peculiarities of Egypt prompts Ceverio to describe what he
has seen of the "strange things of Peru."[63] When he meets "Moorish priests"
in Tripoli, he is moved to state and elaborate a contrast ("Quite different
from the Moorish holy men are the Indian holy men of the West").[64] Anything (not directly related to the holy sites themselves) in the Levant is capable of bringing to Ceverio's mind things he has seen in the New World.[65]

Inclusion of material on the Indies was Ceverio's way of updating
pilgrimage to the Levant. A simple equation is in play: stories about the
Holy Land are like stories about Peru, and vice versa. Arabs and Indians,
or crocodiles and caimans, are understood to be mutually elucidative. As
the *Prologo* made clear, Ceverio's primary ambition was practical rather
than literary. He wished to revive the *practice* of long-distance pilgrimage.
Such a desire stands in high relief because pilgrimage to the eastern Mediterranean as an actual mode of travel was in decline at this very time. Not
only had Europeans been mightily distracted by great voyages of discovery
and great movements of Reformation, both phenomena being accompanied and reenforced by powerful literatures. Geopolitical realities (the
power of the Ottomans, the decline of Venice) had also rendered travel to
the Levant trickier and more dangerous than at any time since the Crusades. An afterglow of the European victory at Lepanto of 1571 did endure
a quarter century after the event—sufficiently so for "the naval battle" to
crop up more than once in Ceverio's narrative[66]—but as far as European

pilgrimage was concerned, 1571 had proved an enduringly disastrous year. The Ottoman capture of Venetian Cyprus had ended any hope of reviving Venetian-directed pilgrimage on any scale at all comparable to its heyday a century or two earlier.

Ceverio wanted Spaniards to follow him to Jerusalem—beyond exhortations in the *Prologo*, he appended at the end an *Itinerario* to assist future travelers[67]—but Ceverio's own text shows that prospects for a revived pilgrimage were not bright. Unable even at the papal court to find others to join him in the journey to Jerusalem, he had set out alone. Nor was there apparently anyone at court to advise him that he was starting out at the wrong time of year for a pilgrimage—something that dawned on him when he found himself deep in snow in the Apennines.[68] Once in Venice, he joined an international group of seventeen pilgrims that included only two other Spaniards.[69]

The Feast of Corpus Christi was the traditional day of departure for the Holy Land, but the grand tradition, except for observance of the day itself, had grown more than a bit tattered. Ceverio explains that the custom had once been for the Republic of Venice to provide and provision a galley for pilgrims, to give them twenty days for sight-seeing once they had landed at Jaffa, and then to return them safely to Venice. Moreover, in the procession of the Blessed Sacrament on the feast day, each senator would take a pilgrim by the right hand. All this had disappeared except for the honored place still reserved for pilgrims in the procession (Figure 33). But even this Ceverio had forgone in order to gain a better view of the festivities.[70]

Such threadbare realities make it difficult to credit Ceverio's overall optimism. Where had he come up with the number of two hundred annual pilgrims to Jerusalem, when his 1595 party, leaving the principal port of departure on the traditional day of departure for pilgrimages, only amounted to seventeen individuals? But even Ceverio, wish though he might for a revival of Spanish pilgrims sailing to Jerusalem, does seem to have realized that pilgrimage's future would be largely literary. He granted that there was an audience of the devout who would need to use his book as a substitute for travel; and for this reason transcriptions of Latin hymns and prayers used at the holy places became a major feature of his text.[71] Printed pilgrimage was destined to provide a *literary experience* for devout stay-at-homes rather than to serve as a practical vade mecum. Ceverio himself must have been keenly aware of the force and importance of pilgrimage as a literature. A book of pilgrimage had, after all, set *him* on the way to Jaffa.

So might his book prove powerful enough at least to turn his reader's thoughts in the direction of the holy places.

Ceverio's own book testifies to the endurance and adaptability, and therefore the vital currency, of early modern pilgrimage, both as a practice of the few but more especially as a literature for the many. A century after the inauguration of the great discoveries and in an Iberia that continued to be the nerve center of overseas exploration and *imperium*, Ceverio brought discovery and pilgrimage into a relationship of association that involved both contrast (pursuits of different sorts of wealth) and comparison (adventures that inspired trepidation, occasions that manifested *maravillas*). That the literature of pilgrimage flourished at century's end and did so in the Iberia of the conquistadores, and partly by incorporating the legacy of Columbus—all of this suggests the cultural bedrock upon which early modern pilgrimage rested. It was difficult to imagine pilgrimage to the Levant ever being washed utterly away or ever purged from the European traveler's consciousness. It was not only that pilgrimage to the East offered the benefit of "true spiritual riches."[72] Pilgrimages to Jerusalem lasted because they were explanatory narratives that recalled Europe's profoundest origins and that continued to hold the attention because they described "the extremely rich wealth of the holy places bathed in the most precious blood of the eternal Son of God."[73]

Ceverio closes out the first century of early modern pilgrimage to Jerusalem. Unlike predecessors and a long line of successors in the studied and studious craft of writing pilgrimages, Ceverio seems not to have been oppressed by the weight of literary inheritance nor to have felt driven to write with an eye on what previous writers had published. Ceverio was wrapped up in executing his own novel scheme—an intellectual innovation, really—of incorporating information and anecdotes from the New World as an explanatory ray of light playing over data derived from the very oldest world. This was not a common method in the works of predecessors. Nor was Ceverio himself steeped to surfeit in the literature of earlier pilgrimage. A single book of pilgrimage had caught him unawares and put him on the road to Venice. Ceverio did not cast himself as one who had longed for the journey and who had meticulously read all that he could get his hands on (a latter-day imitator of Felix Fabri and countless others or a harbinger of Chateaubriand). All that he had done by way of prelude—which could hardly be called preparation—was to encounter a single volume at the papal court when he was at a low point and thinking of returning to Iberia and searching for a book to read in the meantime to lift him out of the doldrums.

Ceverio shows the worth of an amateur within a genre that was not only ancient but also highly referential and doubt-ridden precisely because of the many references internal to the genre made by its typical practitioners. In his finished work, the newcomer to pilgrimage demonstrated the remarkable vitality, but also the undeniable weakness, of the early modern pilgrimage he championed. On the one hand, his book shows the regenerative and evolutionary possibilities of the genre as a literature, its ability to absorb and shape novelties of the age; on the other, even the firmest intentions for writing the book could not thwart the reality that actual pilgrims—in throngs, in boatloads—were largely a matter of the past.

*   *   *

As early modern pilgrimage became a matter more of intellectual and literary history and less of the history of actual movement of persons from Europe to Jaffa, great historical markers that need to be observed are not dates of travels themselves nearly as much as dates of editions and reprints and translations which point to the entry of the idea and *reported* practice of pilgrimage into the European consciousness.

Ceverio's book, for example, appeared in print in Pamplona as late as 1613, one among many printed titles that kept sixteenth-century pilgrimage actively on the scene well into the seventeenth century (and even the eighteenth). The publication of Breydenbach in Cracow in 1610 argues even for an ongoing *fifteenth*-century legacy of pilgrimage. The impressive evidence, however, is of the robust continuation of sixteenth-century printed texts of pilgrimage into the next century and beyond. Noè Bianchi's richly illustrated account of his 1527 pilgrimage that was first printed in 1566 offers perhaps the best example, since the book was still being printed as late as 1742. Its many illustrated editions included four between 1638 and 1697. Perhaps the greatest afterlife of a pilgrimage, simply in terms of the languages in which it appeared, is the case of Zuallart's book of 1587, which only began to be turned into other languages (French, German, Latin) in the next century.

Beyond the weight (and momentum) of inheritance, however, seventeenth-century pilgrimage possessed literary life of its own. New titles came into print, stayed in print, or returned to print across decades. One can argue—and agree with the darkly reiterated worries of pilgrims themselves!—that journeying to and around the holy places was a very old story and much of the data surrounding such overseas experience had been worked and reworked across centuries. The truth of the matter, however, is that many of the printed pilgrimages were centered on the life of the times. Their authors responded to issues and problems encountered either along the way or back in Europe as the accounts were being composed. An item on many pilgrims' agenda was an explicit vindication of pilgrimage *as travel*. Just as Ceverio de Vera at end of last century had brought Levantine pilgrimage into association with New-World discoveries in very explicit fashion—making their relationship strikingly antiphonal—so at the beginning of the seventeenth century there appeared in print the *Hierosolymitana Peregrinatio* (Brunsberg, 1601) of the Polish prince, Nicholas Christoph Radziwill, a work that took equally effective cognizance of pilgrimage's place in the contemporary world. What turned out to be of moment here, however, was not the milieu of discovery, but the practical bearing of Reformation on the nature and future of pilgrimage. There was also a broader recognition, on the part of Radziwill's translator, that the age ("our corrupt times") was unfriendly to pious travel. He is aware, in a faint echo of Ceverio de Vera's theme, that the great discoveries figure in all of this. Travelers such as Radziwill who are steeped in the tradition of pilgrimage, he remarks somewhat obliquely, were not so much disdainful of novelties in making these heroic journeys to the Levant as they were eager to gain spiritual wealth.[74] The point was thus made, without being pressed, that pilgrimage remained an heroic mode of travel in the age of discovery. The critical issue for the Catholic pilgrim, however, at least as presented in the prefatory pages of the *Hierosolymitana Peregrinatio*, was the challenge of the Reformation.

Radziwill's actual pilgrimage had taken place in 1583—two years prior to Ceverio's—but the first printed form of his letters home was this translation into Latin from the Polish original that had survived in manuscripts through the intervening eighteen years. The Latin version of 1601 reappeared in print the following year and in an improved and expanded edition in Antwerp in 1614. There was also a Latin imprint as late as 1753 in Jaurini. A German edition appeared in Mainz in 1603 and was included six years later in the second edition of Feyerabend's *Reyssbuch*. By 1607, a Polish edition had appeared in Cracow, and a Russian version would be printed at St. Petersburg in 1787.[75]

Radziwill's pilgrimage—by the spread of imprints over more than a century and a half, by the range of translations, and by the trouble taken to render a Central European vernacular manuscript into Western tongues (and then, eventually, into Russian)—underscores that Levantine pilgrimage was a living subject matter with a wide radius of circulation. Much the same is suggested by the elaborate care that was taken in the production of the Plantin edition of 1614. A title page of nascent Baroque effusiveness epitomizes the pilgrim's letters to follow. On one side of the title block is a praying figure under whose niche is inscribed: *Devotion Rejoices in God*. On the other side, a figure bearing a cross and with a lamb at her feet stands above the words: *Patience Rejoices in Difficulties*. Above both, a medallion of the Jerusalem cross is suspended from the hands of two angels. And above the medallion and between the angels, an oval surrounds the text of Psalm 131 (132): *We Entered into His Tabernacle: We have Prayed in the Place where his Feet Stood*. This grandly architected page captures the nub of pilgrimage: the prayerfulness of the complete act, the effort and endurance of the journey, and its specific and overriding purpose: *adoravimus in loco*.

The contemporary topicality of Radziwill's *Peregrinatio* arises from the Latin translator's blunt preface, *To the Christian Reader*. Here issues raised by the Reformation are taken up, but under the specific rubric of pilgrimage. Protestants are the heretics of the day who wage war on good works such as pilgrimages, "ranting on with full mouths about 'faith alone' (*sola fide*)."[76] The Latin translator who wrote these words was Thomas Treter, a native of Posnan and priest of Varma as well as a one-time member of the Roman household of the great Polish humanist and leading figure of the Council of Trent, Cardinal Stanislaus Hosius (1505–1579). Indeed, Treter had served as the cardinal's secretary and was himself a considerable practitioner of Renaissance humanism, being the author of the *Theatrum virtutum Divi Stanislai Hosii*, an illustrated biography of his illustrious patron, as well as the first compiler of an index to Horace.[77] That Radziwill's letters attracted such an illustrious editor is yet one more index to the importance of pilgrimage as an early modern subject matter.

Treter's preface to the reader assertively protected pilgrimage in a world where many Reformers despised the very idea of such travel.[78] Treter, indeed, wades into the fray as something of a theoretician in the matter.[79] Under his Catholic scrutiny, pilgrimage evolves in ways that are best explained by the pressure of Reformation critiques to which he was responding. For one thing, Treter locates pilgrimages in general, and pilgrimage to the Holy Land in particular, within a long historical tradition reaching back to classical antiquity. In doing so, he is emphatically conscious of pilgrimage as a form of *travel*. Unlike Protestants such as the Lutheran Menz, who saw pilgrimage as an interruption of an antique travel that he hoped to revive by quashing pilgrimage, Treter interpreted Seneca visiting the villa of Scipio Africanus or Cicero touring Athens in exactly the same light as Christians touring sacred places in Palestine. Travel, for both sensitive pagan and devout Catholic, is essentially a contemplative act that dwells on the places themselves (*ipsa loca*). Such revered places are as suggestive and revealing as the words and deeds (*dicta et facta*) of the illustrious departed.[80] Treter's emphasis on the pilgrim as a pedigreed and recognizable sort of traveler was critical in an era when typical travelers might easily be considered very different sorts of figures, especially to those whose reading material on faraway places was limited to the great collections of travels.

More was at stake, however, than Catholic pilgrims' claim to a traveler's identity on the contemporary scene. Treter's acts of editing, translation, and publication were urgent responses to pilgrimage's contemporary vulnerability. As a species of devout literature in embattled times, pilgrimage had to be protected from those who would alter and corrupt its content— that is, would change it into something other than pilgrimage. Treter's turning Radziwill's letters into Latin was an attempt to protect the text on its way from manuscript to print. Treter viewed pilgrimages, both to holy shrines in Europe and to the Holy Land itself, as very much Catholic enterprises with which the Reformed ("the heretics of our era"), whom he accuses of "blindness and madness," are entirely out of sympathy. He saw their willful and tendentious corruption of texts as a trend of the times. As translator of Radziwill, he reenforces the Catholic nature of one specific pilgrimage. Although taking immense national pride that Poles now have a pilgrim of their own to tell them of the Holy Land in their own language, he sees the appropriateness of turning this work written by a champion of the Catholic faith into the "Catholic—I mean to say the Latin and Roman—language." He assures the reader that he has not departed a bit from Radziwill's meaning, though it has not been a question of rendering the Polish text word for word into the Latin because of the differences of the two languages (the sense of the Latin being "clearer"). Textual rather than linguistic problems, however, are what give Treter's work its urgency. In his role as editor, he sees a lurking danger (*periculum imminere*) in the Polish manuscripts that are scattered about in private hands. He worries about the carelessness (*incuria*) of scribes, but also about the tricks (*machinationibus*) of the evil enemies of Christian belief and of Christian works of piety. Radziwill's letters from the road, he feared, were ripe for alteration and corruption. Thus he secures the best possible text of the letters and publishes a Latin text that can serve as the standard of reference in reading even the Polish original.[81]

Treter, under pressure of Reformation (and broader early modern) realities, made an attempt—rarely so explicity stated in Catholic pilgrimages—to relate actual *peregrinatio* to life after the road when the pilgrim was back in Europe. Life, or *peregrinatio* in a broader sense, continued. Treter claimed that Seneca's literary works, which had aimed at reform of his depraved age, were actually traceable to his pleasurable (but also inspiring) visit to Scipio's haunts. Just so, Radziwill once a pilgrim would always be a pilgrim—"having successfully returned to his own region, he nevertheless thought himself still to be a pilgrim (*peregrinum*) on earth." Treter traces not only Radziwill's virtues, but also the endowed manifestations of those virtues that are visible in society ("churches, colleges, monasteries, inns erected by him"), back to the inspiration won and fortified by his pilgrimage to Jerusalem.[82] Through Treter's explication of Radziwill's journey, pilgrimage became many things: an actual long-distance journey out of society; a continuing sign, upon return, of the pilgrim's spiritual alienation from terrestrial society; *and* a motive force for rejuvenating, reconstructing, and redefining that very same society. Pilgrimage thus appears as a cultural activity and disposition that inheres in, and not merely attaches itself to, early modern society. In this, Radziwill's journey of departure and return resembles other kinds of travel of the times, which were also explicitly thought to justify themselves by meliorative ramifications that entered the traveler's society-at-large upon journey's end.

Although Radziwill's volume was free of illustrations (except for the engraved title page), illustrations figured prominently in many seventeenth-century books of pilgrimage. The general legacy of Breydenbach was great and enduring. It showed up in the much illustrated and much printed guide book composed by Bianchi in the later sixteenth century, in Zuallart's eye-witnessed drawings, and in the engraved images of cities of the Mediterranean that appeared in later editions of Henri de Beauvau's account of Levantine pilgrimage. Bernardino Amico's *Trattato delle Piante et Imagini dei Sacri Edificii di Terra Santa* (Rome, 1609), however, reminds us of Breydenbach, not because of style of depiction or subject matter (Amico, though similar to Breydenbach in sticking to the surface of things, was nevertheless utterly uninterested in portraying either the route between Europe and Palestine or the sociological-ethnic realities on the ground in the Palestine of his day), but because the drawings that Amico did make were products of his own detailed and laborious eyewitnessing and measuring, and also because Amico's *Trattato*, every bit as much as Breydenbach's *Peregrinatio*, was not merely an illustrated travel book, but an example of a book as a grand *production*. In this, the two share a niche all to themselves among early modern pilgrims. In Amico's case, his handiwork demonstrates the adaptability of pilgrimage, its ability to be transformed into something fully of the modern age. Breydenbach had shown the possibilities of pilgrimage as a printed book; Amico showed its possibilities as a certain kind of printed book—a cultural artifact that aestheticized its sacred subject matter. What Amico did, by displaying and concentrating on the architectural and monumental remains of Palestine, was to make the Holy Land into a truly and specifically Baroque subject matter. The idiom of the day was shot through with the architectural.[83] More, perhaps, than ever before, any place (a neighborhood, a square, a city, a province, an entire nation) took shape in a European reader's mind through the delineation of its historical and contemporary architecture. The urban Baroque, in Rome, Paris, London, Naples, and almost everywhere else, issued in grand and ornate constructions of every sort—not merely cathedrals, but churches, chapels, palaces, gardens, fountains, fortifications, convents, civic halls, and on and on. The world came across as a place of design and structure and decoration, an intricately playfully filled-in void. This was not only the reality, but the depicted and conveyed reality, of Europe. When from a distance one learned of, and thought about, Rome, the controlling images were of its architected spaces. One pored over descriptions and depictions of both modern and historical structures. Amico reinterpreted the Holy Land in exactly this contemporary idiom. It was this architectural aura and seal that Amico gave to the Holy Land through his book of sections and plans and drawings. He labored over Jerusalem and Bethlehem in order to fashion them, for the reader, into a distant object of refined longing (Figure 34). He gave to the Holy Land an elegant façade by treating it as a locus of elegant façades (and interiors)—and this despite the poverty of materials with which he had to work, since there was precious little of contemporary vintage to be noticed in Palestine, and even the great historic sites (with the exception of the Church of the Holy Sepulchre and the Church of the Nativity) were humble spots, when not merely rubble with surmised historical associations.

Amico the writer, artist, draftsman, and impressario—much like Breydenbach, who had been the principal author of his own tome—attracted others into his project, both as contributors (Antonio Tempesta and Jacques Callot as engravers) and as patrons (Philip III, the dedicatee of the first edition, and Cosimo II da Medici, to whom the second edition, which had been reengraved at his expense, was dedicated). Amico's book, which, in addition to his verbal descriptions, contained grand and precise architectural plans of buildings, together with interior and exterior views and sections (and panoramas of historical and contemporary Jerusalem), was utterly unlike Breydenbach's work in appearance.[84] For one thing, their circumstances were different. Amico, unlike Breydenbach and Reuwich, was not simply piously passing through the region. In residence as a member of the Franciscan Custody during the years 1593–1597, he held important Custodial posts in both Jerusalem and Bethlehem. Nevertheless, the two works, in their combination of text and illustrations, are the great towering monuments of book production under the category of pilgrimage. There was nothing like Breydenbach until Amico, and nothing comparable to either after Amico. This is true despite the fact that the printed literature of pilgrimage in the early modern centuries was, in the generality, an amply illustrated body of texts. At any rate, the 1609 edition was reissued in Rome in 1612. And eight years later the redone and expanded engravings (Tempesta's being replaced by those of the great, if as yet incompletely renowned, Callot) appeared in a new edition of the book in 1620 in Rome and Florence.[85]

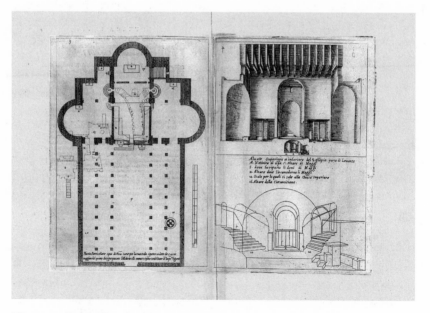

Figure 34. Bernardino Amico, *Trattato delle piante & immagini de sacri edifizi di Terra Santa* (Firenza: P. Cecconcelli, 1620), between pp. 8 and 9.

A year or two later, however, after he had left Rome where he had been working and studying, Jacques Callot (1592–1635) produced a very different set of images (which we have already had occasion to note) depicting a series of down-and-out Europeans who are usually characterized as a gallery of beggars.[86] Among these etched unfortunates were two figures whom Callot clearly outfitted as pilgrims (Figure 14).[87] In fact, as another plate in the series strongly indicates, *all* of these miserable characters were pilgrims. Callot presents us with the grittier reality, the darker side, of making one's way, devout or otherwise, to a shrine in Europe. While the work of 1620, executed at Rome under the favoring eye of the Medici, had suggested the European mind in a lofty, learned, curial state as it devoutly contemplated distant, holy, monumental Jerusalem, the work of 1622–23 documented a world much nearer to home and nearer to the ground—a sordid theater of the lay and the dispossessed that shows pilgrimage as an almost disreputable and certainly inelegant reality on the home scene. Nor was this second work merely expressive of Callot's indulging his love of the bizarre and grotesque. Nor did it simply mirror the grim decades of the Thirty Years' War. Over a century and a half later, pilgrimage within Europe would still offer the illustrator images of the desperate, the maimed, the impoverished (Figure 35).[88]

To peruse Amico—and by and large, most of the literature of early modern pilgrimage to Jerusalem—exposed readers to a gentler and more elevated and more privileged world of devout travel. This is not to say that the rare *act* of going across the sea (or, even more rarely, over land through the Balkans and Anatolia) to Jerusalem was not often a difficult experience filled with desperate risk. Ignatius of Loyola, after all, whatever his comfortable family and illustrious future, chose to be a lone down-and-outer and one not so unlike Callot's beggarly folk at the actual time of his journey across Europe to Palestine.[89] Nevertheless, little of this got into most depictions in the *literature* of pilgrimage to Palestine. It tells a lot, for example, that a visual rendering of Ignatius-as-pilgrim—part of a larger series of pictures illustrating the life of Ignatius, published in 1609 on the occasion of his beatification and reissued in 1622 at the time of his canonization—portrayed him in the garb of stylized and idealized sanctity rather than as a tattered, much less a disreputable-seeming, figure of the road. Rubens rather than Callot was given this assignment (Figure 36).[90] Or there is the example of Jean Thévenot, whose portrait accompanying his text showed him in Jerusalem as a finely clad figure having his feet washed by the resident Franciscans in thoroughly ceremonious fashion and in the comfort

A Pilgrim on his way to Monserrat, an Old Soldier.

Figure 35. Philip Thicknesse, *A Year's journey through France, and part of Spain*, 2 vols., 3rd ed. (London: W. Brown, 1789), vol. 1, frontispiece.

Figure 36. Peter Paul Rubens, *Vita beati P. Ignatii Loiolae Societatis Iesu fundatoris* (Rome: s.n., 1622), plate 27.

of the Convent of Holy Savior in Jerusalem (Figure 37).[91] Europeans'
pilgrimages to the Holy Land expressed a devout, learned, and literary
curiosity. They reported on a grand, even an heroic, experience of the literate traveler. Such a pilgrim was portrayed as pious traveler and cosmopolitan ascetic. The experience of Levantine travel extracted the pilgrim
from home, from Europe. It was left to pilgrimages closer to home—
which took in all of society, including its lowest rungs and its most disastrous histories (such as those depicted by Balbin)—to notice other sorts
of Europeans. Callot's depiction of pilgrims provided commentary on society at large in a manner that rarely, if ever, surfaced in pilgrimages to a
Holy Land that was, after all, far distant from the actual European scene.
Pilgrims in the Levant had other matters on their grandly and devoutly
occupied minds.

That the literature of pilgrimage to Palestine, including Amico's book,
tended to the stylized and elevated, especially compared to the more ele-
mental and demotic experiences of pilgrimage within Europe, does not
mean that the intentions or results of such literature were insipid or desiccated. Amico's agenda, for example, was nothing if not impassioned. He
intended that his drawings should prove an *aide* to religious contemplation on the part of the pious in Europe ("so many pyres of spiritual fire to
enflame minds to the contemplation of the mysteries wrought by the Savior of the world"), but also that they should "excite and enflame the minds
and hearts of Catholic Princes for the recovery of the Holy Land."[92] And
if impassioned, Amico was also quite unapologetic concerning his book.
He did not share fears and hesitations of predecessors that others had
been there and done that. His work was without precedent. Indeed, at the
very end he does refer to previous writers of pilgrimages, but only in order
to take them to task for overestimating the hardships and dangers (from
the sea, from Arabs, from Turks) that might beset the potential traveler.[93]
His own intent was to render the Holy Land as a European-like place, the
kind of grand and substantial destination that the Roman or Parisian or
Londoner would recognize as suitable and understandable as a goal of
long-distance travel.

*   *   *

As an attempt to nay-say gloomy-gusses on the subject of actual pilgrimage to Jerusalem, Amico's book was a failure. A year after Ceverio had visited the holy places and near the end of Amico's stay in Palestine, Joannes

Figure 37. Jean de Thévenot, *Voyages*, 5 vols. (Amsterdam: M. C. Le Céne, 1727), vol. 2, facing p. 574.

Cotovicus, a doctor of laws in Antwerp, visited the Holy Land in 1596. His *Itinerarium Hiersolymitanum et Syriacum* was finally published in Antwerp in 1619. While pilgrimage as a genre had fructified in the writings of such as Ceverio and Amico—who, along with the Latinated Radziwill, suggested luminous prospects of early modern pilgrimage at least in its literary mode—Cotovicus's book was more reflective of the harsh realities that surrounded the present and future of pilgrimage into the Levant. Printed in Latin almost a quarter of a century after his actual journey, the work might have seemed a bit out of date. In fact, in terms of Cotovicus's treatment of his subject matter, the book was urgent and timely and would remain so over a long period. This is true, even though Cotovicus cut a modest figure among the book stalls, his book being issued twice in Antwerp in 1619 and in a Dutch translation the next year in the same city.[94] The *Itinerarium* was an important text, densely packed with observations and information and lavishly illustrated (with Zuallart's images).

What sets Cotovicus apart from contemporary pilgrims is his profound realization that things had changed for pilgrimage to the Levant in the wake of Venice's loss of Cyprus to the Turks in 1571, a full quarter-century before his own visit to Palestine. Unlike Ceverio and Amico, he was under no illusions. The year that had seen Europe's triumph in the western Mediterranean at Lepanto also saw Turkish triumphs in eastern waters. Such events, in a general way, "reconfirmed a naval stalemate,"[95] but the specific loss of Cyprus's Venetian ports as friendly stopovers for ships heading to and from Jaffa permanently damaged the European pilgrim business. After 1571, organized voyages from Venice—or even from Antwerp or Marseilles—of great numbers of pilgrims to Palestine never recovered as a truly popular undertaking. While pilgrimage remained possible, it had become much more arduous. Those who still wished to go to Jerusalem had need of careful planning and provisioning. Cotovicus reminded pilgrims of these new realities and of how to deal with them in a world become more treacherous for pilgrims traveling from Europe. His tone is anxiously methodical. One of the reasons that his book did not have a distinguished publication history is that its densely packed account, filled as it was with practical advice throughout the text proper as well as in the preliminaries, was geared towards the increasingly rare traveler who would actually undertake the journey—few of whom were around after 1571. There is probably no surviving book of pilgrimage that, by tending to the needs of a potential pilgrim of Cotovicus's time, answers more nuts-and-bolts questions about pilgrimage for the later historian.

Cotovicus stood in a long Catholic tradition of pilgrimage, but perhaps felt less weighted down by the testimony of his predecessors precisely because the conditions of pilgrimage had suddenly altered. Cotovicus demonstrated the modernity of pilgrimage not by some intellectual innovation (such as Ceverio's involving the Indies in the Levant, or Amico's shaping the Holy Land into a beautiful object, or Radziwill's translator-editor reconnecting pilgrimage to a classical tradition of travel) but by his grappling with new realities on the ground that hampered or redefined pious venturing into the *Oriens*. His book was something of a rescue operation of pilgrimage, which in the light of current affairs threatened to disappear utterly as an actual undertaking of European travelers. He attacked the overall problem in elaborate preliminaries, especially in the dedicatory epistle, the preface to the reader, and the advice to the reader who plans to make the journey.[96]

In the *epistola dedicatoria*, Cotovicus raises the issue of travel itself, which he praises in the usual terms as the great permanent and enduring reality ("in ancient times and also in our own century") that brings prudence and judgment and sagacity to the individual traveler and outfits him for a role in society. "As the bee gathers honey from diverse flowers, so from these [journeys], he [the traveler] collects things of benefit to the common weal." But, for Cotovicus, however true and accepted all of this has always been concerning ordinary travel (*profana peregrinatione*), just so much more advantageous and beneficial is the particular form of travel, sacred journeying to Jerusalem.[97] The underlying and insistent point is that pilgrimage to Jerusalem remains what it has always been—the crowning form of European *travel*. This theoretical assertion of pilgrimage as the preeminent mode of travel is all the more striking in light of the low ebb of such travel at the time that Cotovicus was writing. Cotovicus himself could recall that there had been a time when every city and town of his region could boast citizens famous for having made the journey to Jerusalem.[98]

Nevertheless, however superior pilgrimage remained among forms of travel, few Europeans took themselves to the sacred places—and "especially in this century."[99] His own journey documents actual numbers and, more importantly, relative numbers of pilgrims. The ship out of Venice held so many persons of such diverse origins and habits and stations that the vessel seemed a city rather than a ship (*urbem non navem*). In this mass of humanity, however, only two other pilgrims (a Portuguese priest and an Italian monk) were on board, in addition to ten Franciscans bound for the Holy Land.[100] As a traveler's activity, devoutly going to the Levant had clearly begun to border on the eccentric. The great fact of Cotovicus's journey was not the impressive public event of pilgrimage itself (such as had been, for example, Breydenach's voyage a hundred and twelve years earlier), but the literary event of his book being published in Antwerp almost a quarter century after the journey. The reader, moreover, had become a key figure in this new universe of pilgrimage. Cotovicus looks to an audience to evaluate his account of experience supplemented by the writings of previous pilgrims, and he is content to "let the sincere reader judge whether I speak the truth."[101]

The fallen fortunes of the highest form of travel may have rendered implausible any popular revival of it as an actual undertaking, but pilgrimage to Jerusalem had not been absolutely refined and reduced to pure literature (or worse, to an imaginary literature composed by a scribe at his desk, matching biblical passages to past travelers' observations). There is more to the contemporary reality than the lone pilgrim writing for a purely ruminative audience. There does exist the *lector* who will also become (conceivably) a *peregrinus*, one who will actually make the journey. And such a one requires advice (*paraenesis*). Under the shadow of the fall of Cyprus almost thirty years before, "almost none, only a few" dare to make the journey to Jerusalem. In the wake of this disaster in the eastern Mediterranean, new dangers and inconveniences have arisen which have dissuaded all but the hardiest. The definition of pilgrimage, however, has grown sharper in such grave circumstances. Actual pilgrims are now moved by "the sole consideration of piety."[102] What we are seeing (through the eyes of Cotovicus), then, is a *two-fold* noumenalization of pilgrimage: on the one hand, general events and Mediterranean realities have meant that pilgrimage itself has become an overwhelmingly literary rather than practical experience; on the other hand, these very same events and circumstances that have reduced the possibilities of actual pilgrimages have also transformed such pilgrimage to the Levant, for the few who still manage the journey, into an even more intensely defined spiritual undertaking. The altered context of Levantine travel explains the first piece of advice that Cotovicus urges upon prospective pilgrims—that such travelers be clear and decisive in their intentions. It is equally important to stress, however, that two-fold noumenalization is not all that is going on in the case of Cotovicus. There still survives the flesh-and-blood phenomenon of actual journeys to the Holy Land, his own and those of other potential pilgrims. Actual travel remains the substratum of early modern writing and reading about pilgrimage. Thus it is that Cotovicus, having urged clarity as to motives and purposes of devout travel, moves on to advice upon more practical matters. Indeed, not just the remainder of the preliminaries but hundreds of pages of the text proper are brimming with advice that is inserted throughout the narrative of Cotovicus's own journey, advice that is aimed at getting the pilgrim through his dangerous journey. There were after all daunting reasons why so few had gone to Jerusalem in the last thirty years. Cotovicus's own accomplishment of pilgrimage within this general context of the times, a context of which he was meticulously aware, renders his volume in some sense the defining work of early modern pilgrimage. It captures the reality of travel. It is what happens in tandem—noumenalization on the one hand, but check-listed practicality on the other—that expresses almost perfectly the tension which went into the realization of pilgrimage during these centuries.

The seventeenth century proved a great era in the literature of pilgrimage to Palestine, even as devout journeys to the Levant continued to decline in numbers and frequency. Circumstances in Europe and the Middle East worked against any revival of devout crowds coming from Europe. The literature of description and celebration nevertheless continued. A cluster of such works appeared in the years after Cotovicus. Nicholas Bénard left Paris in 1616 and sailed from Marseilles to Palestine via Cyprus.[103] The journey resulted in a book of seven hundred and fifty-nine pages, *Le Voyage de Hierusalem et autres lieux de la Terre Sainte*, which was published in 1621, just two years after Cotovicus's first edition, and was still being offered to the public as late as 1657.[104] Also in 1621, Louis Deshayes de Courmenin, a French diplomat doing Louis XIII's business in the Levant, made his way to Jerusalem. His *Voyage de Levant fait par le Commendement du Roy* (Paris, 1624) was a text that would, almost two centuries later, appeal to Chateaubriand.[105] The book went through three more editions at Paris in the two decades following its initial appearance in print.[106] A year after Courmenin had conducted his lofty business, Pacifique de Provins, a Capuchin priest, arrived in Jerusalem. An account of his 1622–23 pilgrimage, which included a missionary journey throughout the Levant, together with an account of his subsequent missionary journey to Persia (in 1626–28, following his return to Paris) first appeared in a Spanish version under the title, *Relación verdadera del Padre Fr. Pacifico de Provins capuchino predicador a los reynos de Oriente* (Granada, 1629). The first French edition of his journeys appeared under the title *Relation du voyage de Perse faict par le R. P. Pacifique de Provins Prédicateur Capucin. Où vous verrez les remarques particulières de la Terre saincte* (Paris, 1631).[107]

All three pilgrims remained as aware as their predecessors of the weight of past travelers' accounts, recognized a need to define pilgrimage as travel while distinguishing it from other forms of travel, and made innovations and modifications that gave a color of its own to their presentations of the age-old journey eastwards. Moreover, in the hands of Courmenin and Pacifique, pilgrimage became involved in larger issues of diplomacy and missions. Bénard and Courmenin continued the hopes (of Ceverio and Cotovicus among others) that readers might against all odds follow them to Jaffa. Courmenin even managed to shape pilgrimage into the kind of travel, or to amalgamate it with a general traveler's interest, that found common ground with popular seventeenth-century views of the traveler as the politician-in-training and of travel itself as a school of civic lessons[108]. Pacifique de Provins, on the other hand, seemed more resigned to the traveler staying at home and thus requiring correct (and corrected) information on what the actual traveler had seen. The book was thought by the printer to have an appeal "for all sorts of persons,"[109] but Pacifique de Provins is specially intent on conveying the actual reality and look of the holy places to the devout reader back in Europe and thereby providing to stay-at-homes an accurate *aide de contemplation* ("Do not imagine in your meditations that the Sepulchre is as the painters represent it, in the form of a low cell covered by a tomb.").[110] Anxiety to correct broad cultural misrepresentations (mainly of easel and pulpit) of the sites of sacred history is a major concern of Pacifique de Provins in his role of pilgrim and reporter (rather than practical guide).[111]

*   *   *

Beyond such works by practitioners of the devout traveler's craft carrying on and fine-tuning a defined tradition, there began to emerge a general and critical issue in pilgrimage-writing as the century progressed. The issue, which distinguished between European residents of the Holy Land on the one hand and European transients on the other hand, might be said to have been lurking for decades,[112] but now came rudely to the fore and went to the heart of what was required, and who were qualified, to write of travel to the holy places. Such a question might seem (at least in retrospect) to be tinged with irony, so small and shrinking was the base of actual travelers from which writers of pilgrimage might be drawn.

In any event, just past mid-century, the Franciscan Antonio del Castillo's *El devoto Peregrino y Viage de Tierra Santa* (Madrid, 1654) appeared in print. Eight years of observant residence in Palestine a quarter century earlier had gone into the making of his book. Castillo, who had held important ecclesiastical posts in both Jerusalem and Bethlehem and was a notable figure at court in Madrid (for many years as Comisario general de Jerusalèn in Madrid), wrote authoritatively on Palestine—on both the Holy Land itself and the nature of devout travel from site to site. Across the early modern centuries, Franciscans were the constant European presence in Palestine. They guarded and administered Catholic interests in the region, dispensed the sacraments, interpreted sites, and served as hoteliers to Catholics and Protestants arriving from the West.[113] Castillo spoke out of this world; and it is no surprise that his voice was attended to. His book appeared in at least twenty-five editions over a period of a century and a half, principally in Madrid, but also in Barcelona. While never translated, *El Devoto Peregrino* did come on the market at least twice in Paris, in 1664 and 1666. Castillo was, in terms of the audience he reached, the first great figure of the seventeenth century who recalls the continuously published pilgrims of the century before.[114] With Castillo, the seventeenth-century literature of pilgrimage comes to full maturity and acquires a profile recognizably its own.

Castillo was at least as keenly aware of the tradition within which he wrote as other pilgrims before him. His worries over the state of pilgrimage were several. For one thing, he defined matters more closely, even more technically, than had previously been usual. In describing holy places, he was quite specific on what constituted such a place: "We identify as sanctuaries not only all those places which Christ Our Savior consecrated by any of his divine works, but also those which Our Virgin Lady, the Apostles, the Prophets, St. John Baptist, and any other illustrious saint sanctified by birth, life, death, or supernatural activity."[115] He also focused on the *act*, and not simply the objects, of pilgrimage. He worked to stay any tendency for pilgrimage to turn into tour. The pilgrim is one who travels to Jerusalem "out of love of God, but without looking to any other goal than that—not out of curiosity to go and see countries, but in order to adore and show reverence to those most holy places."[116] Worry, that the act of pilgrimage was losing clear lines of definition, permeated the book. In the *Prologo al lector*, Castillo urged readers to go to Palestine, but added: "If you are in search of curiosities, stop in your tracks. If devotion is what you are after, keep on."[117] That the *act* of pilgrimage and the actions of pilgrims were as important to Castillo as the places themselves leapt from the engravings in this richly illustrated book, which shows pilgrimage to have moved far

beyond Breydenbach and Reuwich. In an echo (and use) of Zuallart's illustrations, Castillo was aware not only of the things before the pilgrim's eye—
the sacred archaeologia to be reported upon and attended to—but the act
of pilgrimage and the pilgrim himself as actor in the narrative.[118]

When looking back on the tradition of pilgrimage, Castillo's general
concern was quite different from the usual pilgrim-writer's worry over repetition and redundancy. He did not see, or was undaunted by, an established record of descriptions that had been articulated in a long shelf of
books of devout travel. What he did see were instances of carelessness,
error, and gullibility (*facilidad en creer*) on the part of those writers who
hurriedly (*tan de priessa*) passed through the Holy Land. They believed
everything that was told to them, even things that were quite *ridiculos*. From
the point of view of those in situ ("those who know the truth concerning
the place")—that is, the point of view of Castillo—the willingness of such
hurried reporters to believe anything was striking, but even more striking
their rush into print. When Castillo gazed upon a row of imprints, he saw
not so much a full record against which he must compete, as a flawed record
that he felt obliged to emend. His was the perspective of the Franciscan-
in-residence, someone who through eyes-on experience was methodically
in the know. He did not ignore texts of others ("comparing Travels"), but
he was above all the clear-eyed observer who had the leisure, or at least the
time, to take everything in ("I saw, noted, pondered, and wrote very gradu-
ally [*despacio*] all that seemed to me important for executing this work").
Why did he write *El Devoto Peregrino*? In a phrase: "for the disillusionment
(*desengaño*) of some I have written this *viage* (and for the devotion of all)."[119]

All of this sounds like a taskmaster pedant who is picking nits and
steeling the reader for a dry-as-dust account of the sacred Levant in which
quarrels of scribes will block out, for the reader, any view of land and traveler. That such did not happen to be the case was in part due to the fact
that Castillo's book was packed with illustrations. Engravings of the most
notable places accompanied the text "because they give greater understanding than words and they are more moving." And there was an additional
reason: "They are as denuded of rhetorical coloration as the truth itself."
Castillo wanted to move the reader, but to do so in black and white. He
has not only written what he has seen; he has written in unadorned fashion (*sencillamente*). He was after the (sacred) thing-in-itself. The reality of
the Holy Land, accurately marshaled, will speak for itself. If pictures supplemented text, the text itself strove to become like the pictures. Castillo
has written in simple fashion "because you (Christian Reader) should not

be detained in pondering what you read; you should instead travel devoutly (*camines con devoción*), considering what my words signify."[120] It is a measure of the health of pilgrimage in the second half of the seventeenth century and the eighteenth century that a book that was devotional, informational, instructive, and entertaining (moving), but that was also highly self-reflective concerning the purposes and methods of the work, was also a book that ran through so many editions.

Only three years after the first edition of Castillo's book, a very different pilgrimage came on the market, Jean Doubdan's *Le Voyage de la terre-sainte* (Paris, 1657). Doubdan, canon of the royal church of St. Paul in St. Denis and long-time confessor of the Ursuline convent at St. Denis, described the devout journey that he had made to Jerusalem in 1652. Doubdan sets his account of travel in a rich context of the history and liturgy of the Holy Land, but does nevertheless seem to be aware that his account of pilgrimage, when compared to those of others, is somewhat relentlessly focused on the Holy Land itself. "Because the devout voyage to the Levant is rarely made without including Italy," he decided to add some remarks, *en passant* at the end, on the churches of Rome. (He lacked opportunity to see more when his plans for spending a year in Italy were cut short by news of the Fronde, which sent him hurrying back to a miserable scene of unrest and carnage at St. Denis.)[121] Moreover, Doubdan's *Voyage* had the disadvantage, in his eyes, of being even more restrictive in its focus. As a travel book, it had nothing to say about the rest of the Levant, not to mention about the new worlds which were now being converted to Christianity and which possessed *raretéz* which could fill many large volumes. In any case, the *amateurs de la pieté*, who were his real audience, could read in his pages about a "country which ought to be considered the eye and ornament of the world, the center of the habitable earth, and the most worthy portion of the Universe." In doing so, they would provide themselves with food for contemplation.[122]

Doubdan, however, was uneasy (at least rhetorically) about more than the restricted focus of his work. There was the usual worry that "someone will perhaps say that I march in the path of many others who have already handled this subject and that I am undertaking a work which has already been done with the greatest rigor." This seems sufficiently general and vague, more of the usual that by this time has become an almost obligatory trope that would claim little notice. Doubdan may have had acutely in mind several other pilgrims who made the long-distance journey to Jerusalem around the same year as he and who also wrote up their pilgrimages, some

of whose texts were in manuscript while others were, or would subsequently be, published. It was perhaps this consideration—beyond the consideration that so many records of this same journey had been printed for
two centuries before him—that pushed Doubdan to be particularly reflective upon the nature of pilgrimage literature and upon the uses and worth
of any one rendition in a literary universe that included many others. His
own text, at any rate, proved immediately popular, going through five printings between the years 1657 and 1667. The text was richly illustrated.[123]

Something additional, however, and more specific played on Doubdan's mind. He was a canon on holiday from Europe in the Holy Land.
True, he came from one of the most renowned churches of Christendom;
but that did not take away from the fact that he was merely passing through,
catching glimpses, taking notes, forming impressions. He was well aware
of what people might say—"that this material ought not to be treated except
by persons who have grown old in the [holy] places (*blanchy sur les lieux*)
and have a complete knowledge (*connoissance parfaite*) which can only be
acquired by means of a long residence." He clearly had in mind the incomparable expertise of the Custodial Franciscans. He mentions the works of
two (Quaresmio and Roger)[124] and might just as well have mentioned, or
at least have had in mind, the frank and direct words of another, Antonio
del Castillo, on this very question. At any rate, he retreats into the words
of Augustine (to the effect that many may profitably speak in different
styles about the same matter) and takes comfort that the Ursulines back in
St. Denis highly esteem his book "which they prefer to fabulous tales of
fiction."[125] In any event, Doubdan, especially when read in light of Castillo,
hints at an important tension that was developing among seventeenth-
century practitioners of the craft of pilgrimage writing.

The issue remained alive in the work of Jacques Florent Goujon, a
Franciscan who had spent two years (beginning in 1668) making observations, taking notes, and mulling over his experiences in the Holy Land.
His *Histoire et Voyage de la Terre Sainte* (Lyon, 1670), a thoroughly Custodial work, explicitly urged the contrast to be drawn between a pilgrimage
(such as his own) that was composed by a traveler who lived in Palestine
over an extended period of time and a pilgrimage by a traveler who, however devout, was merely passing through.[126] An example of the latter who
comes immediately to mind (though not *expressly* to the mind of Goujon)
is the canon of St. Denis, Doubdan, who had come and gone sixteen years
before Goujon and who indeed had written a large book on the basis of
brief impressions. Tension and competition between pious visitors and

pious residents of the Holy Land became a hovering smoke in the literature of pilgrimage. (Chateaubriand was to feel his own vulnerability on
just these grounds more than a century later—a vulnerability, moreoever,
that would push him to embrace *mémoire* as his metier). Be that as it may,
the bibliographical track records of Doubdan and Goujon were roughly
comparable. The former went through five printings within a decade, all
in Paris; the latter was printed four times at Lyon, between 1670 and 1672,
and once more in 1714.[127]

In Goujon, the perennial problem, of writing something new in a tradition of centuries of reporting on the same places, is related to this matter of the comparison between the resident's thick interpretation of the
Holy Land and the visitor's thin impressions of the same scene. Something
to notice about Goujon is his use of a new style of language. He speaks
of his seeming to "uncover (*desrobant*) the history and outline of the holy
places" and remarks that "each step that Christ took conceals mysteries
(*cache des mystères*) which it is not easy to explain thoroughly." It is for this
reason that one must make repeated visits to individual places. One cannot speak too often of the sacred places. There is always more to say. "These
are the same places sanctified by these august mysteries that I have described. One cannot reflect enough on them. However devout he is, the
Christian cannot often enough mediate upon them."[128]

This is something of a conceptual breakthrough. Within the world of
pilgrimage, Goujon has found a new way to attack the old problem. There
is always need for new books of pilgrimage, and not simply because earlier authors were imperfect or forgetful reporters or because things change
over time or because everyone sees things from a different angle. Goujon
guides the question into a more positive direction. It is the nature of the
places themselves, the spiritual depths that they reveal (and conceal) to
the meditating, contemplating eye, that makes every new effort to look
and see and say productive of something original. And it is the deep and
spiritual nature of the act of contemplation itself that opens up endless
possibilities for travel across sacred terrain. Goujon's attitude towards the
matter made him unembarrassed by predecessors; at the same time, it made
him wonder at those writers who could not linger over the sites because
they were in too great a hurry to move on and to write big books about
that which they had merely glimpsed.[129] Goujon is clearly on the same side
as Castillo on the matter of resident-vs.-transient, but where Castillo's concern was with faulty and inaccurate accounts, Goujon's worry centers on
something deeper. How was one to contemplate on the run? As for himself,

"it has been easy enough for me to see and to examine closely everything at leisure." What Goujon was aiming for was a book for the devout which would "increase their piety," a book moreover that was the product both of his seeing and examining and of his meditation and rumination. All of which activities, he would have said, took time. What he ended up with was a work at once highly reportorial and highly interpretive. He divided the journey into visits, and the visits into days. The whole amounted to thirty-three visits in honor of Christ's thirty-three years on earth. He offered this to the reader:

> Accept, dear Reader, this little work as a mystical rose that combines sweetness and bitterness—although you yourself will not have to touch the thorns. These I have kept for myself alone from among the storms and tempests, the fears and injuries, the menaces and the blows which have served as the sorrows and pains preceding the birth of the rose. I have been comforted by the grace of God and the help of the holy Virgin, his holy Mother, in having avoided some of these trials and having patiently suffered others so that I might, in these places of repose, have the satisfaction of bestowing on you some of the fruit of my labor and pain.[130]

We have entered a new and rarer atmosphere. The air of pilgrimage, always heavily incensed, has now become even more thickly and variously scented. And through the clouds of pondering, the *odeur de méditation*, we are introduced to an autobiographical side of pilgrimage. Such travel requires personal spiritual exertions. The pilgrim who writes of his pilgrimage is (or should be) not a visitor, a passerby, but one who has *lived* in the Holy Land, who has dwelt among *les lieux sacrées,* who has absorbed the meaning, the significance, the spiritual density of the places. A book of pilgrimage suddenly turns out not only to be a tool of contemplation for the pious reader, but itself to be a product of the contemplation (and the suffering and toil) of a pious traveler. Pilgrimage ceases to be prominently about matter-of-fact enumerations of indulgences or identifying rubble or measuring distances between sacred spots. With Goujon, the old question, of what to write when so many have written so much already, appeared in an entirely new light. The question suddenly seemed less urgent, less to the point, when posed of the true pilgrim—the devout traveler with time and leisure to linger devoutly, to loiter with intent, in the Holy Land. Who would have guessed—would Thevet or even Breydenbach?—that *travail et peine* were at the heart of the matter?

Goujon's insight did not, however, take pilgrimage sufficiently by storm to silence perennial second thoughts. As the seventeenth century advanced and the eighteenth century loomed, and despite these new ways (especially Castillo's and Goujon's) of looking at the matter of composing accounts of pilgrimage, there continued to rise up behind the shoulder of any potential writer-pilgrim an intimidating shelf of books, an ever-lengthening literary shadow of guides and narratives and commentaries that recounted pilgrimage to the Holy Land. What had long been a perceived difficulty—to justify yet another account of the Holy Land when so many others were available in printed editions—now seemed a fully hatched predicament that was less and less able to be ignored as the pilgrim set about recollecting his journey in print. The Jesuit Michel Nau wrung his hands over the issue, as had others before him in the century. He did not want "to multiply the infinite number of useless books." He imagined, before consulting the literature, that to add his volume to the shelf would be "to repeat (*redire*) that which had been said and said yet again (*dit et redit*) a thousand times."[131] Thus, he hesitated—at least rhetorically—before bringing into print in 1679 his *Voyage nouveau de la terre sainte*.

Nau meant the title to be taken seriously. He was writing a *modern*, a very up-to-date, narrative. The first edition appeared anonymously, as had his little-noticed travels to the Galilee almost a decade before. The earlier volume had not been a success among the Parisian book stalls. Nau's pilgrimage had been quirky in that, while focused on the Holy Land, it had not included Jerusalem on the itinerary. This gave the book a slightly odd slant and may account for the book's failure to inspire further editions after 1670.[132] In any event, nine years later the still anonymous author produced a popular and more traditional form of pilgrimage. This second effort was also published at Paris. For almost eighty years it would appear again and again, always in Paris. Whatever the competition from pilgrims past and present, Nau's book was received as one of the great accounts of pilgrimage in the waning seventeenth century and into the second half of the eighteenth.[133]

What was it that overcame Nau's hesitation to go into print and thereby launched a publishing history that justified his decision? For one thing, Nau traveled in the entourage of the French ambassador to the Porte, thereby gaining access to places that otherwise might have been closed off to the lone and unsponsored Christian pilgrim. Moreover, Nau cited his experience as a Jesuit in the Levant which had allowed him to make more than one visit to the Holy Land. (In this, he works a variation on a theme played to the hilt by the Franciscan Goujon—and earlier by Castillo). Nau also adds an ingredient not usually mentioned—a facility with Oriental languages which made him more sure-footed on foreign terrain, and less easily deceived or misled by local traditions, than earlier writers of pilgrimages. Finally, when he actually came to read samples of the literature of pilgrimage, he found less than he had expected: "The amplest accounts have omitted the most remarkable things, and the most precise accounts have dealt with only a few places." In fact, in Nau's eyes, this state of affairs is due precisely to the writers' lack of languages and the fact that the typical pilgrim's exposure to the holy places was "a trip of a few days."[134] In Nau, we see an intensification of pilgrimage as a literature of the very few (from the point of view of the composition of that literature) who are equipped by learning and circumstances. The "few" are no longer defined simply by the reality that the opportunity to travel about the eastern Mediterranean was itself rare. Already a heavily clerical literature, it became all the more so as the century progressed and the needs of the genre were defined.

Nau himself, as well as being keenly observant, was also learned and extremely well read, not only in travel accounts, but in a wide range of literature that he applied to the experience of viewing and understanding the places of sacred history. He managed to quote from or refer to an array of writers as disparate as John of Damascus, Bernard of Clairvaux, and Joseph Juste Scaliger. His discussions of the holy sites are constantly being subsumed into a symposium of texts. His large book of travel is, however, something more than a learned tome. Or rather, the sacred learning—scriptural, theological, historical—adds layer upon layer to the pious sentiments that the places themselves initiate. Witness, for example, history enwrapping Nau as he contemplates Nazareth:

At long last we arrived at Nazareth at dusk on Christmas Eve. At first sight while still at a distance, I cannot tell you what various sentiments seized us—sentiments of joy, awe, admiration, love, and devotion. When St. Louis came to visit this holy place, on the Feast of the Annunciation, he had no sooner caught sight of it than he dropped to the ground and, humbly falling to his knees, adored the true God who there became man out of love for us; and he offered the same greeting to the Holy Virgin that the Angel had addressed to her. He chose to go the remainder of the way on foot. Fasting on bread and water and wearing a rough hair-shirt, he prepared to receive in Communion the same Savior whom the Virgin received in the Incarnation.[135]

And not only is Nau himself seized, as it were, by the rich web of associations and allusions constituted by his own literary fashioning of the pilgrim's experience, but he draws into the net of devout feeling the reader at home. Nau places the reader, for example, before Jerusalem and tells him all about the city and tells him to let his imagination leap: "Imagine that you are where we were and that you see what we saw; and determine the reality of the scene from that which simple thought produces in you."[136] Nau is devout, learned, critical, analytical, referential, detached. But as a complete and coherent literary artifact, his book transcends all of this (most of all the detachment) in pursuit, not exactly of emotion as of a sense of (holy) place. It is to the senses and the feelings—*la veuë et le coeur*—of the faithful and devout that the holy places make their appeal.[137] It is the appeal of geography under foot combined with history in the mind.

*   *   *

Sixteenth-century pilgrimages had continued to be printed and to circulate in the seventeenth century. This literary afterlife of editions, translations, and extracts was less striking a phenomenon in the transition from seventeenth-century pilgrimage to eighteenth-century pilgrimage. Continuity did exist, however, and it is crucial to note its existence. Chateaubriand's dark take on the eighteenth century would otherwise have us see only decades of *philosophisme* that led to Revolution and to civilization collapsed in a heap, conditions leaving scarcely any possibility for devout pilgrimage to the Levant. In fact, a few seventeenth-century authors of devout pilgrimages (Linden, Castillo above all, the Protestant Troilo, the Jesuit Nau) did continue to be printed deep into the eighteenth century. There is, too, the longer cord that connects an eighteenth-century audience to interpretations of pilgrimage that had first been printed in the *sixteenth* century. Bianchi's illustrated description of his 1527 journey was still being printed in 1742, as was Bünting's pilgrimage-like book, which had first appeared in 1581. The longevity of Guerrero's book was remarkable, helped along as it was by an altered title in the Valladolid edition of 1785 and turned into another language (Portuguese) in an edition of 1734, almost a century and a half after its original publication. Such retrospective publication testifies to the organic life of long-distance pilgrimage in the eighteenth century. There remained an audience for such literature. If Europeans were still reading decades-old *peregrinationes*, would they not have read similar works produced by pious travelers in their own time? Did not pilgrimage itself endure as a living, current tradition?

   A few Europeans, in the last years of the seventeenth century or in the eighteenth century itself, continued to make their devout way across the Mediterranean to Palestine, and a few of these had their journeys turned into eighteenth-century printed accounts of pilgrimage. This is true,

however desolate the landscape of an entire century appeared to an advo-
cate of revived pilgrimage looking back from the rubble on the far side of
Revolution. There were, contrary to Chateaubriand, signs of peregrinative
life. His pessimism might tempt us to interpret the century as one long
recessional where pilgrimage was concerned. But something like the opposite was true. However hit-and-miss and here-and-there an affair, *dévots*
were up and about, even in the role of long-distance travelers, to contest
the *philosophes*.

Of course, Chateaubriand in the nineteenth century (and Jacobus
Gretser two centuries earlier) did not look upon pilgrimage in the same
light—did not *define* pilgrimage—as onlookers from the twenty-first century might. Consider, for example, Henry Maundrell, who traveled to
Jerusalem from Aleppo in 1697. Gretser was disapproving of his type of
traveler (a century before his person materialized); nor was he at all Chateaubriand's sort of pious traveler a century after Maundrell had departed.
For one thing, Maundrell was Protestant; for another, while observant
and chattily informative on the Levant in general—on places along the
way and places in the neighborhood of Palestine—he withheld from the
sites of the Holy Land itself that careful, detailed, and meditative focus
which was characteristic of the Catholic literature of pilgrimage. Nor did
his take on the holy sites, when he actually considered them, amount to
an entirely reverent picture—not at least from the point of view of Catholic tradition, which was the classic word on the matter. He takes his arrival
before Jerusalem in stride. He leaves the city without emotion. His whole
idea of pilgrimage curiously dissolves in the vapors of labored witticism
when he tells his uncle, to whom he dedicated the account:

When you are tired with reading it, you may support your patience as we did in
travelling it over, by considering, that what you are about is a pilgrimage; that you
need go it but once; and that 'tis the proper nature and design of such perfor-
mances, to have something in them of mortification.[138]

There is a notable want of fervor, or even of substance—even, indeed, of
seriousness—in his observations of the sacred sites. He sounds what seems
a wrong, certainly a jarring, note in sizing up the interior of the Church
of the Holy Sepulchre: "And now being got under the sacred Roof, and
having the advantage of so much leisure and freedom, I might expatiate
in a large description of the several holy places, which this Church (as a
Cabinet) contains in it."[139] To liken the most revered enclosed sacred space
for Europeans in the entire world to a *cabinet* seems clever indeed and

innovative, but would probably have struck the ear of the typical eighteenth-century reader of pilgrimages past and present as an odd, or perhaps a deftly impertinent, choice of word. It broke the concentration—the spell, so to speak—of meditation. The contemplative consciousness had been thrown a curve. Moreover, Maundrell is not after all going to give us the "large description" of the holy sites. Too many, he explains, have done it exhaustively before him. Nor for him the intellectual and spiritual acrobatics of a Castillo or Goujon that would allow him to find his tongue where matters of pilgrimage proper were at issue.

And yet he was a pilgrim of sorts. Not a late Roman or medieval pilgrim, and certainly not an early modern Catholic pilgrim (or even an early modern Protestant pilgrim after the manner of Rauwolf), he was nevertheless some sort of modern pilgrim—and his book a significant variety of modern pilgrimage. He traveled, after all, with Jerusalem as his goal, and traveled, moreover, in Easter time. In his letter to the Bishop of Rochester, he mentions, among the "other satisfactions" of his tenure as chaplain in Aleppo, the voyage to the Holy Land on which he and fourteen others from the factory in Aleppo "visited the several places consecrated by the life and death of our Blessed Lord."[140] And he was capable of religious reflection on what he had seen—although it is perhaps suggestive that such reflection was more likely to crop up in a digression.[141]

Maundrell's book, as a specimen of early eighteenth-century travel writing, threads its way between tour and pilgrimage. He was more than simply a tourist who happened to be abroad at Easter, more (though not a great deal more) than an English *philosophe* (a dandy dressed in the latest notions) on the road. He was a religious tourist—which is *one* passable definition of pilgrimage by the eighteenth century. And in this sense—a limited sense that distinguishes between the identifiably religious sentiment produced by visiting Jerusalem as opposed to, say, the emotional stirrings occasioned by a gaze at the stones of Athens or an inhalation of the salt air around Carthage—Maundrell can be considered a modern pilgrim. As such a creature, Maundrell did not stand alone. We have earlier noted other Protestants who made devout visits to Palestine without embracing Catholic ceremonies, practices, and assumptions. Maundrell himself, moreover, feels himself part of a tradition. However that tradition be defined, he saw himself doing what others had long been doing—traveling to Jerusalem and writing about the experience. Indeed, he felt himself so much a part of the tradition that its weight reduced him to silence on matters about which pilgrims usually had much to say. In explaining his own lack of things to say on the sacred sites, he not only invoked the general tradition of literary pilgrimage—as other pilgrims had long been wont to do when justifying their own writing of a book—but singled out by name the immensely popular Sandys, who had been in the Holy Land almost a century before and who, like Maundrell, was a Protestant Englishman (Figure 38). Sandys's words, Maundrell reasons, "leave very little to be added by after-comers, and nothing to be corrected."[142] Indeed, the publisher in a preliminary note (the book was published posthumously) stated that Maundrell had intended his book to be a supplement to Sandys.[143] For Maundrell, the only identifiable face that the grand tradition wears is that of a Protestant in the person of Sandys.

Maundrell was an amazingly visible, if not a very substantial, figure in print within the overall tradition of European pilgrimage—as much a part of the published scene as the very considerable Sandys in whose tracks he followed. Sandys had loomed large in print for over half a century after 1615, and on the Continent as well as in England. So, too, did Maundrell in the half-century (and beyond) after 1703 enjoy a huge national and international reputation based on the printings of his book of travel. In particular, as a book that was just barely, so to speak, a book of pilgrimage, Maundrell's was one of those rare books of religious travel (Sandys's was another) that found its way into the great collections of travels, both in England and in Europe at large.[144]

Maundrell nevertheless suggests the fading away of pilgrimage before readers' eyes, almost its utter desiccation, as arid a thing offered to the mind of the reader as the desert itself under foot of the traveler-reporter. But there were other contemporaries who provided a more vital alternative for armchair pilgrims. Antoine Morison, a canon of Bar-le-Duc, was in Jerusalem the same year (1697) as Maundrell. An obscure traveler on his own, he was nevertheless firmly planted in centuries-old Catholic traditions of pilgrimage. Although he gave serious accounts of his journey from France to Palestine as well as of the return voyage, his focus was on the essential peregrinative activity of going around the sacred sites. His book of travel was a book of pilgrimage. He immersed himself deeply in the religious experience of his voyage and also in the history of the Holy Land. He was endowed—similarly to Nau, but much more so—with a fine Baroque sense of incongruities that crop up along the road. Where Maundrell was world-weary of pious sentiments and loath to restate the oft-articulated, Morison was devoutly voluble. He was not so much daunted as nourished by pilgrimage's long past. He was one of the great, if now utterly forgotten, travel writers of the eighteenth century.[145]

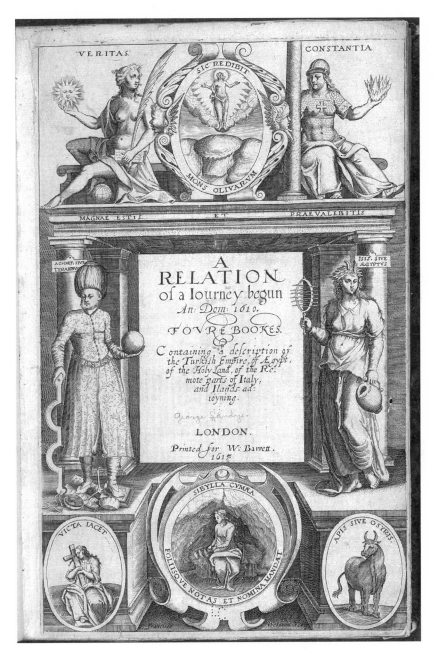

Figure 38. George Sandys, *A Relation of a Journey begun An: Dom: 1610* (London: W. Barrett, 1615), engraved title page.

The contrast between Maundrell and Morison is not only in the substance of each's account (Maundrell the most superficial taster of the scene, Morison all but intoxicated by the spiritual vapors of Terra Sancta). Morison was also entirely overshadowed in his own day by the success of Maundrell (and others) in print. Morison's *Rélation historique d'un Voyage nouvellement fait au Mont de Sinai et à Jerusalem* (Toul, 1704) was printed a second time in the same city the following year. A German edition had appeared in Hamburg in 1704.[146] Emphasis on novelty in Morison's title signified, just as it had in Nau's. Both engaged the ever-green question of justifying yet one more account, a *new* account, of a journey over the same route to the same hallowed destinations. Unlike Nau (and Maundrell), however, Morison does not claim the attention of the historian because he exerted a claim on the audience of his own day. What is significant about his book is not its lack of contemporary appeal, but the fact that it was produced at all, in the early eighteenth century. Morison deserves to be recalled in spite of the fact that he is unremembered, under-appreciated. What catches the historian's eye is the book's intellectual and spiritual force, not any splash among the reading public of its day, nor even any conceivable long-term influence. Indeed, almost as notable as its qualities is this fact that it *didn't* make the splash. Morison pointed the way (not taken), manifested the great potential (unrealized), of eighteenth-century pilgrimage. His volume is an index of *both* strength and weakness in eighteenth-century pilgrimage.

Morison took the insights of Goujon and Nau and added an intensity entirely his own. He had an ardently contemplative, ruminative, lingering, and intensely sympathetic eye for the places of sacred history. And the remarkable thing was that Morison shared Goujon's and Nau's outlook without sharing the circumstances that they took as essential to such an outlook. Morison was a transient rather than a resident. It is as if Morison, deprived of the opportunity of the Franciscan and Jesuit to see over and over again the sites, to *contemplate* the sites through constant exposure to them, developed to a greater extent than they his powers of concentrating upon, of boring in upon, of taking utterly to heart what he had seen on the run. Morison's is a book of extravagant interiorization. And in this, he seems to resolve the tension of last century between residents and transients.

At one point in his text (where he contemplated the ruins of Troy), Morison spoke of himself as "a simple traveler and historian,"[147] which was true enough, except when his travels took him to sacred ground. On Sinai or in Palestine, Morison ceased to be the usual or simple sort of European traveler. He threw himself into the sacred world through which he traveled. He conveyed a sense of raw, unmediated exposure to what was before him. He was seized by passion—by a host of emotions—when his eyes took in Jerusalem or Mount Tabor or any other place that echoed the history of sacred antiquity. Approaching Jerusalem, he spoke to the reader of "the charming trouble" and "amiable confusion" that invested his soul. Jerusalem was "a spectacle so new, so agreeable, and desired for such a long time." His thoughts amount to an orchestrated confusion of contrasts. He gives voice to a rhetoric of interiority and sweet, delicious, blessed disorientation.[148] From Mount Tabor, one looks down upon all Galilee and sees what "eyes, heart, and mind" allow one to see.[149] Mind and heart glide into a common swoon. In Morison, pilgrimage has arrived at its Baroque moment just when the Baroque was waning. His book captured the clash of spirited textual content on the one hand and the increasingly contrary moment in which such content was given expression on the other. The *Relation historique* offered the reader two styles. The serious reader was exposed to the controlled fever of the prose. Any reader at all who picked up the book, however, must have been impressed by the well-behaved look of the thing, the polished surface of the physical book. The *appearance* of the well-made, almost lavishly fashioned book (frontispiece portrait of Louis XIV, precisely engraved map, elegant headpieces) suggested order, discipline, what we think of as the neoclassical ethos. Severity, nevertheless, was a façade that housed a tossing tempest of spirited and expressive prose.

In retrospect, we can spy Morison approaching in the works of Castillo, Goujon, Nau. Morison, however, has gone far beyond these meditating, ruminating travelers. He has turned a book of travel into a book of devotion (without, however—this is the heart of the matter—its ceasing to be a book of travel). It is an observer's meditation on things briefly seen and hurriedly experienced, a meditation of which the reader can partake if he allows himself to see through Morison's eyes. Morison's responses are less mediated—by liturgy, prayer, indulgences, customs of travel—than those of almost any previous pilgrim. He moves about in a cloud of sheer noumenality. It is *mon esprit* and *mon coeur* that take everything in. The mind and the heart are the optical agents that open him up to every possibility of pious ardor. Paired with "sweetest thoughts" is an "inclination bordering on the violent" that drives him, impels him, hurls him, towards Jerusalem and the holy places.[150] In our roster of pilgrims, all the others are in black and white; only Morison is in color. In a highly illustrated genre, Morison's is one of the few books of pilgrimage in which illustrations would have proved a distraction, a threat to the vividness and passion of the text itself.

Morison's rhetoric of the soul can distract from his substantial descriptions of the scenes before him, descriptions which, according to a Jesuit reviewer, were "lively and precise."[151] It is precisely this combination that characterizes Morison. The genre in which he was writing was wobbly on its pins throughout early modernity—at times all but approaching dead-end as a mode of travel, at others pulling itself together with some new insight or method—primarily because of its practitioners' own inner misgivings. Above all, pilgrimage was sagging under heavy worries born of its own success as a printed literature. There was almost a collective neurotic streak in the practitioners of pilgrimage. And no wonder. They practiced a form of travel (and travel-writing) that *did* go over the same routes to the same places; and they did so in an age when other travelers moved across strange waters to exotic remotes and were rewarded by their works' being enshrined in great collections of travels; and these pilgrims did their published writing in a time when printing reigned as the medium of literature and communication—a mixed blessing for pilgrims in particular, in that their predictable accounts were out there, were in circulation, for all to read and to compare. (Thevet saw this at once.) Under pressure of this anxiety, pilgrimage as a variety of travel writing was in danger of faltering—in part because collectors of travels ignored pilgrimage, but also because pilgrims themselves seemed to have progressively less to say. Pilgrimage was less in danger of erasure at the hands of others than it was in danger of losing its grip on its own traditional material. Maundrell reduced himself to silence or smirks when he thought of all Sandys had previously said of the holy sites. The learned Frenchman Jean de La Roque, eighteen years after Morison, was to fasten on a corner of the Holy Land in hopes that a corner would be fresher material than the whole.[152] Such alternatives never occurred to Morison. He filled up the narrative void with fireworks and acrobatics of his own personal spiritual responses to sacred space. And his account was substantial in another sense. However idiosyncratic Morison's departure from pilgrimage-as-usual, his account was not a rejection or denial of tradition. He had devoured the literature of his predecessors. (In this, he was quite unlike the great innovator in pilgrimage from a century earlier, Ceverio de Vera). Indeed, his response to the literature of pilgrimage was as extravagant and ardent as his reaction to the sights and experiences of his own pilgrimage. Morison has gotten us quite beyond any literary worries about repetition of things already stated by others. He had no time for such worries. He may have had little new information to add to the established picture, but the thrust of his work, understood as a traveler's interpretation of things seen, was altogether new. It differed from the books of his predecessors as much as does an embrace from an analysis, or a sonnet from a dissertation. How ever did Morison manage to pull himself away from Terra Sancta, the ruins of which, "these groaning remains," had come alive under his feet—under his eyes, his mind, his heart?

That Morison had little future in the eighteenth century—and that Chateaubriand made no acknowledgment of him in the nineteenth—may say more about the decline of pilgrimage before the Revolution than does any reputed lack of pilgrims and narratives of pilgrimage in the age of *la Lumière*. A half-century earlier, Castillo's remarkable and innovative book had suggested, to judge by its success in print over a span of time, a link between author and audience; Morison's fate in print, on the other hand, suggests the weakening of such a link between pilgrim and audience by the first years of the eighteenth century.

Whether too far ahead of his day (prematurely anticipating Chateaubriand, for example) or too wedded to tendencies (of Castillo, Nau, and others) that perhaps no longer possessed their earlier appeal, or perhaps too much the transient who sounded a note too resident-like, Morison failed to get a hearing among contemporaries—so much so that even those who might have been thought to be sharers of his outlook appear to have missed much of his point. The Jesuits' *Journal de Trevoux* gave the book a strong review; nor was the reviewer unaware of the Morison we have been describing—a traveler who "writes with much passion, portrays things in lively manner, and seizes the reader."[153] He precisely points to Morison's special knack for instilling the same feeling in his readers that he himself experienced at the moment of viewing sacred places.[154] But in a review of twenty-eight pages, references to Morison's expressiveness and riot of spiritual ardor occupy only two or three sentences. Instead of treating Morison as a traveler—high points such as Italy, Alexandria, and Cairo are simply omitted from the review in order to make room for a narrower focus on Sinai and the Holy Land—the Jesuit reviewer regards Morison's text as shedding light, or failing to do so,[155] on certain specific questions and controversies of the day. In part, failure to take Morison whole is because of demands of time and space in a periodical entry. But there is more to the reviewer's approach than that. He is drawn to specific data and opinions in Morison's book because they are seen to provide ammunition to counter ideas of *libertins* and *impies* and especially *philosophes*.[156] *Brièveté* prevents the reviewer from following Morison from place to holy place, but there will at least be opportunity for "remarks certainly worthy of the attention of the intellectuals."[157] This intersection of pilgrim and friendly reviewer tells much about the "age of enlightenment." Not only did the spirit of the times move against a literature of devout travel to the Levant. Even Jesuits who might be expected to sing pilgrimage's praises had more urgent fish to fry and thus found themselves using *peregrinationes* as quarries of arguments rather than as a travel literature of inspiration and entertainment.

*   *   *

Jesuits, as we have seen, acted as more than reviewers of books when it came to the Levant. There is Nau, for example, with his two books of pilgrimage. There appeared in print, too, in Paris in 1725, the fifth volume of *Nouveaux Mémoires des missions de la Compagnie de Jesus dans le Levant*, a series of reports meant (but not exclusively so) for a Jesuit audience in Europe. These accounts detailed the activities of Jesuit missions throughout the Levant. The first item in the book was a "Lettre du Père Neret," the posthumously printed account of the pilgrimage to the Holy Land of a Jesuit missionary who had been stationed in Sidon. Charles Neret had set sail from Sidon, "avec une compagnie de pèlerins," on 7 April 1713, the Monday following Passion Sunday. His report had been long anticipated and had apparently been misplaced (Pierre Fromage, the superior of the Jesuits in Egypt and Syria, remarks in his letter introducing the volume that the text had been promised under his predecessor, and speaks of the *Relation du Voyage du Pere Neret à Jerusalem* as something "which we have fortunately recovered").[158] The text had a life beyond that of a Jesuit publication, being printed in German just two years later in Augsburg and Gratz as part of a larger work, and again in German in 1798 in a collection of Oriental travels.[159]

By this time—the third decade of the eighteenth century—the fact that pilgrimage-writing was a crowded field had become a hurdle that could not be simply kicked over. Authors felt the need to justify yet another version of *pèlerinage* in print. Such anxiety, however, does not appear to have weighed upon Neret himself (who, after all, was not seeing his work into print). Fromage, at any rate, disposes of the issue in a breeze: "This priest is not the only one who has described the places about which he speaks; but that which he has left us has seemed to us to include certain observations and particular circumstances (*remarques et particularitez*) which make his report a pleasure to read."[160]

To be sure, Fromage does not leave the matter quite so unadorned; he does attempt to shore up his claims for Neret's special worth as a writer of pilgrimage. But even if we attend only to Neret's own words, the pages of his text would have been justification enough to the immediate audience of Jesuits back in Europe, who must have felt the full impact of Neret's emotional portrait of himself as spiritually driven by the desire both to serve as a missionary in the Levant and to act the pilgrim in the Holy Land.

Many other qualities might have attracted a general reader to Neret's pages. His deep emotional engagement and expressiveness recall Morison. On the other hand, Neret was very clear-eyed. *Très-exacte* is how Fromage characterizes Neret's take on the Holy Land. He is good in describing the details of sites and ceremonies. He impressively sizes up the present situation of the city of Jerusalem. He has a special knack for spotting what we today would call elements of the tourist trade (but a knack *not* cultivated by him out of any desire to debunk or discredit the whole enterprise of pilgrimage; it merely seems an attendant circumstance, an observable feature, of life in the Holy Land that catches Neret's attention). It is worth noting that he has little to say (again, like Morison) about indulgences attached to sites. His general disposition is to accept what he is told of sites, especially in Jerusalem where local traditions would have been sifted through the interpretive discriminations of the resident Franciscans. It is when local tradition claims to nail down an *exact* spot of sacred history that he sometimes tugs at the reins. Up north, he has no difficulty with the vale between two mountains "where Our Lord multiplied the loaves of bread." When he is told that a plain is called the Plain of Spices because it was there that hungry Apostles uprooted spices on the Sabbath, he puts this down to "common opinion" without further comment. When, however, he has visited the church (now a mosque) on the site of the wedding feast at Cana and moves on to a fountain from which the water was drawn for the jars that were used in Christ's first miracle, he feels the need of an aside: "If the tradition on all these facts is not very accurate (*bien juste*), at least it serves to preserve for us the memory of the actions of the Savior of the world and his Disciples."[161] If this be scepticism, it is of a very pious coloring. Neret's statement assumes a remarkably *modern* understanding of what the pilgrim is about in traveling through the Holy Land—modern not only in contrast to the medieval tradition of pilgrimage, but in contrast as well to that of early modern devout travelers (Catholic and

Protestant). It is a remarkable innovation within this tradition for Neret to be concerned with the general lay of the land of sacred history and with the general (and intense) spirit of devotion that leads one to trample sacred ground in the first place, but at the very same time *not* to hem and haw argumentatively over the correctness of every specific bit of tradition. There is about Neret not only a pious curiosity, but a pious realism (which implies the limits of curiosity) that may explain both his interest in the details of the touristical side of pilgrimage and his willingness to remove issues of traditional attributions from the plane of the merely evidentiary. Neret keeps his eye—it is a crucial act of focusing, a kind of devout squint—on memory ("memory of the actions of the Savior of the world") as the end and reason of history and of travel.

Also unusual in Neret's account is the attention he pays to the monastery of Mar Sabas. His visit to the monastery itself is not without precedent (Nau and Furer, among others, stopped at the famous Judaean site, as had a few much earlier travelers); his probing the life of the sixth-century monk St. Sabas himself, though, is remarkable—and certainly not the typical fare served up to readers of pilgrimages. Pages devoted to the life of Sabas and his monastery suggest nothing so much as perked up ears in Neret's primary audience of Jesuits back home—religious communities in Europe that would have been interested in the life (historical or contemporary) of a celebrated religious community in the Holy Land.[162] Be that as it may, the missionary motif, which Neret articulated in terms both apostolic and Jesuit, is the defining stamp of Neret's journey.

Not surprisingly, Neret invokes the example of Ignatius when he portrays his own longing to go to Palestine and his actual realization of his dream of going on pilgrimage:

> My vocation for Syria had made to spring up in my heart the same desire that Saint Ignatius had after his conversion to go to visit the holy places. I left France with joy and crossed the Mediterranean, hoping to be able soon to offer to God my vows in the Temple of Jerusalem, and at the foot of the Holy Sepulchre of Our Savior.[163]

What Neret did in his day (as had Ignatius in his) was to articulate religious vocation in terms that combined pilgrimage and mission. The combination is what is important. And this fusing of missionary and pilgrim is all the more striking when Neret, in a sense, renews the original Ignatian impulse. As a feature of the early modern European scene—the Renaissance, Counter-Reformation, and Baroque settings—the Jesuits (both in Europe and abroad) took up immense and illustrious cultural space. Jesuit missions are a huge part of the expansion of Europe, for example, just as Jesuit *relations* are a key constituent of the literature of that expansion. In all of this, as in so many other respects, the Levant can get lost from general view. Not entirely, however, was the region lost to view on the part of the Jesuits themselves in their studied refinement of their own corporate self-image—as the volumes of the *Nouveaux Mémoires des Missions de la Compagnie de Jesus dans le Levant* (and earlier Jesuit accounts read by Neret himself in his days as a novice) unmistakably demonstrate. The Levant was a field for Jesuit laborers and, therefore, a field for Jesuit publicists. The proximity of the Holy Land itself to Jesuits laboring in Egypt and Syria offered opportunity for Neret in the eighteenth century, mindful of Ignatius in the sixteenth, to fuse together the missionary and the pilgrim, to articulate the one role in terms of the other. Mission, at least to a Jesuit audience—and probably to a considerably larger audience—imparted to pilgrimage a more intense and more energized life—gave it a new lease on life, a more modern, a contemporary life—than it would have had on its own. (Neret provided a transfusion for pilgrimage at a time when pilgrims themselves were not always confident about the worth of their accounts.)

Desire to be simultaneously pilgrim and missionary is the signature of Neret's text, which begins and ends by pressing home this duality, this inseparability of elements, in his own religious makeup. He traces his longing to go to Palestine, as both pilgrim and missionary, to the early days of his novitiate:

> You know better than anyone, how the missions of our Society in Syria have always had for me an immense attraction. I thought of them in the days of my Noviciate, reading the *Relations* which told us of the works of our missionaries in these vast provinces of an infidel kingdom.
>
> The fruits of their apostolate, and the consolation which they had in walking in the tracks of Jesus Christ, have always made me burn with the desire (*désirer avec ardeur*) to follow in their path, above all in the Holy Land, where Our Savior and his apostles were the first missionaries.[164]

The symbiosis of missionary and pilgrim cannot be pushed further than that! It can, however, be further applied to the contemporary scene. As Neret had followed a tradition, he now offers it to the next generation. His letter is a call for recruits.[165] He lists the Jesuit missions: Aleppo, Damascus, Tripoli, Sidon, Jerusalem, the mountains of the Lebanon, the huge kingdom of Egypt. "All of these lands are holy," he tells his readers, "since they have been sanctified by the birth and the works of the Son of God." Everywhere he goes, he walks in the path of the disciples. Everywhere he preaches, he preaches where the disciples themselves had preached. Sacred history colors every moment, every task, every difficulty. The missionary act in this region—this is the heartfelt core of Neret's letter—cannot but be an act of pilgrimage. The nations among whom Levantine missionaries seek to preserve and defend the faith are the very ones who received the faith from the Apostles. All of this rises to a crescendo—that celebrates the harvest to be made, the thorns and brambles to be endured, the sufferings (of Christ and his disciples) to be imitated—and then it all comes to an end. The text of the letter is unearthed and sent to the printer twelve years later.

After another four years, there appeared in 1729, in the seventh volume of the same *Nouveaux Mémoires des Missions* of the Jesuits in the Levant, the "Lettre du père Sicard."[166] This is a document from what might be called Neret's Greater Holy Land. For centuries, Mount Sinai had frequently been an integral part of the pilgrimage to Jerusalem, going back as far as Breydenbach and well beyond. It was his own journey in the Sinai that Claude Sicard described in his letter. Sicard was a heroic missionary among the Copts, but also an archaeological investigator of sites of sacred and ecclesiastical history in Egypt (the earlier volume containing Neret's report also included Sicard's account of his journey, in company with the Maronite Joseph Assemanni, the Prefect of the Vatican library, to the ancient monastic sites in the Egyptian desert). Indeed, Sicard was acting under royal commission in these investigations.[167] By the time his report on Sinai was published, Sicard was dead from plague contracted in the carrying out of his priestly duties. His Egyptological surveys went unfinished.[168]

Sicard's journey was an act at once of devotion and of scholarly investigation. He and his party sought to determine and follow the route of the Israelites in the desert and to describe places and objects of sacred history along the way.[169] His letter can best be read in the light of Neret's. Both are examples of pilgrimage merging with, or at least being intimately in league with, other than strictly peregrinative enterprises. In Neret's case, pilgrimage formed the other side, or a deeply colored aspect, of his missionary endeavors (Neret, after all, was *primarily* a missionary; he had not been sent by his Jesuit superiors to the Levant in order simply to be a pilgrim). In Sicard's case, devotion to holy sites was translated into tasks of royally sponsored scientific exploration (which themselves focused on *archaeologia sacra*). The two Jesuits shed light on one important part of what was happening to pilgrimage in the modern world. Both represented a religious society that discovered everywhere under foot in the Levant tracks and traces of religious antiquity; and yet, at the same time, the central and continuing purposes of the Jesuits in the Levant (and of these two Jesuits in particular) were not wrapped up in pilgrimage so much as they were directed towards quite other goals and enterprises. These other goals and enterprises which the Jesuits undertook, however, were also religious and ecclesiastical in nature, not secular (not, for example, touristical). They were undertakings either pastoral in nature or dedicated to sacred learning (or, in the case of that earlier Levantine Jesuit, Michel Nau, to ecclesiastical diplomacy). It is perhaps commonsensical to interpret the altered status of pilgrimage in early modern Europe—especially its reduced status in the great collections of travel (and also in the works of travelers who no longer were willing to go long distances primarily or solely in search of sacred sites)—as purely a consequence of some vague but powerful secularization. The Jesuits in the Levant, however, suggest other possibilities. An act of modernization—for example, the treating of pilgrimage differently in the modern world from the way it had been treated in the medieval world—was not always an act of secularization. To be in the Levant—even to be *devoutly* in the Levant—no longer meant that one existed there necessarily or primarily as a pilgrim. To say as much, however, is not to say that Europeans so situated in the Levant could not, and did not, bring powerfully to bear upon their activities the spirit and practice of pilgrimage. Neret and Sicard are both witnesses of such an intensely modern pilgrimage that manifested itself in their accounts of their lives and journeys in the Levant.

The century advanced. Pilgrims continued, now and then, to sail to Jerusalem. Accounts of their journeys continued, here and there, to appear in print. Jonas Korte, a bookseller and schoolteacher in Saxony, and a one-time soldier, shows the capacity of the genre to surprise, even at this late date. If Protestants in general might arrive at the Franciscan convent in Jerusalem without much comment, a Pietist such as Korte making his way from Germany to the Holy Land was probably a sight to behold (and to contend with). But however out of the ordinary, Korte does share (in the very first paragraph of the *Vorrede*) the worry—increasingly common to pilgrims of the age—that adding yet another contemporary account of pilgrimage to the great number already in existence is simply to offer something "superfluous and unnecessary." His hope, that he will not be thought to have placed before the eyes of the world something that is quite useless (*unnutzes*), is based on the fact that he is departing from the common path of such books in ways that are, in his opinion, of more than slight importance. In the event, nevertheless, he does hedge his bets on the matter, retreating to the common proverb: "Many eyes see more than one."[170]

A Protestant ferociously and rigorously opposed to Catholicity, Korte is nevertheless powerfully drawn to the promised land, where he cannot help but encounter causes aplenty to stoke his ire against the papacy and its doings. He disputes the traditional identification of sites (among them Calvary itself), disapproves of Catholic devotions in the Holy Land, and sounds a more general clarion call against all things papistical. Baroque Catholicity and Korte's version of Protestantism had little in common—save the religious desire to be in Palestine. Korte lets fly at Rome with the usual ammunition. The papacy is the devil's work, the pope anti-Christ. Protestants themselves ("theologians as well as politicals") who refuse to see the truth of this are simply proofs of the devil's wiles.[171] At the same time, there is nothing personal—or at least nothing *merely* personal—in Korte's unrelenting lambasting of the pope.[172] He has in his sights everything the pope represents. On the one hand, Catholics are the depraved papacy; on the other, they are a people in need of, and susceptible of, salvation. This hypercharged confessional vehemence, unusual in other pilgrimages, is the living signature of Korte's particular narrative. And there is an incongruity that this heating up of the theological pitch takes place in a rare ecumenical spot of sorts that even Korte recognizes—the Franciscan convent in Jerusalem.

Autobiography—in the sense of the author's *odium theologicum*, but also in the sense of his deeper interior landscape—looms large in Korte's account, because Korte himself is intent on persuading the reader of his deep spiritual longing to go to Jerusalem. What motivates him to travel to Palestine is not the search after "mere novelty" and even less the pursuit of "worldly commerce"—obvious motives for travel in an era of discovery and exploration—but rather "a profoundly interior impulse."[173] We are told much of the personal and anxiety-colored prehistory of his journey—how words of Scripture read by him to youths in a schoolroom sparked his own desire "to see the very land where God especially revealed the magnitude of his goodness and severity"; how his longing seemed "foolish and fanciful" and altogether impossible but then became more of a possibility when he took on a more spiritual view of the world and of his place in it; how he searched for certitude and inner peace and general comfort of soul in respect to his planned trip; how in 1713, in his thirtieth year, he traveled from England through France and Italy and boarded an English ship at Messina and got as far as Constantinople before his spirit flagged; how, back in Europe, his spirit put to rights and his certitude restored, he prepared again for the journey to the Holy Land after, among other preparations, disencumbering himself of his bookseller's business. Breezes of spiritual autobiography—Korte reworked the literature of devout travel into a highly personal literature—waft through the entire book.[174]

Once having got from Venice to Egypt, and from Egypt to Jaffa, he goes from site to site within the Holy Land as generations of pilgrims before him had done. However, his sizing up of his audience—not only the "learned world" but also the "lovers of the divine Word"—leads him to intersperse his traveler's account of things seen with additional reflections (*meditationes*, *Betrachtungen*) on the spiritual meaning of it all.[175] Such writings will provide, for those unable to view the scenes with their own eyes, a witness (*Zeuge*) of what the Lord did in the Holy Land.[176]

Korte is not giving the reader something absolutely new in the line of pilgrimage; but the fuel of his Pietism inflames the already existing contemporary inclination of pilgrims to give vent to a more devotional, personal, and interior disposition. The intensely personal (and combative) tone of Korte's presentation conveys a charged atmosphere. While there is no direct or ostensible connection between Morison and Korte—they are from radically different worlds; neither would have much sympathized with what the other was doing—they actually do share a certain engaged attitude toward things seen and experienced in devout travel. Indeed, if Morison reminds us of Chateaubriand, so also does Korte for the particular reason that he talks seriously and copiously (almost endlessly) about himself—not only about his experiences, but about his motivations and his interior disposition. There is one difference, however, that tends to make all the difference between the nineteenth-century *mémoiriste* and the eighteenth-century Pietist. While Chateaubriand will glory in the role of autobiographer and will assert that autobiography, not travel, is what he is actually writing, Korte pulls up short of such a formulation, even when in the midst of telling us all about himself. He remembers what he is about. He remembers not only the subject matter he is describing, but the form in which he is casting that matter. For example, he mentions "certain difficulties," "certain personal circumstances" that needed to be cleared up before he could finally set out on his journey in 1738. He does not, however, serve them up to the reader, "especially because such matters are deemed inappropriate material for a travel account (*Reise-Beschreibung*) which is not, after all is said and done, an autobiography (*Lebens-Lauf*)."[177] Korte faced the same literary decision that Chateaubriand would confront seventy years later. He simply decided (otherwise than would Chateaubriand) to remain within the tradition of travel-writing. Korte may not have had (to *our* lights) a keenly developed sense of proportion, but he did at least possess a sense of genre.

However odd Korte's emphases (and outbursts) might be when he described the experience of making a religious journey to Palestine, he nevertheless existed well within a long tradition of devout travel to the Levant. His own contribution to the continuation of that tradition was impressively manifested in print for decades. After appearing in Altona in 1741 in German, the text appeared three more times (with supplements) in Halle, which was the great eighteenth-century center of Pietism, and in a Dutch translation in Haarlem (1776) and Amsterdam (1781).[178] Perhaps what secures Korte his place in that tradition is not so much the remarkable coloring—autobiographical, personal, deeply spiritual, harshly polemical—that he contributes to the tradition, but his own sense that he does exist within a tradition. For one thing, Korte gave a substantial grounding to a specifically Protestant pilgrimage. Just as Maundrell invoked Sandys, Korte cited his own sources of information and inspiration—the English Protestant Pococke, for example, and above all Bunyan's *Pilgrim's Progress*.[179] The latter was a highly unusual citation in a genre that usually drew on Jerome, Burchardus of Mount Sion, and other writers of pilgrimages who were timeless touchstones within the Catholic tradition. Finally, however, in seeing Korte as representative of a specifically Protestant tradition of pilgrimage within the larger tradition of pilgrimage, we must not confine Protestant travelers in too narrow a mold. Korte was odd, not only when viewed against the backdrop of a predominantly Catholic world and ethos of pilgrimage, but also when viewed vis-à-vis other Protestant travelers to Palestine—at least as they appeared in their printed accounts. One need only set side by side the homely frontispiece picture of a pilgrim atop a camel ("The manner of Travelling upon Dromedarys") that faces the title page of Crouch's *Two Journeys to Jerusalem* and the frontispiece depiction of forbidding rocks and mountains together with interpretive passages from Scripture that introduces Korte's book to sense a great complexity within Protestantism—even between forms of Protestantism that shared a common urge to go to Jerusalem.

But Korte did far more than substantiate and shore up a specifically Protestant tradition of pilgrimage in his own idiosyncratic manner. Korte, too, serves as convincing example—perhaps the most strikingly persuasive since Feyerabend's tome—of the reality and strength of a fundamentally comprehensive tradition of pilgrimage by Europeans that does manage to transcend (by however close a call) the Catholic-Protestant divide. For though it would be difficult to imagine a Protestant pilgrim more hostile to Rome than Korte, or more willing to use his account of pilgrimage as a tool to express that hostility, yet even he frankly, if selectively, acknowledges the usefulness of Catholic pilgrimage accounts to his own rendition and therefore implies a common substratum serving each party's travels. He devotes an eleven-page chapter (bk. 2, ch. 15) to extracting passages from the intensely Catholic account of Ludwig Tschudi "since they clarify or confirm things that I myself have said [about the Palestinian scene]."[180] Korte shows, at least in interludes between his confessional roundhouses and despite his own deep inclinations (but in ultimate league with the likes of Rauwolf, Feyerabend, and the Franciscan hoteliers and guides to *all* Europeans in Jerusalem), that pilgrimage was an occasion of discourse between Catholics and Protestants, a practice and subject matter over which it was possible to disagree, to agree to disagree, or even on some points to come to more or less modest agreement.

After Korte, we approach mid-century. Pilgrimage perhaps began to strike its tent; or perhaps not. However the scene is envisaged, the genre continued to show signs of life. About this time, there appeared in Swedish Fredrik Hasselquist's *Iter Palaestinum* (Stockholm, 1757). The book was a natural history of the Holy Land rather than a pilgrimage—or, if a pilgrimage, one that was pitched solely from this angle of the natural history of the region. The work was edited by Linnaeus, Hasselquist's teacher and patron, after the author's death in the midst of his explorations of the Levant. Over the decade and a half, following its original edition, Hasselquist's work appeared in various places in translation into German, English, French, and Dutch.[181]

If we are to think at all of Hasselquist (filtered through the editing of Linnaeus) as a pilgrim, it must be as a reluctant or incidental one—a pilgrim in spite of himself. The title page itself of the English edition permits us to regard him in such a light, when it speaks of the observations (of a natural historical, physical, agricultural, and commercial nature) that Hasselquist made "particularly on the Holy land and the natural history of the Scriptures." Hasselquist's book did not, in other words, pretend away the historical significance of Palestine. It was not just a piece of hitherto unexamined terrain. To talk about rocks and plants in Palestine was to be dealing with religiously active material. Moreoever, the company that Hasselquist kept was, by force of circumstances, the company of pilgrims.[182] He admitted—one almost hears a sigh of consternation—that since he was now in the Holy Land, he "therefore had reason to expect continual informations of holy things." Hasselquist did go so far as to tell an enquiring Franciscan to his face that he had not come to Palestine out of devotion. Nevertheless, it turns out that he did accommodate himself to the spirit of the place and did actually participate in pilgrimage. Indeed, he had his own Franciscan guide to lead him through the streets of Jerusalem to one holy site after another.[183]

However much or little Hasselquist himself was influenced by the peregrinative tradition, his book, as the first thorough-going natural historical treatment of Palestine, was the forerunner of that reawakened intellectual interest in the Levant on the part of Europeans that would explode into fashion at the turn of the century with the armies of Napoleon and the production of works such as the *Description de l'Egypte* (Paris, 1809). This revived interest, of course, had less and less to do with the long tradition of religious travel to the Levant. Indeed, the quickened interest in the *realia* of the Levant—its history, archaeology, flora and fauna—will provide the context within which Chateaubriand's efforts at the restoration of pilgrimage will be played out. His *Itinéraire* itself manifested this European turn to the Orient; it also bucked the tide, however, since his focus settled on the Holy Land and its centuries of pious visitors. In some sense, which it is important for us to grasp in trying to evaluate Chateaubriand's efforts to restore pilgrimage, Chateaubriand was conducting a two-front intellectual battle. At home, he was reacting against what Enlightenment and Revolution had wrought. His outlook was both negative and revivalist. In the Orient—or rather in the new Orient that inhabited the minds of Europeans freshly aroused to the lures of the East—he was attempting to stir ashes of a past (a past both remote and not so remote) at the very same time that others were poking about in their own piles of *relicta* that were the detritus of a quite different Levantine past.

It is facile to write off late eighteenth-century pilgrimage—as Chateaubriand himself had done. Pilgrimage was not hopelessly out of step with the march of the times. Pilgrimages continued to appear in print very late in the day. They were a stubborn feature of the literary landscape. In Russia, the two-hundredth anniversary of Trifon Korobeĭnikov's sixteenth-century pilgrimage was marked by the first printed edition of the account of the 1583 journey to Jerusalem, Egypt, and Mount Sinai (St. Petersburg, 1783). The edition was reprinted several times, and fifteen years later (Moscow, 1798) it came out in a wholly new version that was, as the title page has it, "translated into pure Russian for easier understanding, with explanations added for dubious places."[184] Suddenly to bring to printed light a journey made two centuries earlier and then to take the trouble to refashion the text for its easier understanding—both undertakings suggest that printers were still looking for audiences for pilgrimage.

Nor need we look so far to the East to find evidence of pilgrimage's continuing vitality. Evidence exists in the Parisian heart of Europe. On 26 October 1776, the abbé Binos set out from his home in Comminges on a tour of Italy and the Levant. Almost a year and a half later (15 April 1778) he was back in Europe, cooling his heels in the lazaretto at Livorno. It took almost a decade for the account of his journey, in the form of his letters written en route, to be printed under the title *Voyage par Italie, en Egypte, au Mont-Liban, et en Palestine ou Terre Sainte* (Paris, 1787). A German translation was published in 1788 in Breslau and Leipzig; a translation from the German into Russian appeared in 1793 in St. Petersburg. The text even found an audience in Revolutionary France, coming out in a second edition in Paris in 1798/99.[185]

Dominicus Binos, a provincial cleric of some standing—canon of the cathedral of Comminges and vicar general of the diocese of Lescar—undertook a wide-ranging tour. He explains to his reputed correspondent in the very first letter that "I was solely occupied with the desire to satisfy my curiosity."[186] He is very much an eighteenth-century *touriste*, a philosophical traveler who has caught the bug of romanticism in the air, a self-confident traveler seized with the *idea* of travel.[187] He gives us a largely touristical take on Venice. The city offers much to be observed and commented upon, but by the eighteenth century even the pious tourist is not as interested as Breydenbach had been in the fifteenth century to describe the city as a reliquary.[188] And when Binos comes to Loreto, he is delighted to find not simply "an isolated place of devotion" but "a pleasant town" that presents him with many objects of curiosity.[189]

Pilgrimage, however, was what was firmly on his mind. It gave his book shape, weight, motivational drive. At Assisi, for example, while his stop was brief, his attention (unlike that of his contemporary, Goethe) was fixed on the Franciscan church.[190] In Rome, he was "favorably received by the Holy Father who twice requested from me a Mass at the Holy Sepulchre, and his blessing could only increase my desire to undertake this voyage."[191] In his dedicatory letter to Elizabeth of France, Binos spoke of "a journey which zeal for religion has caused me to undertake."[192] More than a third of the text (letters 69–111) was taken up with describing his time in the Holy Land.

In reading Binos, we have very much a sense of being *on the eve*. His

dedication of the book to Elizabeth of France and his meeting with Pius
VI, who was just beginning a long pontificate (1775–1799) that was to endure dark years in the wake of the approaching Revolution, stand for a
world that (unknown to Binos) was on the verge of crashing down. Binos
himself may even have hinted at an awareness on his own part that pilgrimage was a thing of the past, or at least a mode of travel sliding toward the
margins, even in the Mediterranean, when he mentioned "three strangers
recently arrived from different parts of the globe" who shared his quaran-
tine in Livorno. One came from Bactria and claimed to be the son of the
Prince of Chorsan, another was an Anglo-American captain of a merchant
vessel filled with Levantine goods, and the third a German officer who
had come to the Mediterranean on an embassy from the Queen of Hungary to the Porte.[193] And a surer indication of the way adverse winds seemed
to be blowing: in Jerusalem itself, Binos had been astounded to discover
that the traditional Palm Sunday procession from Bethphage to Jerusalem
had been suspended for the past twenty years.[194] Yet, as much as Binos
might appear to a later time—even to the early years of the nineteenth
century—to travel and write from another world, a world almost fading
away before his readers' eyes, his book also provides an impressive bridge
between the worlds of travel before and after the Revolution. There actually appeared a late edition of Binos's *Voyage* in Paris in 1809—that is, in
the period that intervened between Chateaubriand's own journey to the
East in 1806 and the first edition of his *Itinéraire* in 1811. Binos's volumes
do, then, offer a vessel of continuity: he had traveled piously to Jerusalem,
and his account had been published in the last years of the ancien régime.
The book, moreover, continued to appear during the Revolution and in
its aftermath.

Continuity is also suggested by echoes of Binos that will seem to sound
in Chateaubriand.[195] Perhaps even more striking than any specific anticipation of Chateaubriand in Binos, however, is the contrast between the two in
respect to their overall task. Binos is quite comfortable with the "superficial
notions" and the "fleeting impressions" which are the products of a traveler
on the move. He does not deny that he is offering an entertainment, nor
does he take the extreme literary step, as Chateaubriand will do, of retreating from *voyage* into *mémoire* in the face of a realization that others might
be more qualified to report on the scenes he is hurriedly observing and describing. Binos's *Voyage* is not the dense and astounding work of literature
that Chateaubriand's *Itinéraire* turned out to be; the case could be made,
however, that Binos did prove a more deft transporter than Chateaubriand

of pilgrimage across the divide separating an older Europe from post-Revolutionary Europe. He was more confident of his role, more comfortable in the genre and tradition he followed. He admits that he was hurrying along, gathering impressions; but unlike Chateaubriand, he remained a traveler on pilgrimage. What he was writing was an account of travel, no matter how autobiographical his remarks and no matter how clearly he put his own sensibility on show. It was unmistakably a *traveler's* sensibility.

It could be argued that once Binos's late eighteenth-century *Voyage* had been reprinted in the early nineteenth century, there was no great need for the *Itinéraire*, at least not for its grand program of salvage and repair. Pilgrimage had already weathered the Revolutionary storm in the humbler and less elegant craft of the abbé Binos. What requires special notice, moreover, is that Binos's effort, far from being simply a slight and late entry in a field of diminishing importance, shows that pilgrimage still had life in it. For one thing, the oppressive cloud of fear of repetition—the occupational malaise of pilgrim writers for a century and more—is simply cast overboard by Binos. At Loreto, he remarks: "Everyone knows about the miraculous transport of the Holy House to Loreto. I retell it only because it is never possible to repeat too often to men the events that are marked by the seal of the Divine."[196] This is the mark of a pilgrim, one who is not afraid of repetition, one who embraces redundancy—and, we might add, one who knows one of the reasons why readers take up books of pilgrimage. He neither resorts to the wringing of hands and prefatory efforts of justification that had been employed by some seventeenth- and eighteenth-century predecessors, nor does he adopt what will be Chateaubriand's practical fiction on the matter, namely that no one has written or read pilgrimage for so long that one need not fear repetition. Binos simply proceeds with the account of his journey that followed in the footsteps of centuries of previous tellers of the tale. In doing so, he manages to throw new light on old ground—not startlingly new, but sufficiently so to be of interest. He makes clearer than anyone had before him, for example, that when European pilgrims came to Palestine, it was Bethlehem rather than Jerusalem that was of more absorbing emotional interest for many of them.[197] One might have gathered this from earlier pilgrimages, but it was not so frankly stated to be the case. For another example, Binos (or his editors) showed a knack for blending into an organic unity the peregrinative and the touristical-sociological. He could combine curiosity and piety (or, more exactly, general curiosity and pious curiosity), whereas his forerunners (going all the way back to Breydenbach and Reuwich) tended to keep separate the two sorts of information. In this regard, consider the matter of the illustration of costumes. Binos's presentation is visually syntactical rather than paratactical. He combines in one image the "Femme Arabe et vue du Mont Liban" and in another, a "Femme de Jerusalem et vue de la maison d'Elizabeth" (both of which illustrations might be compared to the "Venitienne, Pendant la Foire de l'Ascension").[198] In all three cases, his illustrations combine two separate kinds of information—the religious and the touristical—in one image. This was highly unusual in the iconography of pilgrimages. (One thinks, above all, of Breydenbach's images of representative inhabitants of the Levant in their costumes on the one hand, and his entirely separate images of sacred sites on the other).

For a last example of Binos's novelty, there is this passage:

> I had arrived at the town of Rama. It was called Arimathia at the time when Joseph, who was a native of the town, embalmed Jesus Christ. The hospice of Terra Sancta [i.e., the Franciscan Custody] prides itself (*se flatte*) on being built on the spot where the house of this venerable personage had formerly been located; but its greater glory is to be serving as a refuge for Christian travelers who are going to Jerusalem.[199]

The passage is as remarkable in its way as was Neret's passage on the value of local tradition in keeping alive our memory of the events of sacred history. In both cases, it is the act of pilgrimage, the life suspirant in devout travelers as they move about and mull over the holy sites, rather than the sites themselves, that receives the engaged attention of the pilgrim-writers. In both instances, evidentiary matters have become secondary. Were the waters in the present-day fountain in Cana what local pious traditions said they were? Did the Franciscan hospice in Rama in fact stand on the site of Joseph's house? It did not finally matter—at least not hugely so to either the Jesuit missionary or the cathedral canon. It was not that such matters were unimportant (though they probably would have been more important to *resident* writers of pilgrimages)—still less that they were risible or superstitious. What was undoubtedly important, however, was the act of pilgrimage—an act that folded together prayer, meditation, memory, reflection. The hospice in Rama was a holy spot—a *glorious* spot—for Binos because of its contemporary role of service to pilgrims in quest of sacred history. It was a marker of the continuing history of the holy, quite apart from the matter of its own precise archaeological status.

Conclusion:
Alive and Well and Early Modern

Vicit iter durum pietas. Piety has conquered the arduous road. Against the early modern grain, pilgrimage endured, even if much buffeted and bruised, as a form of travel. The words of Anchises to Aeneas, printed on the eighteenth-century title page of Ambrosio de Morales's sixteenth-century *Viage*, and fittingly so in light of all that had worked to impede or dilute the realization of Morales's *peregrinación* to Compostella, might well have decorated the title page of every book of pilgrimage to the Holy Land printed between Breydenbach and Chateaubriand. Breydenbach's fate—his images to be used for a new sort of travel in 1494, his text to be mangled and abbreviated in a 1625 collection (Purchas's) celebrating that new travel—turned out to be symptomatic of the heavy toll that Discovery and Reformation were to take on the entire genre, not just on one illustrious practitioner, of pilgrimage.

The way to Jaffa for early modern Europeans was an *iter durum* for reasons quite beyond physical hardships. What is essential to notice is the cultural survival of pilgrimage, its survival within the genre of travel. Pilgrimage remained part of the discourse of early modern travel. In spite of the distracting ships of Columbus and Cook, the contrarian pulpits of Luther and Zwingli, the alternative shrines of Loreto and Guadaloupe, Europeans continued to travel to Mediterranean ports in order to sail to Jaffa whence they toured the holy sites of Palestine.[1] No longer the shiploads of earlier centuries, early modern pilgrims nevertheless sufficed to produce an early modern literature of travel that testifies to the early modern reality of pilgrimage to the Holy Land. While it is a great fact of the time that the practice of travel underwent a mighty shift away from the Levant towards new routes and destinations driven by new ambitions that gave rise to a new literature of travel, at the same time there also survived and flourished a travel literature of pilgrimage to Jerusalem. Nor was this literary survival merely at the margins, as might be suggested by celebrated travelers who simply found a place for the Holy Land on their itineraries—a place, moreover, sufficiently subordinate that it could be overlooked by readers with other interests.[2] Adamnan and Mandeville, Tucher and Breydenbach—these travelers and writers of travels did have successors. Pilgrimage to Palestine remained, as it had been for centuries, a notable, if no longer the exclusive, subject matter and theme of travel. While pilgrimage's early modern displacement from the unshared center of travel might now seem to have been inevitable, at the time it may have been more of a near thing. Had, for example, Columbus's true thoughts on Atlantic travel been given an early public voice, or had Ignatius of Loyola's wish to combine Near Eastern missions and pilgrimage been realized, early modern travel might have assumed a different shape that would have allowed more space and color to pilgrimage.

In the event, long voyages to startlingly new places, however massive and plural their other ramifications, were *about travel*, just as long voyages to Jaffa had been similarly occupied in earlier centuries. Discoverers, or their *litterateurs* (especially collector-publishers of travels), heralded new ambitions and destinations for travel. The traveler became what he had not been for centuries—a hero. Memorializations of Columbus sparked references to Ulysses. Religious reformers also helped to redefine travel. Some indicted pilgrimage and sought to be rid of it in contemporary travel, and even in records of past travels. Others practiced a pilgrimage (stripped-down, de-Catholicized) that was recognizable though much altered. Even Catholics of the fervent Baroque, by finding, or refurbishing, Jerusalems closer to home, cleared decks for new travel to new regions and complicated the possibilities of future pious travel to the Levant. As the sixteenth century progressed, centuries-old pilgrimage to the Holy Land declined so markedly in numbers of travelers and infrastructure for such travel that by the early nineteenth century, Chateaubriand could imagine the eighteenth century a dead landscape (or seascape) between Europe and Palestine so far as *peregrinatio causa religionis* was concerned.

Changes in travel seem clear in retrospect, although the image of travel produced by (necessarily) looking at history *à rebours* is not without distortion. The observant present always produces clouds of clarity. In the specific matter of travel, the subject itself can become a somewhat dubious category, and not least because our sense of genre (in both literature and deeds) is more fully defined than was that of early modern Europeans. (It is a trait of the ultra modern to distinguish between Herodotus the historian and Herodotus the writer of travels.) And yet, it is hard to deny that an early modern reality of travel that our contemporary sense of genre appears to detect and approximate did in fact exist, even if not in so sharply outlined a state as we ourselves would have it. Telltale is Europeans' ages-old receptivity to renditions of actual journeys over long distances. Knowledge of remote geographies and topographies—the sheer data of a remote Terra Sancta that was itself a visitable expanse reaching from northern Palestine to Sinai—was often not extracted from experience, but allowed to remain imbedded in more or less fully described experience. Europeans had long wanted to know not only about Terra Sancta, but about the way there and the way from Jaffa to Jerusalem, from Jerusalem to Bethlehem, from Gaza to Sinai. The experience of travel was on their minds. Information never quite trumped story. This was true at least as far back as Adamnan's version of Arculf's travels and remained true a thousand years later in the work of Morison. After Columbus, however, Europeans increasingly wanted to be told new things—and new stories: how one got adventurously to Mexico City or around the Cape of Good Hope or up the Orinoco or from Goa to Macao. New destinations of travel brought new narratives of travel into existence.

But even with all the practical redefinition of travel that was at work in early modernity, piously setting out for Jaffa had not suddenly become a narrow or eccentric or even specialized act that no longer, in the age of Columbus and Francis Xavier and Cook, had much to do with travel proper. Pilgrimage did remain a form of piety, of prayer and devotion and penance; but it also continued to be a form of European travel. That it was so perceived at the time is the first conclusion of our scan of three centuries. To understand early modern travel, one must allow for early modern pilgrimage itself *as a form of travel*. If no longer the conspicuous travelers who never escaped notice, pilgrims did nevertheless remain very much part of the *dramatis personae* of travel.

Changes in travel overall had, of course, come very much at pilgrimage's expense. Collections of voyages that erased pilgrimage, treatises on travel that ignored pilgrimage, the extreme rarity of Levantine pilgrimages coming off New World presses[3]—all point to an altered milieu of travel. Nevertheless, and contrary to the impression created by such evidence, one way that pilgrimage survived was precisely as a mode of travel. When Thomas Treter introduced Radziwill's pilgrimage at the beginning of the seventeenth century, he invoked Cicero and Seneca as travelers who preceded his pilgrim in a grand and unbroken tradition of travel. Gretser in

Ingolstadt, that most expert *amateur* of pilgrimage, acknowledged that pilgrimage was one among various kinds of travel (*peregrinatio*).[4] The celebrated seventeenth-century traveler (but *not* pilgrim), François Le Gouz de La Boullaye, began his great *Voyages et observations* of 1657 with thoughts on books of travel he had read. The seven pages of "Sentiment du Sieur de la Boullaye-le Gouz sur les diverses Relations qu'il a leües des pays estrangers" included pilgrimages in addition to every other sort of travel book. Villamont, in fact, headed a list that also included Columbus, Mendes Pinto, Vasco da Gama, and others.[5] Even as late as the eighteenth century, those who read pilgrimages—to judge by those who arranged books of pilgrimage on shelves—continued to think of them as belonging to a genre of travel. It was hardly odd to find Furer's *Reise-beschreibung*, Bünting's *Itinerarium*, and the second edition (1609) of Feyerabend's *Reise-Buch* in the same category ("Itineraria") with works of very different kinds of travelers such as Mendes Pinto, Chardin, and Tavernier.[6] Similarly, the eighteenth-century catalogue of a Jesuit library placed books by Doubdan, Morison, and other pilgrims alongside those by writers who, though having nothing to say about pilgrimage, did share with pilgrimages the common heading of "Voyages d'Asie, d'Afrique, et d'Amérique."[7]

Contemporaries, then, testify that pilgrimage *ad Terram Sanctam* remained part of early modern travel. Nevertheless, not every contemporary evidence of pilgrimage's general vitality also pertains specifically to its place in the history of travel. Consider the illustrious example of Ignatius of Loyola. His autobiographical reminiscences testify to the transformative role of pilgrimage in an individual life. Ignatius, moreover, was not speaking after a fashion, or in terms of a vague idea of *peregrinatio*, in his conversations in a Roman garden with Luis Gonçalves da Câmara. Ignatius harked back to his actual pilgrimage to Jerusalem undertaken years before. And yet, mulling over the nature of travel itself or asserting pilgrimage's claims within the contemporary travel genre were not on Ignatius's plate. Pilgrimage had shaped his life, but Ignatius was not providing Gonçalves with notes for a *peregrinatio*. Rome was not Iona, nor was Gonçalves playing Adamnan to Ignatius's Arculf. Nor would his autobiographically crucial reminiscences of his journey to Jerusalem, when finally printed in the eighteenth century—or earlier biographies of Ignatius drawing on these reminiscences—be likely to land on a shelf of *itineraria*. Ignatius's pilgrimage-centered memories did not provide a specific matrix for travel or travel literature, though they do show that pilgrimage itself continued as a form of travel to have a richly spiritual and emotional background of its own, even in the age of discovery.

Other (and more typical) early modern pilgrims did, however, view their pious excursions in the specific light of travel. Prominent travelers who were just barely pilgrims and for whom the Holy Land was but one stop *inter alia* along their larger itineraries offer impressive evidence that pilgrimage was still regarded as a mode of travel, even as these same writer-travelers also demonstrate that pilgrimage was no longer the defining center of travel. The gathering together of Mocquet's own travels *placed* pilgrimage within early modern culture in a way that the great collectors of voyages (Ramusio, Hakluyt, Melchisédec Thévenot, Bellegarde, and others) quite failed to do. Mocquet's volume provided a berth for pilgrimage in a roster of wide-ranging journeys. Finally, many other travelers, who were more single-minded in their focus on pilgrimage and whose accounts of their journeys we have also examined, defined what they were doing very clearly in terms of travel. For the great *cosmographe* André Thevet, pilgrims like himself navigated the modern scene as *viateurs*. Ceverio de Vera viewed pilgrimage as both competitive and complementary to voyages of discovery. Cotovicus and Bénard were proof, a century and a half after Columbus, of the survival of the explicit consciousness of pilgrimage as a form of travel. Cotovicus, in particular, insisted on the primary ranking of pilgrimage within the scheme of travel and sought to address the myriad problems that threatened pilgrimage as an actual mode of travel in seventeenth-century Islamic waters. Conviction that pilgrimage was a form of *travel* permeated early modern printed pilgrimages. Indeed, so thoroughly a part of travel was pilgrimage thought to be by pilgrims themselves that the seventeenth-century Franciscan Castillo's anxiety was that pilgrimage not be submerged in other sorts of travel.

This first conclusion, that pilgrimage survived transition from medieval to modern by remaining a mode of travel, is reenforced by a second conclusion, that pilgrim travel as a whole was colored by—almost defined by, certainly energized by—a deep anxiety concerning its ages-old and oft-described subject matter. The first reaction of many pilgrims to the task of writing up pilgrimages was a wringing of hands. Much of this was, of course, trope and boilerplate—this almost tiresome (for twenty-first-century ears) worrying over going the same routes, seeing the same sites, praying the same prayers, listening to (essentially) the same guides, and thinking the same thoughts as pious predecessors.[8] Such worries became ground as heavily trod as the subject matter over which the writers worried! And yet, these worries are a tip-off. Had early modern pilgrimage turned out to be everything one associates with pilgrimage *except* travel—in other words a devotional, penitential, liturgical genre that documented, à la Chateaubriand, the piety and pious curiosity of an individual *dévot*—there would have been little need to express such anxieties. Pilgrimage, however, was part of the reportorial genre of travel, and repetition hence very much its concern—and all the more so in an age of discovery that was also an age of print. The times put a premium on novelty, exoticism, remoteness; and such qualities were all the more precious and perishable in an age when narratives of travelers spread quickly and widely in print. Anxiety on the part of pilgrims, however, did not in the event lead to stupor—or at least not always. It also produced innovative maneuvers, such as Bruyn shifting his line of sight or La Roque picking out a less scoured area of the Holy Land. Worry (however obligatory and rhetorical) turned out to be a sign of life. (Indeed, how up-to-date this genre of travel with its deep medieval roots proved to be can be appreciated when we avail ourselves of the longest possible perspective. Consider that early modern pilgrimage's defining preoccupation, and pilgrims' moves to address what they perceived to be the problem, seem exactly pertinent to worries and anxieties of late modern—post modern? ultra modern?—travelers finding themselves in a world in which all corners of the globe have been discovered, all its interiors penetrated, and all its sites visited. For those oppressed by Waugh's sense that there was a time—but firmly past—when the going was good and by his resigning himself to the status of tourist—rather than traveler— or by Fussell's thesis, nourished on the gloomy likes of Waugh and Lévi-Strauss, that genuine travel no longer exists, the experience of early modern pilgrims might be well worth consulting.[9] It is just possible that pilgrimage offers a way of escape from tourism, since early modern pilgrims' worries and challenges turn out to have become one with those of most would-be travelers in our own discovery-exhausted world.)

But such thought on later times is strictly parenthetical. That pilgrimage survived into early modernity as a mode of travel, and that writers of pilgrimages characteristically fussed with a purpose over the severe limitations of their genre (or subgenre)—these two conclusions keep us to our subject matter of *early* modernity and lead to a third conclusion, that early modern pilgrimage to the Levant turned out to be a living cultural form in early modern Europe, rather than mere cultural detritus from a still earlier stage of Europe's history. Being a part, rather than a relic, of travel—indeed, an alternative to most other, discovery-driven forms of travel—was itself a sign of life productive of various other signs of life. While it is possible to portray early modern pilgrims adhering to a tradition (which they were) and to present them as a continuous band of related travelers following one after the other "in the tracks of" predecessors, even a general scan and survey of three centuries suggests other possible models of historical presentation than the frieze. For one thing, the genre evolved and developed, especially in fundamental matters of perception and expression. Consider, for example, the externalism—the keeping to surfaces, the restraining of personality—in earlier pilgrims such as Tucher, Brasca, and Breydenbach. The observing and recording of immediate data—of indulgences, processions, and ceremonies, of the historical background to Mediterranean realities, of the look of sites and the distances between sites, of the contemporary uses to which historic sites were put, of the costumes and customs of the inhabitants, of the flora and fauna—continued to characterize pilgrimage through much of the sixteenth century. As the seventeenth century advanced, however, things began to alter. A new meditative cultivation of the interiority of the traveler and an emphasis on impressions and emotional reactions slowly began to characterize the rendered experiences of pilgrimage, and all of this culminated in a writer such as Morison, whose book was published at the beginning of the eighteenth century. In the materials we have consulted, the first unmistakable sign of a pivot away from the usual and expected appears in Francisco Guerrero's *Breve Tratado del Viage que hizo à la Ciudad Santa de Jerusalèn*, which was first printed in 1590. Here, the self at the sites begins to come forward as truer subject matter than the sites themselves. Eventually, with Castillo (1654), Doubdan (1657), Goujon (1670), and Nau (1679), travel as a deeply meditative encounter between visitor and place will impart to pilgrimage a new style and substance. This deepening and opening up of the genre through attentiveness to the traveler's emotions and consciousness (including consciousness of himself as a traveler) had never been utterly absent (Breydenbach's fellow traveler, Felix Fabri, is an example, and another is the Breydenbach volume's woodcut portraying pilgrims devoutly at a station of the cross in the plaza of the Holy Sepulchre), and a deeply emotional response to Terra Sancta had not been lacking even in late medieval pilgrimages (many of which remained in manuscript throughout the era).[10] Yet the expressed intensity and fervor of pilgrims traveling and recording their experiences during the second half of the seventeenth century amounted to a new style in the printed literature of pilgrimage. This new *élan* may have developed in part as an answer to fears of repetition. The more individual and idiosyncratic the traveler and the more inward his gaze and the more given to checking his own responses, the less opportunity for authorial echoes. The new coloration of pilgrim narratives may have been due, as well, to the decline in actual numbers of pilgrims going to the Levant. There was less need for that most impersonal and superficial of works, the guide book. As the audience for pilgrimage ceased to be made up of realistically potential travelers, writers could move away from the strictly informational. In any event, the old fear of repetition will somewhat subside because of this new approach, although in its stead a new and perhaps equally defining tension begins to arise, this time between residents and transients. Can one be meditative and insightful, not to mention accurate, on the run? Castillo was among those who thought not. The last decades of the century, for pilgrimage, were a creative fog of boldness and doubts that hung about this question. In any event, Morison's volume of 1704—the scarcely read and insufficiently understood culmination of this late flowering of Baroque pilgrimage—will suggest that the office of pilgrim could be filled startlingly well even by one who had not the time to loiter overlong in the Levant. Morison's significance, however much located in the shadows of his own day, is immense. Beginning at the turn from the fifteenth century to the sixteenth, numbers of actual pilgrims had declined from medieval crowds and shiploads (including regiments of Crusaders) to an early modern few. Now, in the seventeenth century, the active agents of pilgrimage (writer-travelers) threatened, under the influence of Franciscans and Jesuits, to be further drastically reduced to only residents of Terra Sancta. What a case of *reductio ad raram avem* the pilgrim would have become! Moreover, had Castillo and his Franciscan-Jesuit successors completely carried the issue, pilgrimage to the Holy Land would have had its travel content reduced, so to speak, from within. Books of Levantine pilgrimage would have grown similar to books devoted to describing shrines within Europe, becoming in other words less the sort of books of travel that chronicled the *dévot*'s journeys to and from and around holy sites. In any event, the transient Morison's deeply imaginative work was an implicit argument against such suffocating possibilities as well as a marked sign of resistance to further specialization of pilgrimage-writing as a craft as well as a reaffirmation, should one be needed, of pilgrimage as travel.

There are other ways, however, to mark the vitality of pilgrimage beyond tracing a grand line of early modern evolution that carries pilgrimage away from its medieval roots and from the surface of things to depths hitherto largely unexamined and left out of play. Pilgrimage, beyond any general and developing profile, was a vital *presence* on the early modern scene. Much was going on in and around the world of pilgrims. That pilgrimage had become, for example, a highly successful printed literature of multiple editions and translations was the very first sign of its modernity. Equally remarkable, and reflected in its growth as a printed literature, was the transformation of Levantine pilgrimage from an activity of great numbers into a literature produced by a few but read by many (to judge by the editions and translations) who in earlier times would themselves have made the journey across the Mediterranean. This radical change of pilgrimage in early modernity from what it had been through much of the medieval span of centuries may help to account for its becoming lost to the sight of late modern scholars of early modern Europe. Pilgrimage to Jerusalem had not gone away in early modern times but only shifted its place in the European scheme of things. One must look for pilgrimage in a different location once the transition has been made from medieval to early modern. Pilgrimage had not ceased to be popular, but only altered its mode of popularity. Early modern pilgrimage survived through a feat of noeticization or noumenalization, becoming a spiritual exercise at the very time that the *Spiritual Exercises* were coming to the fore. It need hardly be said that in this shift of modes, we are not speaking of pilgrimage as a fossil or anachronism—the fragrance of burnt wax lingering above pinched wicks—or as something that had ceased to be vital and viable in so general a cultural form as travel. Travel before and after the turn to the sixteenth century is not a question of a zero-sum game or of musical chairs in which pilgrimage becomes odd genre out (although there is something of hide-and-seek in the way things turned out). All that had happened was that actual pilgrimage had become the rarest of acts, but those rare acts of pilgrimage sufficed to provoke into existence an entire literature of pilgrimage that flourished in the new medium of print. At the same time, pilgrimage to the Levant never became *purely* literary. It remained a form of travel because this grand literature remained grounded in actual devout travel, however rare, to the Holy Land.

This shift in location within early modern culture of pilgrimage to the Levant is extremely important in at least two very general senses. For one thing, the shift from practice to literature suggests an historiographical argument—that the usual distinctions between high and low culture, between elite and popular history, have gotten in the way of our *seeing* early

modern pilgrimage to the Holy Land. The records of early moderns making their devout way to Jerusalem have slipped through interpretive nets of
later historians. The broadest historiographical categories have left Levantine pilgrimage after the late fifteenth century all but invisible. We are understandably prone to regard pilgrimage to the Levant in medieval times and
pilgrimage to sites within Europe in both medieval and modern times as
productive of data of popular history. But early modern pilgrimage to Jerusalem eludes such expectations. However popular within literary circles, it
had indeed been transformed into something literary (*almost entirely* literary), a matter of writers and readers, by some measure an elitist undertaking, but one which also retained elements of the popular cast of pilgrimage
from the days when it had involved the setting out from Europe of far
greater numbers of actual travelers. The crucial point is that early modern
pilgrimage, from a later historical perspective, is difficult to categorize as
either high or low, elite or popular. Hence pilgrimage of the Baroque, clearly
alive and well and subject to historical study in Bavaria and Rome and
Loreto, is only faintly detectible in Jerusalem, existing as it does in the mists
of an historiographical middle ground.

The alteration in cultural location and appearance of pilgrimage during the early modern period—its movement away from road and shipboard
to desk and armchair—also raises what might be called metahistorical considerations, in that it suggests things about historical change that hypo-
thetically apply to historical subject matter quite beyond early modernity and
pilgrimage. Changes in early modern travel (including changes in pilgrimage) in the wake of printing and global navigation and the Reformation
may be characterized as major historical changes. And when confronted
by radical change, historians are wont to shift language of analysis (or, at
least, characterization and summing-up) from the historical to the natural
historical. The greater the upheaval in history, the more likely a discipline
such as geology is drafted to provide explanatory metaphors. One hears of
movements of tectonic plates or of volcanic eruptions. When subject to
cataclysm and upset, society and culture are thus seen to become things of
nature thrown up, and brought low, by forces deep within the bowels of
the earth of history. Moments, or great spans of time, of change are represented through discussions framed in terms of life and death, succession and replacement. Cultural and societal shifts are thought of in terms
of the largest natural occurrences. In the case of the historical formation
of early modern travel and pilgrimage, however, such metaphors prove
inadequate to capture what occurred. The contours and context of travel

utterly changed as early modernity developed. The complexion of travel as pilgrimage through and through altered, but pilgrimage did not cease as an animate presence on the early modern scene. Nor did travel cease to be one thing and become some entirely other thing. Pilgrimage was not succeeded by another form of travel. Pilgrimage did not even move from the center to the margins (except in the minds of some collector-publishers of travels), did not necessarily or always assume another role, or occupy another position, or stand in different lighting. But pilgrimage to the Holy Land did relocate itself culturally, though such a change is not captured by resort to natural metaphors. It serves the case better to fix on society and culture as continuously self-artifacting entities, to think of them as laminate realities of great variety, as complexities of etched transparencies imposed in complicated fashion one upon another. These layers and transparencies— of ideas, practices, beliefs, customs—are subject over time to alterations in themselves and to rearrangements in relation to other layers and transparencies. What we see in the birth of early modern travel is a shuffle of the historical deck. Pilgrimage did not disappear, even though a certain kind of common sense would see the absence of Crusades or the lack of ships and convoys leaving Venice as indicative of disappearance. Pilgrimage did not even disappear from travel. It remained on the scene and within the genre of travel, even as it altered its mode of being present and active. The most profound alteration-within-continuity is suggested by the experience of pilgrimage to Palestine in early modernity. If long-distance pilgrimage endured, radically altered but intact, on the early modern European scene, perhaps *nothing* ever truly disappears (except through actual material destruction) from a civilized setting. This is one metahistorical hypothesis to be harvested from consideration of early modern pilgrimage. And another is that the choreography of history is complicated. One can't always look in the same place, the usual cultural locus, for the same phenomenon of history. Pilgrimage endured and flourished, but the historian has to figure out where to look for it—a point that is probably most applicable in religious, spiritual, and intellectual domains, particularly in the midst and wake of the Reformation.

Upon the Reformation itself, pilgrimage to Jerusalem had a lively bearing. The literature of pilgrimage offered a rare occasion for the expression of lay piety within the Catholic world (from Tucher and Brasca to Thevet, Radziwill, Bénard, and Courmenin) alongside a predominantly clerical voice (from Breydenbach to Castillo, Morison, Neret, and Binos) that included Franciscans, Jesuits, and other religious as well as secular clergy from throughout Catholic Europe. Lay accounts of pilgrimage, an important challenge to any possible monotonality of spiritual expression that might have threatened to characterize Tridentine Europe, are surely a sign of pilgrimage's cultural life. To the question, "where was everybody else—like the laity?"[11]—everybody else, that is, in early modern Catholic Europe beyond the historians' papacy, Council of Trent, and religious orders—a partial answer would be that they were on pilgrimage across the Mediterranean, and not only that but also writing up their pilgrimages for publication.[12]

Pilgrimage's dual fate in the face of Reformation also shows the genre's contemporary resiliency: on the one hand, Catholic pilgrimage to the Levant survived in terms we have described; on the other hand, and as we have also observed, notable Protestants themselves embraced (with serious modification) a consciously pious travel to the Levant which echoed the attraction they also felt (in common with Catholics) to European shrines that possessed relics of the Holy Land's history. The possibility of such Protestant pilgrimage becoming inarticulate almost to the point of dumbness (on the matter of pilgrimage itself) can be seen by juxtaposing the Protestant Maundrell and the Catholic Morison (who were both in Jerusalem in the same year). On the other hand, Protestantism also gave birth to highly interesting hybrids of pilgrimage in the works of such travelers as Rauwolf and Korte. And there was common ground between Protestant and Catholic pilgrims. They lived ecumenically cheek-by-jowl in the Franciscan hostels of Terra Sancta; and the accounts of Rauwolf and even of the fervently anti-Catholic Korte show that there was a substratum of pious travel and travel reportage that was shared by both Catholics and Protestants.

Pilgrimage was an expressive medium of considerable power, especially for early modern Catholics. One way, for example, that nostalgia for the era of grand Crusade lived on well past its heyday of centuries ago was in books such as those of Beauvau and Amico. Pilgrimages also served as theaters of great erudition. Pilgrims were capable of investing considerable learning in their narratives, as shown by the meticulous gathering and shaping of data by the medieval Burchardus of Mount Sion, whose presentation began to be widely printed in the fifteenth century; by Martin Roth's dense commentaries on Mediterranean realities and histories in Breydenbach's fifteenth-century *Peregrinatio*; by the stress on Oriental languages asserted by the Jesuit Nau in the seventeenth century; and by the laborious researches of Nau's fellow Jesuit Sicard in the following century in the Sinai. At the same time, pilgrimage's appeal proved immense and flexible, being capable, for example, of filling a place in the school curriculum (Linden), or of being shaped into a theatrical drama (Kitscher). A work such as Radziwill's shows (as had Breydenbach's over a century earlier) pilgrimage's impressive ability to penetrate linguistic barriers. Radziwill was to turn up in various languages on the printed scene stretching from Antwerp to St. Petersburg. The popular appeal of pilgrimage can also be judged by illustrations that accompanied and brought to more vivid life so many of the finished texts. Serious resort to illustrations, which began with Breydenbach, continued through Bianchi, Zuallart, Amico, Beauvau, Castillo, and many other colleagues, and remained important in the late eighteenth-century pages of Binos. Beauvau was a writer who caught on, only after his book of pilgrimage had been printed, to opportunities of illustrating his travels, and he took pains to supervise the inclusion of elaborate engravings in later editions. Pilgrimage to the Levant was in general one of the great illustrated genres of early modernity.

While including for the most part a body of individual narratives of travel, the literature of pilgrimage also proved capable of occasionally inspiring grand productions that were all but theatrical in their effects. Breydenbach's great illustrated tome of 1486 both described a devout journey and set it within a learned and wide-ranging context that documented both the historical and the later fifteenth-century Mediterranean scene. Feyerabend's 1584 folio collection of pilgrimages celebrated pilgrimages past and present while demonstrating ecumenical possibilities of pilgrimage across the Reformational divide. The volume also demonstrated the conversational possibilities of pilgrimage when numerous specimens of such travel were gathered within the covers of a volume—the very method used, for decades by Feyerabend's time, to treat travels of Columbus, Magellan, and other discoverers. Amico's book of 1609 depicted Terra Sancta in elaborate architectural terms as a great Baroque destination where readers could imagine themselves travelers strolling and pausing among the monumental edifices and remains of sacred history. Such elaborate books of pious travel were grand cultural artifacts and prominent features of the early modern cultural landscape.

Perhaps no other single work of pilgrimage, save the very different work of Morison, encapsulated more powerfully the resiliency and adaptability and vibrant potential of pilgrimage on the early modern scene than Ceverio de Vera's *Viaje*. Ceverio's most obvious accomplishment was not an authorial plunging below the narrative surface, nor the presentation of the pilgrim as a scrutinized self, but rather his stretching the canvas of pilgrimage to include New World data that he saw to be comparable to, and thus illuminative of, data found in the Levant. In his text, discovery and pilgrimage became intimately, almost antiphonally, related as adventurous undertakings. Ceverio can be seen as one of the earliest practitioners of comparative travel. Nevertheless, the reader (even in the twenty-first century) would have been hard pressed to see Ceverio's methods as a maneuver of secularization. The *Viaje* remained, through and through, a pilgrimage. And there was a second aspect to Ceverio: his freedom from worries concerning *repetitio*. Ceverio was rare among writers of pilgrimage in that his travels and his account of travels were not built upon a heap of previous peregrinative accounts. Ceverio was no Felix Fabri (or even Chateaubriand) prepping for his journey. He had been inspired by only one (unnamed) book of pilgrimage which he had happened upon, so he was not oppressed by fear of going tiresomely over trampled ground. He comes out of a New-World environment where action outshines gloss. Overall and across centuries, inheritance within the genre of pilgrimage had been a strength (however problematical and ambiguous) for writers of pilgrimages. In the case of Ceverio, however, strength is found in the very absence of such a weighty literary past. More hours in a library of pilgrim narratives might have made Ceverio see how genuinely—and startlingly, to the point of discouragement?—unprecedented was his handling of ages-old subject matter. And finally, Ceverio testifies to the tattered state of actual pilgrimage (in Spain, at the papal curia, in Venice), but at the same time demonstrates pilgrimage's flourishing *literary* possibilities. The two conditions are related in his narrative. He longs for the arrival of more pilgrims at Jaffa (especially from Spain), but he seems to come to realize that his wish for a revival of numbers of pilgrims will not in fact happen. His true audience is an audience of readers rather than of future travelers to the Levant.

Ceverio, then, suggests pilgrimage's powers of renewal and adaptation. Indeed, the power of a single volume to rescue Ceverio from ennui and disillusionment in the uninspiring atmosphere of Rome shows the power of the genre, even before he turned his hand to the task. Nevertheless, Ceverio offers only one version of pilgrimage's multifarious vitality. It has been clear time and again in these pages, for example, that pilgrimage's rich millennium of tradition proved a worry and a burden to early modern pilgrims attempting to fashion telling accounts of their own journeys— and it is also plausible that Ceverio's breath of fresh air arose from his relative freedom from that tradition's hold, being as he was an incidental rather than studious reader of earlier pilgrimages—but it is also true that another sign of pilgrimage's vigor was the fact that other pilgrims consciously embraced and cultivated that very same tradition, and even, as in the case of Bénard who came after Ceverio, intensified that tradition. It was Bénard who invoked the Blessed Virgin not simply as an object of pilgrims' devotions manifested at her shrines, but as the great exemplar and originator of the act of pilgrimage itself. It is she who stands in Bénard's pages as first in a line of pilgrims visiting the holy sites of Jerusalem.

*   *   *

Early modern books of pilgrimage to the Holy Land did leave many tracks behind, which reveal pilgrimage to have been part of the spirit of the age and a constituent element of early modern culture. Perhaps most suggestive of its vitality in that world between Renaissance and Revolution, however, is the very precariousness of its position and fortunes as it forged ahead. A crippled but navigable bark, pilgrimage flourished under threat of capsizing. While impressive in itself as a literature of writers and readers who composed and consulted editions and translations of numerous titles across three centuries, that literature was grounded in a humble reality of the fewest possible actual journeys. The anatomy of early modern pilgrimage to Terra Sancta was extremely top-heavy—extremely cerebral— in this respect and its condition therefore necessarily extremely fragile. And perhaps even more suggestive of fragility is that while the literary corpus of pilgrimage was impressive indeed, it must not be forgotten that this array of titles, editions, and translations existed in a world that had given rise to an entirely new genre of travel literature, the collection of travels, which for all practical purposes granted scant recognition to the survival, much less the literary flourishing, of devout travel to the Levant. Pilgrimage was nevertheless a common thread that testified to real continuity between medieval and early modern travel. Such continuity, however, was frayed and weakening and may be said to have come undone with Chateaubriand. The exquisiteness of his *Itinéraire*, and thus its prominence and influence in the post-Revolutionary era, heightened the persuasiveness of his tentative yet adumbrative sense that pilgrimage now existed outside its centuries-old category of travel. Chateaubriand may have removed his own pilgrimage from the genre of travel, but he had not withdrawn himself from the role of traveler—and just how modern a traveler can be seen by the light in which he ultimately cast his pilgrimage. Forty years after his journey to

the Levant and just two years before his death, Chateaubriand is still trying to say a last word on the *Itinéraire*. He adheres to his earlier formulation, by now almost a mantra, concerning "my life being documented hour
by hour in the *Itinéraire*."[13] He then continues, however, in a vein that,
like much in Chateaubriand, leaves the reader calculating whether the words
are meant to count full value. He mentions Julien (his servant and companion) who was with him on his Mediterranean voyage and who had kept
his own *itinéraire* in conjunction with Chateaubriand's. The two of them
were "like those passengers on a ship who keep their individual journal
on a voyage of discovery. The small manuscript which he places at my
disposal will act as a control on my narration. I will be Cook, he will be
Clerke."[14] The image carries weight as a last word on the subject. The *voyage de decouverte* by itself might have floated under our notice, but in combination with the name of Cook, the phrase seems pointed. Chateaubriand
the pilgrim, who had not thought of his *Itinéraire* as a *voyage* at all but
rather as a *mémoire*, does now, at the end, specifically cast himself, on this
particular, long-ago journey (which had been, after all, a long journey from
Paris to Jerusalem), as a *traveler*. And the kind of traveler that occurs and
appeals to him is a discoverer.[15] Invoking Cook—the great man of the seas
of Chateaubriand's youth, the Columbus of the later stages of the Age of
Discovery—makes all the sense in the world, except in the world of pilgrimage. It seems odd as can be that the figure in whose path Chateaubriand *peregrinus* is following—however extravagantly metaphorically—
turns out to be the discoverer of places in the Pacific. The world was changing—which was scarcely a surprise to Chateaubriand. His taking of Cook
as model for himself in such a world was an act of brilliance, like so many
of Chateaubriand's literary feints. Cook was an almost perfect figure of
transition, a harmlessly inspiring figure. And by 1846, life—or, at any rate,
his own life—must have seemed to Chateaubriand to be an affair of one
transition after another.

We conclude, as we began, with Chateaubriand. We called him a
shadow, but he illumines the world of pilgrimage before his day by means
of the contrast that he presents to that earlier world. To understand the
different character of pilgrimage before Chateaubriand, it helps to look at
things through the eyes of Chateaubriand, whose own gaze was constantly
fixed on the example and writings of those pilgrims who had gone to the
Levant before him. Chateaubriand's innovation—turning *voyage causa religionis* into *mémoire* (somewhat less *causa religionis*)—shows all the more
clearly the main route from which he veered, the literary tradition of three

and a half centuries (and more) that he subtly, hesitantly, and yet fundamentally altered. He has—quite unintentionally, it seems—said goodbye to all that. The *res magna* is that printed pilgrimage of whatever kind had flourished as reading matter for Europeans for over three and a half centuries. Of whatever kind? Well, perhaps the kind did matter. Three and a half centuries of conscious literary practice and Chateaubriand's own departure from that practice suggest that it did matter. (It had mattered to Korte, who did not take the step from traveler to autobiographer.) Pilgrimage had survived so long in print precisely as a form of travel literature. As much as pilgrimage may have proved an aid to prayerful Christians performing their spiritual exercises or to writers of spiritual devotions for others—or, at the end, to sensitive Chateaubriand reflecting before the *mémoiriste*'s mirror (and doing his swim of survival between river's banks of past and present)—the literature of pilgrimage had been first and foremost a genre of devout (and devotional) *travel*. Could pilgrimage survive, not only in Chateaubriand's day but on into the future, in any other form? Chateaubriand can be read[16] as the culmination of a grand literary tradition of pilgrimage reaching back at least to the fourth century; but perhaps he is better appreciated as the author of the most crucial departure from that tradition. Was not his *mémoiriste*'s *Itinéraire* the last great act of distraction and erasure (in the name of restoration!) that pilgrimage had to endure along its arduous road through modern times?

Chronological Bibliography of Early Modern Printed Pilgrimages to the Holy Land in the Collections of the Library of Congress

The survival of pilgrimage to the Levant as a subject matter of early modern travel literature is primarily manifested in printed editions of early modern (i.e., post-Gutenberg) pilgrimages to Palestine [*], in printed editions of medieval (i.e., pre-Gutenberg) pilgrimages to Palestine [**], and in printed editions of early modern travel books that included accounts of pilgrimage to Palestine among larger itineraries [***].[1]

The following list records LC's holdings of such editions and forms the evidentiary basis of most of the preceding chapters.[2] The list is arranged chronologically, according to date of first printed edition. The first date indicates the year of first printing (regardless of language of publication and regardless of whether LC possesses an exemplar of the first edition).

c. 1470 **

Mandeville, John, Sir. *Itinerarium* [Italian]. Milan: Petrus de Corneno, 1480. Thacher 505

———. *Das Buch des Ritters Herr Hannsen von Montevilla*. Augsburg: Anton Sorg, 18 July 1481. Rosenwald 79

———. *Reysen und Wanderschafften durch das Gelobte Land, Indien und Persien*. Basel: Bernhart Richel, 1481 or 1482. Incun.X.M29

———. *Itinerarium* [German] Strassburg: Johann Prüss, 1484. Rosenwald 110

———. *Itinerarium*. Antwerp: Gerardus Leeu, ca. 1485. Incun.1485.M3

———. *Tractato de le piu maravigliose cose*. Bologna: Ugo di Rugerii, 4 July 1488. Incun. 1488.M27

———. *Tractato bellissimo delle piu maravigliose cose [e]piu notabile che sitruovino nelle parte delmondo . . . ridocto in lingua Thoscana*. Florence: Lorenzo di Morgiani [e] Giovanni da Maganza, 7 June 1492. Incun. 1492.M27

———. *Ioanne de Mandavilla, nel quale si contengono di molte cose maravigliose*. Venice, 1567. G370.M39

———. *The voyages and travailes* . London: Thomas Snodham, 1612. G370.M2 English Printing

———. *The voiage and travaile* . London: J. Woodman, D. Lyon, & C. Davis, 1725. G370.M24 1725 rare bk col

c. 1472 * *

Robert of Reims. *Histori wie die Türcke[n] un[d] andre Geschlecht der Ungleubigen die cristelichen Kirche[n] vor vil Iare[n] in manigerley Weiss angefochten*. Augsburg: Johann Bämler, 1482. Rosenwald 87

———. *Historien Hertoghe Godevaerts van Boloen*. Gouda: Printer of Historie Hertoge Godevaerts van Boloen, ca. 1486. Rosenwald 493

———. *Een genuechlike hystorie vanden edelen Hertoghe Gouaert van Buloen*. Antwerp: Govaert Bac, after 1500. Rosenwald 556

———. *Die historie van Godevaert van Boloen enn van veel ander Kersten princen en heeren*. Antwerp: W. Vorsterman, 1544. Rosenwald 1163

1475 * *

Burchardus de Monte Sion. *Descriptio Terrae Sanctae* [included with the *Rudimentum novitiorum*]. Lübeck: Lucas Brandis, 5 Aug. 1475. Rosenwald 55

———. ——— [included with *Rudimentum novitiorum* (*La Mer des Histoires*)]. 2 vols. Paris: Pierre Le Rouge, July 1488-Feb. 1488/89. Incun. 1488.R8 Thacher Col. 739

———. ——— [included with *Rudimentum novitiorum* (*La Mer des Histoires*)]. 2 vols. Lyons: Jean du Pré, 20–23 Aug. 1491. Rosenwald 411

———. ——— [included with *Rudimentum novitiorum* (Le premier[-second] volume de la *Mer des hystoires*.)] 2 vols. Lyon: J. Dymantier, 1506. Rosenwald 928

———. ——— [included with *De novis insulis nuper repertis . . . per Petrum Martyrem*]. Antwerp: I. Steelsius, 1536. DS105.B86

———. ——— [included with: Kaspar Peucer, *De dimensione terrae*; and with Philip Melancthon, *Aliquot insignium locorum Terrae sanctae explicatio & historiae*]. Wittenberg: Iohannes Crato, 1554. QB41.P94 1549 Rare Bk Coll.

———. ——— [included with *Rudimentum novitiorum* (Le premier volume de la *mer des histoires*. Auquel et le second ensuyvant]. 2 vols. in one. Paris: Guillaume le Bret, 155-. D17.R8 Rare Bk Coll

———. ——— [included with *Itinerarium Hierosol. Bartholomaei de Saligniaco*].[3] Magdeburg: P. Donatus, 1593 [1587]. DS106.S16 rare bk coll.

c. 1475 * *

Ludolfus de Suchem. *Libellus de itinere ad terram sanctam*. Strassburg: Heinrich Eggestein, c. 1475–80. Hain 10307

———. ———. [Antwerp: Gerardus Leeu, ca. 1485] Incun 1485.L8 Orig. LC

1479 *

Tucher, Hans. *Reise in das gelobte Land*. Augsburg: Hans Schönsperger, 1482. INCUN.82.T88 rare bk col

1481 *

Brasca, Santo. *Viagio del Sepulchro con le sue Ant. e oratione di loco in loco*. Milan: Nicolai di Gorgonzola, 27 September 1519 DS109.4.B737 1519

1486 *

Breydenbach, Bernhard von. *Opusculum sanctarum peregrinationum ad sepulcrum Christi*. Mainz: Erhard Reuwich, 11 February 1486. DS106.B78 Incun Coll / DS106.B78 1486 Incun Coll Vollbehr Coll

———. *Die heyligen Reyssen gen Iherusalem zu dem heiligen Grab und furbass zu der hochgelobten Iungfrauwen und Mertreryn Sant Katheryn*. Mainz: Erhard Reuwich, 21 June 1486. Incun.1486.B84 / Rosenwald 116

———. *Die Fart oder Reysz uber Mere zu dem heylige[n] Grab unsers Herren Ihesu Cristi gen Iherusalem auch zu der heyligen Iunckfrawen Sant Katherinen Grab auf dem Berg Synai*. Augsburg: Anton Sorg, 23 April 1488. Incun.1488.B7 Vollbehr Coll

———. *Die heylighe bevarden tot dat heylighe grafft in Iherusalem*. Mainz: Erhard Reuwich, 24 May 1488. Thacher 5

———. *Peregrination de Iherusalem*. Lyon: Michelet Topie et Jacques Heremberck, 28 Nov.1488. Incun.1488.L52 / Thacher 772

———. *Peregrinatio in Terram Sanctam*. Speier: Peter Drach, 29 July 1490. Incun.1490.B7 / Rosenwald 148

———. *Viaje dela tierra sancta*. Zaragoza: Paulus Hurus, 16 January 1498. DS106.B7818 1486 Incun Coll Vollbehr Coll

c. 1490 **

Hese, Joannes de. *Itinerarius . . . a Hierusalem per diversas partes mundi*. Deventer: Richardus Pafraet, 1499. Hain 8537

———. ———. Cologne: Cornelius de Zyrichzee, ca. 1500. Incun.X.H59

———. ———. Antwerp: Govaert Bac, c. 1500. Copinger 2947

———. ———. Cologne: Cornelis de Zierikyzee, ca. 1500. Hain 8535

———. *Peregrinatio Joan. Hesei ab urbe Hierusalem instituta, et per Indiam, Aetheiopiam, aliasque quasdam remotas mundi nationes ducta* . Antwerp, 1565. G460.H58 rare bks

1501 *

Kitscher, Johannes von. *Tragicocomedia de Ijerosolomitana profectione*. Leipzig: M. Lotter, 1501. In process

1519 *

Salignac, Barthélemy de. *Itinerarii terre sancte: inibique sacrorum locorum: ac rerum clarissima descriptio.* Lyon: Gilbert de Villiers, 1525. DS106.S16 I85 1525

———. *Itinerarium Sacrae Scripturae.*[4] Magdeburg: Ambrose Kirchner, 1593. DS106.S16

1534 *

Vadianus, Joachim. *Epitome trium terrae partium, Asiae, Africae et Europae compendiariam locorum descriptionem continens, praecipue autem quorum in Actis Lucas, passim autem Evangelistae et Apostoli meminere. Cum addito in fronte libri elencho regionum, urbium, amnium, insularum, quorum Novo testamento sit mentio, quo expeditius pius Lectorquae velit, invenire queat..* Tiguri: Christopher Frosch., 1534. Rosenwald 899

———. ———. Tiguri: Christopher Frosch, ca. 1534. G113.V13 1534

———. ———. Antwerp: I. Grapheus, 1535. G113.V13 1535

———. ———. Tiguri: Christopher Frosch, 1548. G113.V13 1548

1540 *

Postel, Guillaume. *Syriae descriptio.* Paris: Hieronymus Gormontius, 1540. DS94.P88 office

1552 ***

Estienne, Charles. *Les voyages de plusieurs endroits de France: et encores de la terre Saincte, d'Espaigne, d'Italie, et autres pays. Les fleuves du royaume de France.* Paris: Charles Estienne, 1552. DC23.E7 rare book col.

1553 ***

Belon, Pierre. *Les observations de plusieurs singularitez et choses memorables, trouvées en Grece, Asie, Iudée, Egypte, Arabie, & autres pays estranges.* Paris: Gilles Corrozet, 1553. DS47.B45 1553 (Office) Spec Col

———. ———. Paris: Guillaume Cavellat, 1555. DS47.B45 1555 Spec Col

———. ———. Paris: H. de Marnef, & la veufue G. Cavellat, 1588. DS47.B45 1588

———. *Plurimarum singularium et memorabilium rerum . . . observationes.* Antwerp: Officina Plantiniana, 1589. QH179.B5

———. ———. Antwerp: Officina Plantiniana, 1605 PH41.L39

1554 *

Thevet, André. *Cosmographie de Levant.* Lyon: Ian de Tournes, et Guil. Gazeau, 1554. DS47.T38 rare bk col

———. ——— . Lyon: Ian de Tournes, et Guil. Gazeau, 1556. DS47.T4 rare bk col

1555 *

Reisner, Adam. *Ierusalem, vetustissima illa et celeberrima totius mundi civitas*. Franckfurt: G. Corvinus, S. Feyerabend, etc., 1563. DS109.R34 office

1563 *

Pascha, Jan. *La Peregrination spirituelle vers la Terre Saincte, comme en Ierusalem, Bethlehem, au Iordan etc.* Louvain: Jean Bogardt, 1566. DS106.P37 1566

1566 *

Bianchi, Noè. *Viaggio da Venezia al S. Sepolcro ed al Monte Sinai*. Bassano: Gio. Antonio Remondini, 1742. DS106.B57

1573 *

Medina, Antonio. *Viaggio di Terra Santa*. Florence: Giorgio Marescotti, 1590. DS 106.M4815 1590 Rare Bk Col

1577 *

Helffrich, Johann. *Kurtzer und warhafftiger bericht, von der Reis aus Venedig nach Hierusalem*. Leipzig: Jacob Berwaldts Erben, 1580. Rosenwald 715

———. ———. Leipzig: Z. Berwald, 1589. Rosenwald 722

1580 *

Meggen, Jodocus von. *Peregrinatio hierosolymitana*. Diling: I. Mayer, 1580. DS106.M49 rare bk col

1581 *

Bünting, Heinrich. *Itinerarium Sacrae Scripturae. Das ist: Ein Reisebuch*. Helmstadt: J. L. Siebenbürger, 1582. 4 Rare Books (Catalogue Reserve no. 67)

———. *Itinerarium Sacrae Scripturae thet ar Een resebook*. 3 vols. in one. Stockholm: Andrea Gutterwitz, 1595. BS630.L3 rare bk

———. *Itinerarium sacrae scripturae. Das ist, Ein Reisebuch*. 3 vols. in one. Magdeburg: Andreas Duncker, 1600 [i.e. 1601?]. BS630.B79 1601 rare bk col

1581 ***

Rauwolf, Leonhard. *Aigentliche Beschreibung der Raiss, so er vor diser Zeit gegen Aussgang, inn die Morgenländer, fürnemlich Syriam, Iudaeam, Arabiam, Mesopotamiam, Babyloniam, Assyriam, Armeniam etc.* Laugingen: Leonhart Reinmichel, 1582. DS47.R353 1582 rare bk col

1582 *

Schweigger, Saloman. *Ein newe Reyssbeschreibung auss Teutschland nach Constantinopel und Jerusalem*. Nürnberg: Caspar Fulden, 1619. DR424.S41 pre 1801

1584 * / **5

Feyerabend, Sigismund (ed.). *Reyssbuch dess heyligen Lands, das ist, Ein grundtliche Beschreibung aller und jeder Meer und Pilgerfahrten zum heyligen Land.* Frankfurt am Main: Johann Feyerabend in Verlegung Sigismund Feyerabendts, 1584. DS 105.R497 1584 fol.

1585 *

Wispeck, Wilhelm. *Hierusalem. Opus praeclarum et privatum. Ein newe Beschreibung der heiligen statt Jerusalem.* München: Adam Berg, 1585. DS103.W573.H547 1585

1587 *

Zuallart, Jean. *Le tresdevot voyage de Jerusalem.* Anvers: Arnould s'Conincx, 1608. G370.Z7 rare bk col

1589 **

Itinerarium burdigalense. In Andreas Schottus and Jerónimo Zurita (eds.), *Itinerarium Antonini Augusti, et burdigalense.* Coloniae Agrippinae: In officina Birckmannica sumptibus Arnoldi Mylij, 1600. DG28.I7 (office)

———. In Petrus Bertius (ed.). *Theatrum geographiae veteris.* Lugduni Batavorum: Isaac Elzevir, 1618. G113.B6

———. In Petrus Wesseling (ed.). *Vetera Romanorum itineraria.* Amsterdam: J. Wetstenius and G. Smith, 1735. DG28.W5 pre 1801

1590⁶ *

Adrichem, Christiaan van. *Theatrum Terrae Sanctae et biblicarum historiarum, cum tabulis geographicis aere expressis.* Cologne: in Officina Birckmannica, sumptibus Hermanni Mylij, 1613. DS104.A2 1613 pre 1801 folio

———. ———. Cologne: Iodocus H. Kramer, 1682. DS104.A2 1682 pre 1801 folio

———. ———. Cologne: Thomas von Collen, 1722. DS104.A2 1722 pre 1801

1590 *

Guerrero, Francisco. *Breve tratado del viage que hizo a la Ciudad Santa de Jerusalen.* Madrid: Josef de Urrutia, 1790. DS109.G85 pre 1801

1590 *

Lussy, Melchior. *Reissbuch gen Hierusalem.* Freiburg: Abraham Gemperlin, 1590. In Process

1593 *

Aveiro, Pantaleâo de. *Itinerario de Terra Sancta, e todas suas particularidades.* Lisbon: Antonio Alvarez, 1596. DS106.P35 1596

1595 *

Villamont, Jacques de. *Les voyages du seigneur de Villamont*. Arras: Guillaume de la Riviere, 1602. DS47.V55 1602 rare bk col.

1597 **

Jacques de Vitry. *Libri duo. Quorum prior Orientalis, sive Heriosolymitanae; Alter, Occidentalis historiae nomine inscribitur*. Duaci: Balthazaris Belleri, 1597. D152.J17 rare bks

1598 ***

Rosaccio, Giuseppe. *Viaggio da Venetia, a Costantinopoli per mare, e per terra, et insieme quello di Terra Santa.*[7] Venice: G. Franco, 1598. DS47.R6 rare bk col

1601 *

Mantegazza, Stefano. *Relatione tripartita del viaggio di Gierusalemme*. Milan: Per l'her. di Pacifico Pontio, & Gio. Battista Piccaglia, 1616. DS106.M29 pre 1801

1603 *

Timberlake, Henry. *A true and strange discourse of the travailes of two English pilgrimes*. London: Thomas Archer, 1608. DS106.T55 1608[8]

1606 *

Tschudi von Glarus, Ludwig. *Reyss und Bilgerfahrt, zum Heyligen Grab*. Rorschach: Bartholomäus Schnell, 1606. DS105.T78 1606

1608 *

Harant, Krystof. *Putowánj, aneb Cesta z Králowstwj Ceského do města Benátek*. 2 vols. in one. Prague, 1608. G460.H35 rare bk col

1608 *

Beauvau, Henri, baron de. *Relation iournalière du voyage du Levant*. Nancy: Iacob Garnich, 1615. DS47.B4 1615 pre 1801

———. ———. Nancy: Iacob Garnich, 1619. DS47.B4 1619 pre 1801

1609 *

Amico, Bernardino. *Trattato delle Piante et Immagini de sacri edifizi di Terra Santa*. Florence: Pietro Cecconcelli, 1620. Rosenwald 1344 NA 5977.A6 copy 2, pre 1801

1609 *

Walter von Waltersweil, Bernhard. *Beschreibung einer reiss auss Teutschland biss in das belobte landt Palaestina*. Munich: A. Bergin, 1610. DS106.W23 pre 1801

1611 **

Bongars, Jacques (ed.). *Gesta Dei per Francos, sive orientalium expeditionum, et regni Francorum Hierosolimitani historia a variis, sed illius aevi scriptoribus, litteris commendata.* Hanover: Typis Wechelianis, apud heredes Ioan Aubrii, 1611. D151.G39 pre 1801

1612 *

Breuning von Buchenbach, Hans Jacob. *Orientalische Reyss.* Strassburg: Johann Carolo, 1612. DS47.B7 office

1614 ***

Ordóñez de Ceballos, Pedro. *Historia, y viage del mundo.* Madrid: J. Garcia Infanzon, 1691. G460.O65 rare bk

1614 ***

Lithgow, William. *The totall discourse, of the rare adventures, and painefull peregrinations of long nineteene yeares travayles, from Scotland, to the most famous kingdomes in Europe, Asia, and Affrica.* London: Nicholas Okes, for Nicholas Fussell & Humphery Mosley, 1632. G460.L65 English Printing, copy 2

———. *Willem Lithgouws 19. Jaarige lant-reyse vyt Schotland, naer de vermaerde koninckrijcken Europa, Asia ende Africa.* Amsterdam: Jacob Benjamijn, 1652. G460.L75 pre 1801

1615 *

Sandys, George. *A relation of a journey begun An: Dom: 1610.* London: W. Barrett, 1615. DS47.S2 1615 office English Printing

———. ———. London: W. Barrett, 1621. DS47.S2 1621 English Printing

———. *Sandys travailes.* London: J. Sweeting, 1652. DS47.S22 pre 1801

———. ———. London: R. & W. Leybourn, 1658. DS47.S23

———. ———. London: J. Williams, Jr., 1673. 4DS 1384

1616–1617 ***

Mocquet, Jean. *Voyages en Afrique, Asie, Indes Orientales, et Occidentales.* Rouen: Jacques Cailloué, 1645. G460.M67 rare bk

———. *Reysen in Afrique, Asien, Oost- en West-Indien.* Dordrecht: Abraham Andriessz, 1656. G460.M68 office

———. *Wunderbare jedoch gründlich- und warhaffte Geschichte und Reise Begebnisse in Africa/Asia/Ost- und West-Indien.* Lüneberg: Johann Georg Lippers, [1688]. G460.M675 rare bk

———. *Travels and voyages .* London: W. Newton, 1696. G460.M673 rare bk

1617 ***

Moryson, Fynes. *An itinerary written by Fynes Moryson gent, first in the Latin tongue, and then translated by him into English*. London: John Beale, 1617. D915.M89 1617 English Printing

1618 *

Amman, Johann Jacob. *Reiss in das gelobte Land*. Zürich: M. Schauffelberger, 1678. G460.S58 Rare Bk

1619 *

Cotovicus, Johannes. *Itinerarium hierosolymitanum et syriacum*. Antwerp: Hieronymus Verdussius, 1619. DS106.C77 pre 1801

1620 *

Furer, Christoph. *Itinerarium Aegypti, Arabiae, Palaestinae, Syriae, aliarumaque regionum orientalium*. Nuremberg: Abraham Wagenmann, 1620. DS47.F87 1620 rare bk col

1624 *

Courmenin, Louis Deshayes, baron de. *Voiage de Levant fait par le commandement du roy en l'année 1621*. Paris: Adrian Taupinart, 1632. DR424.C86.1629 office

1627 *

Bolswert, Boëce van. *Pelerinage de Colombelle et Volontairette*. Antwerp: H. Aertssens, 1636. PT5607.B5 D814

1629 *

Pacifique de Provins, Père. *Relation du voyage de Perse . . . Où vous verrez les remarqus particulieres de la Terre Saincte, et des lieux où se sont operez plusieurs miracles depuis la creation du monde*. Paris: Nicolas et Jean de la Coste, 1631. DS47.P11 pre 1801

1634 *

Linden, Jan Vander. *Heerlyke ende gelukkige Reyze nae het heylig Land ende Stad van Jeruzalem*. Gend: J. Begyn, [ca. 1780]. DS109.L74 1780

1636 *

Heidmann, Christoffer. *Palestina, sive, Terra Sancta*. Wolffenbutel: Sumptibus Conradi Bunonis typis Iohannis Birmarci, 1655. DS106.H45 1655

1643 ***

Stochove, Vincent. *Voyage du sieur de Stochove faict es années 1630. 1631. 1632. 1633*. Brussels: Hubert Anthoine Velpius, 1643. DS47.S8 1643 rare bk col

———. *Le voyage d'Italie et du Levant*. Rouen: Jacques Herault, 1664. DS47.F4 pre 1801

1648 ***

Le Blanc, Vincent. *Les voyages fameux*. Paris: Gervais Clousier, 1648. G460.L4 rare bk

———. ———. Paris: Gervais Clousier, 1649. G460.L4 1649 rare bk

———. *De Vermaarde Reizen*. Amsterdam: Ian Rieuwertsz and Ian Hendrikszx, 1654. KG460.L42

———. *The world surveyed: or, the famous voyages and travailes of Vincent le Blanc, or White, of Marseilles*. London: John Starkey, 1660. G460.L43 office

1649 ***

Somer, Jan. *Zee en landt reyse, gedaen naer de Levante*. Amsterdam: J. Hartgers, 1649. DR424.S69 Rare Bk Coll

1650⁹ ***

Howell, James. *Instructions and directions for forren travell*. London: Humphrey Moseley, 1650. D915.H69 1650

1650 ***

Valle, Pietro della. *Viaggi di Pietro Della Valle il pellegrino*. 3 vols. Rome: V. Mascardi, 1650, 1663. DS7.V15 pre 1801[10]

———. ———. 3 vols. in 4. Rome: B. Diversin, 1658–1663.[11] DS7.V155 rare bk col

———. *Les fameux voyages*. 2 vols. Paris: G. Clovzier, [1662?]-1663. DS47.V3414 1662

———. *The travels . . . into East-India and Arabia Deserta*. London: J. Martin, & J. Allestry, 1665. DS411.9.V18

———. *De volkome Beschryving der voortreffelijcke Reizen*. Amsterdam: Abraham Wolfgang, 1666. DS7.V18

1654 *

Castillo, Antonio del. *El devoto peregrino, viage de Tierra Santa*. Madrid: Joseph Rodriguez, 1705. DS106.C35 pre 1801

1656 *

Dandini, Girolamo. *A voyage to Mount Libanus*. London: A. Roper and R. Basset, 1698. BX182.D313.1698 pre 1801

1657 *

Doubdan, Jean. *Le voyage de la Terre-Sainte*. Paris: Pierre Bien-Fait, 1666. DS106.D55 1666

1663 ***

Neitzschitz, Georg Christoph von. *Sieben-jährige und gefährliche welt-beschauung durch . . . Europa, Asia und Africa.* Budissin: Barthol. Kretschmar, and Johann Barthol. Oehlern, 1673. DS47.N42 pre 1801

1664 ***

Thévenot, Jean de. *Relation d'un voyage fait au Levant.* Paris: Thomas Iolly, 1665. 4DS 13 pre 1801

——. *The travels of Monsieur de Thévenot into the Levant.* London: H. Clark, 1687. DS7.T41 pre 1801

——. *Voyages de Mr. de Thévenot au Levant . . . Premiere partie contenant le Voyage du Levant.* 5 vols. Amsterdam: Michel Charles le Céne, 1727. DS7.T38 pre 1801

1665 *

Sanson, Nicolas. *Geographia sacra ex veteri, et novo testamento desumpta, et in tabulas tres concinnata.* Paris: P. Mariette, 1665. BS630.S25 fol. Pre 1801

1665–1666 ***

Monconys, Balthasar. *Journal des voyages de Monsieur de Monconys.* 3 vols. Lyon: H. Boissart et G. Remeux, 1665–1666. Q155.M72 rare bk. Coll.

1669 *

Rantzau, Henrik. *Denckwürdige reise-beschreibung, nach Jerusalem, Cairo in Aegypten und Constantinopel.* Hamburg: G. Libernickel, 1704. DS49.R3 1704[12]

1670 *

[Nau, Michel]. *Le voyage de Galilée.* Paris: Michel Le Petit et Estienne Michallet, 1670. DS106.N3V69 1670 Rare Bk Col.

1670 *

Goujon, Jacques. *Histoire et Voyage de la Terre-Sainte.* Lyon: Pierre Compagnon et Robert Taillandier, 1671. DS106.G68.H57 1671

1672 *

Crouch, Nathaniel (ed.). *Two Journeys to Jerusalem.* London: Printed for Nath. Crouch, 1709. DS106.C95 rare bk

——. *A Journey to Jerusalem.* Hartford, Conn.: J. Babcock, 1796. DS106.C94 American Imprints

1673 *

Gonsales, Antoine. *Hierusalemsche Reÿse.* 2 vols. Antwerp: Michiel Cnobbaert, 1673. DS106.G6 pre 1801

1676 *

Troilo, Franz Ferdinand von. *Orientalische Reise-Beschreibung.* Dresden: Melchior Bergens sel. nachgelassene Wittwe und Erben, 1677. DS47.T8 pre 1801

1677 *

Dapper, Olfert. *Naukeurige Beschryving van gantsch Syrie en Palestytn of Heilige Lant.* Amsterdam: Jacob van Meurs, 1677. DS106.D23 pre 1801

———. *Genaue und grundliche Beschreibung des gantzen Syrien und Palestins, oder Gelopten Landes.* Nürnberg: Johann Hofmann, 1688–1689. DS106.D21 pre 1801

1679 *

Nau, Michel. *Voyage nouveau de la Terre-Sainte.* Paris: André Pralard, 1702. DS106.N3 pre 1801

1686 ***

Burgo, Giovanni Battista de. *Viaggio di cinque anni in Asia, Africa et Europa del Turco.* 3 vols. Milan: Agnelli, 1686. G460.B95 pre 1801

1687 ***

Carli, Dionigi. *Il moro trasportato nell'inclita città di Venetia, overo Curioso racconto de costumi, riti, e religione de popoli dell'Africa, America, Asia, et Europa.* Bassano: Gio. Antonio Remondini, 1687. G460.C26 rare bk col

———. *Der nach Venedig überbrachte mohr.* Augspurg: L. Kroniger & G. Göbel, 1692. G460.C29 pre 1801

1688 ***

Bruyn, Cornelis de. *Reizen van Cornelis de Bruyn, door de vermaardste deelen van Klein Asia, de eylanden Scio, Rhodus, Cyprus, Metelino, Stanchio, etc. Mitsgaders de voornaamste steden van Aegypten, Syrien en Palestina.* Delft: H. van Krooneveld, 1698. DS7.B88

———. *Voyage au Levant, c'est-à-dire, dans les principaux endroits de l'Asie Mineure, dans les isles de Chio, Rhodes, Chypre, &c, de même que dans les plus considérables villes d'Egypte, Syrie & Terre Sainte.* 5 vols. Paris: J. B. C. Bauche, le fils, 1725. DS7.B9 pre 1801

1699 ***

Careri, Giovanni Francesco Gemelli. *A voyage round the world.* [London, 1704]. G440.G33 pre 1801

———. *Giro del mondo.* 9 vols. Venice: Giulio Maffei, 1719. G460.G29 pre 1801

———. *Voyage du tour du monde.* 6 vols. Paris: E. Ganeau, 1719. G460.G32 pre 1801

———. ———. 6 vols. Paris: E. Ganeau, 1727. G460.G35 pre 1801

1701 ***

Veryard, Ellis. *An account of divers choice remarks . . . taken in a journey through the Low-Countries, France, Italy, and part of Spain; with the isles of Sicily and Malta. As also, a voyage to the Levant.* Oxford: S. Farley, 1701. D975, V57 pre 1801

1703 *

Maundrell, Henry. *A journey from Aleppo to Jerusalem at Easter A.D. 1697.* Oxford: G. Delaune, 1703. DS106.M44 rare bk

———. ———. 4th edition. Oxford: at the Theatre, 1721. DS106.M444 pre 1801

———. ———. fifth edition. Oxford: at the Theatre, 1732. DS106.M446 pre 1801

———. ———. Seventh edition. Oxford: W. Meadows, 1749. DS106.M447

———. ———. Fourth edition. Perth: W. Morison, 1800. DS106.M448 pre 1801

1704 *

Morison, Antoine. *Relation historique, d'un voyage nouvellement fait au mont de Sinaï et a Jerusalem.* Toul: A. Laurent, 1704. DS47.M67 1704

1709 ***

Hill, Aaron. *A full and just account of the present state of the Ottoman Empire in all its branches.* London: John Mayo, 1709. DR425.H64 pre 1801

———. ———. Second edition. London: J. Mayo, and J. Woodward, 1719. DR 542.H54 1710 rare bk col

1712 ***

Lucas, Paul. *Voyage du sieur Paul Lucas, fait par ordre du roi dans la Grece, l'Asie Mineure, la Macedoine et l'Afrique.* 2 vols. in one. Amsterdam: Aux dépens de la Compagnie, 1714. DS47.L88 rare bk col.

1714 *

Myrike, Heinrich. *Reyse nach Jerüsalem und dem land Canaan.* Itzstein: Johann Jacob Haug, 1719. DS106.M9 pre 1801

1717 *

La Roque, Jean de. *Voyage de Syrie et du Mont-Liban.* 2 vols. in one. Amsterdam: H. Uytwerf, 1723. DS94.L32 pre 1801

1723 *

Schmid, Balthasar. *Dess in das gantze Gelobt- und Heilige land zwey mal verreiseten pilgrams Balthasar Schmids, verfasste und ausgefuhrte Reis-beschreibung.* Ulm: Elias Daniel Süss, 1723. DS106.S2 pre 1801

1724 *

Francisco Jesus Maria de San Juan del Puerto. *Patrimonio seraphico de Tierra Santa.* Madrid: En la Impr. de la Causa de V.M. Maria de Jesus de Agreda, 1724. BR1070.F7 rare bk col

1724 ***

Sainte-Maure, Charles de. *A new journey through Greece, Aegypt, Palestine, Italy, Swisserland, Alsatia, and the Netherlands.* London: J. Batley, and J. Wood, 1735. D975.S14 pre 1801

1724 *

Henichius, Adolph Wilhelm. *Dissertatio inauguralis historico-geographica de itineribus religiosis quorundam principum guelphicorum in Palaestina.* Helmstadt: Typis Pauli Dieterici Schnorrii, 1724. DS105.H5

1725 *

Neret, Charles. "Lettre du pere Neret, missionnaire de la Compagnie de Jesus en Syrie. Au pere Fleuriau de la même Compagnie." In *Nouveaux mémoires des missions de la Compagnie de Jesus dans le Levant.* Vol. 5, pp. 1–121. Paris: Guillaume Cavelier, 1725. BX3746.A1.A3 pre 1801

1727 ***

La Mottraye, Aubry de. *Voyages du Sr. A. de La Motraye, en Europe, Asie & Afrique.* 2 vols. A La Haye: T. Johnson et J. van Duren, 1727. D917.L33 rare bk folio

1727 *

Briemle, Vincentius. *Die durch die drey Theile der Welt, Europa, Asia und Africa, besonders in denselben nach Loreto, Rom, Monte-Cassino, nicht minder Jerusalem, Bethlehem, Nazareth, Berg Sinai . . . Pilgerfahrt.* 2 vols.[13] Munich: Georg Christoph Weber, 1727–29. BX2323.B75 1727 rare bk col

1729 *

Sicard, Claude. "Lettre du pere Sicard, missionnaire de la Compagnie de Jesus en Egypte. Au pere Fleuriau de la même Compagnie." In *Nouveaux mémoires des missions de la Compagnie de Jesus dans le Levant.* Vol. 7, pp. 1–27. Paris: Pissot et Briasson, 1729. BX3746.A1.A3 pre 1801

1735 ***

Arvieux, Laurent d'. *Mémoires du Chevalier d'Arvieux.* 6 vols. Paris: C. J. B. Delespine, 1735. DS47.A79 pre 1801

1741 *

Korte, Jonas. *Reise nach dem weiland gelobten, nun aber seit siebenzehn hundert Jahren unter dem Fluche liegenden Lande.* Altona: Verlag des Autoris, 1741. 4DS 275

——. ——. Halle: Joh. Christian Grunert, 1751. DS47.K6 pre 1801

1742 ***

Tollot, Jean Baptiste. *Nouveau voyage fait au Levant, ès années 1731 et 1732.* Paris: André Cailleau, 1742. DS47.T655 1742

1743 ***

Perry, Charles. *A view of the Levant.* London: T. Woodward et al., 1743. DS47.P46 folio pre 1801

1743–45 ***

Pococke, Richard. *A Description of the East, and some other countries.* 2 vols. in 3. London: Printed for the author, 1743–45. DS47.P74 folio

——. *Beschreibung des Morgenlandes und einiger andern Länder.* 2 vols. Erlangen: Walther, 1791- DS47.P745¹⁴

1753 *

A journal from Grand Cairo to Mount Sinai, and back again. Translated from a manuscript, written by the Prefetto of Egypt. London: William Bowyer, 1753. DS110.5.C5 pre 1801 Copies 1 & 2

1753–57 ***

Leandro di Santa Cecilia. *[3 voyages] Palestina, ovvero, Primo viaggio . . . Persia, ovvero, seconda viaggio . . . Mesopotamia, ovvero, terzo viaggio . . . in oriente.* Rome: Nella stamperia di Angelo Rotilj, 1753–1757. DS106.L37 1753

1757 *

Hasselquist, Fredrik. *Reise nach Palästina in den jahren von 1749 bis 1752.* Rostock: Johann Christian Koppe, 1762. QH192.H35 rare bk col

——. *Voyages and travels in the Levant.* London: L. Davis and C. Reymers, 1766. DS106.H36 pre 1801

1757–1758 ***

Egmond [van der Nijenburg], Johannes Aegidius van, and Heyman, Johannes. *Travels through part of Europe, Asia Minor, the islands of the Archipelago; Syria, Palestine, Egypt, Mount Sinai, etc.* 2 vols. London: L. Davis and C. Reymers, 1759. DS47.E32 pre 1801

1769 ***

Mariti, Giovanni. *Voyages dans l'Isle de Chypre, la Syrie et la Palestine, avec l'histoire générale du Levant.* 2 vols. Paris: Belin, 1791. DS47.M34 pre 1801

————. *Travels through Cyprus, Syria, and Palestine: with a general history of the Levant.* 3 vols. London: G. G. J. and J. Robinson, 1791–1792. DS47.M25 pre 1801

1771 ***

Poste per diverse parti del mondo. Con il viaggio di San Giacomo di Galizia, e di Gerusalemme, di Vienna, e Costantinopoli. Ed altre Poste principali di Francia, e Germania. Rome: Casaletti, 1771. DG 793.P67 1771

1778 **

Symon Simeonis. *Itineraria Symonis Simeonis et Willelmi de Worcestre.* Cambridge: J. Woodyer and T. & J. Merrill, 1778. DA610.S95 pre 1801

1783 *

Korobeĭnikov, Trifon. *Puteshestvie moskovskago kuptsa . . . vo Ierusalim.* Moscow: The University Print Shop, 1798. DS109.K68 Yudin Col.

1787 *

Binos, Marie-Dominique. *Voyage par l'Italie, en Egypte au Mont-Liban et en Palestine ou Terre Sainte.* 2 vols.[15] Paris: chez l'auteur & chez Boudet, 1787. DG424.B566 1787

1798 *

Meletiĭ, Hieromonk. *Puteshestvīe vo Ierusalem.* Moscow: A. Reshetnikov, 1798. DS109.M38 Yudin Collection

Abbreviations

B   Leonora Navari. *Greece and the Levant: the Catalogue of the Henry Myron Blackmer Collection of Books and Manuscripts*. London: Maggs Bros. Ltd., 1989.

DHCJ   *Diccionario histórico de la Compañía de Jesús: Biográfico-temático*. 4 vols. Edited by Charles E. O'Neill and Joaquín Ma. Domínguez. Roma: Institutum Historicum, 2001.

ERSM   *Europäische Reiseberichte des späten Mittelalters: eine analytische Bibliographie*. 3 vols. Edited by Werner Paravicini. Frankfurt am Main: Peter Lang, 1994–2000.

G   Johan Georg Theodor Grässe. *Trésor de livres rares et précieux*, 7 vols. in 8. Berlin: J. Altmann, 1922.

Goff   Frederick R. Goff, ed. *Incunabula in American Libraries*. Revised edition. Millwood, N.Y.: Kraus Reprint Co., 1973 (c1964).

NCE   *New Catholic Encyclopedia*. Prepared by editorial staff at the Catholic University of America. 18 vols. New York: McGraw-Hill, 1967–1989.

NUC   Library of Congress. *National Union Catalog, pre-1956 Imprints*. 424 vols. London: Mansell, 1968–1975.

RBG   Reinhold Röhricht. *Bibliotheca Geographica Palaestinae: chronologisches Verzeichniss der auf die Geographie des heiligen Landes bezüglichen Literatur von 333–1878*. Berlin: H. Reuther und O. Reichard, 1890.

RDP   Reinhold Röhricht. *Deutsche Pilgerreisen nach dem heiligen Lande*. Neudruck der neuen Ausgabe. Innsbruck, 1900. Darmstadt: Scientia Verlag Aalen, 1967.

S   Ann Simon. *Sigmund Feyerabend's "Das Reyssbuch dess heyligen Lands": A Study in Printing and Literary History*. Wiesbaden: Ludwig Reichert, 1998.

Sc   Nathan Schur. *Jerusalem in Pilgrims' and Travellers' Accounts: A Thematic Bibliography of Western Christian itineraries, 1300–1917*. Jerusalem: Ariel Publishing House, 1980.

Som   Augustin De Backer & Aloys De Backer. *Bibliothèque de la*

Compagnie de Jésus . . . . *nouvelle édition par Carlos Sommervogel,*
S. J. 10 vols. Brussels: O. Schepens, 1890–1909.

T   Titus Tobler. *Bibliographia Geographica Palaestinae.* Leipzig: Verlag
von S. Hirzel, 1867.

Y   Stefanos Yerasimos. *Les voyageurs dans l'Empire ottoman, XIVe–*
XVIe siècles: bibliographie, itinéraires et inventaire des lieux habités.
Ankara: Imprimérie de la Société turque d'histoire, 1991.

Notes

Introduction

In text and notes, translations into English of both early modern sources and modern scholars' remarks are my own unless otherwise indicated.

1. François Auguste René de Chateaubriand, *Itinéraire de Paris à Jérusalem*, 2 vols., ed. Emile Malakis (Baltimore: Johns Hopkins University Press, 1946). For the chronology of the journey: Bibliothèque Nationale, *Chateaubriand: le voyageur et l'homme politique* (Paris: Bibliothèque Nationale, 1969), pp. xxv–xxvi. For a detailed examination of the pilgrimage portion of the travels: Fernande Bassan, *Chateaubriand et la terre-sainte* (Paris: Presses Universitaires de France, 1959). The biography by Jean-Paul Clément, *Chateaubriand: biographie morale et intellectuelle* (Paris: Flammarion, 1998), includes a chronology (pp. 609–45).

2. *Itinéraire* 1:146; 2:19; 1:164, where he writes: "Some quantity of years separates the Norman pilgrim Robert Guiscard from myself, the Breton pilgrim of today; but in the interval between our two voyages, the seigneur de Villamont, my compatriot, stopped over at Zante." Villamont was in the Levant in 1589–90. His pilgrimage, which appeared in Paris in 1595, was one of the most successful of early modern accounts of pilgrimage. See B 1733.

3. Chateaubriand, *Mémoires d'outre-tombe*, 3 vols. (Paris: Livre de Poche, 1973), 2:36: "The *Génie du christianisme* begins the religious revolution (la révolution religieuse) against the philosophism of the eighteenth century."

4. *Itinéraire* 2:88. *Les Martyrs* (XVII, n. 16) is quoted by the editor in *Itinéraire*, 2:88–89, n. 3. For a very different view of the repairs to the Church of the Holy Sepulchre—the view of Franciscans on the spot who were caught between Eastern Christians and Turkish governors—see "El Incendio del Santo Sepulcro, 12 Octubre 1808, relato del P. Clemente Perez." This was an internal Franciscan document that has been published in A. Arce, *Miscelanea de Tierra Santa*, vol. 2 (Jerusalem: Franciscan Printing Press, 1973), pp. 323–401.

5. *Itinéraire*, Préface de l'Itinéraire pour l'édition des oeuvres complètes, 1:1–2. "The success of the *Itinéraire* was as complete as that of the *Martyrs* had been questionable." *Mémoires d'outre-tombe*, 2:13. On the reception of the *Itinéraire*, see Bassan, *Chateaubriand*, pp. 209–19.

6. *Itinéraire* 2.41–42.

7. Ibid., 2:87–92.

8. See below, Chapter 7.

9. The urgent call of pilgrims themselves for more to follow in their footsteps suggests the gloomy reality. See, for example, Ceverio de Vera and Amico in Chapter 7.

10. *Itinéraire* 2:171. The sole visitor earlier in the year had been Ulrich Jaspar von Seetzen, the complete printed version of whose travels would only appear decades later. Chateaubriand is aware of him as the most modern of his sources, since he was still in the field. Part of his travel accounts had already been published several years before Chateaubriand's publication in 1811.

11. *Itinéraire* 2:171–75.

12. He takes up the matter immediately, in the preface to the first edition. *Itinéraire*, 1:69–70.

13. Ibid., 1:279.

14. See Bassan, *Chateaubriand et la terre-sainte*, pp. 117–19.

15. Chateaubriand, *Mémoires d'outre-tombe*, 1:680: "My life having been on display hour-by-hour in the *Itinéraire*, I will have nothing more to say here about those days." 1:699: "The *Itinéraire* has become thoroughly a part of the very elements that compose my life." Perhaps the most striking evidence, from a late but indefinite date, is the notation, in a secretary's hand, on a manuscript of the journal he kept of his journey: "I destroyed all my manuscripts. The only one that I have retained is that of my voyage to Jerusalem because I wrote it at sea in the midst of storms in the year 1807. I have not had the courage to burn it because it is so intimately bound up with my whole life." Bibliothèque Nationale, *Chateaubriand: le voyageur et l'homme politique*, pp. 76–77, no. 232.

16. But contributory in the profound sense that Hartog means in speaking of antique travelers: "These travellers' journeys through the space of the world can also be read as so many itineraries that leave trails more or less deep and lasting across their own culture." François Hartog, *Memories of Odysseus: Frontier Tales from Ancient Greece* (Chicago: University of Chicago Press, 2001), p. 4.

17. J. R. McNeill and William H. McNeill, *The Human Web: A Bird's-Eye View of World History* (New York: W.W. Norton, 2003), p. 10.

18. For example, Bellegarde at the turn to the eighteenth century, saw the convergence of travel and history. See below, Chapter 3. The idea itself was not new to the eighteenth century nor peculiar to Enlightenment thought. See, for example, *Advis au lecteur* of the earlier traveler, Vincent Le Blanc (1554–c. 1640), in Le Blanc (1648), aiv r–v.

19. Consider even *walking*: "The history of walking is an unwritten, secret history whose fragments can be found in a thousand unemphatic passages in books, as well as in songs, streets, and almost everyone's adventures. The bodily history of walking is that of bipedal evolution and human anatomy. Most of the time walking is merely practical, the unconsidered locomotive means between two sites. To make walking into an investigation, a ritual, a meditation, is a special subset of walking, physiologically like and philosophically unlike the way the mail carrier brings the mail and the office worker reaches the train." Rebecca Solnit, *Wanderlust: A History of Walking* (New York: Penguin, 2000), p. 3.

20. The Turners, following J. J. Jusserand's *English Wayfaring Life in the Middle Ages (XIV Century)*, conclude " that pilgrimage was the main type of mobility in the locally fixated feudal system of landholding and production." Victor Turner and Edith L. B. Turner, *Image and Pilgrimage in Christian Culture: Anthropological Perspectives* (New York: Columbia University Press, 1978), p. 234. And pilgrims were

the great travelers on the medieval scene because they, unlike others (merchants, peasants, women, fishermen, wanderers), were *seen* to be moving about. It was this noted visibility that made pilgrims travelers. On "invisible travelers," see Michael McCormick, *Origins of the European Economy: Communications and Commerce, A.D. 300–900* (Cambridge: Cambridge University Press, 2001), pp. 12, 261.

21. An historical overview of the changes in medieval pilgrimage to Jerusalem is given in Aryeh Grabois, *Le pèlerin occidental en Terre sainte au Moyen Âge* (Paris: De Boeck and Larcier, 1998), pp. 19–51.

22. Largely, but not completely. I have made three principal exceptions by giving attention to three books not among LC's early modern collections: LC's copy of the modern edition of Juan Ceverio de Vera's *Viaje de la Tierra Santa: 1596*, intro. Concepción Martínez Figueroa and Elías Serra Rafols (La Laguna: Instituto de Estudios Canarios, 1964); Houghton Library's copy of Nicholas Christopher Radziwill's *Ierosolymitana Peregrinatio* (Antwerp: Ex officina Plantiniana, 1614); and the Dumbarton Oaks copy of Nicolas Bénard's *Le Voyage de Hierusalem* (Paris: D. Moreau, 1621).

23. By "editions" I mean nothing more than distinguishable appearances on the market. I do not further distinguish between, say, edition, impression, state, and issue, nor even between edition and reprint. I am interested in the broad and fundamental historical fact of a book's being made available for an audience on an identifiable date—in other words, an imprint. For brief discussions of the publication terms, see John Carter, *ABC for Book Collectors* (New York: Alfred A. Knopf, 1978).

24. RBG. There is also an updated reprint of *Bibliotheca Geographica Palaestinae* (Jerusalem: Universitas Booksellers of Jerusalem, 1963).

25. T, pp. 86–87. On Ceverio de Vera, see below, Chapter 7.

26. E.g., Simon Coleman and John Elsner, *Pilgrimage: Past and Present in the World Religions* (Cambridge, Mass.: Harvard University Press, 1995). More than eighty years ago, Febvre noted the permanent factor in history, from antiquity to modernity, from Hellenism and Buddhism and Islam (for examples) to Christendom, of pilgrimage and routes of pilgrimage. Lucien Febvre, *La terre et l'évolution humaine* (Paris: Renaissance des Livres, 1922); trans. *A Geographical Introduction to History* (New York: Barnes and Noble, 1966), pp. 330–34.

27. Ian Rutherford, "Tourism and the Sacred: Pausanias and the Traditions of Greek Pilgrimage," in Susan E. Alcock, John F. Cherry, and Jás Elsner, eds., *Pausanias: Travel and Memory in Roman Greece* (Oxford: Oxford University Press, 2001), pp. 40–52, 40. There seems, too, a need to divest ourselves of "the extreme secularizing tendency among twentieth-century ancient historians" in order to appreciate antique pilgrimage. Peregrine Horden and Nicholas Purcell, *The Corrupting Sea: A Study of Mediterranean History* (Oxford: Blackwell, 2000), p. 447.

28. The sense of the popularity of contemporary pilgrimage to the Holy Land is based on the author's own year-long (1972–73) witnessing of the daily crowds from Europe and America that visited the Christian holy sites in Terra Sancta.

29. The great recent exception to this neglect of early modern pilgrimage to Jerusalem is a study of French Renaissance pilgrimage which underscores this oversight on the part of scholarship, even in the midst of a revival of scholarly interest in the history of early modern travel. Wes Williams, *Pilgrimage and Narrative in*

the French Renaissance: The Undiscovered Country (Oxford: Clarendon Press, 1998), esp. pp. 2–6.

30. Turner and Turner, *Image and Pilgrimage*.

31. E.g., Jean Chelini and Henry Branthomme, eds., *Les Chemins de Dieu: histoire des pèlerinages chrétiens des origines à nos jours* (Paris: Hachette, 1982), pp. 207–92.

32. For examples, see Donald R. Howard, *Writers and Pilgrims: Medieval Pilgrimage Narratives and their Posterity* (Berkeley: University of California Press, 1980); Mary B. Campbell, *The Witness and the Other World: Exotic European Travel Writing, 400–1600* (Ithaca, N.Y.: Cornell University Press, 1988); Jaś Elsner and Joan-Pau Rubiés, "Introduction" to Elsner and Rubiés, eds., *Voyages and Visions: Towards a Cultural History of Travel* (London: Reaktion Books, 1999), pp. 1–56. The latter (p. 31) observes of later medieval travel writing: "This attention to the narration of observed experience, with special attention to human subjects, can in a general sense be seen as the ultimate relocation of the paradigm of travel from the ideal of pilgrimage to those of empirical curiosity and practical science. It results however from the growth and transformation, rather than the mere exhaustion, of the traditional ideologies of pilgrimage, crusade and chivalry under the impact of new religious, political and social concerns." Howard (p. 45) is fond of a late medieval pilgrimage that he nevertheless cuts loose from the subsequent historical progression, finding Felix Fabri both as comparable to Proust (!) and as signifying the "end of an era." By considering the subject matter and focus of chapters in Jean Ceard and Jean-Claude Margolin, eds., *Voyager à la Renaissance: Actes du Colloque de Tours 1983* (Paris: Maisonneuve et Larose, 1987), one might receive the impression that sixteenth-century pilgrimage was thoroughly swamped, though not quite done in, by new and various forms of travel that had arisen after the first discoveries. Nowhere is the idea better stated that "medieval" pilgrimage is now (or at least from some point in the sixteenth century) a thing of the past than in Yvonne Bellenger, "Quelques relations de voyage vers l'Italie et vers l'Orient au XVIe siècle," in *Voyager à la Renaissance*, pp. 453–65, esp. p. 456, n. 57: "Je crois qu'au XVIe siècle, ce genre médiéval s'est si bien transformé qu'il n'existe plus, ou en tout cas de moins en moins. Il s'agit désormais d'autre chose."

33. "About the year 1550 pilgrimage had ceased to be a plausible justification for travel. A new legitimation was needed." Justin Stagl, *A History of Curiosity: The Theory of Travel, 1550–1800*, Studies in Anthropology and History 13 (Amsterdam: Harwood, 1995, repr. 1997), pp. 47ff.

34. Antoni Mączak, *Travel in Early Modern Europe*, trans. 1980, Ursula Phillips (Cambridge: Polity Press, 1995), p. 2.

35. And this scholarly marginalization of the Levant flies in the face of the typical realities of early modern travel, as reflected in the title of a typical traveler's account (translated from the French) such as that of Charles de Sainte-Maure's *A New Journey Through Greece, Aegypt, Palestine, Italy, Swisserland, Alsatia, and the Netherlands*, 2nd ed. (London: J. Batly, and J. Wood, 1735).

36. For Counter-Reformation Europe as a whole, Robert Bireley's rich and vivid *The Refashioning of Catholicism, 1450–1700* (Washington, D.C.: Catholic University of America Press, 1999) gives important attention to pilgrimage, but not to pilgrimage to Terra Sancta (except for a sketch of Ignatius's vocation, to which his

Jerusalem pilgrimage was central). In Diarmaid MacCulloch's *The Reformation* (New York: Viking, 2003), pilgrimage to the Holy Land is prominent only by its absence. For another example, John McManners's detailed treatment of eighteenth-century ecclesiastical history in France does not mention pilgrimage, by Frenchmen or other Europeans, to the Levant. John McManners, *Church and Society in Eighteenth-Century France*, 2 vols. (Oxford: Clarendon Press, 1998). In light of such overall neglect of early modern pilgrimage to the Levant in such historical syntheses, it is scarcely surprising that more focused works—though scarcely *narrowly* focused in their interpretations and searches for data—have little or nothing to say on long-distance pilgrimage. Consider, for example, the silence on the subject in one of the great modern classics of historiography concerned with early modern religion, Keith Thomas's *Religion and the Decline of Magic* (New York: Oxford University Press, 1971). Perhaps most striking of all is the omission of pilgrimage from Edward Said's study of Orientalism, especially since he is interested in "an internally structured archive" produced by European literature describing European experiences in the Levant. Edward W. Said, *Orientalism* (New York: Vintage Books, 1978), p. 58.

Chapter 1. Medieval Pilgrimage into Print

1. Adamnan, *De Locis Sanctis,* ed. and trans. Denis Meehan, Scriptores Latini Hiberniae 3 (Dublin: Dublin Institute for Advanced Studies, 1958). The manuscript tradition is treated by Ludwig Bieler, ibid., pp. 30–34.

2. Ibid., p. 37.

3. Ibid., 2.29, p. 99.

4. Ibid., 2.16, p. 87; 2.26, pp. 95–97; 2.27, p. 97.

5. Adamnan tells the reader that the *relatio* of Arculf concerning Tyre is in complete agreement (*per omnia concordet*) with the extracts from Jerome that have been given to the reader by Adamnan; and similarly that what Adamnan has told the reader of Arculf's experience of Mount Tabor does not in the least depart (*nullo discrepant modo*) from the descriptions of the site to be found in Jerome's writings. Ibid., 2:29, p. 99. See also 2.30, p. 101, on Alexandria: "Concerning the site of this too the account of Arculf differs in no wise from what we learned previously by reading." And the same point is made in regard to information on the Nile in 2.30, pp. 103–05. Ibid., 2.20, p. 91; 2.23, p. 93; 3.6, p. 121.

6. On pre-Constantinian pilgrimage to Jerusalem, see John Wilkinson, "Jewish Holy Places and the Origins of Christian Pilgrimage," in Robert Ousterhout, ed., *The Blessings of Pilgrimage*, Illinois Byzantine Studies 1 (Urbana: University of Illinois Press, 1990), pp. 41–53.

7. Accounts of pilgrimages from the West prior to Arculf are listed and described in Adamnan, *Eines Pilgers Reise nach dem Heiligen Lande (um 670)*, 2 vols., ed. and trans. Paul Mickley, (Leipzig: J.C. Hinrichs'sche Buchandlung, 1917), 2:56–58. Even before the Arab conquest, however, Latins in Palestine appear to have been a much less striking presence than other groups such as Armenians. See Walter E. Kaegi, *Byzantium and the Early Islamic Conquests* (Cambridge: Cambridge University Press, 1992), p. 31.

8. *Itinerarium Antonini Augusti, et burdigalense* (Coloniae Agrippinae: In officina Birckmannica sumptibus Arnoldi Mylij, 1600), pp. 151–54.

9. Ibid., pp. 147, 156.

10. It is less convincing to see Arculf/Adamnan as the last of the early pilgrims, as does Herbert Donner, ed. and trans., *Pilgerfahrt ins Heilige Land: die ältesten Berichte christlicher Palästinapilger (4.-7. Jahrhundert)* (Stuttgart: Verlag Katholisches Bibelwerk, 1979). Arculf came more than a century after his nearest predecessor, the Pilgrim of Piacenza, and much of that dry spell must be chalked up to the prolonged unsettlement in the Levant at the end of the sixth and through most of the seventh century, first because of the Persian-Roman contest and then because of the Arab conquests.

11. On the closeness of pilgrimage and Crusades, particularly at the origins of the latter, see James A. Brundage, *Medieval Canon Law and the Crusader* (Madison: University of Wisconsin Press, 1969), pp. 3–18, 191; Aryeh Graboïs, *Le pèlerin occidental en Terre Sainte au Moyen Âge* (Bruxelles: De Boeck Université, 1998), p. 39; Giles Constable, "The Historiography of the Crusades," in Angeliki E. Laiou and Roy Parviz Mottahedeh, eds., *The Crusades from the Perspective of Byzantium and the Muslim World* (Washington, D.C.: Dumbarton Oaks Research Library and Collection, 2001), pp. 1–22, esp. 11–12, 18–19. Crusade in the period of the eleventh to the thirteenth centuries has been seen as the "contexte particulier" of pilgrimage in Jean Chelini and Henry Branthomme, eds., *Les Chemins de Dieu: histoire des pèlerinages chrétiens des origines à nos jours* (Paris: Hachette, 1982), p. 155. For pilgrimages prior to the Crusades, see Steven Runciman, "The Pilgrimages to Palestine Before 1095," in Marshall W. Baldwin, ed., *A History of the Crusades*, vol. 1, *The First Hundred Years* (Madison: University of Wisconsin Press, 1969), pp. 68–78.

12. "The crusaders are *peregrini* in all the contemporary histories of the First Crusade." Gerhart B. Ladner, *Images and Ideas in the Middle Ages: Selected Studies in History and Art*, 2 vols. (Rome: Edizioni di Storia e Letteratura, 1983), 2: 885, n. 31.

13. On this estrangement between pilgrims and Crusaders in the Levant, see Graboïs, *Le pèlerin occidental*, pp. 38–44.

14. Jacques de Vitry, *Lettres de Jacques de Vitry*, ed. R. B. C. Huygens (Leiden: E.J. Brill, 1960), 6.31–63, pp. 124–25. On Letter 6, which describes events of 1219–1220, see ibid., p. 54; and Philipp Funk, *Jakob von Vitry: Leben und Werke* (Leipzig: B.G. Teubner, 1909), pp. 88–89.

15. De Vitry, *Lettres*, 6.130–32, p. 127.

16. Ibid., 7.37–46, p. 135: "In that stormy and dark time"—after the fall of Damietta—he lambastes the "socalled pilgrims" (*falsi nominis peregrini*).

17. On the Jaffa treaty, see Paul Alphandéry and Alphonse Dupront, *La Chrétienté et l'idée de Croisade*, 1954, 1959 (Paris: Éditions Albin Michel, 1995), pp. 410–14. Also on this "succès éclatant," see David Jacoby, "Pèlerinage médiéval et sanctuaires de terre sainte: la perspective vénitienne," *Ateneo Veneto* 24 n.s. (1986): 28–29.

18. The bibliography of studies on medieval pilgrimage and matters related to pilgrimage is large. For an overview of the history of Latin pilgrimage to the Levant, see Graboïs, *Le pèlerin occidental*, pp. 19–51. For a broader focus that places medieval pilgrimage to Palestine within the framework of medieval pilgrimage in

general, see Jonathan Sumption, *Pilgrimage: An Image of Mediaeval Religion* (London: Faber and Faber, 1975).

19. The identification of crusader and pilgrim began to fade even as soon as the years after the first crusade. Graboïs, *Le pèlerin occidental*, p. 38.

20. The sources have been recently scoured on this question and the evidence marshaled for Germany, France, and the Netherlands. See ERSM, vols. 1–3. For Europe as a whole, a list of pilgrimage accounts written between the fourth and the end of the fifteenth centuries comes to a total of 135, eighty-one of which come from either the fourteenth or fifteenth centuries. Graboïs, *Le pèlerin occidental*, pp. 211–14.

21. Henry L. Savage, "Pilgrimages and Pilgrim Shrines in Palestine and Syria After 1095," in Harry W. Hazard, ed., *A History of the Crusades*, vol. 4, *The Art and Architecture of the Crusader States* (Madison: University of Wisconsin Press, 1977), pp. 36–68, p. 45.

22. For a recent description of the great Venetian era of Latin pilgrimage extending throughout the fifteenth century and a bit beyond, see Deborah Howard, *Venice and the East: The Impact of the Islamic World on Venetian Architecture 1100–1500* (New Haven, Conn.: Yale University Press, 2000), pp. 189–216, and esp. p. 193 for this succinct characterization: "After the loosening of the papal embargo on trade with the Moslem East in 1344, the number of pilgrims surged, reaching a high point in the 1380s when the Venetians shipped hundreds each year. . . . Through the first half of the fifteenth century between two and four pilgrim vessels left Venice each year, and for the rest of the fifteenth century one or two sailings departed annually. . . . At the end of the fifteenth century, problems with the Ottomans provoked a rapid decline in the pilgrimage business, which was dealt a near-fatal blow with the expulsion of the Franciscans from Mount Sion in 1532–4." The fall of Cyprus in 1571 was perhaps the most serious blow in this trend of declining numbers of pilgrims. See also Jacoby, "Pèlerinage médiéval et sanctuaires de terre sainte," pp. 27–58; Beatrice Dansette, "Les pèlerinages occidentaux en Terre Sainte: une pratique de la 'Dévotion Moderne' à la fin du Moyen Age? Relation inédite d'un pèlerinage effectué en 1486," *Archivum Franciscanum Historicum* 72 (1979): 106–33, 330–428.

23. It was in the wake of the Crusades and prior to the revival of classical geographical learning (and prior to the great discoveries) that medieval maps began to emphasize the central position of Jerusalem. J. B. Harley and David Woodward, eds., *The History of Cartography*, vol. 1 (Chicago: University of Chicago Press, 1987), pp. 341–42.

24. Graboïs, *Le pèlerin occidental*, p. 20, n. 1: "Most medieval chronicles mention important personages who derived from the authors' regions and who had made the pilgrimage to Jerusalem, but evidently without writing anything down." See also p. 16, n. 15.

25. See throughout: Adémar de Chabannes, *Chronique*, Collection de textes pour servir à l'étude et à l'enseignement de l'histoire (Paris: Alphonse Picard et fils, 1897). For two other, among countless possible, examples, the early twelfth-century Hariulf's *Chronique de l'Abbaye de Saint-Riquier*, ed. Ferdinand Lot, Collection de textes pour servir à l'étude et à l'enseignement de l'histoire (Paris: Alphonse Picard

et fils, 1894), 4.14, pp. 210–11; and the thirteenth-century *Chronicle of Henry of Livonia*, ed. and trans. James A. Brundage (Madison: University of Wisconsin Press, 1961), p. 192.

26. See below, Chapter 3.

27. On the era of European decline in the Mediterranean, see Halil Inalcik, "The Ottoman Turks and the Crusades, 1451–1522," in Harry W. Hazard and Norman P. Zacour, eds., *A History of the Crusades*, vol. 6, *The Impact of the Crusades on Europe* (Madison: University of Wisconsin press, 1989), pp. 311–53, esp. pp. 350, 353. And see above, n. 22.

28. Of course, the overarching reality of this literature is that there were far more specimens, early or late, that survive only in manuscript. Beatrice Dansette, "Les pèlerinages occidentaux en Terre Sainte," esp. pp. 128–33, provides a list of fifty-five pilgrimages and guides for pilgrims of the fourteenth and fifteenth centuries (including twenty-five that were composed after the invention of printing), almost all of which remained in manuscript throughout the early modern period. For another list of late medieval pilgrimages, see Christiane Hippler, *Die Reise nach Jerusalem: Untersuchungen zu den Quellen, zum Inhalt und zur literararischen Struktur der Pilgerberichte des Spätmittelalters* (Frankfurt am Main: Peter Lang, 1987), pp. 303–11.

29. As noted for France, for example, by Nicole Iorga, *Les Voyageurs français dans l'orient européen* (Paris: Boivin, 1928), p. 6.

30. When thinking of pilgrimage as a cultural artifact, a literary genre, it is worthwhile to ponder Auerbach's distinction between frame and content of a literary work. What Auerbach said of sacred drama could as well be said of devout travel: "Yet it is misleading to speak of a progressive secularization of the Christian passion play, as is generally done. For the *saeculum* is included in this drama as a matter of principle and from the beginning, and the question of more or less is not a question of principle. A real secularization does not take place until the frame is broken, until the secular action becomes independent." Erich Auerbach, *Mimesis*, trans. Willard Trask (1946; New York: Doubleday Anchor, 1953), p. 140. The fact that pilgrimages included much matter that was not (according to our lights) "religious" or "devotional" and that they included more of such matter as the late fifteenth century and the sixteenth century drew near, does not mean that such travels were becoming less peregrinative or more secularized (or touristical). The form or matrix remained pilgrimage. It was not until the frame has been broken or cast aside—i.e., that recorded travel ceased to be framed by pilgrimage and that travel came to be got up in entirely new togs (e.g., tour, scientific travel)— that something culturally revolutionary and discontinuous may be said to have taken place. Finally, such questions, of when a travel is pilgrimage and when a travel so alters as to cease to be a pilgrimage, grow more complex if one accepts, or even simply ponders, a recent remark that "the salient point about pilgrimage is that it need not always be a journey undertaken exclusively or even principally for religious reasons." Peregrin Horden and Nicholas Purcell, *The Corrupting Sea: A Study of Mediterranean History* (Oxford: Blackwell, 2000), p. 445.

31. Though it is perhaps unwise to think of him—as does Donald R. Howard, *Writers and Pilgrims: Medieval Pilgrimage Narratives and Their Posterity* (Berkeley:

University of California Press, 1980), p. 34—as the first "to see the literary possibilities in the genre." On the manuscripts and early modern imprints of Mandeville,
see RBG 196.

32. *The Voyages and Travailes of Sir John Mandevile Knight. Wherein is treated
of the way towards Hierusalem, and of the mervailes of Inde, with other Lands and Countries* (London: Printed by Thomas Snodham, 1612).

33. Ibid., A2r.

34. Ibid., A2v–A3r.

35. Ibid., O1v–O3v.

36. Ibid., M3r–M4v.

37. Ludolfus of Suchem, *Libellus de itinere ad terram sanctam* (Antwerp: Gerardus Leeu, ca. 1485), Aa3r.

38. Goff, p. 389. RBG 195. He was reprinted in Feyerabend's *Reyssbuch* of 1584
and its second edition of 1609. (On Feyerabend's *Reyssbuch*, see Chapter 4.)

39. Joannes de Hese, *Itinerarius a Jerusalem per Diversas Mundi Partes* (Cologne:
Cornelis de Zierikzee, ca. 1500), 2r. On Hese's printed editions, see Goff, p. 296,
and RBG, 227. His pilgrimage is erroneously dated a century later (1489) in Jules
Ludger Dominique Ghislain de Saint-Génois, *Les voyageurs belges*, 2 vols. (Bruxelles:
A. Jamar, 1846?–47?), 1: 36–37.

40. Ibid., 5v.

41. Bernhard Kötting, *Peregrinatio Religiosa: Wallfahrten in der Antike und
das Pilgerwesen in der alten Kirche* (Münster: Regensberg, 1950), pp. 302–7.

42. Modern edition of the single surviving manuscript: Symon Simeonis,
Itinerarium Symonis Semeonis ab Hybernia ad Terram Sanctam, ed. Mario Esposito,
Scriptores Latini Hiberniae 4 (Dublin: Dublin Institute for Advanced Studies, 1960).
Ibid. 4, p. 27 (London), 7, pp. 29–31 (Paris), 14, pp. 35–37 (Venice).

43. Ibid., 6, p. 29; 12, p. 33; 13, p. 35.

44. Ibid., 21–23, pp. 43–45.

45. Ibid., 24–39, pp. 45–65; 48, p. 73.

46. Ibid., 26, p. 49; 80, p. 98.

47. Jacobus Nasmith, ed., *Itineraria Symonis Simeonis et Willelmi de Worcestre.
Quibus accedit Tractatus de Metro, in quo traduntur regulae a scriptoribus medii aevi
in versibus Leoninis observatae* (Cambridge: J. Woodyer, and T. and J. Merrill, 1778),
a5v–a8v.

Chapter 2. Contemporary Pilgrimage ino Print: 1450–1500

1. Edited and translated by Brian P. Copenhaver under the title *On Discovery*,
I Tatti Renaissance Library (Cambridge, Mass.: Harvard University Press, 2002),
2.7, pp. 245–47. Polydore's prediction was on the mark. Two centuries (almost
exactly) after Gutenberg, Hobbes was coolly observing that "the Invention of
Printing, though ingenious, compared with the invention of Letters, is no great
matter." Thomas Hobbes, *Leviathan*, pt. 1, ch. 4, ed. C. B. Macpherson (New York:
Penguin, 1968), p. 100.

2. Tucher: RDP 156–58, T 52–53, RBG 390, S 21–22, 98–99, NUC 603:537,
ERSM 1:82.

3. Hans Tucher, *Reise in das gelobte Land* (Augsburg: Hans Schönsperber, 1482), IV.

4. Ibid., 2v: "Near Venice lies a town called Murano where glass is made. Within the parish church of this place many of the Holy Innocents lie under two altars."

5. Ibid., 73r: "Every year as a rule (*gewonlich*) a ship leaves Venice taking pilgrims to Jerusalem."

6. Ibid., 35v.

7. Ibid., 37r.

8. Ibid., 39r.

9. Ibid., 71r–75r.

10. Ibid., 51r, 70v.

11. Ibid., 10v.

12. Ibid., 70r–71r.

13. Brasca: T 53, RBG 393. A modern edition is in Anna Laura Momigliano Lepschy, *Viaggio in Terra Santa di Santo Brasca 1480 con l'Itineraria di Gabriele Capodilisla 1458* (Milano: Longanesi, 1966), pp. 45–158. LC possesses the 1519 edition. See a description of a fifteenth-century edition in F. B. Maggs, *Voyages and Travels in All Parts of the World: A Descriptive Catalogue*, 3 vols (London: Maggs Brothers, 1942–1951), 1:9–10.

14. Although he does append an account of a journey to Nazareth and Sinai by two Franciscans, who were "in Jerusalem when I was there." Santo Brasca, *Viagio del Sepulchro con le sue Antichita et Oratione de Loco in Loco* (Mediolani: Nicolaus de Gorgonzola, 1519), E5v; 1966 ed, 271, p. 130.

15. Ibid., C4v; 1966 ed., 140, p. 89.

16. Ibid., E4v; 1966 ed., 267, p. 128. See also ibid. A2r ; 1966 ed., 1, p. 45.

17. Ibid., B4r–v; 1966 ed., 62–63, pp. 69–70.

18. Ibid., F1v; 1966 ed., 304, p. 140.

19. In the pilgrimage proper—ibid., A5r–D8r; 1966 ed., 20–237, pp. 53–117— more than a quarter of the text (fifty-five sections) is devoted to formal prayers.

20. Ibid., F5v–F6r; 1966 ed., 320, pp. 149–50: "Insigni viro Sancto Brasche ducali cancellario S.D.P. Ambrosius Archintus mediolanensis."

21. The 1519 edition, which is in the LC collections, reads "pronunciam." The 1966 edition reads "provinciam" which I assume to be an error in transcription from the first edition. Ibid., F5v; 1966 ed., 320 p. 149.

22. Ibid., F5v; 1966 ed., 320 p. 149: "Further, I have read avidly and most carefully your little work which (as they say) you have produced in the midst of the hurried din and the shouts of the oarsmen in the trireme."

23. Donald R. Howard, *Writers and Pilgrims: Medieval Pilgrimage Narratives and Their Posterity* (Berkeley: University of California Press, 1980), p. 35; for the pilgrimage as a whole, pp. 35–52. Two of these writers, Breydenbach and Felix Fabri of Ulm, are compared in Lia Scheffer, "A Pilgrimage to the Holy Land and Mount Sinai in the Fifteenth Century," *Zeitschrift des Deutschen Palästina-Vereins* 102 (1986): 144–51. It is Breydenbach, of the four, who made the great early splash in print.

24. Bernhard von Breydenbach, *Opusculum sanctarum peregrinationum ad sepulcrum Christi* (Mainz: Erhard Reuwich, 1486), 18r.

25. Ibid., 110v.

26. "Lord Bernhard Breydenbach, at that time the camerarius, but now also the dean of the holy metropolitan church of Mainz, was the principal author of this work." Ibid., 103r.

27. Ibid., 107v–108r.

28. For example, ibid., 55v–56r, 90r.

29. Ibid., 29v.

30. On the complexity of this eyewitnessing—its grounding in artistic traditions, its reliance on contemporary sources in the Levant, and the ways Breydenbach and Reuwich were both more and less than proto-photographic in their renderings—see Klaus Niehr, "Als ich das selber erkundet und gesehen hab: Wahrnehmung und Darstellung des Fremden in Bernhard von Breydenbachs *Peregrinationes in Terram Sanctam* und anderen Pilgerberichten des ausgehenden Mittelalters," *Gutenberg-Jahrbuch* 76 (2001): 269–300.

31. T. S. R. Boase, "The Arts in Frankish Greece and Rhodes: Rhodes." In Harry W. Hazard, ed., *A History of the Crusades*, vol. 4, *The Art and Architecture of the Crusader States* (Madison: University of Wisconsin Press, 1977), pp. 229–50, here 237.

32. ". . . asserebat calinus noster . . . " Breydenbach (1486 Latin ed.), 105v.

33. This spot is described in the text at ibid., 31r.

34. Ibid., 124r–127r.

35. Ibid., 127r: "Modon is a city located on the tip of Achaia on the continent near Turkey whence the Turks congregate with the Christians there every week on market day."

36. The ability to return to Europe will be fastened upon as a critical concern common to both discoverer in the distant Indies and pilgrim in the distant Levant by the late-sixteenth century pilgrim Ceverio de Vera. See below, Chapter 7.

37. On Breydenbach, see Hugh William Davies, *Bernhard von Breydenbach and His Journey to the Holy Land 1483–4* (London: J. and J. Leighton, 1911); F. Thomas Noonan, "Bernhard von Breydenbach: *Die heyligen reyssen gen Iherusalem*," in *Vision of a Collector: the Lessing J. Rosenwald Collection in the Library of Congress Rare Book and Special Collections Division* (Washington, D.C.: Library of Congress, 1991), pp. 106–8. *Gesamtkatalog der Wiegendrucke*, Band IV (Leipzig: Karl W. Hiersemann, 1930), pp. 651–59 (nos. 5075–5082). T 55–57, RBG 402, S 15–17, B 204, RDP 164–65, ERSM 1:87. See also Jaime Moll's introduction to the modern facsimile edition of the 1498 Spanish version: Bernardo de Breidenbach, *Viaje de la Tierra Santa* (Madrid: Instituto Bibliográfico Hispánico, [1974]), pp. 5–8.

38. Bernardo de Breidenbach, *Viaje de la Tierra Santa* (Saragossa: Paulo Hurus, 1498), Iiv. On the Spanish translation, see Davies, *Bernhard von Breydenbach and His Journey*, pp. 33–40.

39. Minor alterations are made for the sake of the new audience. For example, the sultan's palace in Cairo is said to be immense—in the Latin original (116r), "almost the size of the town of Ulm, or half the size of Nuremberg"; in the Spanish version (CLIIr), occupying "almost as much space as a city of three thousand residents."

40. *Viaje*, IVv–XLr.

41. Davies, *Bernhard von Breydenbach and His Journey*, p. 34.

42. Compare *Peregrinatio* (1486 Latin ed.), 23v–24r and the *Viaje* LIIIIv.

43. Davies, *Bernhard von Breydenbach and His Journey*, p. 35.

44. That space left in the appropriate places in the text for illustrations of Jacobites, Nestorians, Armenians, Georgians, and Maronites remained empty may reflect the hurrying into print. Breydenbach (1486 Latin ed.), 80v, 81v, 82r, 83r, 84r.

45. Described in Davies, *Bernhard von Breydenbach and His Journey*, pp. 38–40.

46. See below, Chapter 3.

Chapter 3. New Worlds and a New Voice of Travel

1. On the significance of Cheng Ho's career and the Ming's choices, see William H. McNeill, *The Pursuit of Power* (Chicago: University of Chicago Press, 1982), pp. 44–48.

2. A. J. R. Russell-Wood, *The Portuguese Empire 1415–1808: A World on the Move* (Baltimore: Johns Hopkins University Press, 1992), p. 2. It was around this time that the Portuguese king ordered that the inscribed markers should no longer be of wood, but of stone. John Hamilton Moore, *A New and Complete Collection of Voyages and Travels* (London, 1778), p. vii. Can one see this as a grudging step in the direction of publication, a step that would culminate in the Portuguese discoveries being recounted in print after the advent of Columbus made such discoveries items of news? Also for discovery on the eve of Columbus and Portuguese secrecy in such matters, see Donald F. Lach, *Asia in the Making of Europe*, 3 vols. in 9 (Chicago: University of Chicago Press, 1965–1993), 1: 50–58, 151–54.

3. Christopher Columbus, *Epistola . . . de insulis Indie supra Gangem nuper inve[n]tis* (Rome: Stephan Plannck, after 29 Apr. 1493), beginning of unfoliated text.

4. It has been noted that "Polo's story was exceptional because it was recorded, while his travels were not extraordinary." James D. Ryan, "European Travelers Before Columbus: the Fourteenth Century's Discovery of India," *Catholic Historical Review* 79 (1993): 650. On later medieval travel as a period of incubation for many aspects of modern travel, see Gerd Tellenbach, "Zur Frügeschichte abendländischer Reisebeschreibungen," in Hans Fenske et al., eds., *Historia Integra: Festschrift für Erich Hassinger zum 70. Geburtstag* (Berlin: Duncker and Humbolt, 1977), pp. 51–80. J. R. S. Phillips, *The Medieval Expansion of Europe* (Oxford: Oxford University Press, 1988), p. 76, observes that while Rubruck is important to modern readers as a source of information, he was not widely known in the later Middle Ages.

5. The explanation found in Stephen Greenblatt, *Marvelous Possessions: The Wonder of the New World* (Chicago: University of Chicago Press, 1991), p. 37.

6. Marco Polo's text seems a conscious departure from pilgrimage—and even dismissive, in its way, of Jerusalem. Two episodes in *Il Millone* concern the city. In the first, the Westerners go to Jerusalem for the sole purpose of getting oil from the lamps burning at the Holy Sepulcher, which the Khan had requested that they bring back to him (bk 1, chs. 4 and 6). There is no attention given to the holy places or to the holy city. It is not a destination or stopover that they would themselves have chosen. They betray no wish to linger over it. In the second episode,

mention was made of an Abyssinian bishop's pilgrimage to Jerusalem, but the substance of the story had to do with the bishop's mistreatment on his way home at the hands of Adenese—which in turn became a *causa belli* between Abyssinia and Aden. (bk. 3, ch. 44). The only pilgrimage site that attracted Polo's direct attention was the shrine of St. Thomas at Madras—and this, presumably, because it fit into his traveler's aesthetic of the exotic, not into the usual pilgrim's aesthetic of the holy (bk. 3, ch. 27). Marco Polo, *De regionibus orientalibus libri III* (Cologne: Ex Officina Georgii Schulzii, 1671), pp. 4–7, 160–61, 146–47. This translation into Latin was an important text of the time, serving as it did as the edition from which the French translation of Polo, in Bergeron's 1735 *Recueil de Voyages*, was fashioned (on this, see G 4:385 and on Bergeron, below, p. 75). The contrast between pilgrimage accounts and the reports of other travelers to the East was not, however, always so sharp. González de Clavijo, for example also headed deep into the Orient in 1403 on a diplomatic mission from Iberia to the court of Tamerlane. Clavijo, however, placed great emphasis on his interruption of his journey at Constantinople, where he spent much of his time visiting churches and viewing relics. Unlike Polo, Clavijo appears to have seen that a travel narrative had to have something essential to do with visiting holy places. See the account of the embassy's stop in Constantinople in Ruy González de Clavijo, *Historia del gran Tamorlan*, Segunda impresion (Madrid: Antonio de Sancha, 1782), pp. 50–72.

7. William J. Bouwsma, *The Waning of the Renaissance 1550–1640* (New Haven, Conn.: Yale University Press, 2000), p. 70.

8. See Lucien Febvre and Henry-Jean Martin, *The Coming of the Book*, trans. David Gerard. (New York: Verso, 1990), pp. 259, 281–82.

9. Henri Ternaux-Compans, *Bibliothèque asiatique et africaine ou catalogue des ouvrages relatifs à l'Asie et à l'Afrique qui ont paru depuis la découverte de l'imprimerie jusqu'en 1700* (Paris, 1841; repr., Amsterdam, B.R. Grüner, 1968), 514, p. 63. Also Clavijo, *Historia del gran Tamorlan*, p. iii.

10. He passed up opportunities to discuss recent geographical discoveries (*On Discovery* 3.15, pp. 462–70; 3.16, pp. 470–75) and positively bemoaned the fact that "Blinded as we are by a fierce lust for wealth, do we not plow the sea supported by a flimsy board? No, I should say we all but live there" (ibid. 3.15, p. 463).

11. See, for example, Norbert H. Ott, "Zur Ikonographie der Reise: Bilformeln und Strukturprinzipien mittelalterlicher Reise-Illustration," in Dietrich Huschenbett and John Margetts, eds., *Reisen und Welterfahrung in der deutschen Literatur des Mittelalters* (Würzburg: Königshausen und Neumann, 1991), p. 35: "Travel as a literary genre . . . becomes tangible in the travel accounts above all of pilgrims; the medieval journey, which turns out to be fixed in writing, is the journey to the Holy Land, the absolutely chief destination of the journey."

12. Ludolfus of Saxony, *Vita Christi* (Antwerp, 1503), fol. 39r.

13. Transcribed by Antonio Rumeu de Armas in *Libro copiador de Cristóbal Colón*, 2 vols. (Madrid: Testimonio Compañía Editorial, 1989), 2: 435–43. Rumeu de Armas's work includes a facsimile of the text. There is an English translation and study of the text by Margarita Zamora, "Christopher Columbus's 'Letter to the Sovereigns': Announcing the Discovery," in Stephen Greenblatt, ed., *New World Encounters* (Berkeley: University of California Press), 1993, pp. 1–11. See also Zamora's

book on the subject: *Reading Columbus* (Berkeley: University of California Press, 1993).

14. Rumeu de Armas, *Libro copiador*, 1: 85–104. To the importance of Jerusalem as the ultimate objective Columbus would frequently return in subsequent years. His outlook was in accord with apocalyptic, visionary, and crusading ideas of the time. Columbus stands squarely in the tradition of medieval travel—the tradition not only of Mandeville, but of all pilgrimage. Columbus journeying to the East is in search of holy places. See Delno C. West, "Christopher Columbus, Lost Biblical Sites, and the Last Crusade," *Catholic Historical Review* 78 (1992): 519–41; esp. pp. 536–41. Also, for the context of late fifteenth-century crusading desires in Europe, Abbas Hamdani, "Columbus and the Recovery of Jerusalem," *Journal of the American Oriental Society* (1979): 39–48.

15. Christopher Columbus, *The Diario of Christopher Columbus's First Voyage to America 1492–1493: Abstracted by Fray Bartolomé de las Casas*, ed. and trans. Oliver Dunn and James E. Kelly, Jr. (Norman: University of Oklahoma Press, 1989), pp. 290–91.

16. Rumeu de Armas, *Libro Copiador*, 2: 440; Zamora, "Christopher Columbus's 'Letter to the Sovereigns,'" p. 7.

17. Dkelal Kadir speaks of the New World as "a source or mine" of materials necessary for conquering Jerusalem and ushering in the millennium. Dkelal Kadir, *Columbus and the Ends of the Earth* (Berkeley: University of California Press, 1992), p. 164.

18. Pierre Dubois, *De recuperatione terre sancte: traité de politique générale*, Collection de Textes pour servir à l'étude et à l'enseignement de l'histoire (Paris: Alphonse Picard, 1891).

19. Zamora, "Columbus's 'Letter to the Sovereigns,'" p. 1.

20. This was in the *Institución de Mayorazgo* (establishment of a perpetual trust for his heirs). Quoted in West, "Christopher Columbus, Lost Biblical Sites, and the Last Crusade," p. 536. On Columbus's last will and testament, see S. A. Bedini, ed., *Christopher Columbus and the Age of Exploration: An Encyclopedia* (New York: Da Capo Press, 1992, 1998), pp. 750–52.

21. Rumeu de Armas, *Libro copiador*, 1:91–92.

22. "In addition to the expansion of the Christian religion, it would be possible easily to gain unheard of quantities of pearls, spices, and gold." Pietro Martire d'Anghiera, *De orbe novo* 1.1.2. Reproduced in *Selections from Peter Martyr*, ed. and trans. Geoffrey Eatough, Repertorium Columbianum 5 (Turnhout: Brepols, 1998), p. 129.

23. Pierre Chaunu's phrase in his *Conquête et exploitation des nouveaux mondes: XVIe siècle* (Paris: Presses universitaires de France, 1969, 1995), p. 177.

24. It has been famously observed—by J. H. Elliott, *The Old World and the New: 1492–1650* (Cambridge: Cambridge University Press, 1970), p. 17—that early modern Europe came to terms with the New World much more quickly than medieval Europe had coped with the world of Islam.

25. Within five years of Columbus's return, there had appeared twelve editions (not counting the five of Dati's Italian versification) of his letter describing his first voyage: two in Spanish (Barcelona 1493, Valladolid, 1497); nine in Latin

(Rome 1493 [three eds.], Amberes 1493, Basel 1493 and 1494, Paris 1493 [three eds.]), and one in German (Strassburg 1497). See *La Carta de Colón annunciando la llegada a las Indias y al la Provincia de Catayo (China) (Descubrimiento de América): Reproducción facsimilar de las 17 ediciones concocidas*, Introdución y comentaria por Carlos Sanz (Madrid: Graficas Yagües, 1958). There appears to be some question about the 1493 Basel. In the introduction, Sanz mentions a printing at Basel in 1493, but in the facsimiles and table of contents, no date is given for this printing. It has long been assumed, perhaps tenuously, that because the Verardus/Columbus text was printed in Basel in 1494, the illustrated Columbus letter probably came from Basel sometime in 1493. See *The Letter of Columbus on the Discovery of America* (New York: Printed by order of the trustees of the John Lenox Library, 1892), p. x.

On the earliest editions of Columbus's letter, see also John Alden, ed., *European Americana: a Chronological Guide to Works Printed in Europe Relating to the Americas, 1493–1776*, vol. 1 (New York: Readex Books, 1980), pp. 1–2; and George Watson Cole, comp., *A Catalogue of Books Relating to the Discovery and Early History of North and South America Forming a Part of the Library of E. D. Church*, 5 vols. (New York: Dodd, Mead, 1907), 1: 6–11 (no. 3A).

26. The illustrated "Epistola Christofori Columbi de insulis nuper inventis" is included in, and follows, Carolus Verardus, *Bethicae et Granatae obsidio, victoria et triumphus* (Basel: Johann Bergmann, 1494). See F. B. Maggs, *Voyages and Travels in All Parts of the World: A Descriptive Catalogue*, 3 vols. (London: Maggs Brothers, 1942–1951), 2: 389–92.

27. On the character of the second voyage, see J. H. Parry, *The Age of Reconnaissance* (Berkeley: University of California Press, 1963), p. 152.

28. For the fifteenth-century editions of Breydenbach, see *Gesamtkatalog der Wiegendrucke*, Band IV (Leipzig: Karl W. Hiersemann, 1930), pp. 651–59 (nos. 5075–82). The fundamental work on Breydenbach, and the book that noted the connection between depictions of the voyages of Breydenbach and those of Columbus, is Hugh William Davies, *Bernhard von Breydenbach and his Journey to the Holy Land 1483–4* (London: J. and J. Leighton, 1911). And see above, Chapter 2.

29. Felipe Fernández-Armesto, *Millennium: A History of the Last Thousand Years* (New York: Scribner, 1995), p. 365.

30. Columbus himself had begun the *Diario* by invoking the capture of Granada as the context for the royal command that he "should not go to the East by land, by which way it is customary to go, but by the route to the West, by which route we do not know for certain that anyone previously has passed." *Diario*, pp. 18–19.

31. *Bellum Christianorum Principum, praecipue Gallorum, contra Saracenos* (Basel: Henricus Petrus, 1533). See Alden, *European Americana* 1: 38; and Cole, *A Catalogue of Books relating to the Discovery*, 1: 153–55 (no. 66).

32. Hernán Cortés, *Praeclara . . . de Nova maris Oceani Hyspania Narratio* (Nuremberg: F. Peypus, 1524).

33. Melchisédec Thévenot, *Relations de divers voyages curieux*, 4 vols. in 2 (Paris: De l'imprimerie de Jacques Langlois, 1663–1672), 1:aii.

34. Honorius Philoponus, *Nova typis transacta navigatio* (n.p., 1621), p. 4. Authorship is sometimes attributed to Caspar Plautius, the book's dedicatee, who was abbot of the Benedictine monastery at Seitenstetten in Austria.

35. Unless, of course, one followed Ignatius's example (as depicted in his auto-biography) and sought to merge the two motives of missions and pilgrimage.

36. Pierre Joseph d'Orléans, *La vie du père Matthieu Ricci* (Paris, 1693), p. 1.

37. For a recent treatment of the context within which these intellectual organs developed, see Jonathan I. Israel, *Radical Enlightenment: Philosophy and the Making of Modernity 1650–1750* (New York: Oxford University Press, 2001), pp. 119–55.

38. In general, and for discussion of the contents of individual collections, see Max Böhme, *Die Grossen Reisesammlungen des 16. Jahrhunderts und ihre Bedeutung* (Strassburg: Buchdr. von J. H. E. Heitz, 1904; reprint, Amsterdam, 1962, 1968). Also, for the origins of printed collections of travel, see Lach, *Asia in the Making of Europe*, 1: 204–17. An early overview of sixteenth-century collections is A. G. Camus, *Mémoire sur la collection des grands et petits voyages, et sur la collection des voyages de Melchisedech Thévenot* (Paris: Baudoin, 1802), pp. 5–14. For the later period of collections, see Peter Boerner, "Die grossen Reisesammlungen des 18. Jahrhunderts," in: *Reiseberichte als Quellen euopäischer Kulturgeschichte.* Wolfenbütteler Forschungen 21 (Wolfenbüttel: Herzog August Bibliothek, 1982), pp. 65–72. See also the brief comments on travel collections in Justin Stagl, *A History of Curiosity: The Theory of Travel, 1550–1800.* Studies in Anthropology and History, (Amsterdam: Harwood, 1995, 1997), pp. 55–56. "This deskwork," Stagl writes of collections, "actually completed the 'age of discoveries.'" Also, for the travel-collecting enterprise from Ramusio in the sixteenth century to Prévost in the eighteenth, see the remarks of Anthony Pagden, *European Encounters with the New World.* (New Haven, Conn.: Yale University Press, 1993), pp. 84–87.

39. *Novus Orbis regionum ac insularum veteribus incognitarum, una cum tabula cosmographica et aliquot aliis consimilis argumenti libellis* (Basel: J. Hervagius, 1532).

40. The *Paesi*, as part of the *Novus Orbis*, appeared in various editions in various languages throughout the sixteenth century. "It was the most important vehicle for the dissemination throughout Renaissance Europe of the news of the great discoveries both in the east and the west." John Carter, comp., *Printing and the Mind of Man* (London: Rinehart and Winston, 1967), p. 25.

41. Grynaeus recognized the crucial intersection of practical knowledge of the actual world on the one hand and of availability of new knowledge through a new literature on the other: "After these discoveries were made (not without the special beneficence of God) and published (*proditae litteris*), a thing previously impossible was granted to the human race—namely, to go not only in theoretical fashion (*mente et cogitatione*) through the heavenly expanses, but to go about the earth and to traverse the cosmos with one's own eyes." *Novus Orbis*, a 2. And see similar sentiments in Ludovicus Varthema's preface to his work in *Novus Orbis* (1537 ed.), pp. 187–88. Modern scholars have stressed the novelty of Varthema as a traveler who was going in uncharted intellectual waters: "The pioneer Varthema, who had no real models of travel for the sake of mere curiosity to refer to, is uncertain—for instance—as to whether his personal adventures in Mecca, Arab ritual customs, or the two unicorns he claims to have seen were the more interesting objects of his description." Jaś Elsner & Joan-Pau Rubiés, eds., *Voyages and Visions: Towards a Cultural History of Travel* (London: Reaktion Books, 1999), p. 3. For the intellectual milieu of sixteenth-century Basel, and the connections between major

figures, there is much information in Karl Heinz Burmeister, *Sebastien Münster: Versuch eines biographischen Gesamtbildes*. Basler Beiträge zur Geschichtswissenschaft 91 (Basel: Verlag von Helbing und Lictenhahn, 1963).

42. The reader is thought of in the same mold—a *studiosus lector* who is being presented with an *exactissima descriptio* (*fleyssige beschreybung* in the German editions) of the holy places. Everything is being done to present Burchardus's book as a work of scientific geography rather than as a guidebook for the devout. On the evolving meaning of the word "explorer," see Marie-Nëlle Bourguet, "The Explorer," in Michel Vovelle, ed., *Enlightenment Portraits*, trans. Lydia G. Cochrane (Chicago: University of Chicago Press, 1997), pp. 257–315.

43. Skelton thinks the *Novus Orbis* was a haphazard collection of material that simply happened to be available. It may seem so because Skelton has in mind the more systematically *geographical* interests of Ramusio in the 1550s, whereas the *Novus Orbis* seems more concerned with a preliminary task—the establishing of a context for the new literature of travel that was spreading the word about the new discoveries. This seems to be the reason for including Polo and Varthema, and certainly seems to explain the inclusion of Burchardus (whom Skelton doesn't mention). R. A. Skelton, "Introduction" to *Gian Battista Ramusio: Navigationi et Viaggi: Venice 1563–1606*, 3 vols. (Amsterdam: Theatrum Orbis Terrarum Ltd., 1967–1970), 1:xiv. On the *Novus Orbis* as a carefully pondered compilation rather than a jumble of texts, see M. Korinman, "Simon Grynaeus et le 'Novus Orbis': les pouvoirs d'une collection," in Jean Ceard et Jean-Claude Margolin, *Voyager à la Renaissance*, Actes du colloque de Tours 1983 (Paris: Maisonneuve et Larose, 1987), pp. 419–31.

44. Compare the table of contents of the first edition with that of *Novus orbis regionum ac insularum veteribus incognitarum* (Basel: Io. Hervagius, 1555). Ramusio's work came out in three volumes, the first appearance of which spanned the 50s: Giovanni Battista Ramusio, *Primo volume delle navigationi et viaggi* (In Venetia: Appresso gli heredi di Lucantonio Giunti, 1550); idem, *Terzo volume delle navigationi et viaggi* (In Venetia: Nella stamperia de Giunti, 1556); idem, *Secondo volume delle navigationi et viaggi* (In Venetia: Nella stamperia de Giunti, 1559.

45. Thévenot, *Relations de divers voyages curieux*, 1:aii.

46. Lach, *Asia in the Making of Europe*, 1: 207, sees Ramusio as the great model for most of those who followed, but also as the setter of intellectual and scientific standards that the others more or less failed to equal.

47. *Histoire universelle des voyages faits par mer et par terre, dans l'ancien et dans le nouveau monde. Pour éclaircir la géographie ancienne et moderne* (Amsterdam: Pierre Humbert, 1708). It almost immediately thereafter came out in an English translation: *A general history of all voyages and travels throughout the Old and New world* (London: E. Curll and E. Sanger, 1708).

48. Bellegarde, *Histoire universelle*, pp. 1–42: "Discours préliminaire, sur l'Histoire Générale des voyages, faits depuis le déluge jusqu'à nos jours; sur leur excellence, leur utilité, et le fruit qu'on peut tirer de leur lecture."

49. Ibid., *2r–*4v.

50. Ibid., pp. 7, 18, 31, 36.

51. Ibid., pp.32–33: "Those who have neither leisure nor courage enough

to tackle so many large volumes which have been composed by travelers will be compensated by extracts which will be presented to them here. They will find in a few words everything which will satisfy their curiosity."

52. This literature is closely surveyed by Justin Stagl, *Apodemiken: eine räsonnierte Bibliographie der reisetheoretischen Literatur des 16., 17. und 18. Jahrhunderts* (Paderborn: F. Schöningh, 1983). There were important, and not a few, exceptions to the rule of ignoring pilgrimage, prominent among which were the works of John Pits and Jacobus Gretser (on whom, see below, Chapter. 4).

53. Bellegarde, *Histoire universelle*, p. 37.

54. Ibid., pp. 18, 37.

55. Ibid., pp. 39–40.

56. Ibid., p. 5.

57. Ibid., p. 2.

58. Ibid., pp. 4–6, 11–13.

59. Ibid., p. 13.

60. Ibid., pp. 14–15.

61. Ibid., p. 15.

62. Ibid., p. 21.

63. Ibid., pp. 3, 35.

64. Ibid., p. 17.

65. Ibid., p. 14.

66. Ibid., p. 38.

67. Ibid., pp. 38–39.

68. Ibid., pp. 30–31.

69. There is one large exception, Feyerabend, who will be mentioned in the next chapter.

70. Ibid., pp. 41–42.

71. Pierre de Bergeron. *Voyages faits principalement en Asie dans les XII, XIII, XIV, et XV siecles: par Benjamin de Tudele, Jean du Plan-Carpin, N. Ascelin, Guillaume de Rubruquis, Marc Paul Venitien, Haiton, Jean de Mandeville, et Ambroise Contarini: accompagnés de l'histoire des Sarasins et des Tatares, et précédez d'une introduction concernant les voyages et les nouvelles découvertes des principaux voyageurs*, 2 vols. in one (La Haye: chez J. Neaulme, 1735).

72. "Avertissement concernant ce recueil." Two pages following the title page. There is no pagination or foliation.

73. All the works, including the "Traité," have two columns to the page, with columns numbered separately for each work.

74. Bergeron, "Traité de la navigation," cols. 1–2. On Bergeron, see Robert O. Lindsay, "Pierre Bergeron: a Forgotten Editor of French Travel Literature," *Terrae Incognitae* 7 (1975): 31–38.

75. Bergeron, "Traité de la navigation," cols. 101–5.

76. *Recueil ou abregé des voiages, et observations, du Sr. Jean de Mandeville, chevalier et professeur en Medicine, faites dans l'Asie, l'Afrique, &c. Commencées en l'an MCCCXXXII. Dans lequelles sont compris grand nombre des choses inconnues.* In contrast, an earlier German version reads: *Rreysen und Wandershafften durch des Gelobte Land, Indien und Persien* (Basel: Bernhart Richel, 1481 or 1482). And an earlier Latin

version: *Itinerarius a terra anglie in partes ierosolimitanas et in ulteriores transmarinas . . .* (Antwerp: Gerardus Leeu, ca. 1485).

77. John Hamilton Moore, *A New and Complete Collection of Voyages and Travels: containing all that have been remarkable from the earliest period to the present time.* (London: Alexander Hogg, 1778). For his programmatic preliminaries, see ibid., pp. ii–viii.

78. Ibid., pp. ii, vi.

79. Ibid., pp. 677–707.

80. Ibid., p. ii.

81. See below, Chapter 4.

82. Moore, *New Collection*, p. viii.

83. "Finally, a pilot will find in this volume everything that he needs for undertaking to sail a ship to the East Indies without having ever been there." Thévenot, *Relations de divers voyages curieux*, 2: Advis sur l'ordre des pièces de la second partie.

84. *The Naval chronicle: or, voyages, travels, expeditions, remarkable exploits and achievements, of the most celebrated English navigators, travellers, and sea-comanders, from the earliest accounts to the end of the year 1759: by whose wisdom, conduct, and intrepidity, the most useful and important discoveries have been made, and the British commerce extended, thro' Asia, Africa, and America: the many conquests they obtained over the Spaniards, French, and other nations: the unparalelled hardships and sufferings they underwent by shipwreck, famine, and the treachery and cruelty of their enemies. With a description of the religions, governments, customs, manners, commerce, and natural history of the several nations they visited, conquered, or had dealings with. Including the lives of the most eminent British admirals and seamen, who have distinguished themselves by their bravery and love of liberty. In three volumes* (London: J. Fuller, [etc.], 1760).

85. J. G. F. Papst, *Die Entdeckungen des fünften Welttheils oder Reisen um die Welt, ein Lesebuch für die Jugend*, 4 vols. (Nürnberg: Felsseckerischen Buchandlung, 1783–1788). John Adams, *Modern voyages . . . for the amusement and instruction of youth of both sexes*, 2 vols. (London: G. Kearsley, 1790). *Neue Sammlung interessanter und zweckmässig abgefasster Reisebeschreibungen für die Jugend*, 2 vols. (Tübingen: Johann Georg Cottaischen Buchandlung, 1794).

86. Johann Theodor de Bry, *America, das ist Erfindung und Offenbahrung der Neuen Welt . . .* (Francfurt am Main: Nicolaus Hoffman, 1617).

87. Under *Pèlerin*: "There formerly existed an excessive taste for pilgrimages, above all at the time of the crusades." And under *Pèlerinage*: "voyage of devotion (poorly understood); men's ideas have much altered on the merit of pilgrimages. Our kings and princes no longer undertake voyages overseas. . . . There has been a general recovery from earlier eagerness to go to visit distant places in order to obtain in those places heavenly assistance which one can better find at home in good works and in the practice of an enlightened devotion. In a word, journeys of this sort are no longer made except by professional runners, the down-and-out who, because of superstition or idleness or licentiousness, decide to go to Our Lady of Loreto or to St. James of Compostella in Galicia, while asking for alms along the route." *Encyclopédie, ou Dictionnaire raisonnée des sciences, des arts et des métiers. . . . tome douzième* (Neuchastel: Samuel Faulche et cie., 1765), pp. 282–83.

88. *Les Indes Orientales et Occidentales, et autres lieux; représentés en très-belle figures, qui montrent au naturel les peuples, moeurs, religions, fêtes, sacrifices, mosqués, idoles, richesses, cérémonies, festins, tribunaux, supplices et esclavages, comme aussi les montagnes, vaisseaux, commerce, etc.* (Leide: P. Vander Aa, 1700?).

89. The example of the undergraduate Hobbes in the seventeenth century is indicative of the explanatory power and intellectual appeal of the early modern travel genre. In place of the discredited (in his eyes) physics and logic of Aristotle taught in his classes, Hobbes preferred to read accounts of newly discovered lands and to pore over maps that described to the eye a newly developing cosmos. Noel Malcolm, "A summary biography of Hobbes," in Tom Sorell, ed., *The Cambridge Companion to Hobbes* (Cambridge: Cambridge University Press, 1996), pp. 1–44, here p. 16.

Chapter 4. Reformation and the Polemics of Travel

1. The Latin title reads: *Peregrinationes totius terre sancte que a modernis peregrinis visitatur. Et est sciendum quod in illis locis in quibus est signum (crucis) sunt septem annorum et septem quadragenarum de indulgentia. Predicte autem indulgentie concesse fuerunt a sancto Silvestro Papa. Ad preces sancti magni Constantini imperatoris et sancte Helene matris eius.* For transcription of title and for bibliographical information see T 58.

2. Or at least the audience would be less inclusive than heretofore. In the wake of Reformation, pilgrimages and indulgences became causes to be emphasized in Catholic circles—as, for example, in the case of Jesuit preaching reaching back to Francis Borgia and to Ignatius himself. Frederick J. McGinness, *Right Thinking and Sacred Oratory in Counter-Reformation Rome* (Princeton, N.J.: Princeton University Press, 1995), pp. 39–40.

3. Quoted in Euan Cameron, ed., *Early Modern Europe* (Oxford: Oxford University Press, 1999), p. 2.

4. *Histoire de la mappe-monde papistique* (Geneva: Brifaud Chasse-diables, 1567), iiir, iiiir.

5. Ibid., pp. 48–50.

6. The Jesuit Martin Becanus (1563–1624) never brings pilgrimage (whether within Europe or to the Levant) to the surface in his important *Manuale controversiarum*. In the table of contents, at the end of book one (dealing with things which mark off both Lutherans and Calvinists from Catholics), after listing twenty items of contention, pilgrimage not being among them, Becanus adds that "I omit the rest which are of minor importance." Martin Becanus, *Manuale controversiarum in v. libros distributum, quibus hujus temporis controversiae breviter dilucidantur* (Patavii: Ex Typographia Seminarii. Apud Joannem Manfrè, 1727), a4v.

7. On Feyerabend and his travel collections, see Max Böhme, *Die Grossen Reisesammlungen* (Strassburg: Buchdr. Von J.H.E. Heitz, 1904), pp. 97–120; G 6:101; Josephie Brefeld, *A Guidebook for the Jerusalem Pilgrimage in the Late Middle Ages: A Case for Computer-Aided Textual Criticism* (Hilbersum: Verloren, 1994), p. 222; Geoffrey Ashall Glaister, *Glaister's Glossary of the Book* (Berkeley: University of

California Press, 1979), p. 171; S. H. Steinberg, *Five Hundred Years of Printing*, new edition, revised by John Trevitt ((New Castle, Del.: Oak Knoll Press, 1996), p. 16. The most recent and fullest study of the *Reyssbuch* is Anne Simon, *Sigmund Feyerabend's "Das Reyssbuch dess heyligen Lands": A Study in Printing and Literary History* (Wiesbaden: Ludwig Reichert, 1998). The chief study on Feyerabend's work as a whole remains Heinrich Pallmann, *Sigmund Feyerabend, sein Leben und seine geschäftlichen Verbindungen*, Archiv für Frankfurts Geschichte und Kunst n.f. 7 (Frankfurt am Main: K. T. Völcker, 1881).

8. Sigmund Feyerabend, ed., *Reyssbuch dess Heyligen Lands, das ist, Ein Grundtlichebeschreibung aller und jeder Meer und Bilgerfahrten zum Heyligen Lande* (Franckfort am Mayn: Johann Feyerabendt, 1584); 3r includes a passage where Feyerabend, after speaking of Xenophon, Plutarch, Tacitus, and other ancients, adds, "Of a similar sort are the descriptions of the great and perilous journeys and voyages into the new world or the West Indies, I mean those of Christopher Columbus of Genoa and of Amerigo Vespucci and Ferdinand Magellan of Portugal, as well as of others into Asian, African, or even Sarmatian and mysterious regions. But among these certainly must be included the descriptions of the journeys, pilgrimages, expeditions, and Crusades to the Holy Sepulchre and to the Promised Land."

9. For a discussion of the many strands of Feyerabend's aim in publishing a collection of pilgrimages, see S, pp. 40–73.

10. It is perhaps telling of the lack of scholarly notice of pilgrimage as part of the history of modern travel that Donald F. Lach, *Asia in the Making of Europe*, 3 vols. in 9 (Chicago: University of Chicago Press, 1965–1993), 1: 216, makes no mention of the *Reyssbuch* but does treat the *Warhafftige Beschreibunge* when he discusses sixteenth-century printed collections.

11. Pits's 1604 *De peregrinatione* is an extremely rare book. I have been unable to consult, or even to locate, a copy. My comments are based on Justin Stagl, *Apodemiken: Eine Räsonnierte Bibliographie der Reisetheoretischen Literatur des 16., 17. und 18. Jahrhunderts* (Paderborn: F. Schöningh, 1983), p. 83.

12. Jacobus Gretser, *De sacris et religiosis peregrinationibus libri quattuor* (Ingolstadt: A. Sartor, 1606). Gretser's work does not appear in Stagl's *Apodemiken*.

13. On Gretser, see Som 3: 1743–1809; Urs Herzog, "Jakob Gretsers Leben und Werk: ein Überblick," *Literaturwissenschaftliches Jahrbuch* n.s. 11 (1970): 1–36 (which gives a general interpretation and much bibliography); NCE 6: 801; *Die Jesuiten in Bayern 1549–1773*. Ausstellung des Bayerischen Hauptstaatsarchives und der Oberdeutschen Provinz der Gesellschaft Jesu (Weissenhorn: Anton H. Konrad, 1991), esp. pp. 177–81. For bibliography and a near-contemporary sketch, see Philippe Alegambe, *Bibliotheca Scriptorum Societatis Iesu, post excusum anno M.DC.VIII. catalogum R. P. Petri Ribadeneirae Societatis eiusdem Theologi; nunc hoc novo apparatu librorum ad annum reparatae salutis M.DC.XLII. editorum concinnata, et illustrium virorum elogiis adornata* (Antwerp: Ioannis Meursius, 1643), pp. 198–202.

14. Alegambe, *Bibliotheca Scriptorum Societatis Iesu*, p. 199.

15. Stengel, his executor. Quoted in Urs Herzog, "Jakob Gretsers Leben und Werk," p. 26.

16. On Morales, see below, Chapter 5.

17. Alegambe, *Bibliotheca Scriptorum Societatis Iesu*, p. 199.

18. Bk. 1, ch. 9 of Gretser, *De sacris et religiosis peregrinationibus*, pp. 95–113.

19. For the table of contents, see Feyerabend, *Reyssbuch*, 6r.

20. Gretser, *De sacris*, p. 95.

21. Ibid., p. 96.

22. Ibid..

23. Ibid., pp. 102–3.

24. See below, Chapter 6.

25. Gretser, *De sacris*, pp. 102–3.

26. By the turn to the seventeenth century there were several Jesuits who were specialists in the school of doctrinal hard knocks. See Urs Herzog, "Jakob Gretsers Leben und Werk," pp. 17–21. Even this late, however—or even later—a picture of Jesuit rhetoric of slash-and-burn can be overdrawn. The German Jesuit Martinus Becanus distinguished, in his *Manuale Controversiarum* (1624), between different types of heretic and urged for each a different approach on the part of the proselytizer. See N. S. Davidson, *The Counter-Reformation* (Oxford: Blackwell, 1987), p. 54. For a splendidly nuanced characterization of the Jesuits, in terms of both time and geography, vis-à-vis the Reformation, see John W. O'Malley, *Trent and All That: Renaming Catholicism in the Early Modern Era* (Cambridge, Mass.: Harvard University Press, 2000), pp. 127–28.

27. C. V. Wedgwood, *The Thirty Years' War* (London: Jonathan Cape, 1938; repr. London: Methuen, 1981), pp. 317–18.

28. Gretser, *De sacris et religiosis peregrinationibus*, pp. 74–78. I have consulted the copy of the Mergenthal-Weller book in Houghton Library, Harvard University [ASIA 9214.76.9*]. The journeys covered by Weller include, in addition to Albert of Saxony's 1476 pilgrimage, the 1461 pilgrimage of Wilhelm of Saxony, Friedrich of Saxony's 1493 journey, Heinrich of Saxony's in 1506, as well as twelfth-century Saxon pilgrimages. See ERSM, 1: 55, 75, 97.

29. *Itinera sex a diversis Saxoniae ducibus et electoribus, diversis temporibus in Italiam omnia, tria etiam in Palaestinam et terram sanctam facta, una cum brevi narratione, quae ibi relatu digna viderint, et quae inde domum secum reportarint. Additis iis, quae etiam num Hierosolymis praesertim, Romae et Wittenbergae ab advenis observari maxime merentur, studio Balthasaris Mencii Nimecensis. Ab quantum refert, gravis in quae tempora Fato, vel optimi cuiusque virtus incidat* (Wittebergae: excudebat Wolffgangus Meisner, Sumptibus Clementis Bergeri, [1612]). I have used the copy of the University of Illinois, Rare Book Collections. See ERSM, 1: 75.

30. There had been throughout the medieval period a minor, if not always subdued, criticism of, or hesitancy to embrace, pilgrimage to distant parts. See Giles Constable, "Opposition to Pilgrimage in the Middle Ages," *Studia Gratiana* 19 (1976): 125–46; reprinted in Giles Constable, *Religious Life and Thought (11th–12th Centuries)* (London: Variorum Reprints, 1979).

31. The German literary evidence is gathered and analyzed in ERSM 1: 131–371.

32. The Reformation had made Wittenberg. What had once been an undistinguished town—described as located "at the edge of civilization"—became, under the requirements of the Reformation, one of the principal centers of printing in all of Germany. See Steven Ozment, *The Age of Reform, 1250–1550: An Intellectual and Religious History of Late Medieval and Reformation Europe* (New Haven, Conn.:

Yale University Press, 1980), p. 309; and *Oxford Encyclopedia of the Reformation*, 4 vols. (New York: Oxford University Press, 1996), 3: 343.

33. *Itinera sex*, 3r–5r.

34. The first pilgrimage, Duke Albert's 1476 journey to Terra Sancta, for example, had existed in manuscript in German. *Itinera sex*, p. 4: "Just as we have discovered the record of the general course of his journey as well as its particular events written down in German, so we put them down here in Latin translation, with the hope that this historical recital will provide some pleasure to the learned reader (*lectori erudito*)."

35. *Itinera sex*, p. 21.

36. Ibid., p. 5.

37. Ibid., pp. 39–40. The entire text of this journey includes pp. 37–48.

38. Ozment, *Age of Reform*, p. 250, where there is a reproduction of a woodcut, *Frederick the Wise Praying to the Blessed Virgin*, by Lucas Cranach the Elder. See also Euan Cameron, *The European Reformation* (Oxford: Clarendon Press, 1991), p. 14.

39. *Itinera sex*, pp. 44–48.

40. Ibid., p. 50. Henry's first journey is in ibid., pp. 49–77, and the second, pp. 78–100.

41. Ibid., pp. 100–348.

42. Ibid., p. 101.

43. Ibid., p. 105.

Chapter 5. Other Holy Places, Other Holy Lands

1. On antique pilgrimage in the West, see Bernhard Kötting, *Peregrinatio Religiosa: Wallfahrten in der Antike und das Pilgerwesen in der alten Kirche* (Münster: Regensberg, 1950), pp. 228–86. For literary and visual material produced by the major shrines of Europe (and of Terra Sancta), see Thomas Raff, ed., *Wallfahrt kennt keine Grenzen* (Munich: Bayerisches Nationalmuseum und Adalbert Stifter Verein, 1984). For the overall variety and vitality of post-medieval pilgrimage in Europe, see Mary Lee Nolan and Sidney Nolan, *Christian Pilgrimage in Modern Western Europe* (Chapel Hill: University of North Carolina Press, 1989).

2. As early as the second half of the thirteenth century the numbers of European pilgrims to Terra Sancta were beginning to recede, and already among the reasons for the decline was "the growing popularity of pilgrimage shrines in the West." David Jacoby, "Pèlerinage médiéval et sanctuaires de Terre Sainte: le perspective vénitienne," *Ateneo Veneto* 174 (1986): 31.

3. "After fifteen days in Sidon, I embarked on a Karmoussali or Egyptian boat . . . near St. John of Acre is Nazareth, from where it is believed that the house at Loreto was transported in a flash by angels without passing through any actual place. The theologians say that this can happen because when an angel acts through its intelligence, the body cannot resist since its nature is inferior. So, for example, if an angel meant for the Bastille in Paris to be relocated in Rome, it would be there in an instant. On the other hand, philosophers (*les philosophes*) take

it on principle that whatever is able to touch or be touched, to move or be moved, must be corporeal, and that the intelligence of an abstract mind cannot move the body without being united to it. It must, therefore, accommodate itself to the body, the nature of which is to pass through an environment in order to be moved from one place to another." François Le Gouz de La Boullaye, *Voyages et observations* (Paris: François Clousier, 1657), pp. 361–62.

4. Ibid., pp. 360–61. On the reputation of Le Gouz as a traveler, see Donald F. Lach, *Asia in the Making of Europe*, 3 vols. in 9 (Chicago: University of Chicago Press, 1965–1993), 3.1: 408–9.

5. Ambrosio de Morales, *Viage de Ambrosio de Morales por orden del rey D. Phelipe II a los reynos de Leon, y Galicia, y principado de Asturias* (Madrid: A Marin, 1765).

6. On Morales, see NCE 13: 530. Also for Morales, see the remarks of the eighteenth-century editor of the *Viage*, Henrique Florez, in the "Al Que Leyere" to the work and, on pp. i–xxvi, his "Noticias de la vida del chronista Ambrosio de Morales, sacadas, en la mayor parte, de sus obras." Also T. D. Kendrick, *St. James in Spain* (London: Methuen, 1960), pp. 48, 50–51. For Florez, NCE: 5, 975.

7. Morales's work, once Philip's interest was engaged, could not but be an important piece of literature, or at least of documentation. It was, in fact, the locus of intersection of two of the king's great interests—the collecting (especially of relics and books) and the reckoning through quantification of the elements of his kingdom. On which, see Henry Kamen, *Philip of Spain* (New Haven, Conn.: Yale University Press, 1997), pp. 188–89; and Geoffrey Parker, *The Grand Strategy of Philip II* (New Haven, Conn.: Yale Univeristy Press, 1998), pp. 58–65, 98.

8. On Florez, see above, n. 6, and Francisco Mendez, *Noticias sobre la vida, escritos y viajes del Rmo. P. Mtro. Fr. Enrique Florez*, segunda edicion (Madrid: José Rodriguez, 1860).

9. Morales, *Viage*, ¶2v.

10. On Cubero, see Henri Ternaux-Compans, *Archives des Voyages*, 2 vols. (Paris: Arthus Bertrand, 1840–1841), 2: 465–71; B. Sánchez Alonso, *Historia de la Historiographía Española*. 3 vols. (Madrid: Consejo Superior de Investigaciones Científicas, 1941–1950), 2: 351–52; Lach, *Asia in the Making of Europe*, 3: 360.

11. Pedro Cubero Sebastián, *Breve relación, de la peregrinación que ha hecho de la mayor parte del mundo* (Madrid: Iuan Garcia Infançon, 1680), p. 104.

12. The comparison was made by the Jesuit censor, Iuan Cortes Ossorio, in the *Aprobación* to Cubero, *Breve relación*, ¶4r.

13. Because of St. Bernard, St. Francis, St. Catherine, and others, "I have no doubt that Siena is one of the wonders of Italy." Cubero, *Breve relación*, p. 58.

14. Ibid., pp. 263, 268, 276–82, 342–43.

15. Joseph de Castro, *Viage de America à Roma* (Mexico: La Viuda de D. Joseph Bernardo de Hogal, 1745).

16. The imprint on the title page of our copy reads: "Impresso in la Europa; y por su original reimpresso en Mexico por Francisco Rodriguez Lupercio; y áhora nuevamente reimpresso por la Viuda de D. Joseph Bernardo de Hogal. Año de 1745." See Palau 2: 104–5.

17. Castro, *Viage*, p. 2.

18. Antonio Natale, *Tesoro de las copiosas indulgencias* (Mexico: J.B. De Hogal, 1725).

19. Joseph de Avila, *Colección de noticias de muchas de las indulgencias plenarias y perpetuas.* (Mexico: Felipe de Zuñiga y Ontiveros, 1787).

20. Natale, *Tesoro*, p. 12.

21. Jacobus Gualla, *Papie sanctuarium* (Papie: Impressum pro Jacob de Burgofracho, 1505). In 1587 the book was reprinted at Pavia with the title, *Historiae suae patriae, Sanctuarii Papiae appellatae, libri sex.* See Harvard College Library, Dept. of Printing and Graphic Arts, *Catalogue of Books and Manuscripts*, 2 vols. in 4, comp. Ruth Mortimer (Cambridge, Mass.: Belknap Press of Harvard University, 1964–1974), 1: 317–18.

22. *Sancte Ursule Fraternitas ingens perutilis et Christifidelibus multum necessaria.* (Norimbergae: F. Peypus, 1513), reverse of title page and last page.

23. Jacques Callot, *Les gueux* (Nancy: s.n., 1622 or 1623).

24. On Balbin, see NCE 2:24; Som 1:792–808, 8:1729–30; G 1:279; *Dictionnaire d'histoire et de géographie ecclésiastiques*, vol. 6, ed. Alfred de Meyer (Paris: Letouzey et Ané, 1932), pp. 316–19. See also the German summaries in Zuzana Pokorná and Martin Svatoš, *Bohuslav Balbín und die Kultur seiner Zeit in Böhmen* (Köln: Böhlau Verlag, 1993), esp. pp. 270 (Ivana Čornejová, "Der Jesuitenorden in Böhmen zur Zeit Balbíns,"), 273–75 (Jiří Šitler, "Bohemia Sancta von Bohuslav Balbín"), 282–83 (Jan Royt, "Bohuslav Balbín und Wallfahrtsorte des Barocks"). The latter speaks of Bohemia, like other parts of shrine-filled Europe, becoming "einem neuen Heiligen Land."

25. Bohuslav Balbin, *Diva Wartensis* (Prague: Typis Universitatis Carolo-Ferdinandeae in Colleg. Soc. Iesu ad S. Clementem, 1657). On Warta (or Wartha, or Bardo), see *Lexikon für Theologie und Kirche*, 10 vols (Freiburg im Breisgau: Herder, 1930–38), 10: 757.

26. Balbin, *Diva Wartensis*, between pp. 41 and 42.

27. Ibid., between pp. 159 and 160.

28. In the event, Jansenists did, despite the royal hammer, travel to the monastic ruins and take home bricks as relics. The whole business received literary memorialization in Jean-Baptiste d'Etemare's book, provocatively entitled *Gémissements sur la destruction de Port-Royal*, the first volume of which appeared only three years after the act of destruction. See Hubert Jedin and John Dolan, eds., *History of the Church*, 10 vols. (New York: Crossroad, 1980–1982), 6: 55.

29. In general, for these later scenes of the Jansenist drama, see B. Robert Kreiser, *Miracles, Convulsions, and Ecclesiastical Politics in Early Eighteenth-Century Paris* (Princeton, N.J.: Princeton University Press, 1978). Especially good for describing the general context of Jansenism's "determined attempt at vulgarisation, or democratisation, of the religious" in Paris in the early eighteenth century is Daniel Roche, *La France des Lumières* (Paris: Arthème Fayard, 1993), pp. 330–39. See also William V. Bangert, *A History of the Society of Jesus*, 2nd ed. (St. Louis: Institute of Jesuit Sources, 1986), pp. 301, 380, where he writes of the great Jansenist of Louis XV's time, Pasquier Quesnel, that "he lifted Jansenism out of the restricted circle influenced by Port-Royal and brought it to large segments of the middle and even lower classes," and quotes D'Alembert, writing to Voltaire in 1761, on "the Jansenist rabble."

30. Morales, *Viage*, pp. 71–74.

31. D. A. Brading, *Mexican Phoenix: Our Lady of Guadalupe: Image and Tradition Across Five Centuries* (Cambridge: Cambridge University Press, 2001), p. 146.

32. By Gretser's time (1609), it may have been wishful thinking to calculate, as he did, that a printed account represented one percent of those who actually went on pilgrimage. Jacobus Gretser, *De sacris et religiosis peregrinationibus libri quattuor* (Ingolstadt: A. Sartor, 1606), p. 86. On the low ebb of actual pilgrimage to the Holy Land in general as reflected in the evidence of writers of pilgrimage (Ceverio de Vera, Cotovicus, etc.), see below, Chapter 7.

33. Jean Baptiste Gaby, *Relation de la Nigritie* (Paris: Edme. Eouterot, 1689), pp. 3–4.

34. See above, Chapter 3, n. 36.

35. Noted by J. R. Hale for the sixteenth century, *The Civilization of Europe in the Renaissance* (New York: Atheneum, 1994), p. 148, and by Owen Chadwick for the eighteenth, *The Popes and European Revolution* (Oxford: Clarendon Press, 1981), p. 41.

36. On the Campo Santo Teutonico in Rome: NCE:2:1116.

37. In the sixteenth century, Gualla (Papie *Sanctuarium*, 75v -76r) says that those visiting the Church of St. Matthew in Pavia earn a commutation of all a pilgrim's vows—"with the exception of those involving Rome, the Holy Land, and St. James Compostella as well as [the vow] of entering religious life." In the eighteenth century, Antonio Natale gives a scheme of indulgences that suggests Rome ranking before the Holy Land and Compostella. Natale, *Tesoro de las copiosas indulgencias*, pp. 21–28. Jonathan Sumption, *Pilgrimage: An Image of Medieval Religion* (London : Faber and Faber, 1975), p. 239, sees the earlier growth of indulgences at Rome in the fourteenth century as an attempt by Rome to coopt Jerusalem which was then at its peregrinative height.

38. *Mirabilia Romae* [Rome, 151-?], b7v.

39. Ellis Veryard, *An account of divers choice remarks, as well geographical, as historical, political, mathematical, physical, and moral; taken in a journey through the Low-Countries, France, Italy, and part of Spain; with the isles of Sicily and Malta. As also, a voyage to the Levant* (Exon: Printed by S. Farley, 1701), p. 181.

40. Guibert of Nogent, *De vita sua*, 2.1. Guibert de Nogent, *Histoire de sa vie*, ed. G. Bourgin; Collection de textes pour servir á l'étude et a l'enseignement de l'histoire (Paris: A. Picard et fils, 1907), pp. 99–105.

41. John Bossy, *Christianity in the West* (Oxford: Oxford University Press, 1985), pp. 10–11, captures the vagueness of the situation when he speaks of "the discovery about 1470 that the family house at Nazareth had been transported by air to the Italian village of Loreto a century or two before." See also Lucien Febvre, *The Problem of Unbelief in the Sixteenth Century*, trans. Beatrice Gottlieb (Cambridge, Mass.: Harvard University Press, 1982), p. 222, where he says that "we know now the legend grew in the last years of the fifteenth century or the first years of the sixteenth." Early printed accounts of the event give different dates—the *Translatio miraculosa ecclesie Beate Marie Virginis de Loreto* (n.p., 15—), [3r], gives 1296 as the date of the Marian vision that explained the events of Loreto. The Roman edition of the same work, *Translatio miraculosa* (Rome: E. Silber, ca. 1500?), [2r], gives 1386 as the date.

42. LC has the following editions: Orazio Torsellino, *The History of our B. Lady of Loreto. Translated out of Latyn into English* (n.l., 1608); idem., *Lauretanae historiae libri quinque* (Leodii, 1621); Iuan de Burgos Angelopolitano, *Discursos historiales panegyricos de las glorias de la Serenissima Reyna de los angeles en su sagrada casa de Loreto* (Madrid: Joseph Fernandez de Buendia, 1671). And on Louis Richeome's book and its editions, see Som 6:1823–24.

43. Febvre, *Problem of Unbelief,* p. 319.

44. David Alan Brown, *Lorenzo Lotto: Rediscovered Master of the Renaissance* (Washington, D.C.: National Gallery of Art, 1997), pp. 5–13. Michael Kitson, *The Complete Paintings of Caravaggio* (New York: Harry N. Abrams, 1967), pp. 98–99.

45. Baldesar Castiglione, *Il libro del Cortegiano,* ed. Walter Barberis (Torino: Biblioteca Einaudi, 1998), 2.86, pp. 236–38; *Book of the Courtier,* trans. Charles S. Singleton (Garden City, N.Y.: Doubleday, 1959), pp. 182–84.

46. J. C. Beaglehole, *The Exploration of the Pacific,* 3rd ed. (Stanford, Calif.: Stanford University Press, 1966), p. 84.

47. Alexandre de Rhodes, *Sommaire des divers voyages, et missions apostoliques . . . à la Chine, et autres royaumes de l'Orient, avec son retour de la Chine à Rome: Depuis l'année 1618. jusques à l'année 1653* (Paris: Florentin Lambert, 1653), p. 4.

48. Ibid., p. 110.

49. Ibid., a2r.

50. Cubero, *Breve Relación,* pp. 111–20.

51. *Siege of Vienna—Jan III (Sobieski),* King of Poland. Vero disegno e distinto ragguaglio dello stendardo preso a Tuchi sotto Bargam dalla maesta del re de Polonia mandato alla santa casa di Loreto. A single broadside sheet. (Foligno: G. Zenobj, 1684). Entry 515 from *Printed Books and Maps of the Near and Middle East,* Sotheby's Auction: Thursday 23 October 1997. I am indebted to Christopher Murphy, Turkish specialist in the Library of Congress, for knowledge of this artifact.

52. Jean Chelini and Henry Branthomme, *Les chemins de Dieu: histoire des pèlerinages chrétiens des origines à nos jours* (Paris: Hachette, 1982), p. 278.

53. Marie-Dominique de Binos, *Voyage par l'Italie, en Egypte au Mont-Liban et en Palestine ou terre sainte,* 2 vols. (Paris: chez l'auteur et chez Boudet, 1787) 1:83–92.

54. Michel Nau, *Le voyage de Galilée* (Paris: Michel Le Petit et Estienne Michallet, 1670). Nau devotes five chapters (pp. 148–203) to the sites of Nazareth. In 1673–1674, he would again go on pilgrimage to Palestine, an account of which was first published in 1679. On Nau, see B 1185, p. 250.

55. Nau, *Voyage,* p. 152.

56. Gualla, *Pavie Sanctuarium,* 88v–92v.

57. *Relación breve de las reliquias, que se hallaron en la ciudad de Granada en una torre antiquissima, y en las cavernas del mônte Illipulitano de Valparaiso cerca de la ciudad* (Granada: Impresso en la casa la viuda de S. de Mena, 1608).

58. See roster of indulgences of Natale or Avila.

59. Pedro Gonzalez de Mendoza, *Historia del monte Celia de Nuestra Señora de la Salceda* (Granada: Iuan Muñoz, 1616).

60. The riches of the Holy Land and of Alcaria: Gonzalez de Mendoza, *Historia del monte Celia,* pp. 8–13; sacred mountains: ibid., pp. 17–22.

61. Thus is labeled a large illustration of the Marian apparition and miracles: ibid., between pp. 640 and 641. See also p. 145.

62. Matheo de Anguiano, *La Nueva Jerusalèn, en que la Perfidia Hebraica Reiterò con Nuevos Ultrages la Passión de Christo Salvador del Mundo, en su Sacrosanta Imagen del Crucifixo de la Paciencia, en Madrid* (Madrid: En la Imprenta de Manuel Ruiz de Murga, 1709). On Anguiano, see *Enciclopedia universal ilustrada Europeo Americana* 5: 578–79 (which states that he was born at the end of the sixteenth century or the beginning of the seventeenth).

63. Anguiano, *La Nueva Jerusalèn, Prologo al Lector Piadoso,* pp. SS5v–6r.

64. "There is a small chapel, inside which is a place where a great miracle happened. It is there that the wicked Jews scourged an image of Our Savior, and the image shed a great amount of blood." Henri de Beauvau, *Relation iournalière du voyage du Levant* (Nancy: Iacob Garnich, 1615), p. 100.

65. "And in the city of Beirut is a chapel that had once been a Jewish school. Inside the building the Jews tortured a crucifix of Our Beloved Lord, and the crucifix was so covered with blood that it now is in Constantinople. An indulgence of seven years attaches to the chapel." Hans Tucher, *Reise in das Gelobte Land* (Augsburg: Johann Schönsperger, 1482, 32v. Santo Brasca, *Viaggio del Sepulchro* (Milan: Nicolai de Gorgonzola, 1519), E7r–v [Santo Brasca, *Viaggio in Terrasanta,* ed. Anna Laura Momigliano Lepschy (Milan: Longanesi and C., 1966), 287, p. 134)].

66. Noè Bianchi, *Viaggio da Venezia al S. Sepolcro ed al Monte Sinai* (Bassano: G.A. Remondini, 1742), p. 132.

67. Modern edition: *Jacobi a Voragine Legenda Aurea: Vulgo Historia Lombardica Dicta,* ed. Th. Graesse (Leipzig: Impensis Librariae Arnoldianae, 1850).

68. *Legenda Aurea* 137.4 (Graesse ed., pp. 608–9).

69. Anguiano, *La Nueva Jerusalèn,* pp. 218–19.

70. For modern times, Pinto mentions miracles happening at the site in 1726, and the throngs of pilgrims that followed (*immensidade de Romeiros*) and had traveled great distances. And his description of the ceremonies of 1733 includes an engraving that shows men lined up in the form of a cross. António Cerqueira Pinto, *Historia da prodigiosa imagem de Christo crucificado* (Lisboa: Antonio Isidoro da Fonseca, 1737), pp. 32–33, pp. 242–43. On Pinto, see *Grande Enciclopedia Portugeusa e Brasileira* 21: 791. On Matozinhos: ibid. 16: 604–8.

71. Pinto, *Historia da prodigiosa imagen,* p. 62.

72. Pinto, *Historia da prodigiosa imagen,* p. 2: He speaks of the image coming "from the Orient to the Occident, from eastern Palestine in Asia to Matozinhos, the western edge of Europe in Portugal."

73. Febvre, following Geoffroy Atkinson, points this out in *Problem of Unbelief,* p. 343.

74. Diarmaid MacCulloch, *The Reformation* (New York: Viking, 2003), p. 289.

75. Ibid., p. 351.

76. "For Kyhler, Bavaria was the 'Holy Land' of Europe, a place where the march of time was suspended and the biblical story was being continually reenacted. That he should associate Bavaria with the Holy Land was not mere poetic license or rhetoric, for thanks to the enthusiastic promotion by Counter-Reformation propagandists of legends about shrines, the territory had been made more holy

than it had ever been before." Philip M. Soergel, *Wondrous in His Saints: Counter-Reformation Propaganda in Bavaria* (Berkeley: University of California Press, 1993), p. 228. On Rader's *Bavaria Sancta*, see *Die Jesuiten in Bayern: 1549–1773*, Ausstellung des Bayerischen Hauptstaatsarchives und der Oberdeutschen Provinz der Gesellschaft Jesu (Munich: Anton H. Konrad Verlag, 1991), pp. 192–94. Also Euan Cameron, *The European Reformation* (Oxford: Clarendon Press, 1991), p. 16. On the application of the stations of the way of the Cross to Palestine, see Elzear Horn, *Ichnographiae monumentorum Terrae Sanctae, 1724–1744*, 2nd ed. of Latin text with English version by E. Hoade and preface and notes by B. Bagatti (Jerusalem: Franciscan Press, 1962), p. 8.

77. A map shows distribution of shrines holding piece of the True Cross; holy blood from the Holy Land; relic of a Eucharistic miracle. Nolan and Nolan, *Christian Pilgrimage*, p. 180.

78. William H. Forsyth, *The Entombment of Christ: French Sculptures of the Fifteenth and Sixteenth Centuries* (Cambridge, Mass.: Harvard University Press, 1970), esp. pp. 22–23, which show a map of the distribution of entombments

79. Adrien Parvilliers, *Les stations de Jérusalem pour servir d'entretien sur la passion de Jésus Christ* (Paris, 1680). By 1682 it had gone through fourteen editions. It would go through more editions and translations. Cited in RBG 1182, p. 277. Som 6: 319–25.

80. "It is a widespread belief among the people of the Vendôme and those of neighboring provinces that there exists in the Vendôme in the Monastery of the Trinity one of the tears which Our Lord Jesus Christ shed over the death of Lazarus. But this conviction is based on such extraordinary events that are scarcely reliable. One must only expose them to the eyes of the judicious and enlightened in order to render them suspect and apocryphal." J. B. Thiers, *Dissertation sur la sainte larme de Vendôme* (Paris: Claude Thiboust, 1699), pp. 9–10. The book's epigraph is a quotation from Innocent III: "Falsity ought not to be tolerated under cover of piety." This publication (LC also has a 1751 edition that includes "la Réponse à la Lettre du P. Mabillon touchant la prétendue Sainte Larme. Par le même auteur etc.") shows what a live issue relics and pilgrimage were, and had been—Thiers's arguments are made from detailed reliance on Catholic tradition—in Europe, and not only across the Reformational barriers.

81. René François du Breil de Pontbriant, *Pèlerinage du Calvaire sur le Mont Valérien, et les fruits qu'on doit retirer de cette Dévotion. On y trouvera aussi des Prières pour la Messe, la Confession et la Communion, avec les Stations aux saintes Chapelles* (Paris: chez Babuty, 1779), pp. 8, 237–38.

82. Ibid., p. 13.

83. Ibid., p. 15.

84. Ibid., pp. xiii–xv, 122.

85. LC's copy belonged to Jefferson.

86. The uses to which a shrine such as Mont Valérien could be put were, of course, at least potentially as multiple and unpredictable elsewhere, and especially in Paris, as they were on the American frontier. It is worth noting that, among the spoofs and parodies that Chateaubriand's *Itinéraire* inspired in a portion of his audience, there was one entitled *Itinéraire de Lutèce au Mont-Valérien, en suivant le*

fleuve Séquanien et en revenant par le mont des Martyrs, and another entitled *Itiné-raire de Pantin au Mont-Calvaire, en passant par la rue Mouffetard, le faubourg Saint-Marceau, le faubourg Saint-Jacques, etc., et en revenant par Saint-Cloud, Boulogne, Auteuil, etc., ouvrage écrit en style brillant et traduit pour la première fois du bas-breton sur la 9e édition par M. de Chateauterne*. It is surely ironical that on the plane of parody, rather than of piety, a connection is made between the Parisian shrine and the Holy Land itself upon which Chateaubriand, in a spirit of restoration, had reported. See Jean Mourot's edition of the *Itinéraire* (Paris: Garnier-Flammarion, 1968), p. 21 and Fernande Bassan, *Chateaubriand et la terre-sainte* (Paris: Presses Universitaires de France, 1959), pp. 211–12.

    87. Louis Deshayes de Courmenin, *Voiage de Levant fait par le commandement du roy en l'année 1621*, 2nd ed. (Paris: Adrian Taupinart, 1632), p. 461: "The body of St. Nicholas of Bari is very carefully watched over there. It is he who attracts to this city a great number of pilgrims who arrive from all parts of Christendom."

    88. Gretser, *De sacris et religiosis peregrinationibus*, pp. 94–95.

    89. See below, Chapters 6 and 7.

    90. See sketch map of pilgrimage routes to Compostella in Barry Cunliffe, *Facing the Ocean: The Atlantic and Its Peoples 8000 BC–AD 1500* (Oxford: Oxford University Press, 2001), p. 521.

    91. For a sense of the variety of such leavings, throughout the Christian world of Europe and the Near East, consult *Wallfahrt Kennt Keine Grenzen* (see above, n. 1).

Chapter 6. A Second Voice: Terra Sancta inter Alia

    1. Gretser, in his great 1606 book on pilgrimage, sharply distinguished between religious travel and profane travel, but he also recognized a combination of the two—a "certain kind of, so to speak, mixed travel (*mixtae peregrinationis*)" which combined pilgrimage and a tour-like journey. Jacobus Gretser, *De sacris and religiosis peregrinationibus libri quattuor* (Ingolstadt: A. Sartor, 1606), pp. 10–11.

    2. It took Jean Mocquet in the early seventeenth century longer to travel from Paris to Marseilles than to sail from Marseilles to Tripoli. Jean Mocquet, *Voyages en Afrique, Asie, Indes Orientales, & Occientales* (Rouen: Jacques Cailloué, 1645), pp. 367–69.

    3. From the *Préface au lecteur* in Henri de Beauvau, *Relation iournalière du voyage du Levant* (Nancy: Iacob Garnich, 1615).

    4. Ibid., p.157.

    5. Ibid., p. 181: "We the undersigned have read this present *Relation*. In fact, in it we have come across things that inspire trust and belief in the pious traveler (*pieux viateur*) who has written a work that can only bring contentment to its readers. Therefore, it is worthy of being published."

    6. On Careri, see Donald F. Lach, *Asia in the Making of Europe*, 3 vols. in 9 (Chicago: University of Chicago Press, 1965–1993), 3.1: 386–87; and Philippe de Vargas, "Le 'Giro del Mondo' de Gemelli Careri, en particulier le récit du séjour en Chine. Roman ou vérité?" *Schweizerische Zeitschrift für Geschichte* 5 (1955): 417–51.

7. Giovanni Francesco Gemelli Careri, *A Voyage Round the World . . . Written originally in Italian, tr. into English* (London, 1704), p. 289.

8. Examples from LC holdings: Rosaccio (1598), Le Blanc (1648), Veryard (1701), La Mottraye (1727).

9. Charles Estienne, *Voyages de plusieurs endroits de France: et encores de la terre Saincte, d'Espaigne, d'Italie, et autres pays. Les fleuves du royaume de France* (Paris: chez Charles Estienne, Imprimeur du Roy, 1552). The Library of Congress copy is bound with *La guide des chemins de France, reveue et augmentée pour la troisième foix* (Paris, 1553).

10. Estienne, *Voyages de plusieurs endroits*, pp. [3–4].

11. Ibid., pp. 15, 57, 60, 35, 17, 16.

12. Ibid., p. 20.

13. Ibid., p. 51. And see the later, partly repetitious elaboration which describes Rome as "the holy city and chief city of all Italy. See the cloth of Veronica (*la Véronique*) and an infinite number of other relics together with Roman antiquities." Ibid., p. 60.

14. Holy places associated with the relics of saints and Marian devotions attracted Catholics, but those associated with the life and passion of Christ attracted Protestant travelers as well. See Antoni Mączak, *Travel in Early Modern Europe*, trans. Ursula Phillips (Cambridge: Polity Press, 1995), pp. 222–37.

15. Estienne, *Voyages*, p. 67: "A singular journey, of which it has been said that the traveler who has been to St. James but has not been to Holy Savior, has visited the servant and neglected the Lord."

16. On the journey to Jerusalem, see ibid., pp. 67–69. Perhaps a sign of the declining times of actual travel to Jerusalem (in the second half of the sixteenth century) is the slight confusion, in the minds of writers recalling the golden age of such travel, over what had been the exact date of sailing from Venice to Jerusalem. Estienne tells us around mid-century that it was the Feast of the Ascension, Bianchi a decade and a half later that it was the Feast of Corpus Christi, much later (1595) Villamont that it was one or the other, and at almost the end of the century Ceverio de Vera that the great day had indeed been Corpus Christi. It is uncertain whether Villamont was himself unclear on which was the correct feast or whether he thought both were, once upon a time, the great days of sailing to Jerusalem. See below, Chapter 7, notes 50, 56, and 70.

17. Herbert George Fordham, *Les Routes de France: étude bibliographique sur les Cartes-Routières et les Itinéraires et Guides-Routiers de France* (Paris: Librairie Ancienne Honoré Champion, 1929), p. 5. See also idem, "The Earliest French Itineraries," repr. from *The Library* (1921): 197.

18. Guglielmo Grataralo's *Proficiscentium, seu, Magnis itineribus diversas terras obeuntium medicina* (Cologne: Petrus Horst, 1571), a highly practical aid to travelers, lists possible itineraries within Europe. But before beginning the list, he states: "Bernhardus Breitenbachius wrote an *Itinerarium terrae sanctae*, which has been printed." It was as if he were saying that pilgrimage to Jerusalem came first, even in a list of journeys that had nothing to do with pilgrimage. Nor was Estienne's view one that was fading away as time passed. In the 1770s, pilgrimage could still figure at the top of the list in a survey of destinations. See, e.g., *Poste per diverse*

parti del mondo. Con il viaggio di San Giacomo di Galizia, e di Gerusalemme, di Vienna, et Costantinopoli. Ed altre Poste principali di Francia, e Germania. Con la tariffa generale de' pagamenti, per comodo de' viandanti . . . (Roma: Nella stamperia del Casaletti, 1771).

19. On Belon, see B 115. Lach (*Asia in the Making of Europe* 2.2:301) calls Belon's book "one of the most readable travelogues to appear in the sixteenth century."

20. Pierre Belon, *Les observations de plusieurs singularitez et choses memorables, trouvées en Grèce, Asie, Iudée, Egypte, Arabie, et autres pays estranges* (Paris: chez Guillaume Cavellat, 1555), a3v.

21. LC possesses the edition of the year following the book's first appearance: Leonhard Rauwolf, *Aigentliche Beschreibung der Raiss* (Lauingen: Leonhart Reinmichel, 1582). The Staphorst translation also exists in a "second edition corrected and improved" of John Ray, *A Collection of Curious Travels and Voyages*, vol. 2 (London: J. Walthoe,et al., 1738), pp. 1–338, which is in the LC collections. On Rauwolf and his travels, see RBG 758, and K. H. Dannenfeldt, *Leonhard Rauwolf: Sixteenth-Century Physician, Botanist and Traveller* (Cambridge, Mass.: Harvard University Press, 1968), esp. pp. 153–76 for treatment of the pilgrimage section of Rauwolf's book.

22. All of part 3: Rauwolf, *Aigentliche Beschreibung* (1582), pp. 297–480.

23. Ibid., pp. 299–300 (Ray translation, pp. 203–4).

24. Ibid., pp. 428–29 (Ray translation, p. 302: "Their head is the Pope of Rome, who pretends to be the Vicegerent of Christ, and taketh upon himself so much power, as to prescribe to all men laws according to his own pleasure, which Christendom finds every day to its great grief.") Catholics and Franciscans are treated in part 3, chapter 19: "Von den Latinis oder Papisten." Rauwolf (1582), pp. 428–31 (Ray translation, pp. 301–3).

25. Ibid., pp. 342–43 (Ray translation, p. 236).

26. Ibid., p. 299–300 (Ray translation, pp. 203–4).

27. Ibid., p. 315 (Ray translation, p. 215).

28. Ibid., p. 386 (Ray translation, p. 268). See entire passage.

29. Ibid., p. 387 (Ray translation, p. 268).

30. Famous, but not always highly regarded. José Martinez de la Puente's *Compendia de las Historias de los descubrimientos* (Madrid, 1681) lumps him together with that other famous world traveler, Fernan Mendez Pinto, and decides (*Prologo*, p. 2) that both are lacking in "plausibility and seriousness" when it comes to serving as sources of information on parts of the world through which they have traveled. On Ordóñez, whose book appeared in Madrid in 1614, 1616, and 1691, see *Pedros Ordóñez Ceballos: Viaje del Mundo*, ed. Félix Muradás (Madrid: Miraguano Ediciones, 1993), pp. ix–xiv. See also Lach, *Asia in the Making of Europe*, 3.1: 325–26.

31. Ordóñez (1691), *Prologo al Lector* in Pedro Ordóñez de Ceballos, *Historia y viage del mundo* (Madrid: J. Garcia Infanzon, 1691).

32. Ibid., p. 5.

33. Ibid., *Prologo al Lector*.

34. Jean Mocquet, *Voyages en Afrique, Asie, Indes Orientales, et Occidentales* (Rouen: Jacques Cailloué, 1645), pp. 191–92, 210–11. On Mocquet, see Lach, *Asia in the Making of Europe*, 3: 397; and F. B. Maggs, *Voyages & Travels in All Parts*

of the World: A Descriptive Catalogue, 3 vols. (London: Maggs Bros., 1942–1951), 1:254–55.

35. Mocquet, *Voyages* (1645), p. 161: "The previous year's journey to the West Indies had given me such a desire to see the rest of the world that I determined, should convenient occasion arise, to go the East Indies. Thus did I leave Paris on 12 April 1605." He had arrived back in France from his previous journey on 15 August 1604.

36. Ibid., pp. 417–18.

37. Ibid., pp. 420–21, 440–42.

38. Ibid., p. 6.

39. Ibid., p. 213: "As our longings are never completely satisfied in this life, so they are always on the increase and urge us on to new things to the extent that we have already enjoyed the very things that we most wished for. So considering that I was back from my last voyage to Africa, I once again desired to fulfill what had been my first intention, which was to go to the East Indies."

40. Ibid., p. 34.

41. Ibid., p. 4. For the concepts of *via* and *peregrinatio* and other terms that had formed, since antique Christianity, an ideational substratum for wandering and travel as well as for philosophizing and theologizing, see the broad sketches of Gerhart B. Ladner in two classic articles: "Greatness in Mediaeval History," *Catholic Historical Review* 50 (1964): 1–26; and "HOMO VIATOR: Mediaeval Ideas on Alienation and Order," *Speculum* 42 (1967): 233–59. Both are reprinted in idem, *Images and Ideas in the Middle Ages*, 2 vols. (Roma: Edizioni di Storia e Letteratura, 1983), 2: 877–902, and 2: 937–74 respectively.

42. Mocquet, *Voyages* (1645), pp. 367–68.

43. However, almost seventy years after the first French edition, a German translation appeared (Luneburg, 1688) in which the chapter on pilgrimage had grown to almost two hundred and fifty pages (out of a total of six hundred and thirty-two). In the words of Johann Beckmann, *Litteratur der ältern Reisebeschribungen*, 2 vols (Göttingen, 1807–1809; repr., Genève: Slatkine, 1971), 2:114, "The report on the promised land, which is quite short in the French, has here grown, drawing on diverse books, into a detailed description." The German edition is also more heavily illustrated. In addition to the scene of the Syrian dance, there is a fold-out map of ancient Jerusalem showing the three crosses of the Crucifixion.

44. Mocquet, *Voyages* (1645), pp. 386–88, 414–15.

45. Ibid., pp. 411–14.

46. Ibid., p. 398.

47. Ibid., p. 404.

48. Ibid., p. 405. It had always been a common thing to compare, for the easier understanding of the reader in Europe, a Levantine city (Cairo, for example, at which all travelers were amazed) to a known European city. It is a rare thing to do, however, in regard to Jerusalem—the whole point of which, after all, was that it was an incomparable city.

49. Ibid., p. 401.

50. Ibid., pp. 402–3.

51. Ibid., p. 406.

52. For LC copies of such travel accounts, see the triple-starred items in the bibliography.

53. In the *Discours que i'ay dessein de faire à l'Academie en luy, presentans mon Livre*, in Pietro della Valle, *Les fameux voyages*, 2 vols. (Paris,: G. Clovzier, 1662–1663), 2: 77–85.

54. Ibid., 2:80–81. On Valle, see B 1712.

55. On the bibliography of Thévenot's book, see RBG, p. 265; B 1650.

56. Jean de Thévenot, *Voyages de Mr. de Thévenot au Levant . . .troisième édition*, 5 vols. (Amsterdam: Michel Charles le Céne, 1727), 1: *3r–v. Nicolae Iorga, *Les voyageurs français dans l'Orient européen* (Paris: Boivin, 1928), p. 69, credits Thévenot for "a quite interesting personality owing to his total lack of pretension."

57. Jean de Thévenot, *Relation d'un voyage fait au Levant* (Paris: Thomas Iolly, 1665), p. 356: "Upon my return from the journey to Mount Sinai, I thought of making the voyage to Jerusalem and of how the nativity, life, and death of our Savior Jesus Christ make these places so desirable a goal. I waited for Lent in order to be there when the Church celebrates the memory of this sorrowful Passion."

58. Through translations, Thévenot found his way into John Harris's *Collection* (London, 1705) and into the *Sammlung der besten u. neuesten Reisebeschreibungen* (Berlin, 1765). See RBG 1104.

59. Thévenot, *Relation* (1665), pp. 412–13.

60. Ibid., p. 412.

61. Ibid., p. 366.

62. On Bruyn, see B 225.

63. Cornelis de Bruyn, *Voyage au Levant*, 5 vols. (Paris: J. B. C. Bauche, le fils, 1725), 1:1–2: "Since I have always, from tenderest youth, had a great inclination to travel, I pondered very seriously, when I had become a little older, how to prepare myself to travel with success. And since nothing appeared to me more necessary for a traveler than to know how to draw, since by this means not only can one make known the objects which one thinks worthy of the public curiosity, but also because one is thereby able, upon return from the journey, to fashion descriptions as exact as if one where looking at things right before one's eyes, I therefore determined to apply myself to painting, and when I found myself advanced in the art sufficiently (as I judged it) for my purposes, I prepared to get on with my plan. Having learned that the following year 1675 a Jubilee was to be celebrated at Rome, I resolved to go there and to begin my voyages from there."

64. Ibid., *Préface*.

65. Ibid., 2: 237–40.

66. See below, Chapter 7.

67. Laurent d'Arvieux, *Memoires du Chevalier d'Arvieux*, 6 vols. (Paris: C. J. B. Delespine, 1735), 1: x–xi: "They look upon the Levant—that is, the Empire of the Grand Seigneur—as their Indies; it is to the Levant that they send almost all their sons to prepare them for carrying on business in the seaports of this vast country."

68. On Arvieux, see B 50.

69. Jean Baptiste Tollot, *Nouveau voyage fait au Levant, ès années 1731 et 1732. Contenant les descriptions d'Alger, Tunis, Tripoly de Barbarie, Alexandrie en Egypte, Terre Sainte, Constantinople, etc.* (Paris: André Cailleau, 1742). The *Voyage de Jerusalem*

begins on p. 122, and Tollot continues to describe the holy places until p. 201, where he reports on his traveling party's departure from Acre.

Chapter 7. A Third Voice: Pilgrims on Travel and Pilgrimage

1. The Library of Congress does not possess one of these early modern editions. I have used its copy of the modern edition (based on the 1597 edition): Juan Ceverio de Vera, *Viaje de la Tierra Santa: 1596*, edición, introducción y notas por Concepción Martinez Figueroa and Elias Serra Rafols (La Laguna: Instituto de Estudios Canarios, 1964). On Ceverio and his editions, see ibid., xi–xiv. See also T, pp. 86–87; RBG 830; Joseph R. Jones, ed., *Viajeros Españoles a Tierra Santa (siglos XVI y XVII)* (Madrid: Miraguano, 1998), pp. 97–98; and Agustín Millares Carlo, *Ensayo de una Bio-Bibliografía de Escritores Naturales de las Islas Canarias (Siglos XVI, XVII Y XVIII)* (Madrid: Tipografía Archivos, 1932), pp. 170–76; Y pp. 420–21. On Álvar Núñez Cabeza de Vaca's grandfather, Pedro de Vera, see Cabeza de Vaca's *Relación* [f67r] in Rolena Adorno and Patrick Charles Pautz, eds., *Álvar Núñez Cabeza de Vaca: His Account, His Life, and the Expedition of Pánfilo de Narváez*, 3 vols. (Lincoln: University of Nebraska Press, 1999), 1: 278–79.

2. Ceverio de Vera, *Viaje* (1964 ed.), 1: 9–10. On the state of affairs in Rome over the Henrician matter at just this time, see Ludwig von Pastor, *The History of the Popes from the close of the Middle Ages*, vol. 23 (London: Kegan Paul, 1933), pp. 115–17. On Clement's hopes and devices for a Rome-centered reunification and revitalization of Christendom, see Jack Freiberg, *The Lateran in 1600: Christian Concord in Counter-Reformation Rome* (Cambridge: Cambridge University Press, 1995), esp. pp. 161–76.

3. For bibliographical information on these manuscript records of pilgrimage, see the notices (arranged chronologically by year of travel) in Tobler (T) and Rohricht (RBG). Dansette (see above, Chapter 1, n. 22) gives information on modern scholarly editions of these texts that have been published in recent, or relatively recent, times.

4. On the slowly developing organization of learning around the separation of print and manuscript, see David McKitterick, *Print, Manuscript and the Search for Order 1450–1830* (Cambridge: Cambridge University Press, 2003).

5. Machiavelli's *Prince*, which went to many printed editions (and to a place on the Index) is only one prominent example of a work that also had a considerable life in manuscript (circulating within a circle of readers who were in sympathy and in the know) before finally getting into print. See Robert Bireley, *The Counter-Reformation Prince: Anti-Machiavellianism or Catholic Statecraft in Early Modern Europe* (Chapel Hill: University of North Carolina Press, 1990), pp. 14–15. For a recent study on manuscripts as a serious medium of intellectual and scholarly exchange in the age of print, see Harold Love, *Culture and Commerce of Texts* (Amherst: University of Massachusetts Press, 1998).

6. See modern edition of Anselm Adorno's pilgrimage and editorial commentary in Jean Adorne, *Itinéraire d'Anselme Adorno en Terre Sainte (1470–1471)* (Paris: Éditions du Centre National de la Recherche Scientifique, 1978).

7. RBG 968.

8. Henry Maundrell, *A Journey from Aleppo to Jerusalem at Easter A.D. 1699* (Oxford: G. Delaune, 1703), a2.

9. Examples of rhetorical reluctance: Maundrell, *A Journey from Aleppo*, a2; Pacifique de Provins, *Relation du voyage de Perse* (Paris: Nicolas et Jean de la Coste, 1631), p. 2.

10. T, pp. 63–64. B 1206.

11. See Josephie Brefeld, *A Guidebook for the Jerusalem Pilgrimage in the Late Middle Ages: A Case for Computer-Aided Textual Criticism*, Middeleeuwse Studies en Bronnen 40 (Hilversum: Verloren, 1994).

12. The evidence for texts and editions is most comprehensively set out in T and RBG.

13. Antonio de Medina, *Viaggio di Terra Santa* (Florence: Giorgio Marescotti, 1590). See T 66, RBG 592, NUC 373:160. See also Harvard College Library, *Catalogue of Books and Manuscripts*, 2 vols. in 4, comp. Ruth Mortimer (Cambridge, Mass.: Belknap Press of Harvard University Press, 1964–1974), 2:439. The date for a 1594 edition of the Italian translation (but not for one of 1590) is given in Nicolaus Antonius, *Bibliotheca Hispana sive Hispanorum* (Rome: ex officina N.A. Tinassii, 1672) 1:113. See also Samuel Eiján, *España en Tierra Santa* (Barcelona: Herederos de Juan Gili, 1910), p. 67.

14. Harant: T 88, RBG 841, NUC 230:388, G 3:209. See also A. H. Wratislaw, "Adventures of a Bohemian Nobleman in Palestine and Egypt in the days of Queen Elizabeth," *Transactions of the Royal Historical Society* n.s. 3 (1874): 346–71.

15. Jacobus Gretser, *De Sacris et Religiosis Peregrinationibus Libri Quattuor* (Ingolstadt: A. Sartor, 1606), p. 86.

16. "I even dare to assert that there have been authors who, without leaving their studies (*cabinets*), have offered the public voyages which they claim to have made to the Levant." Jean Baptiste Tollot, *Nouveau voyage fait au Levant, ès années 1731 et 1732* (Paris: André Cailleau, 1742), iv–v.

17. T devoted a section (pp. 207–15) to works by authors who probably had not been on the ground in Palestine.

18. St. Thomas More, *Utopia*, ed. Edward Surtz, S.J. (New Haven, Conn.: Yale University Press, 1964), pp. 12–13.

19. On Columbus as more than a discoverer, see Frank E. Manuel and Fritzi P. Manuel, *Utopian Thought in the Western World* (Cambridge, Mass.: Harvard University Press, 1979), pp. 59–62. The authors observe (p. 61) that "Columbus always insisted that his 'execution of the affair of the Indies' was a fulfillment of prophecies in Isaiah and not a matter of mere reason, mathematics, and maps."

20. The great collections of travels, as important constituent agents of early modern culture, are not entirely unrelated to a work such as the thirty-nine volumes of C.-G.-T. Garnier's *Voyages imaginaires, songes, visions, et romans cabalistiques* (Amsterdam, 1746–1795). Its *Avertissement de l'éditeur* describes the overall context of literary endeavor: "History paints for us men such as they have been or such as they are; fictions paint them such as they ought to be; the traveler describes lands which he has visited, tells of his discoveries, and describes that which has happened to him among peoples *previously* unknown to us and whose habits and customs he passes on to us. The philosopher (*le philosophe*), on the other hand, has another

way of traveling (*une autre manière de voyager*). With only his imagination as guide, he transports himself into new worlds where he gathers observations which are neither less interesting nor less valuable. Attend to him in his travels and be assured of gaining as much fruit from our voyages as if we had made a world tour." Ibid., 1:Air. On "fireside travelers" of the later seventeenth and the eighteenth centuries, see Percy G. Adams, *Travelers and Travel Liars: 1660–1800* (New York: Dover, 1962, 1980), pp. 80–131.

21. Bünting's *Itinerarium* heads the list of books under the category of "Itineraria" in Christian Friderich Wilisch's *Index Bibliothecae* (Altenburg: apud Io. Ludou. Richterum, 1721), p. 208.

22. Bünting: T 209, RBG 774, G 1:572. See also H. A. M. van der Heijden, "Henrich Bunting's *Itinerarium Sacrae Scripturae*, 1581: A Chapter in the Geography of the Bible," *Quaerendo* 28 (1998): 49–71. The latter (pp. 69–71) includes a table of the editions of the *Itinerarium*.

23. His contemporary, the artist and traveler Cornelis de Bruyn, took him in this light. He is not ignorant of the fact that Dapper's work was a "compilation," but this does not distract from the fact that he read him pretty much as he read Della Valle and Thévenot, two other Levantine travelers of the seventeenth century. See the *Preface* to Bruyn, *Voyage au Levant* (Paris, 1725), vol. 1. For Dapper, see T 212, RBG 1171, B 449.

24. For a facsimile edition and translation of a fourteenth-century manuscript of Petrarch's guide, see *Petrarch's Guide to the Holy Land*, ed. and trans. Theodore J. Cachey, Jr. (Notre Dame, Ind.: University of Notre Dame Press, 2002).

25. Edward Gibbon, *Memoirs of My Life and Writings* (Staffordshire: Keele University Press, 1994), pp. 110–11. The first phrase was Gibbon's, but was edited out by John Sheffield. On this, see editors' notes, ibid., p. 358.

26. But not unanimously so. Consider, for example, Philip Thicknesse, an English Protestant and Gibbon's contemporary, who was quite taken with Montserrat. Philip Thicknesse, *A Year's Journey Through France, and Part of Spain*, 3rd ed., 2 vols. (London: Wm. Brown, 1789), 1: 207–25.

27. Quoted in Antoni Mączak, *Travel in Early Modern Europe*, trans. Ursula Pillips (Cambridge: Polity Press, 1995), p. 231. On Catholic and Protestant views of relics, ibid., pp. 222–36.

28. Thomas Carve, *Itinerarium* (London: B. Quaritch, 1859), p. 234.

29. Helffrich: T 78, RBG 734, S 22–23, 94–95, RDP 245–246.

30. Johann Helffrich, *Kurtzer und warhafftiger Bericht, von der Reis aus Venedig nach Hierusalem* (Leipzig: Jacob Bersaldts Erben, 1580), Bir.

31. Ibid., Aiiv–Aivr.

32. Salignac: T 69, RBG 610. Christiaan van Adrichem, *Theatrum Terrae Sanctae et biblicarum historiarum, cum tabulis geographicis aere expressis* (Cologne: in Officina Birckmannica, sumptibus Hermanni Mylij, 1613), pp. 287–88, describes Salignac: "sedis Apostolicae prothonotarium, equestris ordinis militem auratum, ac utriusque iuris professorem quod ann. 1522. Expedivit ac descripsit."

33. Thevet: T 73, RBG 686, B 1651, Y pp. 219–20. There is a modern edition: *Cosmographie de Levant*, ed. Frank Lestringant, Travaux d'Humanisme et Renaissance 203 (Genève: Librairie Droz S.A., 1985).

34. André Thevet, *Cosmographi de Levant* (Lyon: Ian de Tournes, et Guil. Gazeau, 1554), pp. 162–80.

35. Ibid., p. 16.

36. Ibid., p. 173: He speaks, for example, of "the Cenacle where the holy Sacrament of the altar was instituted for our salvation and the Holy Spirit was sent to the Apostles to preach the Catholic Faith." Thevet as partisan and practitioner of Catholic pilgrimage remains a public, published fact of the 1554 text, no matter how much Thevet may have moved on from, or even against, pilgrimage in his later travel writings, as argued by Wes Williams in *Pilgrimage and Narrative in the French Renaissance* (Oxford: Clarendon Press, 1998), pp. 266–73. The general scholarly treatment of Thevet's career as traveler and cosmographer is Frank Lestringant, *André Thevet: Cosmographe des derniers Valois*, Travaux d'Humanisme et Renaissance 251 (Genève: Librairie Droz S.A., 1991).

37. Thevet, *Cosmographie*, p. 176.

38. Ibid., pp. 3–6 (the dedicatory epistle), pp. 13–16 (the preface).

39. Ibid., p. 15.

40. Ibid., p. 4.

41. Ibid., pp. 4–5.

42. Ibid., pp. 13–14.

43. Zuallart: T 83–85, RBG 797, B 1873 and 1874, S 117. On Zuallart's voyage, see also J. L. D. Ghislain de Saint-Génois, *Les voyageurs belges*, 2 vols (Brussels: A. Jamar, 1846?–1847?), 2: 37–55.

44. These remarks are from the second page of the *Au pèlerin dévot* in Jean Zuallart, *Le trèsdévot voyage de Jérusalem* (Anvers: Arnlould s'Conincx, 1608).

45. Ibid., bk. 1, pp. 12–13.

46. The image reappears at the place in the narrative where the pilgrims are actually approaching Jerusalem. Zuallart (1608), bk. 3, p. 25.

47. Ibid., bk. 3, p. 1; bk. 3, p. 10; bk. 3, p. 15.

48. Ibid., bk. 3, p. 142.

49. T.S. R. Boase, "Ecclesiastical Art in the Crusader States in Palestine and Syria." In Harry W. Hazard, ed., *A History of the Crusades*, vol. 4, *The Art and Architecture of the Crusader States* (Madison: University of Wisconsin Press, 1977), pp. 69–139, here pp. 69–72.

50. Noè Bianchi, *Viaggio da Venezia al S. Sepolcro ed al Monte Sinai* (Bassano: G.A. Remondini, 1742), pp. 8, 7. On Bianchi, see Y, pp. 163–64; F. B. Maggs, *Voyages and Travels in All Parts of the World: A Descriptive Catalogue*, 3 vols. (London: Maggs Brothers, 1942–1951), 2:93–94.

51. Guerrero: T 86, RBG 809, NCE 6:833. See also Nicolaus Antonius, *Bibliotheca Hispana sive Hispanorum* (Rome: ex officina N. A. Tinassi, 1672) 1:329, where Guerrero's title is given as "Portionarius et Choragus cantorum almae Ecclesiae Hispalensis." The second title of the *Viage* was *Breve tratado del viaje que hizo a la ciudad santa de Jerusalem D. Franc. Guerrero en cual se da noticia veridica de todos los santuarios sitios y lugares en que Nuestro Redentor Jesu Cristo estavo dode nacio y murio.* See also Samuel Eiján, *España en Tierra Santa* (Barcelona: Herederos de J. Gili, 1910), p. 69.

52. Francisco Guerrero, *El Viage de Hierusalem (Seville, 1592)*, ed. R. P. Calcraft

(Exeter: University of Exeter, 1984), p. 56. This passage has apparently disappeared from the later and differently titled editions (such as LC's 1790 Madrid edition).

53. "It is impossible to describe the great devotion, tenderness, and piety that we feel here when we consider that everything that we read in the Gospel was enacted in that place." Francisco Guerrero, *Breve Tratado del Viage que hizo a la Ciudad Santa de Jerusalen* (Madrid: Josef de Urrutia, 1790), p. 87.

54. Villamont: T 85–86, RBG 812, B 1733, Y pp. 400–2. See also Louis Loviot, "Les voyages de Villamont (1595)," *Revue des Livres Anciens* 2 (1916): 237–53.

55. Jacques de Villamont, *Les voyages du seigneur de Villamont* (Arras: De l'Imprimerie de Guillaume de La Riviere, 1602), pp. 36 (Siena), 110–122 (Loreto), 27 (Bologna), 53 (St. John Lateran), 247–48 (rosaries).

56. Ibid., pp. 166–67. This is 1589, when there is no longer a Jerusalem-bound ship leaving Venice on the Feast of the Ascension or on the Feast of Corpus Christi (*la feste Dieu*) for the sole purpose of transporting pilgrims. Ibid., p. 171.

57. Ibid., pp. 2–3.

58. Ibid., p. 166.

59. On Feyerabend's comparison of the great navigators with pilgrims going to the Levant, see above, Chapter. 4, n. 8.

60. Ceverio de Vera, *Viaje* (1964 ed.), pp. 7–8. Quotations in this and the following paragraph are from this 2-page *Prologo*.

61. Ibid., p. 85.

62. Ibid., pp. 85–88.

63. Ibid., pp. 100–7.

64. Ibid., pp. 118–22.

65. See also ibid., pp. 128–35, 144–49.

66. Ibid., pp. 17, 28.

67. He provided information for those traveling from Rome, which made sense because he himself had followed that course and the first edition of his book was printed in Rome; but he followed that up with further instructions for those setting out from Spain. Ibid., pp. 156–58.

68. "Unable to find a companion, I all alone . . . commenced my journey." Ibid., p. 10.

69. Ibid., pp. 22–23.

70. Ibid., p. 23.

71. Speaking of their making the holy rounds in Jerusalem: "From that altar we began the solemn station, opening the gate to the contemplation of such high mysteries as they happened in those holy places. Both because it seemed to me that dolorous hymns and prayers were quite appropriate to these places and also because it would be a comfort for those devout persons who, not being able personally to visit the places themselves, would recite them in their places of prayer, I decided to write them down." Ibid., pp. 52–53.

72. Ibid., p. 8.

73. Ibid., p. 7.

74. Nicholas Christopher Radziwill, *Ierosolymitana Peregrinatio* (Antwerp: Ex officina Plantiniana, 1614), *4r.

75. There may have been a second Polish edition in 1617; and there were further

editions of the *Reyssbuch* (a third in 1629 and a fourth in 1659). On the biblio-graphical record of Radziwill's text, see RBG 787; also S, p. 116; Maggs, *Voyages and Travels*, 3: 303; Y pp. 352–54. The Library of Congress does not possess a copy of this important pilgrimage; I have used Houghton Library's copy (Asia 9215.83.23F*) of the 1614 Antwerp imprint.

76. Ibid., *3r.

77. This index—according to Isaac Verburg (ca. 1680–1745), who corrected and expanded his predecessors' work in his own version of the index attached to Bentley's eighteenth-century edition of Horace—had been compiled by Treter, assisted by Stanislaus Drozinus, in 1573, when both lived in the Hosius establish-ment in Rome. See Verburg's preliminaries to *Q. Horatius Flaccus, ex recensione et cum notis atque emendationibus Richardi Bentleii*, 3rd ed. (Amsterdam: R. et J. Wet-stenios et G. Smity, 1728). On Stanislaus Hosius and his world, see Henry Damien Wojtyska, *Cardinal Hosius: Legate to the Council of Trent* (Rome: Institute of Eccle-siastical Studies, 1967). See also NCE 71:154; and *The Oxford Encyclopedia of the Refor-mation*, 4 vols. (New York: Oxford University Press, 1996), 2: 256.

78. Radziwill, *Ierosolymitana Peregrinatio*, *2r–*5v.

79. Treter's theoretical bent may have been encouraged by one of his cited sources, the Franciscan Johannes Dubliulius, the title of whose own *peregrinatio* has something of an abstract ring: *Hierosolymitanae peregrinationis hodoeporicum septem dialogorum libris explicatum, in quo de ratione itineris in Palaestinam, de sanctis locis vicinisque provinciis, de illarum gentium religione et moribus aliisque eo pertinentibus accurate disseritur* (Cologne: G. Grevenbruch, 1599). Cited in RBG 844, p. 221.

80. Radziwill, *Ierosolymitana Peregrinatio*, *2r–v.

81. Ibid., *5r–v.

82. Ibid., *4v.

83. The architectural mode of European consciousness is lavishly analyzed and illustrated throughout Henry A. Millon, ed., *The Triumph of the Baroque: Archi-tecture in Europe 1600–1750*, 2nd English ed. rev. (New York: Rizzoli, 1999).

84. Boase speaks of Amico as belonging to "a more scientific approach" to depicting structures in the Holy Land, an approach that he traces back to Zuallar and which he contrasts to the woodcuts in Breydenbach. T. S. R. Boase, "Ecclesi-astical Art in the Crusader States in Palestine and Syria." In Hazard, *A History of the Crusades*, vol. 4, pp. 69–116; here, p. 69.

85. Amico: T 87, RBG 837, B 31. See also the preface and notes of B. Bagatti to *Fra Bernardino Amico. Plans of the Sacred Edifices of the Holy Land*, trans. T. Bel-lorini and E. Hoade. (Jerusalem: Franciscan Press, 1953). Also A. Arce, "Bethlehem: el culto de San José in Belen," in idem., *Miscelánea de Tierra Santa*, vol. 2 (Jerusa-lem: Franciscan Printing Press, 1973), pp. 27–28. And Serge Sauneron, ed., *Voyages en Égypte des années 1597–1601* (Paris: Institut français d'Archéologie orientale, 1974), pp. iii–iv.

86. Jacques Callot, *Capitano de baroni* (or, among other titles, *Les Gueux*), ([s.l.:s.n.], 1622–23).

87. The third illustration in his *Les Gueux*. On which, see J. Lieure, *Jacques Callot: Catalog of the Graphic Works*, vol. 5 (New York: Collectors Editions, 1969), no. 481 (pp. 41–42).

88. The frontispiece to volume one of Thicknesse's *A Year's Journey* portrays a rag-tag, hobbled soldier on his way to Monserrat. A large fold-out engraving (facing 1: 208) shows the great variety of sorts of pilgrims that visited the great shrine.

89. The sections of Ignatius's autobiography (nos. 35–53) describing his travels from Spain to Jerusalem and back cast the entire journey in this light. *A Pilgrim's Journey: The Autobiography of Ignatius of Loyola*, ed. and trans. Joseph N. Tylenda, S.J. (Collegeville, Minn.: Liturgical Press, 1985, 1991), no. 35, p. 42.

90. *Vita beati P. Ignatii Loiolae Societatis Iesus fundatoris* (Rome, 1622). For Ignatius as a pilgrim to the Holy Land, see pls. 22–29, and especially pl. 27. On this volume, see the Estudio Preliminar of Antonio M. Navas Gutiérrez in P. P. Rubens y Jean Baptiste Barbé, *Vida de San Ignacio de Loyola en Imágenes. Edición Facsimil*, Biblioteca Teológica Granadina 27 (Granada: Facultad de Teologia, 1993), pp. ix–xlix.

91. Jean de Thévenot, *Voyages de Mr. de Thévenot au Levant . . . troisième édition*, 5 vols. (Amsterdam: Michel Charles le Céne, 1727), 2: facing p. 574.

92. Bernardino Amico, *Trattato delle piante et immagini de sacri edifizi di Terra Santa* (Firenza: Pietro Cecconcelli, 1620). The first quote comes from the dedicatory epistle to Francesco de Castro, the Spanish ambassador in Rome, and would have been in the first edition. The second quote comes from the 1620 edition's dedication to Cosimo II of Tuscany (Bellorini and Hoade trans., pp. 38–39).

93. Amico, *Trattato*, pp. 63–65 (Bellorini and Hoade trans., pp. 142–44).

94. Cotovicus: T 87–88, RBG 839, B 416.

95. William H. McNeill, *Europe's Steppe Frontier: 1500–1800* (Chicago: University of Chicago Press, 1964), p. 55.

96. *Admodum reverendo Domino Arsenio Schayck, Primarii Belgicae Monasterii S. Petri Archimandritae*: Ioannis Cotovicus, *Itinerarium Hierosolymitanum et Syriacum* (Antwerp: Hieronymus Verdussius, 1619), a2r–a4v. *Praefatio ad Benevolum Lectorem*: ibid., e1r–e2v. *Ad lectorem Peregrinantem Paraenesis*: ibid., *2r–**1v.

97. Ibid., a2v: "While all these things can be truly said and commended concerning profane travel, who would not readily assert that more results and benefits are to be anticipated in the case of sacred travel to Jerusalem?"

98. Ibid., a4v.

99. Ibid., e2r.

100. Ibid, p. 3.

101. Ibid., e2v.

102. Ibid., †2v: Many are dissuaded by Near Eastern dangers and troubles. "But such reasons do not delay him who has already firmly decided to undertake this journey. He should consider that he is going not on a profane or pleasurable journey but on a sacred journey, which is undertaken not because of lucre or vain glory or ambition but from the sole motive of piety, so that he might offer grateful allegiance to God and bear the Cross with Christ."

103. Nicolas Bénard, *Le Voyage de Hierusalem et autres lieux de la Terre Sainte faict par le Sieur Bénard . . . Avec une ample description des choses plus remarquables et une Instruction nécessaire pour les pèlerins voyageurs ès Sts. Lieux cy dessus de Hierusalem* (Paris: D. Moreau, 1621), p. 43. He mentions elsewhere that for a Frenchman going to Palestine, he must leave from either Marseilles or Venice. Ibid., p. 6.

104. LC does not possess a copy of Bénard's book. I have used the Dumbarton

Oaks copy of the 1621 edition, cited in the previous note. On Bénard, see RBG 949, T, pp. 96–97.

105. François René Chateaubriand, *Itinéraire de Paris à Jérusalem*, 2 vols., ed. Emile Malakis (Baltimore: Johns Hopkins University Press, 1946), 2:91–95.

106. Deshayes de Courmenin: T 97, RBG 968, B 479.

107. Great controversy swirled about the text from the beginning. It seems to have been printed without the author's permission and was ultimately disavowed by him. The editor mentions the troubles but asserts that the reader will find in the book "many things quite useful as well as remarkable." Pacifique de Provins, *Relation du Voyage de Perse* (Paris: Nicolas et Iean de la Coste, 1631), following p. 215 and facing the beginning of the *Table des matières*. On the controversy over authorship of the 1631 edition and of the 1632 edition at Lille see Godefroy de Paris et Hilaire de Wingene, eds., *P. Pacifique de Provins: Le Voyage de Perse et brève relation du voyage des îles de l'Amérique*, ed. Godefroy de Paris et Hilaire de Wingene, Bibliotheca Seraphico-Capuccina, Sectio Historica 3 & 4 (Assisi: Collegio S. Lorenzo da Brindisi, 1939), pp. lxv–lxix (where it is said that "les variantes du texte sont infimes").

108. See, for example, Herman Conring's "De prudentia peregrinandi," ix; in *Dissertationes academicae selectiores* (Lugduni: Floridus Martin, 1686), fol. Kk7r, where he speaks of travel as improving the traveler and as benefiting the state as well, because the traveler learns from the particular political arrangements of other polities. On the other hand, while Conring recognizes that there are other sorts of travelers than his aspiring statesman—soldier, merchant, tourist, diplomat, even the exile—he makes no mention of the pilgrim. Conring, "De prudentia peregrinandi," ix, fols. Kk7v–Kk8r.

109. Pacifique de Provins, *Relation du Voyage*, a2r.

110. Ibid., p. 208.

111. "Most painters, indeed nearly all, when they represent to us this action of Pilate, when he said *Ecce Homo*, in fact misrepresent the mystery because of their ignorance. As a rule, they picture this action taking place on a high stairway or on steps, or on a low balcony enclosed in trellis-work or balusters. But the setting is in fact in the following manner." Ibid., p. 195.

112. It had long been recognized that there were two sources of information on the holy sites. Zuallart, for example, had challenged the great Baronius over the location of the house of Zachary, on the basis both of travelers' accounts (going back to the Middle Ages and coming forward to his own time) and of the tradition of residents. Zuallart, *Le trèsdévot voyage*, bk. 3, pp. 225–26.

113. On the Franciscan Custody: A. Arce, "The Custody of the Holy Land," in A. Arce, *Miscelánea de Tierra Santa*, vol. 3 (Jerusalem: Franciscan Printing Press, 1974), pp. 141–55; and idem, "De Origine Custodiae Terrae Sanctae," pp. 75–139.

114. Castillo: T 98, RBG 989. Castillo's contemporary, Nicolaus Antonius—*Bibliotheca Hispana sive Hispanorum*, 1: 85—remarks on him: "On account of his goodness and pleasantness as well as his religious probity and humility, he is so dear to our Court that almost never for these many years would he be absent from it." See also Arce, "Bethlehem: el culto de San José in Belen," p. 28.

115. Antonio del Castillo, *El Devoto Peregrino, Viage de Tierra Santa* (Madrid: Imprenta Real, por Joseph Rodriguez, 1705), p. 347.

116. Ibid., pp. 94–95.

117. Ibid., ¶¶5v.

118. Ibid., p. 142. See also the illustration of Jaffa with travelers and ships in harbor: ibid., p. 140. See also, ibid., pp. 144, 146–48.

119. Ibid., *Prologo al lector*, ¶¶4v–5v.

120. Ibid., ¶¶4v–5r.

121. Jean Doubdan, *Le Voyage de la Terre-Sainte . . . troisiesme edition* (Paris: chez Pierre Bien-Fait, 1666), a4r: After sailing to Marseilles, he traveled by way of Lyon to Paris and St. Denis, "where I found all in lamentation and tears, and a horrible mess of war and death which had carried off many of my relations, eight of my fellow Canons, and many of my closest friends."

122. Ibid., a3r–a4v, pages which contain the *Au lecteur*, where Doubdan vents his concerns and ambitions for his pilgrimage.

123. Doubdan: T 104–5, RBG 1079.

124. Doubdan, *Le Voyage*, a4r–v. Francesco Quaresmio's *Historica, theologica et moralis Terrae Sanctae Elucidatio: In qua pleraque ad veterem et praesentem ejusdem Terrae statum spectantia accurate explicantur, varii errores refelluntur, veritas fideliter exacteque discutitur ac comprobatur* appeared in Antwerp in 1639. Quaresmio had resided in Terra Sancta from 1616–1626. Eugène Roger's *La Terre Saincte; ou Description topographique tres-particuliere des saincts Lieux et de la Terre de Promission* (Paris, 1646) tells of his pilgrimage of 1631 and of much more (the title continues: *Avec un Traitté de quatorze nations de differente Religion, qui l'habitent, leurs moeurs, croyance, ceremonies et police. Un discours des principaux points de l'Alcoran. L'histoire de la vie et mort de l'Emir Fachr ed-din, Prince de Damas*). The book was reissued in 1664 and 1666. See RBG 948 and 1012.

125. Doubdan, *Le Voyage*, a4v.

126. Goujon treats of the complicated history of Nazareth, including the saga of the transference of Mary's house to Loreto. He then adds: "I cannot actually say how so many persons are able to write of the Holy Land after having been here so briefly, and above all of this holy house of Nazareth where no stopover at all is made. I am speaking of pilgrims who allow four or five days to visit [the Holy Land] and its environs." Jacques Goujon, *Histoire et Voyage de la Terre-Sainte* (Lyon: Pierre Compagnon, et Robert Taillandier, 1671), pp. 67–69.

127. Goujon: T 111–12, RBG 1142.

128. Goujon, *Histoire et Voyage*, in the introduction to the reader, e1re–e2v.

129. Ibid., e1r: "What strikes me is how our pilgrims who write large volumes concerning the Holy Land, and this after a month's visit at most, are convinced that they are able to say all that there is to say concerning it."

130. Ibid., e2r.

131. Michel Nau, *Voyage Nouveau de la Terre-Sainte* (Paris: chez André Pralard, 1702), first page of (unpaginated) *Preface*.

132. On the earlier book by Nau: T 110–11, RBG 1138.

133. On the later book by Nau: Som 5:1595–96; T 110–11; RBG 1138; B 1185; DHCJ 3:2802–3.

134. Nau, *Voyage Nouveau*, the five-page preface deals succinctly and frankly with Nau's motives and ambitions for writing up his travels.

135. Ibid., p. 604.

136. Ibid., pp. 50–53.

137. Ibid., p. 275.

138. Henry Maundrell, *A Journey from Aleppo to Jerusalem at Easter, D.D. 1697*, 4th ed. (Oxford: Printed at the Theater, 1721), b4r.

139. Ibid., p. 68.

140. Ibid., b2r.

141. Ibid., p. 49.

142. Ibid., p. 68.

143. Ibid., a2r–v.

144. Maundrell: T 116–17, RBG 1235, B 1095.

145. In the modern book trade, his volume is considered "très rare." *Bibliothèque de feu M. Ch. Chadenat*, 2 vols. (Paris: Editions du Vexin Français, 1980), no. 5101.

146. Morison: T 118, RBG 1237, B 1155. See also *Le Voyage en Egypte d'Antboine Morison, 1697*. Présentation et notes de Georges Goyon ([Cairo]: Institut français d'archéologie orientale du Caire, 1976), pp. i–xxvii. There was a contemporary review in the Jesuits of Trevoux's *Mémoires pour l'histoire des sciences et des beaux arts* (Février 1705): 187–215.

147. Antoine Morison, *Relation historique, d'un voyage nouvellement fait au mont de Sinaï et a Jerusalem* (Toul: A. Laurent, 1704), p. 626.

148. Ibid., pp. 248–51.

149. Ibid., pp. 210–11.

150. Ibid., pp. 1–2.

151. *Mémoires pour l'histoire des sciences et des beaux arts* (Février 1705): 202.

152. Jean de La Roque, *Voyage de Syrie et du Mont-Liban*, 2 vols. in one (Amsterdam: H. Uytwerf, 1723), *5r: "After so many *rélations* on the Levant and the Holy Land, we were not yet at all thoroughly informed concerning all that which includes the vast region of the Lebanon, one of the most beautiful countries of the Orient, and acclaimed in our religion for its many different sites." The author's time in the Levant also produced two other volumes, the *Voyage de l'Arabie heureuse* (Paris, 1716) and *Voyage dans la Palestine* (Paris, 1717). On La Roque: T 114–15, RBG 1208. See also commentary in: *Voyage de Syrie et du Mont-Liban par Jean de La Roque*, ed. Jean Raymond, Voyageurs d'Orient 1 (Beirut: Editions Dar Lahad Khater, 1981), pp. v–xxviii.

153. *Mémoires pour l'histoire des sciences et des beaux arts* (Février 1705): 187–215. Ibid., p. 188.

154. "The expressions that he uses cause to enter into the hearts of his readers the same pious emotions which the sight of these sacred monuments has inspired in him." Ibid., p. 201.

155. Ibid., p. 189. "M. Morisson seems poorly informed on the origin of the Nile. It is no longer a mystery since Father Jerome Lobo, a Portuguese Jesuit, has discovered the source of the river. One can read about this discovery in the latest edition of Moreri's *Dictionnaire Historique*, as well as the fourth collection of the letters of several Jesuit missionaries, which is about to appear." Ibid., p. 201.

156. Ibid., pp. 190–91, 200.

157. Ibid., pp. 201–2.

158. *Nouveaux mémoires des missions de la Compagnie de Jesus dans le Levant,* vol. 5 (Paris: Guillaume Cavelier, 1725), b1r. Neret's letter, entitled "Lettre du pere Neret, missionnaire de la Compagne de Jesus en Syrie," appears on pp. 1–121.

159. Neret: Som 5:1635–36, T 124, RBG 1361. On Pierre Fromage, see Som 3:1039–44.

160. *Nouveaux mémoires,* vol. 5, b1r–v.

161. Neret, "Lettre," pp. 108–10.

162. Ibid., pp. 89–98.

163. Ibid., pp. 3–4.

164. Ibid., 1–2.

165. Ibid., pp. 120–21.

166. Sicard: Som 7:1185–89; DHCJ 4:3567–68. Sicard's "Lettre" describing the journey into the Sinai is in *Nouveaux mémoires,* vol. 7 (Paris: Pissot et Briasson, 1729), pp. 1–27.

167. "His undertakings as a missionary, which he considers essential to his [Jesuit] Profession, have not prevented him from executing the orders that he received from the King—which orders are for him to continue his research of ancient monuments which he has discovered in Upper and Lower Egypt." *Nouveaux Mémoires des Missions de la Compagnie de Jesus dans le Levant* 5(1725): b1v–b2v. On the royal orders, see DHCJ 1:805.

168. *Nouveaux Mémoires* 7(1729): iv: "He has often let us know that his continual missions to instruct a people more ignorant than schismatic have not been a hindrance to his enlarging daily the collection of his discoveries. However, the services that he felt obliged to continue to render to the pest-ridden poor did cause his death. Thus it is that his writings have come down to us in an imperfect state."

169. Ibid., pp. 4–5: "At the outset, we took the route of the Hebrews, and we followed it from the passage of the Red Sea until Sinai. We have traversed, just as they did, the deserts of Sur, Etam, Sim, and Raphidin. Scripture tells us that they drank from the waters of Mara and Elim, and so also did we."

170. Jonas Korte, *Reise nach dem weiland Gelobten . . . Lande* (Halle: Joh. Christian Grunert, 1751), a2r. The very important "Vorrede an den geneigten Leser" takes up pp. a2r–b6v.

171. Ibid., b4r.

172. Ibid., b3v: "But since much is said of the Pope as Antichrist in this book, I wish to make myself clear in this regard, namely that throughout these words are meant to apply not simply to the person of the Pope, but to the entire clergy with him."

173. Ibid., a3r.

174. For this autobiographical prelude to the actual voyage to Jaffa, see ibid., a3r–a6r.

175. For example, in bk. 2 of ibid., pp. 321–29, 401–9: ch. 19: "Meditation on the Resurrection of Jesus Christ . . . "; ch. 20, "Meditation on the physical miracles of Our Lord Jesus Christ, and how the Christ as a child performed greater miracles than even his Lord and Master, according to John 14, 12"; ch. 25, "On the expectation of better times. Es. 58, 8."

176. Ibid., a6r–v.

177. Ibid., a6r.

178. Korte: T 128–29, RBG 1395.

179. Korte, *Reise*, pp. 51–52.

180. Ibid., p. 277. Excerpts from Tschudi footnoted by Korte follow (ibid., pp. 277–87). Indeed, a striking aspect of Korte's approach here is that his notes can invoke the testimony of another Catholic pilgrim (Goujon, for example, in ibid., p. 278, n. 1) to support his position on a point vis-à-vis Tschudi. One is given a sense of Korte as well tuned in to a peregrinative discourse (that is largely Catholic in its participants), but in a way that it would be too simplistic for us to characterize or dismiss as nothing but contrarian and nay-saying.

181. Hasselquist: T 130, RBG 1435, B 792.

182. The reader is told, in the preliminaries by Linnaeus, that Hasselquist traveled from Cairo "to Jerusalem with the pilgrims who intended to celebrate their Easter there." Fredrik Hasselquist, *Voyages and Travels in the Levant in the Years 1749, 50, 51, 52* (London: L. Davis and C. Reymers, 1766), v.

183. Ibid., pp. 117, 121 ff.

184. Korobeĭnikov: T 82; *Russian Travellers to the Greek World* (Moscow: Indrik, 1995), 81–82.

185. Binos: T 134, RBG 1507, B 144. For dates of departure and of return to Livorno: Marie-Dominique Binos, *Voyage par l'Italie, en Égypte au Mont-Liban et en Palestine ou Terre Sainte*, 2 vols. (Paris: chez l'auteur et chez Boudet, 1787), 1:6, 2:354.

186. Ibid., 1:2.

187. Ibid., 1:150–51, where the author is seized by the charms of the Italian landscape.

188. Venice: Ibid., 1:159–87.

189. Loreto: Ibid., 1:83–84.

190. Johann Wolfgang Goethe, *Italienische Reise mit vierzig Zeichnungen des Autors*, 2 vols. (Frankfurt am Main: Insel Verlag, 1976, 1979)1:153–57.

191. Assisi: Binos, *Voyage*, 1: 98–10; Rome and the Pope: ibid., 1:138.

192. Ibid., 1:vi–viii.

193. Ibid., 2:355.

194. Ibid., 2:248: "It is not known why this ceremony has been in suspension for twenty years. It is shocking that Christians have abandoned a custom which represented so well one of the beautiful events in the life of Our Savior."

195. Compare, for example, Chateaubriand, *Itinéraire*, 2:87 and Binos, *Voyage*, 1:2.

196. Ibid., 1:86.

197. Ibid., 2:148.

198. Ibid., 2: facing p. 145; 2: facing p. 196; 1: facing p. 198.

199. Ibid., 2:133.

Conclusion: Alive and Well and Early Modern

1. A 1635 Franciscan document ("Informatione delle cose di Terra Santa e di Levante (del P. Diego [di] San Severion, già guardiano di Gierusalemme") speaks

of Marseilles, Venice, Livorno, Genoa, Messina, and Malta as the usual points of departure of pilgrims heading for Jerusalem. Edition in G. Golubovich, *Biblioteca Bio-Bibliografia della Terra Santa e dell'Oriente Francescano* n.s. 1 (1921): 363–64.

2. Desfontaines, reading Arvieux's traveler's *mémoires* in the 1730s, underscored the great variety of information that Arvieux's Levantine mercantile travels provided, but gave no indication that among such variety was Arvieux's significant attention to pilgrimage in the Holy Land. Pierre-François Guyot Desfontaines, *Observations sur les écrits modernes*, 3:49–60 (*lettre* 33). In idem, *Observations sur les écrits modernes, 1735–1743*, 34 vols. in 4 (Genève: Slatkine Reprints, 1967), 1: 198–201.

3. The only North American imprint in the LC collection is Nathaniel Crouch's *A Journey to Jerusalem* (Hartford, Conn.: J. Babcock, 1796).

4. "In the strict sense, we take travel as the departure and absence from our own country in the situation of this life. But there is a kind of travel that because of the diversity of its purposes one not inconveniently divides into profane travel and sacred or religious travel." Jacobus Gretser, *De sacris et religiosis peregrinationibus libri quattuor* (Ingolstadt: A. Sartor, 1606), pp. 4–5.

5. François Le Gouz de La Boullaye, *Les Voyages et Observations* (Paris: chez François Clousier, 1657), eiv–e4v.

6. C. F. Wilisch, *Index Bibliothecae* (Altenburg: Io. Ludov. Richter, 1721), pp. 208–12.

7. *Catalogue des livres de la bibliothèque de la maison professe des ci-devant soidisans Jesuites* (Paris, 1763), pp. 325–28.

8. Such, however, was not entirely boilerplate. An historian of travel, looking back on earlier pilgrimage, wrote in the mid-nineteenth century of the "exhausting monotony" of pilgrimage accounts and praised one author—"at least he is amusing"—though he had little else to recommend his narrative. Jules Ludger Dominique Ghislain de Saint-Génois, *Les voyageurs belges*, 2 vols. in 1 (Bruxelles: Jamar, 1846?–1847?), 2: 187.

9. Paul Fussell, *Abroad: British Literary Traveling Between the Wars* (New York: Oxford University Press, 1980). Evelyn Waugh's *When the Going Was Good* (Westport, Conn.: Greenwood Press, 1976) was originally published in 1946 as a condensation of his *Labels, Remote People, Ninety-Two Days*, and *Waugh in Abyssinia*, four books that had been published between 1929 and 1935.

10. Just before Fabri was the never printed (until recent times) pilgrimage of Anselm Adorno who, at Golgotha, exclaimed: "What Christian of today could see without moans and tears and a tremor of heart and a compassion of mind this place where our blameless Redeemer and Creator was handed over to death." Jean Adorne, *Itinéraire d'Anselme Adorno en Terre Sainte (1470–1471)*, ed. and trans. Jacques Heers et Georgette de Groer (Paris: Éditions du Centre National de la Recherche Scientifique, 1978), pp. 265, 266. For both the presence and absence of the personal element in earlier pilgrimages, see J. K. Hyde, "Italian Pilgrim Literature in the Late Middle Ages," *Bulletin of the John Rylands University Library* 72 (1990): 3–33.

11. Posed by John W. O'Malley in his overwhelmingly elegant *Trent and All That: Renaming Catholicism in the Early Modern Era* (Cambridge, Mass.: Harvard University Press, 2000), p. 56.

12. The line between clerical and lay is not, however, absolute in pilgrimage

to Terra Sancta. All pilgrims, including lay, were expected to receive a papal license for going to Jerusalem (or, alternatively, from the Custody upon arrival without license in Jerusalem). In addition, for cleric and layman alike, the main source of information on the holy sites would come from the Franciscans resident in Terra Sancta. Even a pilgrimage account by so prominent a layman as Radziwill was edited and translated by the cleric Treter. And Beauvau's book of travels was a pilgrimage, in part because the Franciscan censors of Toul said that it was.

13. To be sure, the point of the statement here is factual rather than theoretical or interpretive: he is not explaining the nature of his earlier book, but clarifying the basis of the record of his life (during his year abroad in the Mediterranean) for purposes of the present work, the *Mémoires d'outre tombe*, which is full-fledged autobiography.

14. *Mémoires d'outre-tombe* 1:680. The entry is dated Paris, 1839. The further indication is "Revu en decembre 1846." Clerke was the first officer on Cook's final voyage.

15. But he also resorts, elsewhere, to a more antique model of his sort of traveler, when he speaks of Julien as "le camarade d'Ulysse." *Mémoires d'outre-tombe* 1:709. If, then, we look upon Chateaubriand specifically and exclusively as a *traveler*, he seems a complete convert to one modern view of things. Even though he was a pilgrim (*and* a voracious reader of pilgrimages *and*, in this instance, a traveler to Jerusalem) pilgrimage has no place in the equation: the contemporary traveler is a discoverer (or discoverer-like figure) and his roots are antique (Ulysses). There isn't much, for Chateaubriand or for the great collectors, in between. It is something of a surprise to find Chateaubriand in such company.

16. For example, by Dansette ("Pèlerinages occidentaux en terre sainte," pp. 122–23): "Accounts of pilgrimage constitute a veritable literary genre the history of which is very extensive. In effect, with the exception of St. Jerome's letters telling of his pilgrimages around the Holy Places, the first known account, that of the 'Anonymous of Bordeaux', who was a pilgrim in Jerusalem in 333, stands at the beginning of the long uninterrupted succession of accounts rendered by Westerners, all the way up until the nineteenth century, which latter was made illustrious in this regard by the much celebrated *Itinéraire de Paris à Jérusalem* of Chateaubriand."

Chronological Bibliography

1. This refers to an *individual* traveler's printed travels, not to more general printed collections of travels (Hakluyt, Purchas, etc.). The latter are not listed in this bibliography.

2. The bibliography records, in addition to those pilgrimages that were part of an individual traveler's wider travels, separate printings of pilgrimages (as opposed to the rare examples of pilgrimages as parts of the great travel collections). The bibliographical reality is historically complicated, especially when the matter in question is a printed version of an antique pilgrimage (the *Itinerarium burdigalense*) or of a medieval pilgrimage (the travels of Burchardus of Mt. Sion, or of Symon

Simeonis). There are some pilgrimages that, while separately printed in the sense that they were not part of such collections, were not, however, *entirely* separate printings. The best example of how such works are treated in the bibliography is the entry for Burchardus of Mt. Sion, where his appearance in the *Novus Orbis* (one of the earliest great collections of travels) is not recorded (although it is discussed in the text), but his printed appearances in combination with the *Rudimentum Novitiorum*, with the excerpted *Decades* of Peter Martyr Anghiera, and with the *Itinerarium* of Barthelemy de Salignac, are all recorded. Burchardus and his like were, however, exceptional cases and are taken to be so in this bibliography.

3. Copy is imperfect. Salignac's Itinerarium is wanting.

4. See previous note.

5. Feyerabend's *Reyssbuch*, which includes both medieval and modern pilgrimages, is the one great example of pilgrimage as part of the grand tradition of travel collecting.

6. One component of the *Theatrum*, the description of Jerusalem in the time of Jesus, was printed as early as 1584; but the complete work (the description of Jerusalem, the geography of Terra Sancta, and a world chronicle to the death of John the Baptist) first appeared in 1590. See: B 7.

7. Imperfect copy. Folios 50, 52, 53 wanting.

8. Also printed in Crouch 1672. See below.

9. Work was first published in 1642; 1650 is first edition with appendix that expands the work into a text that includes matters of pilgrimage.

10. Only vols 1 & 3 on shelf.

11. Mixed set—i.e., 1662, 1658, 1658, 1663.

12. This volume is missing from the shelves of LC.

13. LC has volume one only.

14. LC set imperfect: volume of plates only.

15. LC has volume one only. Vol. 2 contains the chapters on pilgrimage in Terra Sancta. I have consulted the copy at Catholic University of America.

Index

Page numbers in **bold** type indicate entries recorded in the Chronological Bibliography

Abraham, 71
Adam, 71, 105
Adamnan, 17–18, 22, 28, 127, 163, 236–38
Ademar of Chabannes, 20
Adorno, Anselm, 317 n.10
Adorno, Jean, 155
Adrichem, Christiaan van, **258**
Aeneas, 71
Albert of Saxony, 95, 292 n.28, 293 n.34
Alexander the Great, 18, 71, 78
Alexander VI (pope), 54
Amico, Bernardino, 190–93, 196, 198–99,
    246–47, **259**, 271 n.9
Amman, Johann Jacob, **261**
Anghiera, Peter Martyr, 54
Anguiano, Matheo de, 118–20
Apollonius of Tyana, 71, 74, 82
Archinti, Ambrogio, 34–35
Arculf, 17–18, 22, 31, 163, 237–38
Aristotle, 166
Arvieux, Laurent d', 151–52, **266**
Ascension, Feast of the, 156, 234, 301 n.16,
    309 n.56
Assemanni, Joseph, 224
Assisi, 231
Auerbach, Erich, 278 n.30
Augustine, St., 206
Augustus of Saxony, 96
Aveiro, Pantaleâno, **258**
Avila, Joseph de, 106

Balbin, Bohuslav, 107, 109, 196
Banks, Joseph, 27
Baronius, Cesare, 154, 312 n.112
Baumgarten, Martin von, 77

Beauvau, Henri de, 119, 131–33, 136, 190,
    246–47, **259**
Becanus, Martin, 290 n.6, 292 n.26
Bellarmino, Roberto, 154
Bellegarde, Jean Baptiste Morvan de, 68–75,
    130, 239, 272 n.18
Bellenger, Yvonne, 274 n.32
Belon, Pierre, 135, **256**
Bénard, Nicholas, 201–2, 239, 245, 249, 273
    n.22
Benedictines, 61
Bergeron, Pierre, 75
Bernard of Clairvaux, 210
Bianchi, Noè, 27, 119, 175, 186, 190, 211,
    247, **257**
Binos, Marie Dominique de, 231–34, 245,
    247, **268**
Bireley, Robert, 274 n.36
Bolswert, Boëce van, **261**
Bom Jesus de Bouças, Shrine of, 120
Bongars, Jacques, **260**
Bordeaux Pilgrim. *See* Itinerarium
    burdigalense
Bougainville, Louis Antoine de, 60
Bramante, Donato, 116
Brasca, Santo, 32–36, 44, 100, 119, 125, 157,
    169, 241, 245, **255**
Brendan of Clonfert, St., 61
Breuning von Buchenbach, Hans Jacob, **260**
Breydenbach, Bernhard, 20, 29, 31, 32,
    35–45, 56, 60, 64, 100, 125–28, 130, 133,
    136, 153, 156, 157, 168–69, 175, 177, 186,
    190–92, 200, 204, 208, 224, 231, 233–36,
    241, 245–47, **255**
Briemle, Vincentius, **266**

Bruyn, Cornelis de, 149–53, 240, **264**
Bry, Johann Theodor de, 78, 80; and
　Theodor de, 67, 105
Buil, Bernardo, 61
Bünting, Heinrich, 158–60, 211, 238, **257**
Bunyan, John, 228
Burchardus of Mount Sion, 21, 66–67, 74,
　128, 228, 246, **254**
Burgo, Giovanni Battista de, **264**
Burgos Angelopolitano, Iuan de, 115

Cabeza de Vaca, Álvar Núñez, 154
Callot, Jacques, 107–8, 191–93, 196
Calvin, John, 85, 161, 182
Campbell, Mary B., 274 n.32
Câo, Diogo, 49
Capuchins, 118
Caravaggio, Michelangelo Merisi da, 115
Careri, Giovanni Francesco Gemelli, 132–33,
　264
Carli, Dionigi, **264**
Casas, Bartolomé de las, 51
Castiglione, Baldesar, 115
Castillo, Antonio del, 175, 202–6, 209, 211,
　213, 219, 239, 241–42, 245, 247, **262**
Castro, Joseph de, 105, 112, 128
Cavendish, Thomas, Sir, 104, 142
Ceverio de Vera, Juan, 10, 154–55, 163,
　181–87, 196, 198–99, 202, 218, 239,
　247–49, 271 n.9, 273 n.22, 281 n.36
Chardin, John, Sir, 238
Charles V, 49, 60, 95
Chateaubriand, François-René de, 1–7, 11,
　22, 35, 37, 42, 82–83, 87, 149, 155, 157, 167,
　185, 201, 207, 211–12, 219, 227, 230, 232–33,
　235–36, 240, 248, 249–51, 318 n.15
Cicero, 189, 237
Clavijo, Ruy González de, 50
Clement VIII (pope), 154
Clement X (pope), 104
Collège Louis le Grand, 73
Columbanus, St., Tomb of, 26
Columbus, Christopher, 9, 19, 44– 45,
　49–64, 68–70, 72–74, 76–78, 81, 84, 87,
　93, 98, 130, 143, 146, 153–54, 157–58, 162,
　181–82, 235–39, 247, 250, 306 n.19

Compostella, 86, 96, 103, 112, 128, 134, 296
　n.37, 235
Constantine the Great, 84
Conring, Herman, 312 n.108
Cook, James, 60, 81–82, 235, 237, 250
Corpus Christi, Feast of, 175, 184, 301 n.16,
　309 n.56
Cortés, Hernán, 49, 60, 100
Cosimo II da Medici, 191
Cotovicus, Joannes, 175, 196, 198–202, 239,
　261
Courmenin, Louis Deshayes de, 126, 155,
　201–2, 245, **261**
Crusades, 2, 9, 11, 18–20, 51, 59, 76–77, 86,
　157, 181, 183, 242, 245–46, 276 nn.11–17,
　289 n.87
Crouch, Nathaniel, 228, **263**, 317 n.3
Cubero Sebastián, Pedro, 104–5, 107, 112,
　116, 128

Dampies, Martin, 42–45
Dandini, Girolamo, **262**
Dapper, Olfert, 150, 160, **264**
Dati, Giuliano, 55
Democritus, 73
Description de l'Egypte, 230
Desfontaines, Pierre-François Guyot, 317
　n.2
Dominicans, 35, 40
Doubdan, Jean, 205–7, 238, 241, **262**
Drake, Francis, Sir, 60, 104, 142
Dubliulius, Johannes, 310 n.79
Dubois, Pierre, 53

Ecklin, Daniel, 90
Egmond van der Nijenburg, Johannes
　Aegidius van, **267**
Einsiedeln, 161
Elizabeth of France, 231–32
Elsner, Jaś, 274 n.32
Empedocles, 73
Encyclopédie, 81
Erasmus, 12, 115
Escorial, 121
Estienne, Charles, 133–35, **256**
Euripides, 18

Fabri, Felix, 185, 241, 248, 274 n.32
Ferdinand of Aragon, 54
Feyerabend, Sigismund, 30, 41, 86–91,
    98–99, 135, 161–62, 167, 181, 187, 228–29,
    238, 247, **258**, 288 n.69
Flórez, Enrique, 103–4
Francis Xavier, St., 61, 73, 100, 105, 112, 237
Franciscans, 19, 26, 105–6, 122, 132, 136,
    144–45, 150, 152, 156, 192–93, 199, 203–4,
    206, 209, 216, 221, 225–26, 229–30, 234,
    239, 242, 245–46, 271 n.4, 318 n.12
Francisco Jesus de San Juan del Puerto, **266**
Franck, Sebastian, 87
Frederich II, 19
Frederick III the Wise of Saxony, 93, 95–96
Fromage, Pierre, 220–21
Fronde, 205
Furer, Christoph, 222, 238, **261**
Fussell, Paul, 240

Gaby, Jean Baptiste, 112
Gama, Vasco da, 31, 76–77, 146, 238
Garnier, C.-G. T., 306 n.20
Gemelli Careri, Giovanni Francesco. *See*
    Careri, Giovanni Francesco Gemelli
George of Saxony, 96
Geufroy, Antoine, 41
Gibbon, Edward, 161
Goethe, Johann Wolfgang von, 231
Goicoechea, Juan de, 112
Gonçalves da Câmara, Luis, 238
Gonsales, Antoine, 178, **263**
González de Clavijo, Ruy. *See* Clavijo, Ruy
    González de
Gonzalez de Mendoza, Pedro, 118
Goujon, Jacques Florent, 178, 206–9, 213,
    216, 241, **263**
Grataralo, Guglielmo, 301 n.18
Gregory XIII (pope), 141
Gretser, Jacobus, 88–92, 98, 100, 126, 135,
    157, 161–62, 212, 237–38, 288 n.52, 296
    n.32, 300 n.1
Grynaeus, Simon, 66, 73, 78, 166, 286 n.41
Guadalupe, Our Lady of, 112, 235
Gualla, Jacobus, 107, 117, 296 n.37
Guerrero, Francisco, 175, 177, 211, 241, **258**

Guibert of Nogent, 113
Gustavus Adolphus, 92
Gutenberg, Johann, 9, 25, 28–29, 44, 130, 153

Hakluyt, Richard, 67–68, 85, 99, 130, 159, 239
Hannibal, 18
Harant, Krystof, 156–57, **259**
Hasselquist, Fredrik, 229–30, **267**
Heidmann, Christoffer, **261**
Helena, St., 84, 113
Helffrich, Johann, 90, 162, 167, **257**
Henichius, Adolph Wilhelm, **266**
Henry II (king of France), 164
Henry II the Pious of Saxony, 93, 96
Henry IV (king of France), 143, 145, 154
Hercules, 71, 78
Herodotus, 236–37
Hese, Joannes de, 21, 24–25, 28, **255**
Heyman, Johannes. *See* Egmond
Hill, Aaron, **265**
Histoire de la mappe-monde papistique, 85–86,
    98
Ho, Cheng, 49
Hobbes, Thomas, 279 n.1, 290 n.89
Homer, 82, 94
Hooghe, Romaine de 81
Horace, 94, 188
Hosius, Stanislaus, 188
Howard, Donald R., 274 n.32
Howell, James, **262**
Hussites, 109
Hythlodaeus, Raphael, 158

Ignatius of Loyola, St., 126, 193, 195, 222,
    236, 238–39, 286 n.35
Innocent IV (pope), 86
Isabella of Castile, 54
Itinerarium burdigalense, 18, 28, 127, 163,
    258, 318 n.16

Jacobus de Voragine, 119
Jacques de Vitry, 18, 21, **259**
Jaffa, Treaty of, 19
James III of Scotland, 155
Jansenism, 109, 111, 295 nn 28–29
Jason and the Argonauts, 71, 78

Jefferson, Thomas, 124–25
Jenson, Nicholas, 29
Jerome, St., 17, 31, 166, 228
Jesuits, 81, 86, 89, 106–7, 112, 115–16, 122,
    209–11, 216, 219–25, 238, 242, 245–46,
    290 n.2, 292 n.26, 314 n.155
Jews, 118–19
John George of Saxony, 97–99
John the Baptist, 26
John of Damascus, 210
Journal de Trevoux, 219, 314 n.46
Journal from Grand Cairo to Mount Sinai,
    267
Julius Caesar, 94, 134

Kitscher, Johannes von, 247, **255**
Korobeınikov, Trifon, 230, **268**
Korte, Jonas, 225–29, 246, 251, **267**
Kyhler, Benigno, 122

Labre, Benedict Joseph, 116
La Harpe, Jean-François de, 76
La Mottraye, Aubry de, **266**
Landriano, Antonio, 32
La Pérouse, Jean-François de Galaup de, 60
La Roque, Jean de, 218, 240, **265**
Leandro di Santa Cecilia, **267**
Le Blanc, Vincent, **262**, 272 n.18
Le Gouz de La Boullaye, François, 101–3,
    112, 117, 126, 238
Le Nain de Tillemont, Louis-Sébastien, 89
Lepanto, 183, 198
Lévi-Strauss, Claude, 240
Linden, Jan Vander, 211, 247, **261**
Linnaeus, Carolus, 229
Lithgow, William, **260**
Lobo, Jerome, 314 n.155
Loreto, 86, 101, 105–6, 115–18, 120–21, 125,
    127, 180, 231, 233, 235
Lotto, Lorenzo, 115
Louis IX, St., 210
Louis XIII, 123, 201
Louis XIV, 109, 217
Lucas, Paul, **265**
Ludolf of Saxony, 51
Ludolfus of Suchem, 24–25, **254**

Lussy, Melchior, **258**
Luther, Martin, 45, 84–85, 93, 95, 98 130,
    153, 161, 235

MacCulloch, Diarmaid, 275 n.36
Machiavelli, Niccolò, 305 n.5
Mączak, Antoni, 12
Magellan, Ferdinand, 60, 87, 98, 104, 142,
    146, 247
Mandeveille, John, Sir, 21–25, 28, 50–51, 53,
    75, 128, 160, 236, **253–54**
Mantegazza, Stefano, **259**
Mariti, Giovanni, **268**
Maundrell, Henry, 77, 155, 212–16, 218, 228,
    246, **265**
McManners, John, 275 n.36
Medina, Antonio de, 156, **257**
Meggen, Jodocus von, **257**
Melanchthon, Philipp, 93, 95–96
Meletií, Hieromonk, **268**
*Mémoires pour l'histoire des sciences et des
    beaux arts. See Journal de Trevoux*
Mendes Pinto, Fernão, 238, 302 n.30
Menz, Balthasar, 92–99, 100, 188
Mergenthal, Hans von, 92
Mirabilia Romae, 113–14
Mocquet, Jean, 141–46, 148, 153, 177, 239,
    260, 300 n.2
Monconys, Balthasar, **263**
Montaigne, Michel de, 63
Montgeron, Louis Basile Carré de, 109, 111
Montserrat, 133
Mont Valérien, 123–25
Moore, John Hamilton, 76–79
Morales, Ambrosio de, 89, 103–4, 112, 128,
    235
More, Thomas, St., 158
Morison, Antoine, 153, 214, 216–21, 227,
    237–38, 241–42, 245–47, **265**
Moritz of Saxony, 96
Moryson, Fynes, **261**
Moses, 113
Myrike, Heinrich, **265**

Napoleon I, 1, 9, 230
Natale, Antonio, 106

Nau, Michel, 116–17, 209–11, 214, 216, 219–20, 222, 225, 241, 246, **263**, **264**
Neitschitz, Georg Christoph von, **263**
Neret, Charles, 220–24, 245, **266**
Neri, Filippo, St., 154
Noe, 71
Noort, Olivier van, 142
Nouveaux mémoires des missions de la Compagnie de Jesus dans le Levant, 220, 223–24
Nova typis transacta navigatio, 61–62
Novus Orbis, 65–67, 70, 74, 85, 166
Nuestra Señora de la Salçeda, Shrine of, 118
Núñez Cabeza de Vaca, Álvar. *See* Cabeza de Vaca, Álvar Núñez

O'Corrain, Thomas, 161
Ordóñez de Ceballos, Pedro, 141, 145, **260**
Origen, 17, 166
Orléans, Pierre Joseph d', 61
Ovid, 94
Oviedo, 112, 134

Paciencia de Christo, Convento de la, 118–20
Pacifique de Provins, père, 201–2, **261**
Paesi novamente retrovati, 65
Pâris, abbé de, 109, 111
Parvilliers, Adrien, 122
Pascha, Jan, **257**
Paul, St., 71
Pennant, Thomas, 27
Perry, Charles, **267**
Petrarch, Francesco, 160
Philip II, 103–4, 121
Philip III, 191
Philip IV, 118
Pietism, 227–28
Pinto, António Cerqueira, 120
Pits, John, 88–89, 288 n.52
Pius VI (pope), 232
Plato, 71, 73, 166
Pliny, the Elder, 70–71, 73, 131, 166
Pococke, Richard, 77, 228, **267**
Polo, Marco, 50, 53, 66, 71, 74–75, 82
Pontbriant, René François du Breil de, 123–25

Poste per diverse parti del mondo, **268**
Postel, Guillaume, **256**
Prévost, abbé, 67, 76
Protestants (Reformers), 85–100, 134–41, 145, 160–64, 167, 189, 203, 211–14, 225–29, 236, 246, 301 n.14, 307 n.26
Ptolemy, 166
Purchas, Samuel, 41, 67–68, 85, 235
Pythagoras, 71, 73

Quaresimo, Francesco, 206
Queirós, Pedro Fernando, 115, 142–43

Rader, Matthaeus, 122
Radziwill, Nicholas Christoph, 187–90, 198–99, 237, 245, 247, 273 n.22
Ramusio, Giovanni Battista, 67, 70, 74, 92, 99, 239
Rantzau, Henrik, **263**
Raphael, 116
Rauwolf, Leonard, 90–92, 135–41, 147, 160–61, 213, 229, 246, **257**
Ray, John, 135
Reisner, Adam, **257**
Reuwich, Erhard, 35–36, 43, 169, 192, 204, 233–34
Rhodes, Alexandre de, 115–16
Richelieu, Alphonse Louis du Plessis de, 123
Richeôme, Louis, 115
Robert of Reims, 59, **254**
Roger, Eugène, 206
Röhricht, Reinhold, 10
Rosaccio, Giuseppe, **259**
Roth, Martin, 35, 246
Rubens, Peter Paul, Sir, 193, 195
Rubiés, Joan-Pau, 274 n.32
Rubruck, William of, 50

Sabas, St., 222
Said, Edward, 275 n.36
Sainte-Maure, Charles de, **266**, 274 n.35
Salignac, Barthélemy, 163, 169, **256**
Sandys, George, 175, 214–15, 218, 228, **260**
Sanson, Nicolas, **263**
Scaliger, Joseph Juste, 210
Schedel, Hartmann, 43

Schmid, Balthasar, **265**
Schweigger, Solomon, 167, **257**
Scipio Africanus, 189–90
Seetzen, Ulrich Jaspar von, 272 n.10
Seidlitz, Melchior, 90
Seneca, 188–90, 237
Shaw, Thomas, 77
Sicard, Claude, 224–25, 246, **266**
Siena, 104
Sixtus IV (pope), 32
Socrates, 71, 166
Somer, Jan, **262**
Stagl, Justin, 12
Staphorst, Nicholas, 135
Stations of the Cross, 121–23
Stephen, St., 117
Stochove, Vincent, **261–62**
Strabo, 71, 131, 166
Suetonius, 94
Symon Simeonis, 26–28, 126, **268**
Sylvester I (pope), 31, 84

Tamerlane, 50
Tasman, Abel Janszoon, 60
Tatars, 109
Tavernier, Jean-Baptiste, 70, 238
Tempestata, Antonio, 191–92
Thévenot, Jean, 146–50, 193, 196–97, **263**
Thévenot, Melchisédec, 60, 67–68, 99, 105,
   146, 159, 239
Thevet, André, 163–68, 177, 208, 218, 239,
   245, **256**
Thicknesse, Philip, 194, 307 n.26
Thomas, Keith, 275 n.36
Thomas the Apostle, Tomb of, 22, 25,105,
   141, 283 n.6
Timberlake, Henry, **259**
Tobler, Titus, 10
Tollot, Jean Baptiste, 152, **267**
Torsellino, Orazio, 115

Trent, Council of, 246
Treter, Thomas, 188–90, 237
Trinité, Monastère de la (the Vendôme),
   122–23
Troilo, Franz Ferdinand von, 211, **264**
Tschudi von Glarus, Ludwig, 229, **259**
Tucher, Hans, 29–32, 34–36, 41, 44, 119,
   125, 153, 156–57, 164, 236, 241, 245, **255**
Turner, Edith L. B., 12
Turner, Victor, 12

Ulysses, 71, 81, 94, 236
Ursula, St., Fraternity of, 107

Vadianus, Joachim, **256**
Valle, Pietro della, 146, 150, **262**
Varthema, Ludovicus, 66, 286 n.41
Verardi, Carlo, 59
Vergil, Polydore, 29, 50–51, 64
Veryard, Ellis, **265**
Vespucci, Amerigo, 81, 87, 146, 158
Viaggio da Venetia, 156
Villamont, Jacques de, 50, 177, 180–81, 238,
   259
Virgil, 71
Volney, C.-F., 148
Voyages faits principalement en Asie, 74–75

Walter von Waltersweil, Bernhard, **259**
Wartha, 107, 109–10
Waugh, Evelyn, 240
Weller, Hieronymus, 92, 98–99
Wilhelm of Saxony, 292 n.26
Williams, Wes, 273 n.29
Wispeck, Wilhelm, **258**
Wormsber, Jacob, 90

Zuallart, Jean, 167–75, 177, 186, 190, 198,
   204, 247, **258**
Zwingli, Ulrich, 98, 161, 235

Acknowledgments

I am grateful to the Library of Congress for various reasons—in the first place for having gathered and guarded across generations the early modern travel books that are the subject matter of this essay, and in the second place for having encouraged and tolerated my own labors over these books while I have been on staff, not, to be sure, across generations but nevertheless through three regimes of leadership within the Rare Book and Special Collections Division—those of the late William Matheson, Larry Sullivan, and Mark Dimunation. Moreover, shortly after my arrival at the Library, Kathleen Mang, at the time the Library's Curator of the Lessing J. Rosenwald Collection, introduced me to the splendid editions of Bernhard Breydenbach, books that were to prove crucial to this study. Later, great generosity toward the Library on the part of Abraham and Julienne Krasnoff made possible a Krasnoff-Billington fellowship that the Library bestowed at a crucial stage in my work. Clark Evans, the guiding hand and spirit of the Rare Book Reading Room during much of this time, has never allowed my requests for help in searching out books or my moving books hither and thither to seem unreasonable or inconvenient. Over a period of years, George Chiassion, in his capacity as Special Assistant to the Chief of Rare Books & Special Collections, has expertly contributed in numerous ways as I have sought to navigate the manuscript through the shallows and currents of a large institution. Ralph Eubanks, the Library's Director of Publishing, and the anonymous readers and the editors (especially Jerome Singerman, Alison Anderson, and Mariana Martinez) of the University of Pennsylvania Press also worked to see that a manuscript became a book. Margaret Kieckhefer worked to the same end by ensuring that the many images in the book were properly photographed. To all of the above I am grateful.

I am indebted to others for the opportunity of consulting books in their collections: Georgetown University and in particular, Joseph N. Tylenda, S.J., Librarian of the Woodstock Library at Georgetown, 1994–2003; the libraries of the Catholic University of America; Houghton Library, Harvard University; the Dumbarton Oaks Research Library and

Collection; the Rare Book Library of the University of Illinois Library (at Champaign-Urbana); and the Folger Shakespeare Library.

I am immensely grateful to William H. McNeill, who generously gave a close reading to the first draft of the manuscript and offered detailed comments and encouragement. Anthony Grafton read the introduction, and Declan Murphy and Molly Pyle read the manuscript. Mark Chello read part of the text. Jason Cober and I chatted at length on the book and subject matter. I thank them all for their valuable suggestions.

I owe the greatest debt of gratitude to my family, to my sisters Mary Ann Noonan and Regina Noonan Cober, and above all to my parents, who have been a constant and sustaining source of interest, encouragement, and inspiration throughout this long *via peregrinationis* and to whom the book is dedicated.